A MOST DETESTABLE CRIME

A Most Detestable Crime

New Philosophical Essays on Rape

Edited by
KEITH BURGESS-JACKSON

New York   Oxford
Oxford University Press
1999

Oxford University Press

Oxford   New York

Athens   Auckland   Bangkok   Bogotá   Buenos Aires   Calcutta
Cape Town   Chennai   Dar es Salaam   Delhi   Florence   Hong Kong   Istanbul
Karachi   Kuala Lumpur   Madrid   Melbourne   Mexico City   Mumbai
Nairobi   Paris   São Paulo   Singapore   Taipei   Tokyo   Toronto   Warsaw

and associated companies in
Berlin   Ibadan

Copyright © 1999 by Oxford University Press, Inc.

Published by Oxford University Press, Inc.
198 Madison Avenue, New York, New York 10016

Oxford is a registered trademark of Oxford University Press

Library of Congress Cataloging-in-Publication Data
A most detestable crime : new philosophical essays on rape / edited by
Keith Burgess-Jackson.
p.   cm.
Includes bibliographical references and index.
ISBN 0-19-512075-2
1. Rape—Philosophy.   I. Burgess-Jackson, Keith.
K5197.M67   1999
306.7′01—dc21   98-26835

Excerpt from *Sula*, copyright Toni Morrison, *Sula* (New York: Alfred A. Knopt, 1974),
pp. 42–44. Reprinted by permission of International Creative Management.

All royalties from the sale of this book go,
in equal measure, to the National Clearinghouse on
Marital and Date Rape (NCMDR) and the National
Coalition Against Sexual Assault (NCASA).

1 3 5 7 9 8 6 4 2
Printed in the United States of America
on acid-free paper

To women, that they may live lives of
dignity, equality, respect, and safety

Acknowledgments

A great deal of intellectual, organizational, physical, and emotional labor has gone into the production of this volume, but it has been, for me at least, a labor of love. The book would not exist had it not been for the encouragement and advice of a friend, Nathan Jay Schwartz, who, at a crucial juncture, persuaded—or rather, *reminded*—me that the project had merit. Spirits do flag from time to time. I also thank those among the volume's contributors who committed to it early on: Pat Smith, Larry May (with his coauthor Ed Soule), and Nancy Snow. These individuals took a chance on an unknown scholar with no formal editing experience long before Oxford University Press (or any other publisher) expressed interest in the project. At the time, I must confess, it was more hope than plan. I thank them, as well as Oxford's anonymous reviewers, for their faith and trust, which do my heart good.

Others to whom I am indebted are the many wonderful people in the Interlibrary Loan Office of The University of Texas at Arlington, my home institution. These tireless, cheerful, *dogged* individuals worked above and beyond the call of duty to acquire books and articles for me over a period of many months. One of my aims in editing this book was to provide philosophers and other scholars with a wide-ranging, accurate, and useful (albeit noncomprehensive) bibliography on the subject of rape. I believe I have done that, for which my sincere thanks go to Rachel Robbins (Head of Access Services), Beatrice Cantu (Interlibrary Loan Coordinator), and their respective staffs (with particular thanks to Diana Hines and Judd Knight for their diligence and good cheer).

Finally, but no less importantly, I thank the philosophy editor of Oxford University Press, Cynthia A. Read, for the confidence she expressed in me from the outset. I also thank her successor in that office, Peter H. Ohlin, for guiding the manuscript through what appears (to me) to be a publication maze. Editorial assistants Gene Romanosky and Catharine A. Carlin were helpful and courteous to me on numerous occasions. It has been a pleasure working with the good people of Oxford University Press. Every scholar should be so fortunate.

As the subtitle suggests, all of the substantive contributions to this anthology are new in the sense of being previously unpublished. Some of the material, however, has appeared in print elsewhere. Chapter 1 ("A History of Rape Law") is a revised version of chapters 3 and 4 of my monograph, *Rape: A Philosophical Investigation* (Aldershot, England: Dartmouth Publishing Company, 1996). It is reprinted here by kind permission of Dartmouth Publishing Company, for which I am grateful. I renew my thanks to Dartmouth's managing director, John L. Irwin, and to Tom D. Campbell, the general editor of Dartmouth's Applied Legal Philosophy Series (in which my monograph appeared). A revised version of "A Chronology of Philosophical Publications on Rape" appeared in *The American Philosophical Association Newsletter on Philosophy and Law* [97 (spring 1998): 105–7]. I thank Richard Nunan, the newsletter's editor, for allowing it to appear there, knowing that it would eventually be published in this anthology.

I am proud to report that all royalties from the sale of this volume will go directly from Oxford University Press to two worthy organizations: the National Clearinghouse on Marital and Date Rape (NCMDR) and the National Coalition Against Sexual Assault (NCASA). Now in its twenty-first year under the able and inspired direction of Laura X, NCMDR's mission is "to bring about social, legal, political, psychological, economic, and religious change through [its] vast resource network of information and support, in order to make intimate relationships truly egalitarian."[1] NCASA's mission is "to eliminate sexual assault and all forms of oppression." It does this by (among other things) training professionals and activists; advocating on behalf of sexual-assault coalitions, rape-crisis programs, and survivors of sexual assault; working with national media to educate the public; monitoring public policy; supplying testimony to Congress and other legislative and judicial bodies; filing legal briefs; and hosting national conferences and Women of Color Institutes.[2]

The idea for such a donation was my own, but until I corresponded with Peter Unger, whom I knew only in name at the time, the mechanics were obscure. Professor Unger, I learned, had donated all royalties from his book *Living High and Letting Die: Our Illusion of Innocence* (New York: Oxford University Press, 1996) to Oxfam America and the U.S. Committee for UNICEF. When I queried him on the subject by e-mail, he graciously explained the process in a way that made it seem not just feasible but morally mandatory. I agree with him that scholars such as us need to engage the world as well as reflect on, theorize about, and expound upon it. Donating royalties from our published work is the perfect way to demonstrate to cynics—of whom, unfortunately, there are legions—that our motives are, if not entirely selfless, not altogether self-serving.

I think I speak for all the book's contributors when I say that I am honored to play a role, however small, in ameliorating the effects of rape, a task that goes hand in hand with rape prevention. If the latter of these tasks succeeds—and with enough hard work it will—the former will be unnecessary. My hope is that the present volume will stimulate discussion among ordinary citizens, lawyers (including judges), therapists, scientists, scholars, social theorists, and policymakers at every level and in every branch of government. One consequence of such discussion, should it come to pass, will be to refute the prevailing (and scurrilous) notion that philosophy, as a discipline and as a profession, is irrelevant to people's lives and concerns. Nothing, to my mind, is further from the truth.

Fort Worth, Texas   K. B.-J.
8 June 1998

Notes

1. For more information about NCMDR; to use NCMDR's consulting, speaking, and publication (e.g., law-charts) services; or to make a gift of time, money, or resources, visit NCMDR's Web site (from which the quoted language is taken) at http://ncmdr.org.

2. This information, and some of the language, is taken from the NCASA brochure. For more information about NCASA, including details about how to become a member, visit its Web site at http://www.ncasa.org.

Contents

Contributors

DAVID ARCHARD is Reader in the Department of Moral Philosophy at the University of St. Andrews in Fife, Scotland. He studied philosophy and politics at Oxford University and received his doctoral degree from the London School of Economics. From 1976 to 1995, he taught philosophy at the University of Ulster, Northern Ireland, and has been at St. Andrews since 1995. He has published *Marxism and Existentialism: The Political Philosophy of Jean-Paul Sartre and Maurice Merleau-Ponty* (1980), *Consciousness and the Unconscious* (1984), *Children, Rights, and Childhood* (1993), and *Sexual Consent* (1998). He is the editor of *Philosophy and Pluralism* (1996). He has also published numerous articles and chapters on social, political, and moral philosophy.

BRENDA M. BAKER is Professor of Philosophy at the University of Calgary, Alberta, Canada, where she teaches philosophy of law, ethics, political philosophy, bioethics, and environmental ethics. Her main research interests are in responsibility, excuses, punishment theory, and women's issues in the criminal law. She has published essays in *Ethics, Canadian Journal of Philosophy, Law and Philosophy, Social Theory and Practice, Dialogue, Hypatia,* the *Canadian Journal of Law and Jurisprudence, Utilitas,* and in various collections. She is active in the Canadian Section of the International Association for Philosophy of Law and Social Philosophy, of which she is past president, and is a member of the Canadian Society for Women in Philosophy.

BAT-AMI BAR ON teaches philosophy and women's studies at the State University of New York at Binghamton. Her primary theoretical and activist interests are in violence—although she escapes them by pursuing other activities.

KEITH BURGESS-JACKSON is Associate Professor of Philosophy at the University of Texas at Arlington, where he teaches courses in philosophy of law, ethics, philosophy of religion, and feminism. He received M.A. and J.D. degrees (the former in history) from Wayne State University, Detroit, Michigan, in 1983 and M.A. and Ph.D. degrees (in philosophy) from the University of Arizona, Tucson, in 1985 and 1989, respectively. He is coauthor (with Irving M. Copi) of *Informal Logic* (2d ed. 1992; 3d ed. 1996) and author of *Rape: A Philosophical Investigation* (1996). A licensed attorney, he has published more than 45 articles, chapters, critical notices, reviews, and encyclopedia entries in legal, historical, and philosophical journals.

VICTORIA DAVION is Associate Professor of Philosophy at the University of Georgia, Athens. Since 1990, she has been a faculty affiliate there in the Environmental Ethics Certificate Program. She received her Ph.D. degree from the University of Wisconsin, Madison, in 1989. Davion specializes in feminist philosophy, ethical theory, applied ethics, and social and political philosophy. She publishes in a variety of journals, such as *Hypatia, Social Theory and Practice*, and the *Journal of Social Philosophy*. She is the editor of the journal *Ethics and the Environment* and is coediting a volume (with Clark Wolf) concerned with the recent writings of John Rawls.

JEFFREY A. GAUTHIER is Associate Professor of Philosophy at the University of Portland, Oregon. He received his Ph.D. degree from the University of Michigan, Ann Arbor, in 1992 and has taught at the University of Michigan and at Bowling Green State University, Ohio. He is the author of *Hegel and Feminist Social Criticism: Justice, Recognition, and the Feminine* (1997) and has lectured and published on topics in ethics, political philosophy, nineteenth-century German philosophy, and feminism. He currently serves on the board of directors of the Sexual Exploitation Education Project, a program aimed at educating and reforming men convicted of crimes in the sex industry.

JEAN HAMPTON was, at the time of her death (at age 41) in 1996, Professor of Philosophy at the University of Arizona, Tucson. She also taught at the University of Pittsburgh, Pennsylvania; the University of California, Los Angeles; and the University of California, Davis. Hampton was the author or coauthor of four books, coeditor of one book, and author of over 40 articles in the areas of political philosophy, ethics, philosophy of law, rational-choice theory, and feminist theory. Her books are *Hobbes and the Social Contract Tradition* (1986); *Forgiveness and Mercy*, coauthored with Jeffrie G. Murphy (1988); *Political Philosophy* (1997); and *The Authority of Reason* (1998). Hampton was a contributing editor, with David Copp and John E. Roemer, of *The Idea of Democracy* (1993).

LINDA LEMONCHECK teaches feminist theory in the Gender Studies Program at the University of Southern California, Los Angeles. She is editor of the "Studies in Feminist Philosophy" book series for Oxford University Press. Her publications focus on the role played by current conceptions of gender in women's sexual and reproductive lives. She is the author of *Dehumanizing Women: Treating Persons as Sex Objects* (1985), *Loose Women, Lecherous Men: A Feminist Philosophy of Sex* (1997), and coauthor, with Mane Hajdin, of *Sexual Harassment: A Debate* (1997). She is currently coediting a volume on sexual harassment (with James P. Sterba) for both the academic and popular markets. Linda lives in Seal Beach, California, where she supports local women's organizations and community arts projects.

LARRY MAY is Professor of Philosophy at Washington University in St. Louis, Missouri. He received his Ph.D. degree from the New School for Social Research in 1977, where he was Hannah Arendt's last research assistant. Before going to Washington University in 1991, he taught at Purdue University, West Lafayette, Indiana; the University of Wisconsin, Madison; and the University of Connecticut, Storrs. He has writen four books—*The Morality of Groups* (1987), *Sharing Responsibility* (1992), *The Socially Responsive Self* (1996), and *Masculinity and Morality* (1998)— and coauthored a fifth, *Praying for a Cure* (1999). He has also coedited six books: *Collective Responsibility* (1991), *Rethinking Masculinity: Philosophical Explorations in Light of Feminism* (1992; 2d ed. 1996), *Applied Ethics: A Multicultural Approach* (1994; 2d ed. 1997), *Mind and Morals: Cognitive Science and Ethics* (1996), *Hannah Arendt: Twenty Years Later* (1996), and *Liberty, Equality, and Plurality* (1997). He is currently working on a book entitled *Legal Guilt and Moral Sensitivity*.

PATRICIA SMITH is Professor of Philosophy at Baruch College, the City University of New York, where she specializes in legal and political philosophy and feminist jurisprudence. She is author of *Liberalism and Affirmative Obligation* (1998) and editor of *The Nature and Process of Law: An Introduction to Legal Philosophy* (1993) and *Feminist Jurisprudence* (1993), as well as numerous articles on these topics. She is currently working on a book entitled *The Reproductive Revolution*, which is concerned with the challenges presented to traditional values and legal and social institutions by the sexual revolution of the twentieth century.

NANCY E. SNOW is Associate Professor of Philosophy at Marquette University, Milwaukee, Wisconsin. In addition to various articles on specific virtues, such as compassion and humility, she has published on self-blame and the blame of rape victims and has edited *In the Company of Others: Perspectives on Community, Family, and Culture* (1996). She is currently coediting a philosophy of law textbook with Larry May and Angela Bolte of Washington University in St. Louis, Missouri. Her current research interests are in moral psychology and the philosophy of law.

EDWARD SOULE is Senior Lecturer at the University of Missouri, St. Louis, where he teaches and writes about economic theory and business ethics. He recently published an essay in *Business Ethics Quarterly* in which he explored the connection between trust and managerial responsibility. He recently returned to philosophy— receiving a Ph.D. degree from Washington University in St. Louis, Missouri—after a career in business in which he held senior-level positions in the financial services industry.

A MOST DETESTABLE CRIME

Introduction

[W]e understand what we are and where we are in the light of what we are not yet.

Sandra Lee Bartky, 1975[1]

The title of this anthology derives from a posthumously published work by Sir Matthew Hale, a seventeenth-century English jurist who has been described as "the most eminent lawyer and judge of his time."[2] Hale, who served as Chief Justice of the King's Bench from 1671 to 1676 (the year of his death), did as much as anyone in his day (or afterward) to articulate, and in some cases to transform, the law of rape, which was by then several centuries old.[3] It may surprise the reader to learn that Hale's imprint on the law of rape remains—more than three hundred years after his death and in jurisdictions (such as Utah and Missouri) that he could not have imagined, much less sought to influence.

Among the doctrines for which Hale is given credit—or blame, as the case may be—are the marital-rape exemption (which, as the name implies, exempts husbands from rape charges)[4] and the cautionary instruction (in which the trial judge informs the jury prior to its deliberations that rape "is an accusation easily to be made and hard to be proved, and harder to be defended by the party accused, tho never so innocent").[5] The marital-rape exemption was abolished in New York in 1984,[6] Georgia in 1985,[7] and Illinois in 1992,[8] although it continues to exist in one form or another elsewhere.[9] The cautionary instruction was eliminated from Florida law in 1986,[10] but it was still being given in "over half of the states" as of 1988.[11] It is no exaggeration to say that Hale, for better or worse, is still with us. If I were to amend Professor Bartky's epigraph, it would be to say that we understand what we are and where we are in the light of *where we have been* as well as what we are not yet. Rape law has a past, and a heavy one, not just a future.

Until recently, rape was all but ignored by philosophers.[12] This is doubly unfortunate: first, because rape is endemic in our society, and philosophy might make a contribution to eradicating it; and second, because the subject is philosophically fecund. Take rape itself; the very concept cries out for analysis. Is it an act? A practice? An institution? Could it be more than one of these at the same time? Some scholars have argued that rape is sui generis among crimes.[13] How might this be, and what theoretical and practical differences (if any) should it make? What, *exactly*, is the wrong or harm of rape (for surely it is both wrong and harmful)? This is a surprisingly difficult question to answer. Is rape best conceived as an offense against property, against the family, against public morals, against liberty, against bodily integrity, against security, against autonomy, against equality? The idea that rape offends against equality is a recent one, as ideas go. It suggests (rightly, in my opinion) that rape belongs to the domain of social and political philosophy as well as moral and legal philosophy, to which it has usually been relegated. Indeed, there are aspects of rape and rape law that touch upon every branch of philosophy. Logicians, metaphysicians, epistemologists—as well as value theorists—can find something in it to which to apply their analytical and critical skills.

Few philosophers, today, believe that philosophy is limited to the analysis of concepts,[14] but certainly conceptual analysis is one of the discipline's distinctive concerns and activities.[15] This is because questions of public policy (including law) have an abstract dimension. They employ or presuppose *concepts*, some or many of which may be unclear. Think of the concepts of mistake, belief, consent, will, act, force, coercion, harm, recklessness, and punishment, all of which arise in the law of rape (as elsewhere). Until these and other relevant concepts are clarified and situated in a larger scheme of thought, there is little hope for consensus or resolution—or, if there is consensus, it may rest on divergent understanding.

Most philosophers, at least in English-speaking countries, are trained to distinguish various questions or propositions, often classifying them as conceptual (about concepts, ideas, or categories of thought), evaluative (about values, norms, or standards), and factual (about facts or the way things are). Until a particular question is classified in this way, it will not be clear which method or methods should be used to answer it—or who, if anyone, is equipped to do so. The result may be confusion rather than elucidation. The working assumption of most philosophers is that clear, careful, critical thinking is necessary (although perhaps not sufficient) for meaningful social action.

Among the conceptual questions to be asked about rape, besides those set out above, is whether it is an instance of sex, violence, or both. Assuming that rape is *some* kind of sexual intercourse (an assumption that may well deserve to be questioned),[16] should it be conceived as forced sex, violent sex, coerced sex, compelled sex, nonconsensual sex, pressured sex, exploited sex, involuntary sex, expropriated sex, objectified sex, unwanted sex, nonmutual sex, or bad sex? (These are just some of the possibilities.) Here the philosopher must do more than provide a definition. He or she must formulate a *theory*. Not a theory of the sort a scientist propounds, which takes the concept of rape for granted and seeks to understand its causal antecedents and consequents, but rather a theory of the *concept*. The philosopher's task, in other words, is to reconstruct the *idea* of rape, showing that a particular understanding—that is, a particular location among allied concepts—illuminates the various objects or phenomena that fall under it. It may be that no single theory accommodates all of the data, in which case the most we can hope for is a theory that illuminates more data than any other. What a *philosophical* theory of rape is, and what should be expected of it, is itself a matter of philosophical disagreement—as it should be.

As anyone who reads philosophical literature knows, philosophers are as adept at argumentation as they are at analysis. They take, and defend, positions. This is the evaluative, normative, or prescriptive aspect of the discipline. Examples: Should the marital-rape exemption be abolished? Reasonable people disagree about this. There is no reason why philosophers should be of a single mind on the matter either. Should defense attorneys who represent accused rapists be allowed to introduce evidence concerning the alleged victim's prior sexual history? If so, should the evidence be limited to the victim's sexual history with the defendant? If not, why not? What values are at stake, and how important are they? Again, there is a diversity of opinion on the matter, both in and out of philosophy. Should the law incorporate a defense of mistaken but reasonable belief in consent? If so, how is reasonableness to be understood in this context? Is a man's belief reasonable if it is based on empirically confirmable generalizations about "what women want"? Should there be a crime known as "statutory rape," in which having sexual intercourse with a person below a specified age is forbidden—even though both parties consent to the act? If so, what is the appropriate age of consent, and why? Finally, should rape be punished by death? If not, what punishment do convicted rapists deserve, and on what basis?

Very often, evaluative questions such as these are interwoven with factual or empirical questions. For example, asking whether rape should be punished by death is an evaluative question; but how one *answers* it may well depend on the facts, such as whether punishment by death deters those who might otherwise rape, and whether there is a reasonable chance that rapists can be rehabilitated. While the philosopher qua philosopher has no expertise on factual matters, he or she is no less competent than anyone else to marshal facts in support of a conclusion. Most philosophers (and others) who argue about rape draw on a rapidly growing body of scientific research on the subject.[17] Both natural and social scientists have inquired into the etiology of rape, many of them using the most sophisticated techniques of their disciplines. To what extent is rape a biological phenomenon? To what extent is it psychological? To what extent is it social? How is rape related, causally, to such phenomena as pornography, low self-esteem, and the will to dominate? What motivates rapists? The philosopher who wishes to write intelligently (and intelligibly) about rape must attend to the scientific, literary, and autobiographical literature on the subject, which is vast and growing.

The present volume reflects this diversity in approach and method (without pretending to reflect every approach or every method, which would be impossible in a single anthology, even a very large one). It shows philosophers both detached and engaged, seeking understanding as well as change, asking questions as well as providing answers (some, admittedly, tentative)—in short, doing all the things that philosophers do. Part I of the anthology, entitled "Understanding Rape," is primarily descriptive and explanatory in nature. In chapter 1, Keith Burgess-Jackson sketches a history, not of rape as act or as institution, about which others have written with great eloquence and erudition, but of rape as crime. This chapter, which includes a discussion of recent developments and trends, is designed to provide a factual background for the more specific analyses and arguments to come.

In chapter 2, Patricia Smith argues that rape is a paradigmatic expression of the traditional double standard of acceptable male and female sexual behavior. One function of the double standard, she claims, is to reinforce patriarchal values such as hierarchy, exploitation, male dominance, masculinity (understood as strength and authority), and femininity (understood as weakness and dependence). Against this background, Smith maintains, rape appears as but one of the self-perpetuating tendencies of social systems, which reproduce themselves by reinforcing certain beliefs, attitudes, and behaviors, while retarding or punishing others.

Part II, entitled "Analyzing Rape," is primarily conceptual in nature. Brenda M. Baker begins the discussion in chapter 3 by analyzing one of the oldest and most controversial elements of rape, that of consent (or rather, the lack thereof). Her point of departure is Canadian law, which in 1983 underwent a profound transformation. That year, Canada's crime of rape was replaced by a new offense known as "sexual assault." The new law, Baker says, was designed (among other things) "to emphasize that sexual aggression against women and other persons should be viewed as a crime of violence and domination rather than one of sexual passion." In Baker's view, consent is best understood not as a mental state, attitude, or disposition, but as a "normative, permission-giving act." Her chapter is an elaboration of this innovative and interesting idea.

Like Baker, Jeffrey A. Gauthier believes that rape is best conceived as nonconsensual sex, but he is worried that much of what *passes* for consent in a "sexually exploitative system" such as ours fails to reflect the choices of "genuinely consenting agents." Under such conditions, women's consent to sex is not a "meaningful expression" of their "interests and desires." In chapter 4 he addresses this problem by "considering the nature of sexual relations under the coercive conditions of a sexist society," ultimately concluding that the state has an interest in "restricting certain coercive proposals." Gauthier's argument relies on an analogy between labor-market regulations, which are designed to promote worker autonomy by preventing the worst sorts of exploitation and abuse by their employers, and the "bargaining" that often occurs between sexual partners, one of whom has disproportionate power over the other. The aim of such regulations, Gauthier says, is to help women "achieve the position of genuinely consenting agents."

In the past two decades there has been growing disenchantment among legal scholars and practitioners with the definition of "rape" as nonconsensual sex. Part of the problem is the way the concept of consent has been understood and applied by legal actors, including legislators and judges; but there are deeper and more intractable problems as well. In chapter 5, Keith Burgess-Jackson argues that the consent standard is not just misapplied in practice but misplaced in principle. To avoid the problems to which it gives rise, he sets out a theory of rape in which consent plays no direct role. Rape, he argues, is best conceived as coerced sex, where "coerced" includes both forced sex and sex accomplished by threat of harm. The model for rape, Burgess-Jackson suggests, should be *robbery* rather than assault, battery, larceny, trespass, or some other crime (which is not to say that sex is a commodity).

Jean Hampton comes at things differently in chapter 6. Rape, she says, is some sort of "morally wrongful sex," so if we are to understand the species (rape), we must first understand the genus (morally wrongful sex). But in order to understand morally wrongful sex, we must understand the nature of a morally wrongful act generally. Wrongful action, Hampton writes, is that which inflicts a "moral injury," which she defines in Kantian terms as an injury to the "realization and acknowledgment of the victim's value" as a person. It is not that the injury *really* degrades the person, for in Kantian thought, nothing could do that, but it *appears* to degrade and may be *intended* to. Hampton calls the appearance of degradation "diminishment." It is, she says, "the normal result of an immoral action, and that which constitutes the moral injury inflicted by a wrongdoing." To inflict a moral injury, therefore, is to engage in behavior the meaning of which is that the victim has diminished value. This, according to Hampton, is precisely what occurs in rape.

One virtue of Hampton's analysis is that it shows how rape can injure women as a class as well as particular women. The rapist, in raping, acts qua male upon an individual qua female, thus conveying the idea (to her and to anyone else who observes or learns about it) that women are diminished in value relative to men. As Hampton puts it, "Rape confirms that women are 'for' men: to be used, dominated, treated as objects." Another virtue of Hampton's analysis, at least to some theorists, is that it does not rest on consent. Consent, Hampton says, is at most a necessary condition of the moral rightness of a sexual encounter; it is not sufficient. The reason it is not sufficient is that one can consent to an act that is experienced as demeaning or damaging to one's understanding of one's worth. Hampton stops short of advocating that all instances of morally wrongful sex be criminalized, suggesting only that the most egregious acts of sexual diminishment be prohibited and punished as rape.

Parts III and IV are primarily evaluative in nature. Part III, entitled "Situating Rape," continues the effort begun in Part II to analyze rape, but with an emphasis on how rape is situated relative to other acts, other crimes, and other forms of oppression. In chapter 7, Linda LeMoncheck criticizes what has come to be known as "the continuum model of sexual violence against women." This model views rape as continuous with, rather than as distinct from, such crimes as battering and sexual harassment. Those who employ the model—whom LeMoncheck refers to as "radical feminists"—believe that it makes sense of "the institutionalized male dominance referred to as patriarchy." Critics of the continuum model, many of whom are themselves feminists, argue that it has a number of deleterious effects, to wit: It reinforces stereotypes of men and women; it "reduces all heterosexual sex to sexual exploitation"; it trivializes rape by placing it on a continuum with acts of lesser gravity; and it leaves no logical space for female agency or resistance.

LeMoncheck, who is deeply concerned about "divisiveness among feminists," develops a new model—an overlapping-frames model—that "exposes the pervasive and systemic character of men's sexual violence against women without implying, or appearing to imply, that women are the perpetual victims of male sexual abuse." Among the many virtues of this model, according to LeMoncheck, is that it makes sense of both women's oppression at the hands of men and women's "capacity to resist and transcend that oppression." It also reflects "the culturally located and context-specific expression of particular acts of violence against women," thus avoiding the criticism that feminism speaks only to the experiences of women of a certain race, class, culture, place, or time.

One of the acts (or act-types) that is situated near rape on the continuum model of sexual violence against women is sexual harassment. In chapter 8, Larry May and Edward Soule discuss the relationship between these acts. They argue that the class of sexually harassing acts is broad and diverse—so diverse, in fact, that some of its members ought to be dealt with by criminal sanctions of the sort usually applied to rape and battery. This is a departure from current law, which views sexual harassment as a civil wrong—a kind of sex-based discrimination—calling for compensation from the wrongdoer (and perhaps the wrongdoer's employer) to the victim. May and Soule accept the general framework of sex-discrimination law, but wish to draw attention to a subset of sexually harassing acts that are so coercive and so harmful to their victims as to be criminally punishable. Toward this end, they develop a "typology of forms of sexual harassment." The form that most closely resembles rape, and which ought to be punished as "a form of nonviolent rape," is quid pro quo sexual harassment, in which the perpetrator threatens "significant harm" to another unless he or she submits to sexual intercourse. One incidental benefit of punishing the most egregious instances of sexual harassment, the authors say, is that the other members of the class will "be taken more seriously and attempted less frequently."

In chapter 9, Bat-Ami Bar On maps the intersection of rape, race, gender, and class, using a particularly disturbing case, that of "the Scottsboro boys," as the focus of discussion. This case, or collection of cases, involved the alleged rape of two poor white women in Alabama by nine African American temporary workers. After a number of trials and appeals stretching over a period of years, several of the defendants were sentenced to long terms of imprisonment. This, even though one of the prosecuting witnesses recanted and worked with defense attorneys. The cases were brought to the attention of scholars and the larger public through the work of Susan Brownmiller,[18] who viewed the cases as another instance of male domination of women. Subsequently, Brownmiller was criticized for ignoring the racial dimension of the cases. What this criticism shows, Bar On says, is that we need a more expansive and nuanced conception of rape that takes into account such factors as race and class. This conception would allow us to see that in cases such as that of the "Scottsboro boys," those charged with rape may themselves be victims of a racist and classist society. It would allow us to see that some women (white, affluent, heterosexual women, for example) are situated as oppressors and that some men (nonwhite, poor, homosexual men, for example) are situated as victims.

Part IV, entitled "Evaluating Rape Law," contains three essays that address and criticize particular aspects of rape law. In chapter 10, David Archard considers the *mens rea* or required mental state of rape. Traditionally, in jurisdictions that define "rape" as nonconsensual sexual intercourse, the prosecutor must prove beyond a reasonable doubt that the defendant *believed* that the prosecuting witness was *not* consenting to intercourse. The defendant would sometimes concede that intercourse had occurred and that the witness had not consented to it, but he would claim that he believed that she consented—and that the mistaken belief was reasonable under the circumstances. If this claim were accepted by the factfinder, he would be acquitted. The question courts have had to grapple with is how reasonableness is to be understood in this context. Archard explores the concepts of mistake and reasonableness and concludes that in some cases, even "an honest mistake" about a woman's consent is unreasonable, therefore culpable. What makes it unreasonable, he says, is that the man supplants "the authoritative voice of [the] woman" with some other authority, such as convention (how women typically behave in such circumstances) or the testimony of others about what the woman wants. This supplanting of authority is the sort of defiance that the requirement of *mens rea* is meant to capture.

In chapter 11, Victoria Davion uses rape as a vehicle for discussing a larger debate within the feminist movement, the so-called difference debate. The underlying assumption of the disputants is that men and women differ in their biological capacities, which shapes their experiences, which gives rise to differing perspectives on the world. The question that has divided theorists is whether these differences (again, assuming they exist) should be ignored or accommodated by laws and other public policies. For example, only women can become pregnant. Should public policy ignore this fact or take it into account? What does equality require? Among those who would accommodate women's interests and perspective is Lois Pineau, who, in 1989, argued that "the law can protect women better against nonaggravated date rape by regarding sex from 'a woman's point of view.'"[19] In particular, the law should incorporate the idea that "it is not reasonable for women to consent to aggressive noncommunicative sex." Consequently, "acquiescence under such conditions should not count as consent." When such acquiescence does occur, the woman has been sexually assaulted for legal purposes.

Pineau has been criticized for, among other things, "essentializing" women; that is, for assuming that it is of the essence of women to have certain characteristics, interests, needs, desires, or experiences. Why, the critics ask, should it be assumed that all and only women desire "communicative sex," or that the "end" of a sexual encounter is pleasure? Davion takes a different tack. Pineau's work, she says, "is essentialist, but this is not what is wrong with it." Essentialism may have strategic value in certain circumstances. What is wrong with Pineau's work is that it is *needlessly* essentialist. Actively ensuring that one's sexual partner is consenting is not something only men should do; it is something *any* person can and should do out of respect for another. Davion's essay is a defense of what she calls "a minimum standard of sexual decency" that is "gender-neutral" in the sense that it applies to men as well as women. One advantage of this standard, she says, is that it does not require that men "understand sexuality from 'a woman's point of view,'" which some critics (for example, David Adams)[20] have found objectionable on grounds of unfairness. Davion concludes that her standard of consensual sex is preferable to that of Pineau because it creates fewer problems.

Finally, in chapter 12, Nancy E. Snow defends what are known as "rape shield laws." These laws, which now exist in every state as well as in federal courts, exclude certain forms of relevant evidence on grounds that it unduly prejudices the factfinder against the prosecuting witness. Specifically, rape shield laws exclude evidence of "the victim's past sexual conduct" with the defendant or with other men. They are also designed to prevent humiliating, intimidating, and abusive cross-examination by defense attorneys, which, it is thought, will make rape victims more willing to report their rapes to authorities.

Rape shield laws, while well-intentioned, have certain failings that need to be corrected, according to Snow. First, the laws contain "loopholes," such as allowing sexual-conduct evidence to show the origin of semen, that allow judges to avoid their strictures. Second, they fail, in practice, to deter zealous defense attorneys from abusing prosecuting witnesses. Third, they cannot, even if rigorously applied, counteract various myths about rapists and their victims, one of which is that "good" women cannot be raped. Snow argues that rape shield laws "could be bolstered by showing that complainants have a constitutionally guaranteed right to a zone of privacy in cross-examination." She also advocates creation of "specialized sex-crimes courts" that are modeled on family courts, juvenile courts, and bankruptcy courts. The personnel of these courts, including judges, would have expertise in the area of sex crimes that would help them understand the special vulnerabilities, needs, and fears of rape victims. Ultimately, the solution is for all of us—in and out of the court system—to "re-educate ourselves about men, women, sex, and rape." Only then will rape shield laws accomplish their purpose, which is to treat both rape defendants and their accusers fairly.

For the reasons I have given, the divisions of this book are somewhat arbitrary. A different editor might well have arranged things differently—and with equal justification for so doing. The factual and explanatory chapters presuppose analyses of various concepts (such as rape itself) and invoke various interpretive and explanatory norms. The conceptual chapters not only propound theories and analyses that have an evaluative dimension; they draw on the empirical (including historical) literature of rape for cases and examples that test the reader's intuitions and judgments. The evaluative chapters presuppose both analyses and facts in their arguments. My division of the essays is therefore one of emphasis rather than of type.

Each essay reflects the richness, diversity, and power of contemporary philosophical thought. That, in fact, has been the goal in preparing this anthology: to allow the contributors to focus on what *they* take to be the most interesting and urgent questions concerning rape. I believe that this feature of the anthology, more than any other, will make it useful to nonphilosophers, many of whom (lawyers, for example) are so immersed in their work that they lack the time, training, or inclination to explore the underlying conceptual issues. My hope, as editor, is that by bringing out the abstract dimension of rape and rape law and by showing where and how that dimension underlies the factual and evaluative issues being discussed, the collection does what Hale's *Pleas of the Crown* did in the seventeenth century; namely, reshape the dialog on rape for many years to come. I will be happy, however, if it does no more than contribute to a dialog already begun.

Notes

1. Sandra Lee Bartky, *Femininity and Domination: Studies in the Phenomenology of Oppression* (New York and London: Routledge, 1990), p. 15 (essay originally published in 1975).

2. P. R. Glazebrook, introduction to *Historia Placitorum Coronæ [The History of the Pleas of the Crown]*, by Sir Matthew Hale, 2 vols. (London: Professional Books Limited, 1971), vol. 1, p. [1]. Hale's *Pleas of the Crown* was originally published in 1736, 60 years after

his death. The titular quotation appears at vol. 1, p. *635 (the asterisk indicating original pagination).

3. See chapter 1 of this volume for a history of rape law.

4. In Hale's (in)famous words, "the husband cannot be guilty of a rape committed by himself upon his lawful wife, for by their mutual matrimonial consent and contract the wife hath given up herself in this kind unto her husband, which she cannot retract." Hale, *Pleas of the Crown*, vol. 1, p. *629.

5. Ibid., p. *635. Judges do not necessarily use Hale's *words*, which I just quoted, but the intent, and probably the effect, are the same. Here is the instruction given in Idaho until its prohibition by the state Supreme Court in 1978: "A charge such as that made against the defendant in this case is one, which, generally speaking, is easily made, but difficult to disprove even though the defendant is innocent. Therefore, I charge you the law requires that you examine the testimony of [the alleged victim] with caution." *State v. Smoot*, 99 Idaho 855, 863, 590 P.2d 1001, 1009 (1978).

6. *People v. Liberta*, 64 N.Y.2d 152, 474 N.E.2d 567 (1984), cert. denied, 471 U.S. 1020 (1985).

7. *Warren v. State*, 255 Ga. 151, 336 S.E.2d 221 (1985).

8. *People v. M. D.*, 595 N.E.2d 702 (Ill. App. Ct.), appeal denied, 602 N.E.2d 467 (Ill. 1992).

9. See, e.g., Jaye Sitton, "Old Wine in New Bottles: The 'Marital' Rape Allowance," *North Carolina Law Review* 72 (November 1993):263 ("significant resistance to abolishing all laws distinguishing between marital and nonmarital rape has persisted, leading a number of jurisdictions to replace the traditional exemption with what might instead be termed a 'marital rape allowance.' In general, the allowance creates a lesser crime for wife rape than for other rapes" [citations omitted]). For a critique of the arguments that have been advanced in support of the marital-rape exemption, see Keith Burgess-Jackson, "Wife Rape," *Public Affairs Quarterly* 12 (January 1998):1–22.

10. *Marr v. State*, 494 So. 2d 1139 (Fla. 1986).

11. A. Thomas Morris, "The Empirical, Historical and Legal Case Against the Cautionary Instruction: A Call for Legislative Reform," *Duke Law Journal* (February 1988):156. See also Denise R. Johnson, "Prior False Allegations of Rape: Falsus in Uno, Falsus in Omnibus?," *Yale Journal of Law and Feminism* 7 (1995):243–76.

12. See *A Chronology of Philosophical Publications on Rape* at the end of this volume.

13. See, e.g., Robin L. West, "Legitimating the Illegitimate: A Comment on *Beyond Rape*," *Columbia Law Review* 93 (October 1993):1449.

14. For a defense of the view that philosophy *is* so limited, see Alan R. White, "Conceptual Analysis," in *The Owl of Minerva: Philosophers on Philosophy*, ed. with an introduction by Charles J. Bontempo and S. Jack Odell (New York: McGraw-Hill, 1975), pp. 103–17, esp. pp. 114–15. White claims that the value of philosophy, so conceived, is in discovering "certain important features which no other study can discover, namely, the necessary characteristics of anything, the characteristics in virtue of which it is what it is and is what it is called. How important this discovery will be depends on how important the things it studies are." Ibid., pp. 116–17.

15. See, e.g., J. L. Mackie, *Truth, Probability, and Paradox: Studies in Philosophical Logic* (Oxford: Clarendon Press, 1973), p. vii ("Philosophy, to be any good, must be analytic; but conceptual analysis is not the whole of philosophy"); Joel Feinberg, *The Moral Limits of*

the Criminal Law, vol. 1: *Harm to Others* (New York: Oxford University Press, 1984), p. 17 ("Conceptual clarification is the most distinctively philosophical of enterprises").

16. Here is the argument, which, as far as I know, has not been made elsewhere in the literature. Etymologically, "intercourse" means "to run between." *The Compact Edition of the Oxford English Dictionary* (Oxford: Oxford University Press, 1971), vol. 1, p. 1461. Originally it referred to "Communication to and fro between countries, etc.; mutual dealings between the inhabitants of different localities." Ibid.; see also Eugene Ehrlich et al., *Oxford American Dictionary* (New York: Oxford University Press, 1980), p. 345 ("any dealings or communication between people or countries"). The term incorporates an ideal or norm of mutuality (as opposed to unilaterality), which presupposes communication rather than dictation. One can see this in the fact that nobody calls robbery "commercial intercourse." Robbery is not intercourse at all. It is a corruption, betrayal, denial, or mockery of intercourse. Therefore, it is not *commercial* intercourse; therefore, it is not, as someone might claim, *nonconsensual* commercial intercourse.

Sexual intercourse, on this understanding, is communication, or mutual dealing, of a *sexual* nature between individuals (leave aside the question of what makes something sexual). But surely rape, whatever else it is, is neither mutual nor a form of communication! Conceiving of rape as sexual intercourse is therefore oxymoronic: both communicative and dictated; both mutual and unilateral. This shows that rape is not intercourse at all. As in the case of robbery, it is a corruption, betrayal, denial, or mockery of intercourse. Hence, it is not *sexual* intercourse; hence, it is not, as many theorists claim (see, e.g., John H. Bogart, "Commodification and Phenomenology: Evading Consent in Theory Regarding Rape," *Legal Theory* 2 [September 1996]:253–64), *nonconsensual* sexual intercourse. Rape is dictated, unilateral—in a word, *compelled*—sex (or sexual contact), just as robbery is compelled delivery of personal property. For the long version of this argument, culminating in a theory of rape as coercion, see chapter 5.

17. See the *Selected Bibliography* at the end of this volume.

18. Susan Brownmiller, *Against Our Will: Men, Women and Rape* (New York: Simon and Schuster, 1975), chap. 7 ("A Question of Race").

19. The internal quotation is from Lois Pineau, "Date Rape: A Feminist Analysis," *Law and Philosophy* 8 (August 1989):217–43, reprinted in Leslie Francis, ed., *Date Rape: Feminism, Philosophy, and the Law* (University Park: The Pennsylvania State University Press, 1996), pp. 1–26.

20. See David M. Adams, "Date Rape and Erotic Discourse," in *Date Rape: Feminism, Philosophy, and the Law*, ed. Leslie Francis (University Park: The Pennsylvania State University Press, 1996), pp. 27–39.

PART I

UNDERSTANDING RAPE

KEITH BURGESS-JACKSON

A History of Rape Law

Nearly a quarter century ago, Susan Brownmiller published a history of rape that by all indications set many of her readers to thinking about the subject for the first time.[1] Rape had to that point been conceived as either pathology (the act of a disturbed or diseased man) or deviance (the act of a bad man), both of which portray it as the act of one individual against another. Brownmiller's detailed research and forceful presentation made it possible to see rape as something else: a highly regulated practice or institution. In words that must have sent chills down many of her readers' spines, she wrote, "From prehistoric times to the present, I believe, rape has played a critical function. It is nothing more or less than a conscious process of intimidation by which *all men* keep *all women* in a state of fear."[2]

Brownmiller's aim in writing *Against Our Will* was to "give rape its history" in order to "deny it a future."[3] My aim in this chapter is considerably less ambitious. It is to provide a sketch, not of rape qua act or even qua institution, but of the history of rape *law*. These histories—of rape as act or institution on the one hand and of the legal rules and procedures that have been developed to govern rape on the other—are not just parallel; they are related in subtle, complex, and interesting ways.

One may wonder, for example, about the extent to which law in general, and rape law in particular, influences people's values, beliefs, attitudes, and behavior. Perhaps the law is an *expression* or *register* of certain values, beliefs, and attitudes. This seems to be the case with respect to criminal law, at any rate.[4] Needless to say, I cannot inquire into these large and difficult issues here, even if I were competent to do so, but I do assume the following: (1) that the law of a given time and place (including the law of rape) reflects some part, if not the whole, of prevailing sentiment toward that class of acts; and (2) that law (again including the law of rape) has some causal connection to how people think, what they value, and how they behave (however grudgingly). If law were unconnected in any of these ways to ordinary life, its study would be "purely academic" in the worst sense, meaning irrelevant to what most of us as persons and as citizens deem important.

"The first rape law," it has been written, "appeared in Babylon, 1900 B.C., in the Code of Hammurabi."[5] This law made sexual intercourse with "the betrothed wife" of another a capital offense. Rape was also a criminal offense in Ancient Greece. According to historian James Brundage, "Greek law . . . penalized rape, whether of a man or a woman, sometimes by fines, sometimes by more severe measures."[6] Interestingly, the Greeks treated seduction as a more serious offense than rape because seduction, unlike rape, affected one's feelings and loyalty, which were viewed as more of a threat to those who mattered; namely, husbands, fathers, and guardians. In both cases, the wronged party was a male to whom the nominal victim was related. This understanding would remain prominent in the law for many centuries. Vestiges of it appear even today.

Jewish or Hebrew law drew a distinction between married and unmarried rape victims, punishing those who victimized the former more severely than those who victimized the latter. The English jurist William Blackstone reported that in Jewish law (citing Deuteronomy 22:25),[7] rape of a Jewish woman was punished with death if the victim were married and a fine of "fifty shekels" (payable, significantly, to the victim's father) if she were unmarried—and the unmarried victim was required, willing or not, to marry her rapist.[8] Brundage says that in Ancient Judaism rape was conceived as a civil wrong rather than as a "moral offense." The wrong was for stealing a young woman's virginity from its rightful owner, her father, "thus decreasing her value on the marriage market."[9] If Scripture is to be believed, these penalties were actually inflicted in at least two cases.[10]

Early Roman law did not view rape as it is viewed today, as a distinctively sexual offense. *Raptus*, which was originally a private wrong against a man and only later a public wrong,[11] consisted in the carrying off of a woman by force, with or without intercourse.[12] In modern terms it is an abduction or kidnapping. The "raptor" (compare the bird type) removed the woman from "the person under whose authority she lived"—usually but not necessarily her father. As Brundage puts it, "The emphasis in the law relating to *raptus* generally centered on the damage that the household suffered, rather than on the personal hurt and injury done to the victim."[13] The modern term "rape" derives from this Latin word "raptus."[14]

Eventually, as the Roman civil law developed, "Either abduction or sexual relations procured by force or fear, or any combination of these elements, counted as *raptus*."[15] Rape, in other words, became a sexual offense. Interestingly (some might say "perversely"), a woman who consented to being "taken away" was punishable to the same extent as her abductor—on the grounds that she should have prevented the incident.[16] The punishment, moreover, was severe. The Roman "crime of ravishment," as Blackstone described it,[17] had always been punishable by death. But during the late or imperial Roman period, Justinian added confiscation of property.[18] Two other features of Roman law bear noting. One is that it was deemed impossible for a man to rape a prostitute,[19] and the other is that a husband could conceivably rape his wife.[20] This latter feature, as we shall see, is remarkably modern.

Medieval canon law became a well-organized legal system in about 1140, with the publication of Gratian's *Decretum*, which borrowed heavily from Roman law.[21] Gratian defined "rape" as "unlawful coitus, related to sexual corruption." In the late eleventh and twelfth centuries, rape began to be understood as a crime of violence and as a sexual offense against the person, rather than as a property crime.[22] Rape (force) was distinguished from seduction (promise). The former was treated as "the most serious sexual offense, one that merited more severe punishment than other violent crimes."[23] Gradually, four distinct elements of rape emerged: (1) the use of violence; (2) abduction; (3) coitus; and (4) lack of free consent.[24]

Canonists, who worked out the law of rape in considerable detail during this period, determined that, while strenuous resistance on the part of the victim was not required as proof of lack of consent, crying out was necessary. Unlike Roman law, canon law carved an exception for husbands—the first marital-rape exemption. It was held, moreover, that a man cannot rape a prostitute.[25] The punishment for rape, keeping in mind that these are ecclesiastical and not secular authorities, was excommunication, public penance, imprisonment, whipping, monetary fine, enslavement,[26] and infamy (inability to accuse or testify against another).[27] Any or all of these penalties could be meted out for a single offense.

As in Roman law, canon law provided that marriage could save the rapist from punishment. By the late twelfth century, canonists required that "the [rape] victim be restored to her family and that the attacker submit to their will. The family head could, if he so chose, enslave the assailant, who nonetheless retained the right to buy back his freedom if he had sufficient resources."[28] These are the penalties *as written*. "In practice," Brundage points out, "ravishment and abduction were rarely punished with anything like the severity that either secular or ecclesiastical law prescribed. This was especially true, of course, when the victim consented to abduction and, as sometimes happened, even cooperated in the affair."[29]

Blackstone writes in his *Commentaries* that "the Saxon laws" punished rape with death,[30] until William the Conqueror reduced the punishment to "castration and loss of eyes."[31] The rationale for the latter was put by Bracton as follows: "Let him lose his eyes which gave him sight of the virgin's beauty for which he coveted her. And let him lose as well the testicles which excited his hot lust."[32] Rape is obviously being understood as a crime of passion rather than as a crime of violence or domination. The historians Pollock and Maitland say in a note that if the rapist were married, his wife might intervene in the case to prevent his castration—or what Pollock and Maitland call "emasculation."[33]

Chief Justice Matthew Hale of the King's Bench subsequently defined "rape" as "the carnal knowledge of any woman above the age of ten years against her will,"[34] terminology that, despite its patent vagueness, survived for centuries.[35] Blackstone, a hundred years later, defined "rape" or "raptus" as "carnal knowledge of a woman forcibly and against her will."[36] Originally the punishment for rape in English law was death, but in 1275 the Statute of Westminster[37] reduced this to two years imprisonment and a fine—at the King's pleasure.[38] Among other provisions, the statute gave the victim 40 days in which to make her complaint to authorities. Ten years later,[39] rape was made a capital felony again,[40] a status it retained until 1840.[41]

Rape victims, like other victims of violent crime, were required by English law to raise a hue and cry so as to alert the community to the offense.[42] As in Roman law, an English victim could spare her rapist by marrying him. Unlike Roman law, however, English law made it possible for prostitutes to be raped on grounds that they may have "retreated" from that "unlawful course of life." Blackstone gave the standard rationale:

> The civil [i.e., Roman] law seems to suppose a prostitute or common harlot incapable of any injuries of this kind: not allowing any punishment for violating the chastity of her who hath indeed no chastity at all, or at least hath no regard to it. But the law of England does not judge so hardly of offenders, as to cut off all opportunity of retreat even from common strumpets, and to treat them as never capable of amendment. It therefore holds it to be felony to force even a concubine or harlot; because the woman may have forsaken that unlawful course of life.[43]

Blackstone goes on to (mis)quote Hale's dictum that rape "is an accusation easy to make, hard to be proved, but harder to be defended by the party accused, though innocent."[44] This, the so-called cautionary instruction, read by judges to jurors in rape cases, crept into American law and has been widely criticized by feminists and others. One motive for a woman to lie, according to Pollock and Maitland, was to induce the accused man to wed her and thus to "marry upward."[45] The law came to reflect this male concern (one might say "fear"). Hale, who seems to have drawn controversy to himself,[46] is also responsible for another contentious feature of English law: the marital-rape exemption.[47] The crime of statutory rape was created in 1576 during the reign of Elizabeth.[48]

Rape remained a common-law crime in England until 1976, when the British Parliament enacted some of the recommendations of a specially appointed advisory group. This group had been commissioned by the Home Secretary "to consider whether legislation should be drafted to amend or reverse"[49] the decision in *Director of Public Prosecutions v. Morgan*,[50] in which the House of Lords ruled that an honest or sincere belief that one's sexual partner is consenting to intercourse, *even if unreasonable*, provides a defense to a charge of rape.[51] The decision created a firestorm of controversy that led to the creation of the advisory panel. The result, the Sexual Offences (Amendment) Act 1976, defined "rape" as "unlawful sexual intercourse with a woman who at the time of intercourse does not consent, the man knowing she does not consent or being reckless as to whether she does."[52] Prior to this act, intention was the requisite mental state for rape. Afterward, either intention or recklessness suffices, so in principle it is now easier for the prosecutor to secure a rape conviction.

Brownmiller, with forgivable exaggeration, says that little in the English law of rape changed from the thirteenth to the twentieth centuries.[53] The American colonies, as part of their wholesale adoption of English law in the seventeenth and eighteenth centuries, brought the English law of rape into their fledgling legal systems—some of them using Blackstone's exact words.[54] The earliest Massachusetts statute, in 1642, provided that "If any man shall forcibly and without consent ravish any maid or woman that is lawfully married or contracted, he shall be put to death." The statute went on to specify that "If any man shall ravish any maid or single woman, committing carnal copulation with her by force, against her will, that is above the age of ten years, he shall be either punished with death, or with some other grievous punishment, according to circumstances, at the discretion of the judges."[55]

According to the official commentary on the *Model Penal Code*, "Older decisions and derivative American statutes defined the offense [of rape] in a number of different ways, but the central notion has always been unlawful sexual intercourse committed upon a female by imposition."[56] The various "ways" being alluded to, three of which are represented in the Massachusetts statute just quoted, include "without her consent," "against her will," "by force and against her will," and "forcible ravishment against her will."[57] In 1870, in one of the earliest reported judicial decisions on the subject, the Massachusetts Supreme Judicial Court defined "rape" as "the having carnal knowledge of a woman by force and against her will." The court ruled that the expressions "without her consent" and "against her will" were, for legal purposes, synonymous.[58]

In May 1955, the American Law Institute produced and considered a tentative draft of a *Model Penal Code* (hereafter "MPC") that addressed the topic of rape. The official draft of this document was approved and published in 1962,[59] before the rise of the modern women's movement. The MPC, which constituted "a massive effort to codify the entire criminal law, including both general principles of criminal liability and definitions of specific offenses,"[60] has been influential in many, although not all, states.[61] Since its rape provisions will be discussed in various places throughout the anthology, and since many of them have been challenged by feminists and other critics, the MPC provisions bear quotation in full:[62]

Section 213.1 Rape and Related Offenses
(1) Rape. A male who has sexual intercourse with a female not his wife is guilty of rape if:
(a) he compels her to submit by force or by threat of imminent death, serious bodily injury, extreme pain or kidnapping, to be inflicted on anyone; or
(b) he has substantially impaired her power to appraise or control her conduct by administering or employing without her knowledge drugs, intoxicants or other means for the purpose of preventing resistance; or
(c) the female is unconscious; or
(d) the female is less than 10 years old.

Rape is a felony of the second degree unless (i) in the course thereof the actor inflicts serious bodily injury upon anyone, or (ii) the victim was not a voluntary social companion of the actor upon the occasion of the crime and had not previously permitted him sexual liberties, in which cases the offense is a felony of the first degree.

(2) Gross Sexual Imposition. A male who has sexual intercourse with a female not his wife commits a felony of the third degree if:
(a) he compels her to submit by any threat that would prevent resistance by a woman of ordinary resolution; or
(b) he knows that she suffers from a mental disease or defect which renders her incapable of appraising the nature of her conduct; or
(c) he knows that she is unaware that a sexual act is being committed upon her or that she submits because she mistakenly supposes that he is her husband.

Section 2.02 of the MPC requires that the accused, whether in cases of rape or any other offense, have "acted purposely, knowingly, recklessly or negligently . . .

with respect to each material element of the offense."[63] Some critics of the MPC have argued that rape should be a strict-liability offense, while others claim that only purposeful or knowing conduct should be punishable. Still others maintain that negligence should suffice for liability.

The astute reader will have observed that there is no mention of consent in the MPC sections on rape or gross sexual imposition. A later section (2.11) of the MPC, however, provides that "The consent of the victim to conduct charged to constitute an offense or to the result thereof *is a defense* if such consent negatives an element of the offense."[64] Since consent presumably negates the element of force or threat contained in the definition of "rape," it serves as a defense to that charge. In recent years there has been much confusion and debate concerning the relations among consent, compulsion, force, threat, coercion, submission, and resistance. Just how these concepts are related to one another is a difficult and interesting philosophical question. Several of the chapters in this volume address that topic.

The MPC, despite its reformist, modernizing spirit, did not change the long-standing rule that exempted a husband from raping his wife. Indeed, it *extends* the rule by treating cohabiting couples—i.e., "persons living as man and wife"[65]— as married for purposes of the rape and gross sexual imposition statutes. This issue has generated as much controversy as any other in the law of rape. The reader will note in addition that the MPC, in section (1)(d) quoted above, treats as rape sexual intercourse with a female who is less than 10 years old. Another part of the MPC (section 213.6(1)) precludes a defense of reasonable belief that the victim was 10 years or older, thus making statutory rape, in those circumstances, a strict-liability offense.

The prescribed punishment for convicted rapists depends on two factors: first, whether, in the course of the rape, the rapist "inflicts serious bodily injury upon anyone" and, second, whether the victim was "a voluntary social companion of the actor upon the occasion of the crime."[66] If there was serious bodily injury *or* if the victim was not a voluntary social companion of the rapist (or both), rape is punishable by as little as one year imprisonment and by as much as life imprisonment. If the victim was a voluntary social companion of the rapist *and if* no person (including the victim) suffered serious bodily injury during the incident, the range of imprisonment is 1–10 years. The punishment for gross sexual imposition, which is considered a lesser offense but still a felony, is 1–5 years.[67] The MPC's graded approach to rape is one of its more distinctive and modern features.[68]

Looking back on the development of rape law, it appears to have increasingly emphasized the individualized rather than collective nature of the harm of rape. Rape came to be seen as an offense against an individual (usually, but not always, a woman) rather than as an offense against the (male-headed) family, community, or society in general. This shift might be described as one from conservatism (or traditionalism) to liberalism. Radicals such as Brownmiller have taken the liberal critique one step further, emphasizing the fact that rape harms women not just as individuals (although it surely does that) but *as women*. Neither the liberal critique of conservatism nor the radical critique of liberalism has been entirely successful to this point, and the law of rape currently reflects all three understandings. I now sketch some of the recent developments and trends in rape law.[69]

Substantive Changes

As late as 1975—coincidentally, the year in which Brownmiller's *Against Our Will* appeared—Michigan's rape statute provided that "any person who shall ravish and carnally know any female of the age of 16 years or more by force and against her will . . . shall be guilty of a felony."[70] Other states, either by statute or by court decision, defined "rape" as unlawful sexual intercourse with a female not the wife of the accused without her consent.[71] Whether the language in question is "by force," "against her will," "without her consent," or some combination of the three, the focus of rape law and practice has been on the victim's mental state and behavior.[72] This fact about the law of rape has struck many reformers, liberal and radical alike, as misplaced, unjust, and intolerable, and has led to the enactment of statutes that eliminate nonconsent as an element of the offense.

Michigan's reform statute, for example, which became effective in April 1975,[73] emphasizes the force or coercion used by the rapist, not the resistance (or lack thereof) of the victim.[74] This, it is claimed, brings rape in line with other violent felonies. No prosecutor has to prove beyond a reasonable doubt that a *robbery* victim did not consent to the taking of his or her money or that a *murder* victim did not consent to being killed; so why should a prosecutor in a rape case have to prove that the *rape* victim did not consent? So goes the argument. This development goes to the core of the legal understanding of rape and has therefore generated heated controversy. Much has been written about the Michigan experiment in particular.

Another change in the traditional law of rape has been to eliminate or reduce the scope of the marital-rape exemption, which precludes a charge of rape against a husband—however premeditated, however violent, and however injurious his act may be. Only a handful of states now confer what one critic has called a "marital-rape allowance."[75] Most have abolished the exemption entirely. Many legislators and judges have apparently been persuaded by the argument that married women should have at least as much legal protection against rape as their unmarried cohorts. The scholar and activist Diana E. H. Russell has been at the forefront of efforts to abolish the exemption, which, like other rape-law doctrines, has centuries-old roots.[76]

Other developments in the law of rape, some of which occurred in only a few jurisdictions, include (1) eliminating the *mens rea* requirement, thus making it a strict- or absolute-liability offense;[77] (2) prohibiting unconsented-to (or forcible) anal and oral penetration as well as vaginal penetration, which the law traditionally required;[78] (3) creating a hierarchy of sexual offenses rather than just one all-purpose offense; (4) making the crime of rape sex-neutral rather than sex-specific, so that women as well as men can be perpetrators and men as well as women can be victims;[79] and (5) changing the name of the offense from "rape" to "sexual assault" or "sexual conduct."[80] One motive for the latter development is to avoid the stigma of being a rapist and therefore make a jury less reluctant to convict an admittedly culpable defendant.[81]

These changes in the substantive law of rape, even where less than universal, are significant. They reflect the essential contestedness of the concept of rape.[82] The law of rape is in a state of flux *because* there are different theories or understandings of the nature of the underlying offense. Each theorist seeks to make the law of rape reflect what he or she takes to be the wrong or harm of rape.[83] Since no theorist—conservative, liberal, radical, or otherwise—can control the process of change, the law remains a mélange. Here, as elsewhere, law mirrors the sentiments of society.

Procedural and Evidentiary Changes

One of the more widespread and controversial developments in recent years has been the enactment by state legislatures of so-called rape shield statutes, the aim of which is to narrow the circumstances in which inquiry may be made into the sexual history of a rape victim.[84] Where nonconsent is an element of the offense, as it has been traditionally and remains in most states, a significant percentage of rape trials come down to the question whether the victim consented to intercourse with the defendant on the occasion in question, the defendant often admitting that intercourse occurred. He says she consented; she says she did not. Defense attorneys seek to show that the victim consented to sexual intercourse with the defendant on one or more prior occasions, the implication being that she consented on the occasion in question. Evidence is also introduced to the effect that the victim consented to intercourse with *other men* under relevantly similar conditions. Some states have gone so far as to allow evidence of the victim's reputation for (un)chastity.[85]

These sorts of evidence, whether intended to do so or not, are likely to inflame a jury. Feminists have argued that sexual-history evidence unduly prejudices the jury against the victim and encourages them to apply stereotypes of "loose women" and "innocent boys" to the parties. In effect, it puts the rape *victim*, rather than (or in addition to) the defendant, on trial. Liberals tend to be ambivalent about rape shield laws, with some arguing that such statutes infringe on a defendant's right to a fair trial. If a defendant may not introduce evidence of prior acts of consensual intercourse by the complaining witness, the liberal argues, he is denied the opportunity to raise a reasonable doubt about an essential element of the offense. Some states have compromised the point by allowing evidence of prior consensual sex with the *defendant*, but not with others. Michigan's new sexual-conduct statute, for example, allows evidence for this purpose as well as to show the origin of pregnancy, disease, or semen. Recently, rape shield laws have come under attack on a different ground: for infringing on the constitutional right of a criminal defendant to effective assistance of counsel.[86] The controversy has been, and continues to be, a live one.[87]

Other procedural or evidentiary rules that have come under fire in recent years are (1) the corroboration requirement, which in practice prevents a defendant from being convicted solely on the basis of the victim's testimony;[88] (2) the utmost-resistance requirement, which prohibits a conviction for rape where the victim submitted to sexual intercourse, even if she were paralyzed with fear and did not consent to it;[89] (3) prompt-notice or prompt-reporting requirements, which are modern vestiges of the hue-and-cry requirement of English law;[90] and (4) a cautionary instruction from the judge to the jury to the effect that "rape is an easy charge to make but a difficult one to defend against."[91] In addition, there have been changes made to the rules by which rape victims' names are released by court officials to the public[92] and to the procedures used by police departments and prosecutors' offices in investigating and processing rape charges.[93]

Some radicals have argued that since rape victims are, as a matter of fact, viewed by jurors as codefendants (the charge, they say, is "consenting to sexual intercourse," which "good girls" are not supposed to do), they should have the same constitutional protections as are accorded defendants.[94] No state, to my knowledge, has accepted this argument or tried to implement its conclusion. As a general matter, liberals insist that rape be treated like any other violent crime. Their aim has been to remove special rules such as the corroboration and utmost-resistance requirements, rules that do not apply to felonies such as murder or robbery.[95] Radicals, on the other hand, have tried to show why rape, being essentially a crime of men against women, *is* special among violent crimes and therefore *requires* accommodation by the legal system—although not in the traditional way. Both theorists challenge the conservative approach to rape, which, as we have seen, views rape as a crime against male privilege (patriarchy).

Penal Changes

For those individuals who believe that rape is a serious offense and that rapists ought to be punished accordingly, which is just about everyone, the traditional punishment for rape—death or a lengthy term of imprisonment[96]—is viewed as counterproductive. Jurors have been reluctant, perhaps understandably so, to inflict such severe punishment on admittedly guilty defendants, but since these jurors have no alternative other than to acquit, acquittal is often the result. Jury nullification occurs and rapists go free.[97] Both liberals and radicals are disturbed by this phenomenon (the latter more than the former) and have sought to change the punishment for rape so as to make conviction more likely.[98] In states with one rape offense and one prescribed punishment, this has led to abolition of the death penalty or to decreases in the length of prison terms or both. In other states, it has produced gradations of punishment depending on the presence of certain "aggravating" factors.[99] Some states have reduced both the penalty *and* the judge's discretion, providing more or less mandatory sentences for convicted rapists.[100]

In Michigan, to illustrate this development, the "carnal knowledge" statute has been replaced by four degrees of "criminal sexual conduct (CSC)." First-degree CSC, defined as aggravated sexual penetration (where aggravation includes any or all of the following: the victim being below 13 years of age; the actor being in a position of authority over the victim; the actor committing a felony during the act; the actor using a weapon; there being aiders and abettors; personal injury being inflicted), is punishable by life imprisonment. Second-degree CSC, which is aggravated sexual *contact* (touching as opposed to penetration), is punishable by up to 15 years' imprisonment, as is third-degree CSC, which is defined as nonaggravated sexual penetration. Fourth-degree CSC, defined as nonaggravated sexual contact, is punishable by up to 2 years' imprisonment and a fine of $500. Michigan has no minimum punishments for these offenses, a fact that has generated criticism.[101]

As these developments and trends indicate, the law of rape has been in a state of flux for at least a generation. The liberal has tried, in many cases successfully, to promote equality and neutrality in the law of rape by taking the sex out of it—by insisting that rape be viewed as a crime of violence. Rape, the liberal says, is in principle no different from murder, robbery, arson, or larceny. In each case, one individual transgresses the property or autonomy rights (or both) of another. The role of the criminal law is to identify and punish such transgressors. That rape is predominantly a crime of men against women is of no moment, at least to the criminal law.

The radical sees things differently. The radical sees rape as essentially sexual in nature but also as violent—indeed, *as sexual violence*. To take the sex out of rape is to make it something it is not. One legal scholar has argued that rape is special (among crimes) in at least three ways: (1) "[I]t is predominantly a crime of male perpetrators and female victims, and there is . . . a 'power' differential between men and women in our society"; (2) "the conduct that is criminalized by rape laws is, absent force or some other unacceptable 'imposition,' [a] frequently engaged in and desirable activity"; and (3) "social stereotypes have had and continue to have a profound influence upon the law."[102] If rape is indeed sui generis, as this line of thought suggests, then the law ought to reflect it not only substantively but in the procedures, evidentiary rules, and penalties it provides.

Another way to frame the point is to say that while the liberal *and* the radical are concerned with sexual equality, the radical seeks to promote equality somewhat differently: by noticing and then trying to change the ways in which even neutrally phrased doctrines and procedures are *applied* in cases of rape.[103] The radical views traditional rape law as fundamentally sexist, as reflecting certain assumptions about how men and women are by nature. The doctrine of consent, for instance, which appears to be a neutral and even-handed means for distinguishing rape from lawful or ordinary sexual intercourse, appears to the radical as an effective means to perpetuate sexual *inequality*, for it assumes, falsely, that women have as much control as men do over the terms and conditions of sexual intercourse.[104] Under conditions of inequality, sexual submission rooted in fear and powerlessness looks like consent. In short, the radical agrees with the liberal that consent counts, but disagrees about what counts (or should count) as consent.

Amid the flux of scholarly debate and practical reform, one thing is clear: The law of rape has not ceased, and in all likelihood will not cease, to evolve.[105] Nor, arguably, should it, for the law of rape, like any body of law—perhaps *more* than other bodies of law—reflects changing social attitudes and conditions, normative as well as material. Exactly where the law of rape goes from here depends to a large extent on the arguments that theorists and practitioners muster for and against various changes. It is to articulating and evaluating some of these arguments that the remaining chapters of this volume are devoted.

Notes

1. Susan Brownmiller, *Against Our Will: Men, Women and Rape* (New York: Simon and Schuster, 1975). For a critique of Brownmiller, see Edward Shorter, "On Writing the History of Rape," *Signs* 3 (Winter 1977):471–82.

2. Brownmiller, *Against Our Will*, p. 15 (italics in original).

3. Ibid., p. 404.

4. Joel Feinberg has argued that one function of criminal punishment (and presumably also of the statutes that provide for punishment) is to express society's condemnation of the behavior for which the individual is being punished. See Joel Feinberg, "The Expressive Function of Punishment," in *Doing and Deserving: Essays in the Theory of Responsibility* (Princeton, NJ: Princeton University Press, 1970), pp. 95–118 (essay originally published in 1965).

5. Sally Gold and Martha Wyatt, "The Rape System: Old Roles and New Times," *Catholic University Law Review* 27 (1978):696. For details on the Code of Hammurabi, see ibid., pp. 696–99; Brownmiller, *Against Our Will*, pp. 18–19.

6. James A. Brundage, *Law, Sex, and Christian Society in Medieval Europe* (Chicago: University of Chicago Press, 1987), p. 14.

7. "But if a man finds a betrothed young woman in the countryside, and the man forces her and lies with her, then only the man who lay with her shall die." *Holy Bible: Containing the Old and New Testaments*, The New King James Version, Red Letter Edition, The Open Bible, Expanded Edition (Nashville: Thomas Nelson, 1985), p. 195.

8. Sir William Blackstone, *Commentaries on the Laws of England*, 4 vols. (Chicago and London: The University of Chicago Press, 1979), vol. 4, p. *210 (facsimile of first edition, published in 1765–69) (citing Deuteronomy 22:25–29); see also Brundage, *Law, Sex, and Christian Society*, p. 56; Gold and Wyatt, "The Rape System," p. 698; Brownmiller, *Against Our Will*, pp. 19–20. The asterisk (*) before a numeral indicates that the reference is to the original page number.

9. Brundage, *Law, Sex, and Christian Society*, p. 55 (citation omitted).

10. Brundage cites Genesis 34:1–31, Exodus 22:16–17, Deuteronomy 22:25–29, and 2 Kings 13:1–34. See ibid., pp. 56, 56 n. 31.

11. The Emperor Constantine made it a public offense, punishable by death. See James A. Brundage, "Rape and Seduction in the Medieval Canon Law," in *Sexual Practices and the Medieval Church*, ed. Vern L. Bullough and James Brundage (Buffalo, NY: Prometheus Books, 1982), p. 142; Brundage, *Law, Sex, and Christian Society*, p. 107.

12. "Both medieval and modern notions of rape emerged from the *raptus*—literally carrying off by force—of the Roman law." Brundage, "Rape and Seduction," p. 141.

13. Brundage, *Law, Sex, and Christian Society*, p. 48 (citation omitted).

14. See, e.g., D. P. Simpson, *Cassell's Latin Dictionary*, 5th ed. (New York: Macmillan, 1968), p. 807 (first edition published in 1959).

15. Brundage, *Law, Sex, and Christian Society*, p. 48.

16. Ibid., p. 107.

17. Blackstone, *Commentaries*, vol. 4, p. *210; see also Brundage, "Rape and Seduction," p. 145.

18. Brundage, "Rape and Seduction," p. 142; Brundage, *Law, Sex, and Christian Society*, p. 47.

19. Blackstone, *Commentaries*, vol. 4, p. *212.

20. Brundage, "Rape and Seduction," p. 144.

21. Ibid., p. 142.

22. Ibid., pp. 142–43; Brundage, *Law, Sex, and Christian Society*, p. 209.

23. Brundage, "Rape and Seduction," p. 143.

24. Ibid.

25. Ibid., p. 147; Brundage, *Law, Sex, and Christian Society*, p. 466.

26. Brundage, "Rape and Seduction," p. 145; Brundage, *Law, Sex, and Christian Society*, p. 398.

27. Brundage, "Rape and Seduction," p. 146; Brundage, *Law, Sex, and Christian Society*, p. 209.

28. Brundage, *Law, Sex, and Christian Society*, p. 313.

29. Ibid., p. 472 (citation omitted).

30. Brownmiller adds "dismemberment." Brownmiller, *Against Our Will*, p. 24.

31. Blackstone, *Commentaries*, vol. 4, p. *211; see also Frederick Pollock and Frederic William Maitland, *The History of English Law Before the Time of Edward I*, 2nd ed., 2 vols. (Cambridge: Cambridge University Press, 1968), vol. 2, p. 490 (reissue of 1898 2nd ed.); *Model Penal Code and Commentaries* (Official Draft and Revised Comments), Part II (Philadelphia: The American Law Institute, 1980), p. 275 n. 1; Brownmiller, *Against Our Will*, p. 25.

32. Quoted in Brownmiller, *Against Our Will*, p. 25.

33. Pollock and Maitland, *History of English Law*, vol. 2, p. 492 n. 6.

34. Sir Matthew Hale, *Historia Placitorum Coronæ* [*The History of the Pleas of the Crown*], 2 vols. (London: Professional Books Limited, 1971), vol. 1, p. *628 (originally published in 1736) (quoted in Gold and Wyatt, "The Rape System," p. 699).

35. Michigan's rape statute, enacted in 1846, used the words "ravish and carnally know" until its repeal in 1975. See Kenneth A. Cobb and Nancy R. Schauer, "Legislative Note: Michigan's Criminal Sexual Assault Law," *University of Michigan Journal of Law Reform* 8 (Fall 1974):219 n. 13.

36. Blackstone, *Commentaries*, vol. 4, p. *210.

37. 3 Edw. 1, Westm. 1, ch. 13.

38. The offense was reduced to a trespass. See *Model Penal Code*, p. 275 n. 1.

39. 13 Edw. 1, Westm. 2, ch. 34.

40. An historian who studied the matter found no executions between 1285 and 1330. See G. Geis, "Lord Hale, Witches, and Rape," *British Journal of Law and Society* 5 (1978): 26–27 (citing J. M. Kaye, "The Making of English Criminal Law: (1) The Beginnings—A General Survey of Criminal Law and Justice Down to 1500," *The Criminal Law Review* [1977]:4–13).

41. Roy Porter, "Rape—Does It Have a Historical Meaning?," in *Rape: An Historical and Cultural Enquiry*, ed. Sylvana Tomaselli and Roy Porter (Oxford: Basil Blackwell, 1986), p. 217.

42. Brownmiller, *Against Our Will*, p. 26.

43. Blackstone, *Commentaries*, vol. 4, pp. *212–13 (citations omitted).

44. Ibid., pp. *214–15. Hale's actual words were "it must be remembered, that [rape] is an accusation easily to be made and hard to be proved, and harder to be defended by the party accused, tho never so innocent." Hale, *Pleas of the Crown*, vol. 1, p. *635.

45. Pollock and Maitland, *History of English Law*, vol. 2, p. 491.

46. Among other things, he presided over a witchcraft trial that resulted in two women being hanged and had a scandalous second marriage to his housekeeper. See Geis, "Lord Hale," for details.

47. See ibid., p. 40. As Hale put it, "the husband cannot be guilty of a rape committed by himself upon his lawful wife, for by their mutual matrimonial consent and contract the wife hath given up herself in this kind unto her husband, which she cannot retract." Hale, *Pleas of the Crown*, vol. 1, p. *629. For a critique of arguments for the marital-rape exemption, see Keith Burgess-Jackson, "Wife Rape," *Public Affairs Quarterly* 12 (January 1998):1–22.

48. 18 Eliz., ch. 7, sec. 4. See Brundage, "Rape and Seduction," p. 264 n. 25. For a discussion, see Keith Burgess-Jackson, "Statutory Rape: A Philosophical Analysis," *The Canadian Journal of Law & Jurisprudence* 8 (January 1995):139–58; reprinted in *Human Sexuality*, ed. Igor Primoratz (Aldershot, England: Dartmouth, 1997), pp. 463–82.

49. Leigh Bienen, "Mistakes," *Philosophy & Public Affairs* 7 (Spring 1978):230.

50. [1975] 2 All E.R. 347, 1976 App. Cas. 182 (H.L. 1975).

51. For critiques of *Morgan*, see E. M. Curley, "Excusing Rape," *Philosophy & Public Affairs* 5 (Summer 1976):325–60; Anthony Kenny, "The Mental Element in Crime," in *Controversies in Criminal Law: Philosophical Essays on Responsibility and Procedure*, ed. Michael J. Gorr and Sterling Harwood (Boulder, CO: Westview Press, 1992), pp. 17–31 (essay originally published in 1978).

52. Quoted in Bienen, "Mistakes," p. 231 n. 18.

53. Brownmiller, *Against Our Will*, p. 30.

54. Blackstone's definition of "rape," Brundage writes, "has been incorporated, often verbatim, into modern statute law in many jurisdictions." Brundage, "Rape and Seduction," p. 262 n. 2.

55. *Commonwealth v. Burke*, 105 Mass. 376, 380 (1870). Gold and Wyatt write: "Both the Bible and the English common law accompanied American settlers across the Atlantic, and in 1648 [*sic*] the first codification of these principles occurred in Massachusetts." Gold and Wyatt, "The Rape System," p. 700.

56. *Model Penal Code*, p. 275. According to Gold and Wyatt, the "typical common law definition of rape states that '[a] person commits rape when he has carnal knowledge of a female, forcibly and against her will.'" Gold and Wyatt, "The Rape System," p. 701 (citing many statutes).

57. *Model Penal Code*, p. 275.

58. *Commonwealth v. Burke*, 105 Mass. at 377.

59. *Model Penal Code*, p. 274.

60. H. S. S., "Recent Statutory Developments in the Definition of Forcible Rape," *Virginia Law Review* 61 (November 1975):1501. Wallace Loh says that "Most state criminal laws were developed piecemeal since the turn of the century, and were ad hoc responses to immediate law enforcement exigencies. The [Model Penal] Code was a massive effort to bring a sense of order to the antiquated, prolix body of state laws by proposing model criminal legislation." Wallace D. Loh, "Q: What Has Reform of Rape Legislation Wrought? A: Truth in Criminal Labelling," *Journal of Social Issues* 37 (1981):34 (citing Herbert Wechsler, "The Challenge of a Model Penal Code," *Harvard Law Review* 65 [1952]:1097–1133).

61. "By 1970," Loh writes, "over thirty jurisdictions had started or completed revisions modeled after the [Model Penal] Code." Loh, "Q: What Has Reform of Rape Legislation Wrought?," p. 34 (citing S. J. Fox, "Reflections on the Law Reforming Process," *Journal of Law Reform* 4 [1971]:443–60). Some states emulated New York's alternative approach. Others, such as Michigan, struck out on their own. See H. S. S., "Recent Statutory Developments," pp. 1500–503.

62. Article 213 of the MPC is entitled "Sexual Offenses." Its sections are entitled, respectively, "Definitions" (213.0), "Rape and Related Offenses" (213.1), "Deviate Sexual Intercourse by Force or Imposition" (213.2), "Corruption of Minors and Seduction" (213.3), "Sexual Assault" (213.4), "Indecent Exposure" (213.5), and "Provisions Generally Applicable to Article 213" (213.6). Section 213.4, on sexual assault, governs sexual *contact* rather than sexual *intercourse*, the latter of which is defined as "some penetration [vaginal, anal, or oral] however slight." *Model Penal Code*, sec. 213.0(2).

63. Ibid., sec. 2.02(1).

64. Ibid., sec. 2.11(1) (emphasis added).

65. Ibid., sec. 213.6(2).

66. Ibid., sec. 213.1(1).

67. Ibid., sec. 6.06.

68. For a concise but useful discussion of the history of the MPC, see *Model Penal Code*, pp. 279–81.

69. For a discussion of the effects of certain reform measures such as those implemented in Michigan and Washington, see Loh, "Q: What Has Reform of Rape Legislation Wrought?" Loh's study found that reform brought "no change in the overall rates of convictions and pleas" and "no change in the overall rate of charging" by prosecutors. Revised penalties, however, made punishment for rape more certain (if not more severe). Loh's conclusion is that "the main impact of the statutory reform has been a symbolic and educative one for society at large, rather than an instrumental one for law enforcement." Ibid., p. 28.

70. Mich. Comp. Laws sec. 750.520 (1967). This statute was enacted in 1846. See Cobb and Schauer, "Legislative Note"; Margaret T. Gordon and Stephanie Riger, *The Female Fear: The Social Cost of Rape* (Urbana: University of Illinois Press, 1991), pp. 63–65 (originally published in 1989).

71. See *Black's Law Dictionary*, 6th ed. (St. Paul, MN: West, 1990), p. 1134 (s.v. "rape") (citing *State v. Lora*, 213 Kan. 184, 515 P.2d 1086, 1093 [1973]) (first edition published in 1891).

72. See "Forcible and Statutory Rape: An Exploration of the Operation and Objectives of the Consent Standard," *The Yale Law Journal* 62 (December 1952):55 n. 3 ("Statutes may define forcible rape with such phrases as 'against her will,' or 'by force.' But these expressions are generally considered synonomous [*sic*] with 'without her consent'" [citations omitted]). See also Robin D. Wiener, "Shifting the Communication Burden: A Meaningful Consent Standard in Rape," *Harvard Women's Law Journal* 6 (Spring 1983):143–46.

73. Loh calls Michigan's reform statute "The sharpest departure from, and the most sweeping revision of, common law statutes of rape." Loh, "Q: What Has Reform of Rape Legislation Wrought?," p. 44. The Michigan statute has served as a model for many other states. Ibid.; see also H. S. S., "Recent Statutory Developments," p. 1502.

74. See Cobb and Schauer, "Legislative Note," pp. 223–26. The word "consent" does not appear in the Michigan statute. Ibid., p. 226 n. 73.

75. Jaye Sitton, "Old Wine in New Bottles: The 'Marital' Rape Allowance," *North Carolina Law Review* 72 (November 1993):261–89.

76. See, e.g., Diana E. H. Russell, *Rape in Marriage*, exp. and rev. ed. with a new introduction (Bloomington and Indianapolis: Indiana University Press, 1990) (originally published in 1982 by Macmillan). Subsequent references are to the expanded and revised edition.

77. See *State v. Reed*, 479 A.2d 1291 (Me. 1984); *Commonwealth v. Williams*, 439 A.2d 765 (Pa. Super. Ct. 1982); *Commonwealth v. Grant*, 464 N.E.2d 33 (Mass. 1984).

78. The law of rape traditionally covered only vaginal penetration, "however slight," and emission of semen was not required. See Russell, *Rape in Marriage*, p. 18.

79. See Gordon and Riger, *The Female Fear*, p. 65. In 1975, the House of Delegates of the American Bar Association issued a resolution urging a number of rape-law reforms. Among these was the "redefinition of rape and related crimes in terms of 'persons' instead of 'women.'" "House of Delegates Redefines Death, Urges Redefinition of Rape, and Undoes the Houston Amendments," *American Bar Association Journal* 61 (April 1975):465 (quoted in Vicki McNickle Rose, "Rape As a Social Problem: A Byproduct of the Feminist Movement," *Social Problems* 25 [October 1977]:82). As early as 1973, Camille LeGrand had argued that "Men who are sexually assaulted should have the same protection as female victims, and women who sexually assault men or other women should be as liable for conviction as conventional rapists." Camille E. LeGrand, "Rape and Rape Laws: Sexism in Society and Law," *California Law Review* 61 (May 1973):941. LeGrand's rationale was that this "might do much to place rape law in a healthier perspective and to reduce the mythical elements that have tended to make rape laws a means of reinforcing the status of women as sexual possessions." Ibid.

80. Other names that have been used or proposed are "sexual battery," "sexual inter-

course without consent," "gross sexual imposition," "aggravated felonious assault," and "felonious sexual penetration." See H. S. S., "Recent Statutory Developments," p. 1542 n. 220. The author of this student note advocates "complete elimination of the word 'rape' from criminal codes" on grounds that it "would help eliminate some of the traditional social reactions which have placed such a strain on the legal system." Ibid., p. 1542; see also Jennifer Temkin, "Women, Rape and Law Reform," in *Rape: An Historical and Cultural Enquiry*, ed. Sylvana Tomaselli and Roy Porter (Oxford: Basil Blackwell, 1986), p. 24 ("[T]he word ["rape"] evokes images and associations which are not altogether helpful in a modern context. For rape, as the dictionary states, is a taking or carrying off by force, the ravishment or violation of a woman or of a country. Arguably today, the law should seek to protect the right of every woman to choose whether to have sexual intercourse or not and its language should reflect this objective").

81. This may be a mixed blessing from the standpoint of the radical. On the one hand, as indicated in the text, removing the stigma associated with being a rapist may increase the number of rape convictions, which the radical desires; but on the other hand, removing the stigma eliminates the opportunity for society to express its condemnation of men who rape. As Loh points out, "to brand someone as a rapist is a kind of 'status degradation,' whereby he is 'transformed into something looked on as lower in the social scheme of social types.'" Loh, "Q: What Has Reform of Rape Legislation Wrought?," p. 37 (quoting H. Garfinkel, "Conditions of Successful Status Degradation Ceremonies," *American Journal of Sociology* 61 [1956]:420). Since, in the radical view, rape is a kind of degradation, it is arguably fitting, and therefore in keeping with retributive principles, that the rapist be degraded.

82. The concept of an essentially contested concept, which, if the literature is any indication, is itself an essentially contested concept, comes from W. B. Gallie, "Essentially Contested Concepts," *Proceedings of the Aristotelian Society* 56 (1956):167–98.

83. See Keith Burgess-Jackson, "Rape and Persuasive Definition," *Canadian Journal of Philosophy* 25 (September 1995):415–54.

84. According to John Dwight Ingram, "All fifty states and the federal government now have enacted some kind of rape-shield law, either by statute, judicial opinion, or rule of court." John Dwight Ingram, "Date Rape: It's Time for 'No' to Really Mean 'No,'" *American Journal of Criminal Law* 21 (Fall 1993):15 (citation omitted).

85. "[B]efore 1981, Virginia's rape law assumed that a woman with prior sexual experience would be casual and unselective in choosing sexual partners and thus would be more likely to have consented to the act in question. And generally, a sexually experienced woman was assumed to be morally deficient, and thus more likely to lie in bringing a charge of rape." Ibid., p. 12 (citations omitted).

86. See Joel E. Smith, "Constitutionality of 'Rape Shield' Statute Restricting Use of Evidence of Victim's Sexual Experiences," *American Law Reports 4th* 1 (1980):283–305.

87. The evidence scholar John Henry Wigmore said that no evidentiary question has been more controverted than whether to allow evidence of a rape victim's prior sexual conduct. See H. S. S., "Recent Statutory Developments," p. 1508 (citing John Henry Wigmore, *Evidence*, 3rd ed., vol. 1, sec. 200, p. 682 [1940]). For a discussion and critique of rape shield statutes, see Kristine Cordier Karnezis, "Modern Status of Admissibility, in Forcible Rape Prosecution, of Complainant's Prior Sexual Acts," *American Law Reports 3d* 94 (1979): 257–86; Peter M. Hazelton, "Rape Shield Laws: Limits on Zealous Advocacy," *American Journal of Criminal Law* 19 (Fall 1991):35–56; Elizabeth Kessler, "Pattern of Sexual Conduct Evidence and Present Consent: Limiting the Admissibility of Sexual History Evidence in Rape Prosecutions," *Women's Rights Law Reporter* 14 (Winter 1992):79–96.

88. See "The Rape Corroboration Requirement: Repeal Not Reform," *The Yale Law Journal* 81 (June 1972):1382 ("The corroboration requirement, in effect, is a prior determina-

tion that if the prosecution's case stands solely on the testimony of the complainant, the defendant shall win"). The corroboration rule may rest on a belief that women are vengeful liars. See Brownmiller, *Against Our Will*, pp. 22, 228, 238, 278 n. *, 364, 369, 370, 371–74, 386–87.

89. "This 'utmost resistance' formulation of 'against her will' involved two separate requirements. First, the victim must have resisted intercourse to the 'utmost' of her physical capacity. Second, she must have resisted to the utmost in the sense that this resistance must not have abated during the struggle." H. S. S., "Recent Statutory Developments," p. 1506. For a discussion and critique of this requirement, see Brownmiller, *Against Our Will*, pp. 360, 384–85; Brundage, *Law, Sex, and Christian Society*, pp. 107, 311–13, 396–98, 469–72; Gordon and Riger, *The Female Fear*, pp. 59–60; Kurt Weis and Sandra S. Borges, "Victimology and Rape: The Case of the Legitimate Victim," *Issues in Criminology* 8 (Fall 1973):84; Susan Estrich, *Real Rape* (Cambridge: Harvard University Press, 1987), pp. 29–41. Angela Davis asks the following rhetorical question: "Is a businessman asked to resist the encroachment of a robber in order to guarantee that his property rights will be protected by the courts?" Angela Y. Davis, "We Do Not Consent: Violence Against Women in a Racist Society," in *Women, Culture, and Politics* (New York: Random House, 1989), p. 41 (essay originally published in 1987).

90. See Brundage, *Law, Sex, and Christian Society*, p. 484.

91. Russell, *Rape in Marriage*, p. 18. As we saw, the rule derives from the English jurist Matthew Hale.

92. See Cobb and Schauer, "Legislative Note," p. 231 (discussing the Michigan statute).

93. According to Loh, "King County [Washington] prosecutors claim that they have adopted a more aggressive filing posture since the new [rape] law went into effect. The office has bolstered its enforcement capability by establishing a specialized Sexual Assault Unit, recruited more women prosecutors, sensitized its staff to the unique problems posed by rape, and generally pursued a tougher filing policy." Loh, "Q: What Has Reform of Rape Legislation Wrought?," pp. 40–41.

94. See Gold and Wyatt, "The Rape System," pp. 695–727.

95. Estrich is prominent here. See Estrich, *Real Rape*.

96. As of October 1971, "Seventeen states and the District of Columbia [could] sentence rapists to death." Diane K. Shah, "Women Attack Rape Justice," *The National Observer* 10 (9 October 1971):21. The student author of a June 1972 note in *The Yale Law Journal* says that "Sixteen states still prescribe capital punishment for rape." "The Rape Corroboration Requirement," p. 1381. The United States Supreme Court subsequently ruled, however, that the death penalty for rapists is unconstitutional (a violation of the Eighth Amendment). *Coker v. Georgia*, 433 U.S. 584 (1977). On the history of capital punishment for rape, see Brundage, *Law, Sex, and Christian Society*, pp. 47–48, 119, 133, 530–33.

97. "The Rape Corroboration Requirement," p. 1381.

98. See Rose, "Rape As a Social Problem," pp. 81, 82, 84.

99. See ibid., p. 82. Another commentator says that "the general trend in the last decade has been to specify degrees of forcible rape and further to identify specific aggravating circumstances to distinguish between them, as exemplified by the Model Penal Code." H. S. S., "Recent Statutory Developments," p. 1522.

100. See Rose, "Rape As a Social Problem," p. 81.

101. For analysis, discussion, and a critique of Michigan's statute, see Cobb and Schauer, "Legislative Note."

102. James J. Tomkovicz, "On Teaching Rape: Reasons, Risks, and Rewards," *The Yale Law Journal* 102 (November 1992):489–90. I do not know whether it is accurate to classify Tomkovicz as a radical or whether he would welcome the label, but he *is* making a radical case that rape is special.

103. See ibid., p. 505 n. 65.

104. For an argument that nonconsent should be eliminated as an element of rape, see Gold and Wyatt, "The Rape System," p. 726.

105. Reform can occur quickly and on a wide scale, largely through mimicry. Loh reports in 1981 that "Since the enactment in 1974 by Michigan of the first comprehensive reform rape legislation in the nation, some forty states have modified existing or passed new statutes on rape." Loh, "Q: What Has Reform of Rape Legislation Wrought?," pp. 28–29 (citations omitted).

PATRICIA SMITH

Social Revolution and the Persistence of Rape

By and large, an effective change in law requires a substantial revision of cultural attitude, not the other way around. Still, some legal reform, as long as it is incremental, can encourage cultural evolution. Certainly there has been enormous social upheaval with regard to sexual relations between men and women during the second half of the twentieth century—so much so, in fact, that it is often called a sexual revolution. One might think that recent cultural change, then, is sufficient to support some needed legal reform. But the changes, while undeniable, are difficult to assess. In some ways they are cataclysmic; in others, barely discernible. Rape, for one thing, is as prevalent, menacing, and limiting to women as it has ever been.[1] Assuming that rape, like slavery, is an evil that we would like to see evolve out of existence, I would like to consider what has changed, what hasn't changed with regard to sexual attitudes, as well as what might be changed—especially in law and legal enforcement— to encourage the decline of rape in our culture.

What Has Changed and What Hasn't

Although it is an oversimplification, it is still generally true that women were the sexual property of men for most of the history of civilization in virtually the entire world. This manifested itself in two forms: reproductive property and "recreational" property. Both almost totally eliminated the autonomy of women. Very few women ever were or could be independent.[2] All customs, attitudes, and institutions concerned with sex (and almost everything else as well), including attitudes, customs, and laws about rape, reflect that history. Thus, one earth-shattering change in modern society has been the decline during the past two centuries of the general view of women as property and the emergence of the idea of women as autonomous (or at least individual) human beings with interests of their own.[3] This was a very novel idea—every bit as astounding and transformative as the idea that all men were created equal, which appeared only a bit earlier.

There is no question that before the 19th century the crime of rape was a crime against men (as owners of their wives and daughters). This was demonstrated by many legal policies. One common one, for example, was that a man charged with rape (which was, like horse thievery, a capital offense) could exonerate himself by marrying his victim and paying her father a sum equal to her estimated value on the marriage market (so to speak).[4] This suggests that women were viewed more or less like valuable livestock or perhaps uniquely prized possessions. Women, especially virgins, were very valuable property.[5] But since their value was conditioned on their sexual purity, they could be very easily ruined, and consequently required strict and careful guarding. This produced the dual male role of predator and protector of the female prey, all of which has survived in many subtle forms, even though the idea of women as property has declined. Of course, it was always the case that only certain women could be raped—only women of value, that is, women who were owned by men of property. All other women—slaves, serfs, servants, peasants, racial and ethnic minorities, and all working class women were used with something close to impunity as recreational sex objects since they could not be raped. No one would expect a lord to marry a peasant girl for the privilege of "wenching," although it was not a bad idea to leave a few coins to assuage her husband or father. The point is that no one asked the woman how *she* felt about it. She simply had no individual interests or standing of her own.[6] All this was reflected in the rape law of the time, and the history of law, as noted by Holmes, has its effect.

In the nineteenth century, some of this began to change. Coverture laws were repealed; the Married Women's Property Acts were introduced, enabling women to have a legal identity, to sign contracts, own property, to have both rights and obligations.[7] The ideal of romantic love (always an underground force) replaced family arrangement as the predominant basis for marriage.[8] The Industrial Revolution transformed both Europe and the United States into urban societies, pulling masses of young men and women into factories and mills, and away from the watchful eyes of parents.[9] And middle-class Americans, while claiming to constitute the classless society, became as class-conscious as any Europeans, guarding the purity of their daughters with chaperones and watchful parlor visits.[10] Women may not have been property anymore but they certainly were prey, and they certainly were sex objects. During the nineteenth century, the feminine virtues of delicacy, fragility, and deference were developed to a high art in the middle classes, while working-class girls either emulated middle-class values of chastity or were considered "loose women" and fair game.[11]

Rape law at this time was (and basically still is) defined as "carnal knowledge by a man of a woman (not his wife) by force and without her consent."[12] Class presumptions (and racial prejudice) remained such that working-class women—much less Blacks, Latinos, Asians, or Native Americans—had little chance of prosecuting a rapist. Even a middle class woman would never bring a charge against a man she knew. It was understood that rape was something committed by a stranger, a predator of low class, and very probably Black.[13] If an (otherwise) "good" woman should have the misfortune of being forced into sex with a man she knew, it was her shame and defilement, a secret she could never reveal. And it had to be her fault for several reasons.

First, she should not allow herself to be in a situation in which such an incident could occur. Women were not entitled to freedom without endangerment. Protection was available, but only at the price of restriction. It was a woman's responsibility to see to it that she remained within the bounds of safety. If she exceeded those boundaries she was engaged in behavior that could be considered provocative and thus construed as consent. A woman who presumed to be independent could not look to the law to protect her. Such were the presumptions of the time. During the course of the twentieth century this particular set of attitudes was both challenged and maintained as women became increasingly independent and recognized as entitled to freedom but still viewed as fair game for utilizing it. If the law would not restrict women (that is, ban them outright from places and practices), it would not protect them either, certainly not from acquaintances within their own class.

Second, a woman should not tempt a man, who could not be expected to control himself in the face of temptation. Thus, her sexual history, her style of dress or manner, her behavior, and so forth were relevant inquiries for whether a rape could have been committed. If a woman did anything that could be construed as provocative (and this could include merely allowing herself to be in the wrong place at the wrong time), she could not be raped, since in effect this constituted consent.

Third, if she should "get herself" into such a situation, she should be willing and able to resist somehow—perhaps, to fight to the death to defend her purity. Only force necessary to overcome the "utmost resistance" of a woman of honor would meet the element of force necessary for rape. And in the last analysis, her resistance was the only evidence a woman could provide that she did not consent. Saying no was certainly not sufficient, nor was crying or begging or struggling weakly.[14] Only "utmost resistance" was enough and it ordinarily required the testimony of a corroborating witness, since women could lie about such things. Consequently (corroborating witnesses being in short supply), the rape of a woman by a man she knew was exceedingly rare. Rape law may be said to protect women, but it was very sympathetic to the potential perpetrator as long as he was not a stranger.

Finally, whatever the reason, whatever the excuse, the fact of defilement remained. If the Ming vase is broken, it is broken. What loses its value is the Ming vase. If a woman was defiled she was better off living with her secret, since the person with the most to lose was her. This set of attitudes pervaded the first half of the twentieth century. A friend of mine in the 1960s had an insanely jealous husband. He constantly forbade her to go anywhere alone because she might be raped. She could not go to the grocery store because she might be raped or go to the PTA meeting because she might be raped. Tired of the single focus, one day she angrily said, "You know, it could be worse. I could be killed." To this her husband replied, "That would not be worse. If you get raped you might as well crawl off and die, because you would be useless to me after that." Words spoken in anger, no doubt exaggerated, but illustrating the point. Even in the 1960s, women were widely considered to be priceless possessions that could be ruined by the touch of another.

All the points just listed illustrate both the evolution and the persistence of attitudes and presumptions about women, men, and sexuality. They were still powerful in the 1960s and persist in fragments even today. These developments and fragments are now and have been for some time grossly inconsistent and highly confusing for both women and men. In the United States, these inconsistent attitudes reached a palpable crisis level as women of the 1950s were expected to emulate Debbie Reynolds on the one hand and Marilyn Monroe on the other. By this time women were somehow supposed to manage to be both recreational and reproductive sex objects. All women were supposed to be seductive teasers who love sex themselves but somehow magically remain pure. Thus, Debbie and Doris struggled with themselves as well as their pursuers. And Marilyn was always saved by accident. There was the doorbell, the telephone, the potted plant falling from an upstairs balcony. Something always saved Marilyn; she didn't do it herself. That's what made her such a special dream in the 1950s. But it was a dream that no one could live (unfortunately, not even Marilyn) and by the mid '60s hippies and teenagers were extolling the virtues of drugs, sex, and rock and roll. *Playboy* was in full power and the virtue of virginity was becoming quaintly obsolete. Freedom, especially sexual freedom, was the value and demand of the day, yet little legal change occurred for the benefit of women, and the topic of rape was not appropriate in polite company, even among hippies.

In the early '70s, angry feminists gave up being polite, declared rape the "All American Crime" and a "male protection racket" that kept women off the streets, confined to their homes, and unsafe even there.[15] Thus, one big change in the '70s was that rape became a topic of discussion—the silence was broken. Once it could be discussed, anomalies of law and custom were exposed to scrutiny. These "anomalies" are evidence of changing cultural attitudes about women—what they are and what they are for and what they are entitled to. Indeed, the fact that rape law and sexual practice could be questioned at all was the culmination of the gradual cultural evolution regarding the nature and position of women and their proper relations with men that took place over the nineteenth and twentieth centuries, cresting in the 1960s and 1970s. By the end of those two decades, women were recognized as free individuals, with interests of their own, entitled to determine their own lifestyles and futures, to direct their own lives, and to participate in any activity (sexual or otherwise) as they see fit (with the possible exception of military combat and some religious positions, which is still under debate.) Since none of these views was accepted 100 years ago, taken together, they constitute an enormous change in public opinion about women.

This change of cultural attitude is reflected in many legal reforms, but surprisingly few reforms in rape law. The marital exemption has been largely repealed. The "utmost resistance" test has been reduced, and the requirement of corroborative testimony has been eliminated. Rape shield laws have been enacted that protect the victim to some extent from examination of her past history, at least her sexual history. And it is now recognized that anyone can be raped, even a prostitute, even a Black prostitute. In practice, it may be (and is) very difficult to obtain a conviction, but no one is preemptively excluded from legal protection. These are important changes, but the basic definition of rape remains unchanged: Both force and nonconsent must be proven as separate elements of the crime.[16]

While in many ways these changes, both legal and social, are important, substantial, even cataclysmic, in many ways, life has barely changed at all. In particular, the threat of rape remains a clear limit on the freedom and security of women.

Some statistics suggest that the incidence of rape has increased in recent decades. There is no way to assess these data. It may be that rape has not increased so much as the reporting of it. On the other hand, because of increased freedom, more women are exposed to the possibility of rape. In any case, there is no evidence that it has decreased despite the public outcry of angry women for the past 30 years. One might hope for some greater progress than that in the reduction of a clear evil. So one wonders, What is blocking the way? Where should our focus be aimed? What needs to be changed at this point, and how should the change be accomplished to secure a greater respect and protection for the freedom and security of women?

Forcible Rape and Protection from Violence

In the feminist literature, discussion of rape developed in several strands or perhaps stages, and these various foci are reflected in several elements of rape law. To review the developments as chronological stages, it can be noted that the first angry outcries of the early '70s were protests against the restriction of women by the constant threat of violent rape on the streets. The demand to "Take Back the Night" was a claim to a right to equal security and freedom to participate in society at large.[17] It was a demand for freedom of movement and safe streets. If we consider the object of this anger, it was the traditional threat of rape by the violent and predatory stranger. It was rather quickly discovered (or realized), however, that the bulk (an estimated 80%) of forcible sexual intercourse was not perpetrated against women by strangers, but by men with whom they were acquainted.[18] This discovery changed the focus of the discussion. The marital rape exemption was challenged, and the idea of date rape or acquaintance rape was introduced. Since then, a great deal of the discussion and debate has centered on the notion of date rape, and much of that has been focused on the construction of consent.[19]

Roughly corresponding to these developments are two strands of analysis suggesting legal reforms that focus on the two major elements of the crime of rape: namely, force and nonconsent. What is sometimes called the liberal analysis (following a well-known article by Susan Estrich) emphasizes the protection of sexual autonomy, suggesting that the crime of rape be defined as nonconsensual sex and then graded on whether and how much force accompanies it.[20]

What is often called the radical analysis of rape (following the work of Catharine MacKinnon) focuses on the crime as a violation of bodily integrity and as a tool of domination, terror, and control.[21] The radical legal proposal is to drop the consent requirement. If force is shown, then rape is proven. It is this proposal that I would like to consider and defend here.

I'm not a radical, myself. In fact, I consider myself a liberal, but on this particular issue, the radicals had it right (or at least largely right) to begin with, and we (liberals and feminists) have been diverted by endless discussions of the constitution of consent, from preventing an obvious evil. Rape—violent rape—is an act of terror and overt humiliation. It should be clearly distinguished from nonconsensual sexual intercourse without threat of violence. I do not mean to suggest that I do not sympathize with those women who are tricked or pushed into sex, but it is not the same and not as bad as being terrorized into submitting to sex out of fear of death or bodily harm. The latter is rape; the former is not, although it is certainly a bad thing that ought to be a punishable offense. By merging these two, I fear that we are doing ourselves a grave disservice in several ways.

The first is that which I just mentioned. Because of the fear of unclear definition, we remain in a quagmire of discussion over the nature of consent within the sexual context. Some important theoretical headway has been made toward clarifying this concept, but we have far to go before we reach anything approaching consensus—especially the consensus that would be needed before legal reform can be accomplished. In the meantime, forcible rape remains tied to an unclear consent element that lets violent rapists off the hook. The consent element should be eliminated and rape defined simply as sexual intercourse by force or threat of bodily harm.

We all want reform, but we are not getting it. Why not? One possibility is that traditional rape has gotten tied to a vague idea of date rape that terrifies some ordinary men who are not sure whether they themselves have crossed over the line of committing it. Consequently, many are leery of legal reforms, the implications of which are not clear. By contrast, if these two issues (violent rape v. nonviolent sexual coercion) were sharply divided, by all the (highest) statistics we have, at least 80% of all men in this country know for a fact that they have not and will not (even accidentally) commit a violent rape. Most men are not violent and even fewer are violent rapists. Wouldn't women be better off dividing the issue, keeping the issue of consent out of it and enlisting the cooperation of the nonviolent 80% of men to oppose violent rapes, by limiting the crime to clear cases of violence?

This is a pragmatic point. Any good legislator knows that the best way to kill a bill (or any legal reform) is to make it big and comprehensive. If you want to get something passed, pass it in pieces. It also corresponds to what was said earlier about legal reform and social evolution. It all has to be incremental. It can only proceed in little steps.

Second, even if somehow we can manage to get a big reform statute passed, criminalizing a broad range of reprehensible but nonviolent sexual misconduct as rape, it will not be enforceable. Either prosecutors will not prosecute vigorously or jurors will not convict (or both). This is because defining rape without force is too controversial. It does not correspond closely enough to widely held intuitions about the nature of rape, even if those attitudes are inchoate and confused. Here is why I think so.

I am an academic feminist. By comparison with society at large (which is what juries are made up of), that probably puts me morally and politically close to the radical left-wing fringe. But I don't think that a man who tricks a woman into having sex with him has committed rape. It just doesn't fit my intuitions. But I suppose that if I don't think it is rape, then most of the country doesn't think so either, because most of the country is more conservative than I am. I conclude that before it will do us any good to get a statute broadening the definition of rape to include nonviolent behavior, a good bit of social evolution will have to take place that reforms what people think rape is. It will not work the other way around. That is, we will not be able to reform what people think by enacting a broader statute, because the conceptual jump is too big. As I said before, the steps have to be little. As we have known at least since the time of Bentham, legal reforms that jump too far ahead of common consensus simply are not enforceable.

On the other hand, what does seem to me ready for the push of legal reform is the clarification of force and the elimination of the consent element. The opposition to violence, including violent rape, is widely enough held that it could be taken to eliminate consent presumptively or automatically. That is, people are ready to be persuaded that women (like anyone else) who are coerced, threatened, or physically compelled to do anything (even engage in sex) are not in a position to disagree and therefore cannot freely consent. Thus, the question of consent in the face of violence is moot. Force overpowers any possibility of consent.

There will be objections made even to this, but I think such objections could be overcome and something close to consensus reached on this issue. That may not be everything, but it would be better than the law we now have. By holding out for everything (a broad definition of rape) we are getting nowhere.

Third, by merging the issues we (women) may accidentally be restricting ourselves. The number of men who rape women who are strangers to them is very low, considerably lower than the number who might resort to violence with women whom they know. This should be common sense, but it gets obscured. A recent survey, for example, of some college campuses indicated that one in five women said that they had been forced into sex. Of those, 80% said the rapes were perpetrated by men they knew.[22] That means that 4% (not 20%) were raped by strangers. That figure (four in one hundred) is in itself highly unacceptable, and we should have protections—better lighting, better transportation, escort services, cooperative arrangements, legal enforcement, etc. to prevent it. It is a very bad thing, but it is not even close to the one-in-five figure that wound up being the focus of the report and subsequent discussion of it. If we are afraid to go out on the street, is it partly because we have confused the 4% with the 20% or merged the 4% within the 20% that are all rapes after all? If we are doing this, we are contributing to our own restriction and our own fear. To avoid it, we must be careful to keep these numbers straight, and the major factor in not keeping them straight is merging everything together under a blanket term of rape. This is especially suspect if merging violent and nonviolent sexual interactions, since it make the numbers terrifyingly high. If the result is that women walk around terrified, we are not doing ourselves any favors. Nor are we helping ourselves or anyone else if we create the impression that violence and rape are so common as to be normal. Normal men are neither violent nor rapists. It is not normal to be so. If statistics are inflated, even accidentally, to create the impression that it is common and thus normal, the result will surely be harmful to women, and this can happen by merging all the numbers together.

For all these reasons, I suggest that rape should be defined simply and narrowly as sexual intercourse by force or threat of bodily harm and prosecuted vigorously as such, in those terms and no others. Everything else we should call something else—sexual misconduct, perhaps. That way we could prosecute forcible rape, while we debate the nuances of defining and specifying and grading the seriousness of any and all other infractions.

Such a proposal immediately raises certain objections. The first and the most important is that such an approach requires a theory of force. I would suggest in response a simple and narrow definition: physical coercion and/or threat of bodily harm. A threat could be assessed by considering what a reasonable woman in similar circumstances would consider threatening. This is far from ideal but no worse than tests currently used. Alternatively, threat might be defined as any statements and/or gestures calculated or intended to produce fear. This, at least, would have the virtue of focusing the interrogation on the accused rather than the victim. Force could be defined as any physical restraint that prevents a woman from leaving or physical exertion that does bodily harm. That seems to me straightforward and clear. No man is entitled to hit a woman, to throw her down or pin her down or rip off her clothing. Any such behavior constitutes force. It can be identified without any consideration of consent whatsoever. The only question in assessing the crime is, Did the accused do it or not? As with virtually all other crimes, in this definition, there is no need to assess the mental state of the victim, least of all whether she ultimately acquiesced in cooperating with her assailant. Such an assessment would never be considered relevant to the commission of any other crime, and it should not be considered relevant here.

Two objections will be raised to this position. First, it will be objected that it is overbroad. It will chill the consensual behavior of those who prefer a racier brand of sexuality that includes violence or the threat of it as part of the thrill of risk or danger. My quick answer to this view is that if the thrill of danger is what turns you on, this new law will help you out, because now you can add the further risk of being prosecuted later for rape. That should make it really exciting. But supposing sarcasm to be unappreciated, the real answer, as noted by other feminists,[23] is that some practices are too costly to maintain. If the cost of maintaining the freedom of a few to play sexual games with the risk of violence is that no woman can prove a claim of rape without proving the impossible negative that she did not find it erotic, then the cost is too great. There are always trade-offs in any policy decision. In this case, we will be trading the freedom of a few, who entertain themselves as they will, for the security of many from experiencing serious bodily harm. In my view, this is not one of the difficult choices.

The second objection is more difficult. It is that the definition is too narrow, too much is left uncovered that is not only immoral or even reprehensible, but genuinely coercive. What if a woman has sex with a man to keep him from beating her children or her elderly parent? What if he threatens her job or her future rather than bodily harm? Such threats are no less coercive for not being aimed directly at her own body. Shouldn't the definition of coercion be broadened to include other serious threats that make refusal of sex impossible?

This is a much more difficult objection for me. There is no question that serious coercion can take many forms, and women (or men) subjected to it should have recourse to legal remedy. I am very sympathetic to the problem, but it is clearly the beginning of a slippery slope. I fear that if we start down it, we will be quickly returning to the quagmire of vagueness that plagues rape law and stalls all attempts at reform. Because of this, I suggest that we stick with the clear and narrow definition of rape I offered earlier and deal with these other problems in other ways. A clear specific definition of rape should make it easier both to enforce and to prosecute because consensus against it will be clear. That consensus needs to be enlisted, mustered for the significant cause of eliminating violence against women. Nearly everyone opposes violent rape. Focusing in this way on eliminating physical violence, even if narrow, is not an easy or unworthy goal and should not be diluted by attaching controversial riders to the crime of forcible rape that weaken the consensus.

Nonconsent and Protection of Sexual Autonomy

If rape should be defined narrowly, what should be done about the many sexual infractions that will be left out of it? A number of proposals have been made. One that I find particularly attractive was articulated recently in an article by Stephen Schulhofer.[24]

Schulhofer proposes a new cause of action for the nonviolent impairment of sexual autonomy: to criminalize sexual intercourse without consent per se. This is a radical proposal that Schulhofer presents with admirable diplomacy. Part of his strategy in defending his proposal is to point out that sexual intercourse without consent has long been illegal in theory. Admittedly, defined as rape, illegal nonconsensual intercourse has always been reduced to forcible compulsion except in those special cases in which consent is precluded by status or incapacity. That is, consent is assumed in the absence of demonstrable force, unless nonconsent can be presumed on the basis of characteristics of the victim that do not rely on her testimony, specifically, that she was incompetent, unconscious, or underage. This point is important for several reasons.

One of them is that it underscores the abiding distrust of the testimony of women in sexual matters: Women may change their minds on reflection about what happened. They may be unhappy or want revenge for numerous reasons. They may lie. It also indicates a continuing concern to protect supposedly innocent men who may have been just a little too passionate, or a little too overbearing, or who may have misread the signals or lack of signals of their unwilling sexual partners. Both these concerns assume the realities of the sexual game of predator and prey—or sex as conquest—as inevitable, natural, or good, and consequently reflect a concern for the difficulty or impossibility of distinguishing real rejection from playing the game. If the game is conquest, then "no" cannot mean no or it ends the game at the outset; and even resistance cannot initially be taken seriously, for what is conquest without resistance? If this is the baseline from which we are operating, the concern of legislators (especially male ones) is not hard to understand. If sex is conquest, then the distinction between legitimate sexual intercourse and rape is a fairly fine one that turns entirely on the subjective mental state of the parties. More specifically, assuming that the predator thinks that he is playing with someone who is also playing, the entire distinction between sex and rape turns on whether he is right that she is playing. If she is not playing then he is committing rape. Should he be able to tell the difference? Many people think so, but many legislators are not so sure.

Schulhofer's proposal would obliterate the conquest game altogether, and it is high time as far as some people are concerned. I always thought it was a dumb game myself, and the sooner gone, the better for all of us. Clearly, some might mourn its passing as some gentlemen of honor mourned the loss of dueling or trial by combat. But even if some like the game of sex as conquest, it wouldn't be very safe for any man to play if he could then be held criminally liable for sexual misconduct. That would put "sex as conquest" in a category similar to that of having relations with underage women—who are, after all, affectionately known as "jail bait." That means that Schulhofer's proposal would make the game of sex as conquest almost as dangerous for men as it has always been for women. Some men no doubt would still risk it, but at least the risk would be clear; the victims would have recourse; and the public standard or message would be one of disapproval.

As Schulhofer suggests, another reason that his approach is important is that the acknowledgment of the special cases—women who are underage, incompetent, or unconscious—as falling within the law of rape shows that nonconsent is the unifying principle that spans all cases. The significance of nonconsent (in theory) accords with statutory language as well as with the representations of legal treatises on the topic of rape. The language of the *Model Penal Code* Commentaries is typical in noting that, "The law of rape protects the female's freedom of choice . . ." and its "unifying principle . . . is the idea of meaningful consent."

In the words of rape law expert, Susan Estrich: "Not exactly." One of the interesting features of traditional rape law that continues despite efforts for reform is its double speak about the significance of nonconsent. While rape law purports to protect the sexual autonomy of women, the fact is, it never has done so. It does not do so even now, despite reform efforts. It may be that it is difficult to establish clearly and exactly what it would take to do so. Schulhofer's proposal is certainly a step in the direction of making clear what it would take to protect sexual autonomy, thereby raising in an unavoidable way the question of whether we should do it. This is a question that needs to be faced squarely. If sexual autonomy is not considered appropriate for legal enforcement, it would be better to face it and defend that position, rather than to pretend that rape law accomplishes, or is even intended to accomplish, this purpose.

One of the virtues of Schulhofer's treatment of the topic is his recognition of the need to accommodate, or at least to acknowledge, ordinary conceptual understandings and ordinary language usage. As he points out, five centuries of legal recognition of "statutory rape" have convinced no one that statutory rape is "real rape." The conceptual distinction is maintained between the two despite the legal subsumption of both under the same name. This is a clear case because it turns factually consensual sex into rape by legally invalidating the consent of the woman (or child). But most cases are not so clear, and the basic problem becomes one of determining what should count as consent. The question is whether Schulhofer's proposal helps with this problem. Why should we think it will?

Schulhofer believes that it will help clarify the law by instituting a cause of action that is separate from rape. What are the implications and potential effects of such a move? Simply calling the offense a different name has no particular effect in itself, as we have seen from statutory revision such as that introduced by the Michigan law of criminal sexual assault. This reform effort attempted to eliminate the use of the term "rape" and to mark off degrees of seriousness to allow the law to more effectively handle a broader range of conduct. Yet, the conceptual foundations for these distinctions of degree remain unclear, and criminal sexual assault is apparently translated into rape in the minds of attorneys, judges, and jurors.

Schulhofer is attempting conceptual clarification. He wants his new proposed cause of action to distinguish violent, nonconsensual intercourse—which is rape—from nonviolent, nonconsensual intercourse—which might be called sexual misconduct. The point of the felony of rape is to prohibit forcible sexual intercourse. The goal of the felony of sexual misconduct is to prohibit impairment of sexual autonomy. Sexual misconduct is intended to be a serious offense (a felony) although, presumably, not as serious as rape. What would such an offense include?

Schulhofer proposes that sexual misconduct be recognized in any case in which there is no particular reason for a man to assume that a woman is agreeing to sexual intimacy. This would include cases involving clear refusals and also ambiguous acquiescence or silent passivity. As he puts it, "intimate genital contact and especially, sexual intercourse . . . unquestionably involve profound intrusions on the physical and emotional integrity of the individual. For such intrusions, as for surgery, actual permission, nothing less than a crystallized attitude of positive willingness, should ever count as consent."

One interesting thing that this proposal accomplishes is to create a separate offense that reverses the presumptions regarding consent that apply to traditional definitions of rape (but not in the treatment I proposed in the previous section). In the traditional offense of rape, consent is presumed in the absence of affirmative evidence to the contrary. In the offense of sexual misconduct, nonconsent would be presumed in the absence of affirmative evidence of consent. This raises a number of interesting questions.

Would such an offense accord with common moral understandings of sexual misconduct? That is a complex question that turns on a variety of factors. One question is whether most people think that sexual misconduct without violence is a serious offense. This raises a concern that as long as it is classified as a felony, it will be equated with rape, and if equated with rape, convictions will not occur. In fact, not only may convictions not be forthcoming, prosecution may not be attempted. As Schulhofer himself noted, in the three jurisdictions where it would be possible, there have been no prosecutions for nonconsensual intercourse without force.[25] Of course, one of the statutes is fairly new, and the other two jurisdictions still label the offense as rape. So, it may be that while prosecutors are not willing to pursue nonconsensual intercourse as a form of rape, they might be willing to prosecute as a separate offense.

On the other hand, it may be that most people do not think that nonconsensual intercourse without clear force or violence should be a criminal offense, or at least a felony, even though most of them think it is immoral. Most people think that lying is immoral but do not think that it should be illegal and certainly not criminal, except in special circumstances. Perhaps common views on sexual misconduct are similar.

This might be overcome with careful jury instruction, if statutory revision of this sort were to be accomplished. Statutory revision of this sort does seem a real possibility, since some states have moved in this general direction already. What would be involved in drafting such a statute?

There are several possibilities. One is to draft the statute to correspond as closely as possible to ordinary settled understandings. Drafting statutes in this way has the virtue of the highest probability of effectiveness or compliance. It is also generally the easiest sort of law to defend, since it is simply the legal enforcement of the settled standards of the community. That is not to say that such laws are always defensible or effective, but only that enforcing the will of the people at large is the most common defense for legal restrictions. The problem with accomplishing this in this area, however, is that attitudes are not apparently settled about what constitutes sexual misconduct outside of forcible rape. Indeed, this is an area of considerable social upheaval and change. That being the case, there is no way to enforce community standards, for community standards are unsettled and confused. There are two possible responses. One is to keep law out of the matter and let community standards evolve through personal interactions, socialization, or other modes of social influence. That is the situation we are presently in.

Another possibility is to draft a statement that is intended to reform common attitudes, to encourage behavior in a particular direction. Antidiscrimination laws are examples of such reforms. Reform statutes tend to be both less effective and harder to defend than those that unambiguously reflect settled community standards. That does not mean that reform laws are not defensible at all, but they require a level of rigorous justification that is not generally required of mere enforcements of community standards.

And enforcement is likely to be difficult, especially if the moral case is not successful. Witness the attempt to prohibit nationally the sale of alcohol. This was a disastrous attempt at reform on the part of an ineffective minority that failed to convince the general public of the moral grounds for general prohibition. Of course, there are important differences between prohibiting the sale of alcohol and criminalizing nonconsensual intercourse, the latter being much more like an antidiscrimination law, in that it attempts to discourage certain conduct by providing victims with legal protection. Without question, Schulhofer's proposal would be a reform statute of this type. When is such a view defensible? Antidiscrimination laws are presumably defensible reforms, but prohibition of alcohol was not. What distinguishes the two?

Both, presumably, involved a well-meaning and powerful minority that attempted to discourage behavior that is clearly harmful to some members of society. The obvious difference between the two is that alcohol prohibition attempted to prevent harm (perhaps even moral harm) to the actors themselves, thus being a blatantly paternalistic (and/or moralistic) reform. Antidiscrimination law, on the other hand, prohibits people from harming others, thus falling under the clearest justification for restricting behavior, often called the harm principle.[26]

If this is the relevant comparison, then arguably impairment of sexual autonomy should be prohibited, since it falls under the harm principle that has long been the centerpiece of liberal democratic law and thus is in line with the core of the criminal law that prohibits individuals from harming others.

I don't believe that anyone today could seriously, or at least successfully, argue that impairing sexual autonomy is not a harm, even for a woman. Making this point relies again on the social evolution that has occurred during the past two centuries. Claiming sexual autonomy (or any other kind of autonomy) for women a hundred years ago would have been outrageous, but today its time has come. I suspect that many people, a majority, are ready to recognize this claim as a cause of action in law—as an infraction against women that should have a legal remedy, even though most people would not be willing to call it rape.

For these very practical reasons, I want to suggest that legal reform calculated to reduce the incidence of rape in our society at this time should take the form of a cause of action like that proposed by Schulhofer, criminalizing sexual misconduct but clearly distinguishing nonviolent conduct from forcible rape. At the same time, forcible rape should be defined simply as sexual intercourse by force or threat of harm—period. No further elements should be needed, and no further violence against women should be tolerated.

Notes

1. Statistics suggest that the incidence of rape has risen in recent decades, but the many variables make these data impossible to assess. There is reason to believe that much more rape is reported now than it was in the past, especially among what were then the great mass of unconsidered lower classes. Furthermore, through exchange of information, consciousness-raising and social evolution, what is now considered to be rape, at least among women, has expanded. All this suggests that the incidence may not have increased so much as perceptions and reporting of it. On the other hand, social upheaval, especially the new challenge of women to traditional positions and expectations, creates tension, resentment, and misogyny that may be expressed in an increase of rape as well as other violence against women. And there is more unsupervised interaction of men and women, more independent (and thus unprotected) women, more women alone and at large, so there are more targets. Whether the occurrence of rape is increasing or decreasing, with some current studies placing the rates in the United States at one woman in five, the statistics are alarmingly high either way.

2. Women who provided recreational sex were largely outlaws, especially if not owned or "kept" exclusively by one man, and in any case could not be raped. Rape law therefore applied to reproductive property only.

3. That women were not considered separate beings with interests of their own in the eighteenth century (and before) is fully evident in legal doctrines like coverture, which dissolved the legal identity of all married women into that of their husbands. Before their marriages, women and girls were the wards of their fathers. See, e.g., Rhode, D. *Justice and Gender* (Cambridge, MA: Harvard Univ. Press, 1989).

4. Ibid. for this and other examples.

5. This was demonstrated cross culturally by Levi-Strauss, C. *The Elementary Structures of Kinship*, trans. Gora, F. Jardine, L. and B. Roudiez (New York: Columbia University Press, 1980).

6. See, e.g., Rhode, *Justice and Gender*, or Beauvoir, S. *The Second Sex*, trans. H.M. Parshley (New York: Vintage, 1989).

7. Ibid. for historical review.

8. See D'Emilio J. and E. Freedman, *Intimate Matters: A History of Sexuality in America* (New York: Harper and Row, 1988). *Fiddler on the Roof* is the story of a man who experiences these developments as they are manifested in the increasing freedom and rejection of (his) traditional authority by his daughters.

9. Ibid.

10. Ibid.

11. Ibid. This is an overstatement but still generally correct. Working girls in the late nineteenth and early twentieth centuries did have more freedom than their middle-class counterparts, but being without any real legal protection or recourse, they were also more susceptible to predators.

12. See Rhode, *Justice and Gender.*

13. Indeed, the myth of the black rapist was a powerful tool for controlling both black men and all women. See D'Emilio and Freedman, *Intimate Matters* pp. 215–221.

14. Some feminists have noted the inconsistency of expecting passive, demure, deferential behavior as a condition of femininity and breeding and on the other hand requiring a woman (to be able) to fight like a man to defend her "honor." See, e.g., Rhode, *Justice and Gender.*

15. See, e.g., Griffin, S. "Rape: The All-American Crime," *Ramparts* (Sept. 1971); Brownmiller, S. *Against Our Will* (New York: Simon and Schuster, 1974); or Peterson, S. "Coercion and Rape: The State as a Male Protection Racket," in *Feminism and Philosophy*, ed. Vetterling-Braggin, M. Elliston, F. and J. English (Totowa, NJ: Rowman and Littlefield, 1977).

16. See, e.g., Estrich, S. *Real Rape* (Cambridge: Harvard University Press, 1987); or Schulhofer, S. "Taking Sexual Autonomy Seriously: Rape Law and Beyond," *Law and Philosophy*, vol. 11 (1992) for good reviews of the elements and developments in rape law.

17. *Take Back the Night* (New York: Morrow, 1980), Laura Lederer, ed. is a book of essays opposing pornography but it is also a name taken by many organizers of marches, rallies, and demonstrations that protest rape and violence against women.

18. See, e.g., Rhode, *Justice and Gender*, or Estrich, *Real Rape.*

19. See, e.g., "Special Issue: Sex and Consent," parts 1 and 2, *Legal Theory* 2, no. 2 and no. 3 (1996).

20. For discussion, see Estrich, *Real Rape*; West, R. "A Comment on Consent, Sex, and Rape," *Legal Theory*, 2, no. 3, (1996); or MacGregor, J. "Why When She Says No, She Doesn't Mean Maybe, and Doesn't Mean Yes: A Critical Reconstruction of Consent, Sex, and Law," *Legal Theory*, 2, no. 3, (1996).

21. See, e.g., MacKinnon, C. *Toward a Feminist Theory of the State* (Cambridge: Harvard University Press, 1989), especially chap. 9.

22. See Sweet, E. "Date Rape: The Story of an Epidemic," *Debating Sexual Correctness*, ed. Adele Stan, (New York: Delta/Doubleday, 1995), citing study by researchers at Auburn University, Auburn, AL, University of South Dakota, Vermillion, and St. Cloud State University, St. Cloud, MN.

23. See, e.g., MacGregor, "Why When She Says No" or West, "A Comment on Consent."

24. Schulhofer, "Taking Sexual Autonomy Seriously."

25. Schulhofer made this assessment in 1992, but subsequent data suggest that nonviolent rape will not be prosecuted.

26. See Feinberg, J. *Harm To Others: The Moral Limits of the Criminal Law* (New York: Oxford University Press, 1984); or John Stuart Mill, *On Liberty* (New York: Hackett, 1956).

PART II

ANALYZING RAPE

3

BRENDA M. BAKER

Understanding Consent in Sexual Assault

In 1983, Canada replaced its rape law with the offense of sexual assault. The sexual assault law took the form of a multitiered offense recognizing different severities of sexual violation, incorporating sexual assault, sexual assault with a weapon, threats to a third party or causing bodily harm, and aggravated sexual assault. The new classification was designed both to respect gender neutrality as required by the *Canadian Charter of Rights and Freedoms*[1] and to emphasize that sexual aggression against women and other persons should be viewed as a crime of violence and domination rather than one of sexual passion. It acknowledged feminist arguments that rape is not about sex but about power. At the same time, legal reforms were introduced to help strengthen women's equality by removing obstacles to legal enforcement of their claims to sexual security and sexual integrity. These also served to bring sexual assault law into line with broader principles of criminal law and criminal procedure. They included removal of spousal immunity, removal of any requirement for corroboration evidence, lifting of statutes of limitation, and the introduction of constraints on the use of evidence of past sexual history.

The Canadian law of sexual assault is governed by Canada's law of assault[2] and so incorporates its basic defining elements; namely, the application, or threat of application, of force, and consent. Assault occurs when one person "without the consent of another person applies force intentionally to that other person, directly or indirectly" or "attempts or threatens . . . to apply force to another person," where he has or is reasonably believed to have the ability to carry out his purpose.[3] Consent in assault is not defined but is clearly distinguished from submission or lack of resistance that does not amount to consent. Section 261(3) says that no consent is obtained where the complainant submits or does not resist by reason of

(a) the application of force to the complainant or to a person other than the complainant;

(b) threats or fear of the application of force to the complainant or to a person other than the complainant;

(c) fraud; or

(d) the exercise of authority.

In addition to these conditions where submission or lack of resistance does not amount to consent, Section 273.1(1) of the Canadian Criminal Code states that for purposes of sexual assault, "consent" means "the voluntary agreement of the complainant to engage in the sexual activity in question," but that (Section 273.1(2)) no consent is obtained where

(a) the agreement is expressed by the words or conduct of a person other than the complainant;

(b) the complainant is incapable of consenting to the activity;

(c) the accused induces the complainant to engage in the activity by abusing a position of trust, power, or authority;

(d) the complainant expresses, by words or conduct, a lack of agreement to engage in the activity; or

(e) the complainant, having consented to engage in sexual activity, expresses, by words or conduct, a lack of agreement to continue to engage in the activity.

Section 273.1 expressly leaves open the possibility that other conditions than those itemized in Subsection (2) may establish no consent, by adding (Section 273.1(3)):

(3) Nothing in subsection (2) shall be construed as limiting the circumstances in which no consent is obtained.[4]

In this chapter, I want to consider how consent should be analyzed in Canada's law of sexual assault. I will begin with some general remarks on the sexual assault model.

The model integrates sexual assault into Canada's law of assault. In so doing, it emphasizes commonalities between the idea of a right to bodily integrity or security of the person and a right of sexual integrity or sexual security, both of which are legally protected against interference by others unless access is given by the agent's consent. This linkage serves to acknowledge the important role that sexual security plays in personal autonomy. Common assault also offers a framework in which both violent and nonviolent interferences with the person are thought of as wrongs. Touching without consent can constitute the force needed for an assault, indeed, assaults can occur without touching and even where merely threatening words occur. So the notion of "force" invoked in the model of sexual assault is a very flexible one; it includes, but does not require, the use of physical force or coercion and can accommodate cases involving implicit force or threat of force or even the threat of other pressures that could constrict choice. This gives the offense of sexual assault greater breadth and range than the offense of rape, which is traditionally associated with threats or exertions of physical force or coercion and actual or risk of bodily harm. The former can cover sexual offenses of greater and lesser degrees of seriousness, including wrongful nonviolent exercises of power over women that coerce sexual cooperation. Even if there is some risk of rapes being handled as lesser offenses under an assault regime, this may turn out to be compensated for by higher reporting and conviction rates. An assault-based offense can also recognize among harms to be prohibited certain wrongful violations of sexual self-determination or security that are distinct from the act of penetration or sexual intercourse itself, as in Section 273.1(2). In contrast, rape is confined to the harm and violation constituted by sexual intercourse.[5]

Unlike some recent attempts to reform rape law, Canada's sexual assault provisions retain the idea of consent as a pivotal one in understanding what the offense of sexual assault is. However, the legislation itself gives somewhat mixed signals about what consent consists of. It says that "consent" means "the voluntary agreement of the complainant to engage in the sexual activity in question" but does not explain what this entails or excludes. But does it regard "voluntary agreement" as necessary for consent, or further, as sufficient for consent? This last is doubtful, since the legislation disallows consent where the accused "induces the complainant to engage in the activity by abusing a position of trust, power, or authority," a situation where the complainant's actions might be thought (at least sometimes or, by some, conceptually and always) to be voluntary, and because it holds that there is no consent where there is no complainant resistance as a result of fraud or the exercise of authority, situations where the question of whether the complainant's conduct was voluntary might well be moot. The legislation suggests that voluntary agreement, or the lack of agreement, is "expressed by words or conduct," but it says nothing about whether such (overt) expression is necessary for agreement (or lack of agreement) to exist or be established, and it does not explain whether the relationship between the agreement and its expressions is to be construed evidentially or in some logically tighter way.

This chapter will explore how consent in sexual assault should be understood. I want to argue that consent cannot be fully or adequately understood in terms of the idea of voluntary agreement or voluntary assent, and that it is central to its understanding that we recognize certain rights of sexual security and sexual autonomy that entitle persons to control intimate access to themselves through the exercise of certain normatively significant permission-giving acts.[6] One reason why the idea of a right is important is that a right can be violated without any distress or coercion or fear or other constraints on choice being experienced by the right holder. In fact, a right can be violated without any force or violence being used, and even when the right holder is not aware of and never becomes aware of its violation. The ways in which voluntariness can be impaired or reduced or vitiated are more limited than this and often take a different form; an act may be less that fully voluntary, or not voluntary, because it results (at least in part) from the operation of external physical force, coercion, fear, pressure to choose a certain option, or otherwise act against one's will (Aristotle's compulsion). It can also be impaired or reduced by impaired capacities or understanding that affect one's ability to act on choices that properly reflect one's desires and preferences. However, there are cases where there is voluntary assent or agreement to engage in sexual relations yet where the conditions for giving another permission to one's body that are consonant with exercising a right of sexual security or autonomy have not been satisfied.[7] These are cases where sexual interactions may be voluntary but are done without consent and are therefore illegitimate.

In addition, I will maintain that trying to understand consent in terms of voluntariness runs the risk of regarding consent as wholly determined by the mental states, attitudes, and dispositions of the consenter, whereas in fact the norms governing valid or genuine consent include factors independent of the consenter and his or her experience of the interaction. Valid consent, then, is not determined entirely by the psychological dispositions of the consenter.

Consenting as a Normative Permission-Giving Act

In this chapter, I continue to support the view, developed by Nathan Brett in a number of perceptive papers,[8] that consenting is something that we do, and is an action that has normative significance in that it gives permission to someone to do what otherwise he or she would not be entitled to do. I think Brett has shown this "performative" account of consenting[9] to be superior to the attitudinal account of consent often favored by courts, which conceives consent as expressing certain states of mind or attitudes of the consenting subject. Consenting, like promising, is an act directed to someone else[10] that alters the prevailing pattern of rights and obligations between that other person and the actor, although the specific changes brought about are different in the two cases. Because of its permission-giving force, consenting is not something that can be understood purely as a description of what is transpiring in the mind or understanding of the one who consents, nor is its existence simply a matter of the presence of certain psychological attitudes or subjective mental states and dispositions of the consenter. One person's consent brings about changes in the normative situations of individuals, and that sort of change cannot depend on a private experience of the consenter that is only contingently and uncertainly evidenced by the consenter's behavior.[11] Consenting is interpersonal in its intention, and it is appropriate that its presence or absence should be knowable by criteria that are interpersonally accessible. Secondly, the normative force or function of consenting means that the boundaries of consent will be importantly shaped by norms, conventions, and public policy considerations.

There are some misconceptions about a performative account that we should guard against. It does not imply that there is a fixed set of moves that needs to be gone through in order to give consent. Consent can be given through words, gestures, body language, or without any speech at all, and it can be differently communicated on different occasions. Nor does a performative account of consenting imply any sort of behaviorism. The performative account claims that consenting is something that we do, but the fact that it emphasizes performance does not imply that it excludes or denies as essential certain mental conditions of the performer. Many actions that we do, such as stealing or lying, require necessary mental components of belief, intention, or will in the agents who do them. And most performative doings, like christening and marrying and promising another, require someone who acts with certain states of belief, understanding, or awareness. Consenting is itself clearly not something that a person can do while unconscious or without being mentally competent in the sense of being able to recognize and understand the circumstances relevant to the normative character of her act. She will need to have more than a rudimentary understanding of the customs and conventions that make possible her behavior as a permission-giving act. This is why the agreement or cooperation of young children, who are too young to understand rights of self-determination or how structures of rights and obligations can be legitimately altered by individuals, cannot be said to amount to consent to certain actions or interactions. They lack the mental and moral understanding needed to be able to give a permission to another that could release them from obligations not to interfere or to undertake certain advances.

The operations of consent in medical contexts, while far more formalized than those governing consent in sexual contexts, show clearly that specific mental requirements are needed for acts of consent. Patients must be of normal competence, not suffering from some temporary mental or emotional disturbance that might lead them to make choices not consonant with their known values, and they must be given full information about the nature of the treatment to which they are consenting, the conditions under which it will be given, the attendant risks, and available alternatives. The example shows that a reasonably sophisticated cognitive mental involvement is required for an agent to be able to consent. It is not possible to understand either proxy consent or the construction of living wills without presupposing that the standard case of consent is consent by someone who is competent, cognitively aware of the circumstances of her action, and who is acting intentionally in giving consent.

Voluntariness and the Normative Nature of Consent

In addition to these general mental requirements, does consenting require a voluntary act, and what does the element of such voluntariness consist of? Does it consist of some element of desire or positive feeling, so that spontaneity or sincerity of feeling is a requirement of consensual sexual relations, for instance? It has been argued that the essential feature needed for genuine consent is that the act of giving it should be fully voluntary, and that requires that the act be something that we want to do and are not averse to doing.[12] While it may be true that all clear cases of giving consent are cases of voluntary action, the attempt to understand voluntariness in terms of wants or desires unduly narrows the kinds of agent features that are relevant to it. The idea of voluntary action has important connections with desire and wants, but also with the will, with choice and purposeful action, and with questions of responsibility and accountability.[13]

Aristotle's famous discussion of voluntariness illustrates some of the complexities of the notion and its associations. Aristotle describes as voluntary the coordinated purposeful behavior of children and animals, and actions issuing unthinkingly from our passions and appetites; what is voluntary includes more than what is consciously chosen. Yet his idea that action is voluntary if the "moving principle is in the agent himself" is encompassing enough to include as expressions of personal agency actions based on a variety of kinds of reasons and chosen on a balance of reasons. His view fits with our own that our chosen and intended actions are commonly considered voluntary, even where they entail our acting contrary to some of our preferences and desires. We often regard them as fully voluntary from the point of view of responsibility in that we accept full responsibility for them and their consequences. At the same time, the Aristotelian idea that actions are not voluntary if they are done under compulsion makes clear that there are limits, created by severe situational or intentional constraints on choice, which can make even some of our chosen actions sufficiently contrary to our values and "against our wills" to make us deny full responsibility for them.[14] It is clear that the conception of the voluntary that we find in Aristotle is subtle and many-faceted and cannot be represented as concerned primarily with the role of desire or wants in shaping conduct to the exclusion of purposeful, chosen, or intended behavior.

Of course, it could be argued that our choice to act contrary to existing preferences and desires really represents a deeper and more powerful desire or preference that we have, so that what we choose is always what we most deeply or strongly desire. But the view that what is chosen is always the most strongly or deeply desired action, and so is voluntary, makes it impossible to distinguish voluntary actions from those that are coerced or compelled (since these actions are also chosen—as the lesser evil, out of necessity or duress). An account of human motivation that makes every intentional action or choice desire-driven, and so voluntary, has no way to distinguish between intentional behavior that is genuinely consensual and that where there is no consent due to force or coercion or fear of these.[15]

The boundaries of our concept of voluntary action are fuzzy in places where the concept of consent is clearly defined. Consider the case of young children and those who are not competent to understand the nature or moral significance of sexual interactions they may have been persuaded to participate in. They may have engaged in certain acts, say of stroking and kissing, willingly and with no qualms. In so doing, they may have been aroused by the actions of others and acted as they wanted to, or in some cases they may have regarded their interaction as some kind of cooperative game that they took enjoyment in. Should we characterize such acts of children and noncompetent persons as voluntary? Their acts may be done spontaneously, in accordance with their desires, and there is no experience of compulsion or coercion or threat that would support our saying that they are constrained to act against their will or their predominant desires. In these respects, their behavior looks voluntary. But at the same time, they act without any understanding of their actions as sexual, and this ignorance of the sexual nature of these acts may incline us to say that they did not engage in these acts voluntarily. There is at least, we might say, no voluntary performance of sexual acts by these individuals. But the idea of voluntariness does not yield any settled single way of describing the respects in which what is done here is or is not voluntary. Some of us might prefer to say that while the children's actions were voluntary, it was simply not the case that they were engaging in any sexual acts at all. Their actions were innocent. Here the perspective of the children is used to characterize what they were doing and to limit what they could be considered responsible for. We may hang on to some description of what they did as voluntary, while abandoning a more precise normatively and evaluatively sophisticated action-description as appropriate to describe what they were doing, or we may instead qualify that more complex description by saying that the doing of acts so described was not voluntary.[16]

This suggests that our judgments of the voluntariness of behavior are sensitive in a loose way to beliefs about what the agents were aware of or could understand themselves as doing. We are not very comfortable about calling "voluntary" actions under descriptions that assume a level of agent understanding of what they were doing that may not have existed in the particular case. While we will not necessarily say that the actions in question were not voluntary or nonvoluntary or involuntary, we may simply decline to locate the action so described on any scale of voluntariness. In this way, the idea of voluntary action may be quasi-intentional.

J. H. Bogart, in a very thoughtful and interesting discussion of the respective claims of voluntariness and consent models to capture the nature of rape,[17] argues that nonvoluntary behavior results where action is done under compulsion, threats of coercion, physical constraints, or where circumstances or internal psychology compels conduct. But he holds that where sexual intimacy is secured through deception of adults or exploitation of children or others who lack understanding, yet there is no violence or coercion or suppression of dissent or resistance through fear of coercion, the sexual acts of the victims are voluntary. "So, when one is deceived and acts on the lie, one still acts voluntarily."[18] Therefore, the woman who has sex believing it is something other than sexual intercourse, or when deceived into thinking she is having it with her husband, has acted voluntarily. "They have done voluntarily what they would not have done had they known the truth."[19]

In these remarks, I think Bogart is too quick to assume a uniform use for various distinct locutions of voluntariness and too ready to interchange "acting voluntarily" with "performing a voluntary action." None of our predications of voluntariness are completely unaffected by the description being used to identify what was done. This is especially true of "doing something voluntarily," which often carries the implication that the subject of the action done voluntarily knew he or she was doing something of that description. So in the examples given by Bogart, there may be *some* less-complete description(s) of what was done that we are willing to regard as voluntary on the part of the woman who is deceived into thinking her sexual partner is her husband (e.g., performing the actions involved in sexual intercourse), but we certainly would not characterize her as "having intercourse voluntarily with someone who was in fact not (turned out not to be) her husband." We might allow "voluntary sexual intercourse with someone who pretended to be her husband" or "voluntary intercourse with someone whom she honestly believed to be her husband." But these accounts do qualify what was voluntary by reference to some agent perception of the action situation. In other words, they exhibit some of the quasi-intentional character I outlined above.

Still, this disagreement with Bogart is a minor one. And it is true that in some cases of sexual interaction marked by failure of victim understanding, there may be no coercion and a more positive participation than acquiescence, with the victim acting sincerely on innocent desires that have been exploited. Exploitation is standardly distinguished from coercion, because it does not constrain desires or choices but depends on them as on strings to be played. Its wrongness has been explained as lying, not in constricting the desires or voluntary actions of its victims, but in deliberately taking unfair advantage of those desires and voluntary actions. These considerations support talk of voluntary action. Furthermore, there are many different kinds of cases, and cases involving exploitation may shade into cases where the victims have more (but still limited) understanding of what they are doing—their participation is arguably more clearly voluntary, although they may still be considered too immature to give consent to sexual intercourse. I will discuss such cases shortly.

The point to be made here is that whether or not Bogart and I would agree about the range of actions that are voluntary, we are agreed that there are cases of voluntary sexual intercourse that are not cases of consensual sexual intercourse.

By contrast with voluntariness, the idea of consent as a permission-creating act clearly requires the one who gives consent to have full information and understanding about what is being consented to as well as a more general understanding (possibly unarticulated) of what it is to change the normative status of an action, and associated relationships, by this means. If the act has social or moral significance in the society or has serious ramifications, this too must be understood by someone who is in a position to consent to it. Because children and some mentally impaired persons lack these competencies and knowledge requirements with respect to acts of sexual intimacy, they are unable to give consent to them. Any participation of theirs in sexually intimate acts is therefore done without their consent.[20]

These requirements for consent have been legally important in explaining how fraud can vitiate the informed consent needed to avoid the crime of rape. The maxim traditionally used in Canada is that consent is not "effective" or "valid" if it was "obtained by false and fraudulent representations as to the nature and quality of the act."[21] For instance, in *Bolduc* (1967), Justice Hall held that the consent needed for rape "demands a perception as to what is about to take place, as to the identity of the man and the character of what he is doing."[22] Similarly, in *Williams* (1923), the English Court of Appeal upheld the judgment that a girl who believed that she was undergoing a medical operation to improve her voice did not consent to intercourse and so was raped.[23]

This reasoning moves from the kind of act that consenting is to the requirements that must be met by individuals who are able to give consent. The requirements include not only certain agent understandings of what the situation of choice is but also the present possession by persons of competencies and abilities that qualify them as able to consent, including a general understanding of the social significance of giving consent and giving it in this context. They may also include other normative or moral standards specifying who is and who is not eligible to give consent. It is clear from this set of requisites that what it is to consent cannot be understood simply by considering the consenter's perception of the situation and his or her psychological dispositions, attitudes, and desires with respect to the subject of consent as she perceives it. Voluntary engagement in sexual activity, as determined by the actor's perceptions and dispositions, does not ensure the cognitive and mental understanding necessary for consent and therefore is not sufficient to establish consent to the activity.

Now consider two cases that illustrate more specifically the role of consent as a permission-giving act. These two cases involve exploitation of adolescent victims by others who abuse their authority and/or use deception to accomplish their ends. In the first case, a family friend or stepfather persuades a girl of 11 that her initial resistance and anxiety about a sexual liaison is mistaken, by subtly representing her cooperation as something to which he is entitled and as an appropriate expression of feelings of affection between them. She has some understanding of what intercourse is and its consequences, but has no sense of her own rights with respect to others' sexual access or of how to assert her autonomy socially. A variant of this case is one where the 11-year-old is initially favorably disposed and cooperates willingly, yet shows no mature understanding of why the liaison might be unacceptable. The second case would be one satisfying Section 273.1(2)(c), where one person "induces another to engage in sexual activity by abusing a position of trust, power or authority." I will use this description to identify the kind of case where there is a more overt securing, by someone with power or influence, of an adolescent's assent to sexual access by making it a condition of her securing a job or a promotion. It is clear that Section 273.1(2)(c) is intended to cover more kinds of cases, including those involving two adults, but I will exclude these for the sake of simplicity.

In at least some of these examples, the "victim's" behavior is not merely a matter of submission or nonresistance but is arguably voluntary. There may be some element of obedience to or respect for adult or familial authority in some cases, but that need not vitiate voluntariness. In each of these examples, one party is vulnerable because of moral or social immaturity, inexperience, imperfect or inchoate understanding of the significance or implications of sexual interaction, and undeveloped autonomy. These are examples where we regard sexual activity as wrong or impermissible, because it involves unjustified and inexcusable exploitation of these vulnerabilities. If we tie the idea of consent to that of a normative permission-giving act that removes an obligation not to behave in a certain way, then we can say that the actions of these vulnerable individuals—even if they are voluntary or show willing compliance or are assented to—do not make sexual acts permissible when they otherwise would not have been. Therefore, they do not establish consent in the appropriate normative sense. We might give a number of different reasons for regarding these cases as cases of "no consent." We might hold that wherever there is some uncertainty about whether both parties are acting with full information, knowledge, and appreciation of what they are doing, the conditions for consent are not met or should be treated as not met. Or we might hold that individuals with certain kinds of immaturities or inexperience that make them susceptible through persuasion to wrongful (invasions of their rights by means of) exploitation can be protected from these wrongs by holding that their cooperation or assent does not amount to consent.[24] So gaining their assent/agreement is not enough to make permissible the interaction assented to.

Either way, it is clear that certain moral or social policy considerations are playing a role in our decisions about where to draw the boundaries of consent. Consent is being treated as incorporating a number of different and distinct normative conditions required for acceptable or permissible sexual intercourse. This way of conceptualizing consent fits well with the idea that rights of sexual security and sexual self-determination are the major values to be protected by prohibiting forms of sexual assault. These rights can be violated through the use of force or coercion that constrains someone's will or voluntariness, but they can also be violated without any exercise of physical force, compulsion, or coercion, or any extension of these ideas as in fear of "implicit force." Some nonforceful infringements of such rights involve refusals to respect consent by not refraining from sexual initiatives with persons whose exercise of consent is not completely developed and in so doing amount to wrongful violations of those rights. Where the invasion of rights involves sexual intercourse, it may be thought sufficiently serious to be classified as sexual assault.

Consent in medical contexts provides a useful analog. The adult patient's right to decide what should be done to his or her body serves to determine what constitutes informed consent, and this in turn is held to rightly determine the standard of the physician's obligation to disclose information. In the well-known U.S. case of *Canterbury v. Spence*,[25] Judge Spotswood W. Robinson III was explicit in rejecting as standards of adequate disclosure "good medical practice" and "what a reasonable practitioner would have supplied" in favor of one that provides all information pertinent to the patient's decision about treatment, saying: "the patient's right of self-decision shapes the boundaries of the duty to reveal."[26] This illustrates an analogous though nonidentical way in which taking a right of bodily integrity as central results in the establishment of certain standards governing others' interactions with us (impermissible sexual intercourse, impermissible nondisclosure) that will be required for full consent.[27]

While Canada's sexual assault law gives primacy to the idea of consent as an expression of a right to bodily integrity and control, there is no need for criminal sexual offense provisions to be designed around this model. Michigan has chosen not to make consent a crucial or even a necessary feature of sexual misconduct.[28] The Michigan statute defines criminal sexual conduct by reference to the presence of one or other of a range of objective circumstances, including the use of force or coercion by the accused to accomplish sexual penetration or contact, the knowledge or reasonable belief of the accused that the victim is mentally handicapped or helpless, and so on. The legislation omits any reference to consent as a negative defining condition or a defense. Developed as a result of women's initiatives, it has been praised for its gender neutrality, its inclusion of sexual contact as well as penetration, and its avoidance of misogynous and insulting tests for consent such as lack of resistance or passivity. However, the Michigan law is very complicated and is unwieldy to apply. By excluding consent, it also excludes the complainant's perspective, judgments, and opportunities for self-determination and self-affirmation in sexual encounters. For example, because it allows no role for the complainant's choice, it does not recognize consent in the (admittedly rare) instance where a person knowingly and freely agrees to intercourse accompanied by force or objective evidences of force. Yet this is undoubtedly a case where adult fully informed consent can be given; and where it is given, however aberrant, it marks an expression of an autonomous sexual choice. While it is true that the Canadian legislation, by itemizing certain unacceptable influences that vitiate consent as permission-giving, leaves complainants to withstand pressures for sex that are not itemized,[29] it also provides a basis for hearing complainants' reasons for responding as they do. It enables their perspectives to be represented.[30] The presentation of these perspectives has resulted in legal reforms recognizing specific normative constraints on what can establish valid consent. Examples of such reforms are to be found in the provisions of Section 261(3), which disallow inferences to consent from lack of resistance and silence, and in the Section 273.1(2) provisions upholding verbal nonconsent and withdrawal of consent. These provisions show how consent can be normatively refined as a useful vehicle expressing a structure of rights and corresponding obligations.

There remain significant feminist criticisms of the consent model for sexual offenses.[31] But I will later argue that this model provides a good framework for strengthening further the position of women in such sexual interactions.

Material Conditions for Consent

The formal outline of what is required for consent can yield different contents as to what amounts to consent, depending on the context and the purposes for which consent is required. In most legal and medical contexts, the criteria for consent are more formalized than in more everyday social contexts. They often require those giving consent to go through a set of specific, overt procedures, such as reading documents and meeting with professionals to ensure that the terms of the agreement are fully understood, followed by giving some conventional sign of acceptance or endorsement (e.g., a signature) of an official statement of the understood terms. Many public sporting and social events have ritualized conventions expressing consent and associated transfers of rights, ranging from simple handshakes at the beginning of sporting contests (showing consent to play fairly by the rules) to elaborate rituals such as those transferring the authority to host national and international events. Even more complex are the conventions governing parliamentary consent and other forms of institutionalized political consent, which blend elements of tradition, history, political and moral value, spectacle, and practicality in their governing norms.

In more informal situations, consent is often conveyed by colloquial phrases or by body language, gestures, and responsive actions; no set expressions or forms of words or customary gestures need to be used, though it is important that the one who consents communicate by his or her behavior agreement to the proposal in question. In some areas, what communicates consent may be unsettled, variable, and individual; there may be few agreed-on standard responses, and sensitivity to both context and the personalities involved may be important in determining whether or not consent is being given. This is especially true in encounters broaching sexual activity between strangers or acquaintances who do not know one another well.

Given the variety of forms and contexts in which consent can be given, how plausible is it to think that every act of genuine consent expresses some sympathetic disposition or pro-attitude of the consenter toward the object of her consent? Could we say, for instance, that genuine consent must be to something that we want to do or desire to do rather than are averse to doing, or that the act of consenting itself must be something we want to do? If these mean no more than that the act of consenting must be minimally voluntary, they may be unobjectionable. But if they claim some stronger requirement of positive feeling or overall pro-attitude to exist toward either our act of consent or what we consent to, then the sheer variance in what is needed for consent in different contexts proves this wrong. Most obviously, where consent involves going through a set of conventional or formal procedures, I can do this, provided that I am normally aware and conscious of what I am doing and the circumstances do not compel or coerce my doing so. I need not have any enthusiasm or other positive desire for what I consent to for it to have permission-granting effect. I may sign a medical consent form or a bill of sale when indifferent to it or without bothering to give any careful attention to it. I may give consent to a course of action about which I entertain, and continue to entertain, doubts and misgivings, and I may consent even where I think that, on balance, the reasons against the action outweigh those for it, so my consent is unwillingly given.[32] In such cases, consent aligns much more closely with what I intend or choose to do than with the orientation of my desires or sympathetic dispositions.

But are there not more limited contexts in which consent is supposed to express some favorable disposition of the consenter toward what is consented to? Sometimes consent is supposed to convey approval of or a positive desire to do what is consented to—that is one of its social functions. However, consent can occur without being what it should be. It is important not to confuse the sincere expression of a desire for something with consent to that thing. Consent to sexual intercourse should, at least ideally, reflect a genuine interest in and desire for sex, but it does not always do so. Sincere expressions of desire for sex can overlap with consent to have sex with another, but they are different kinds of actions and they need not occur simultaneously. Consent—and consent to sex—can be given insincerely, just as a promise can.

Having acknowledged this diversity in behaviors that amount to consenting, we may still want to say that wherever consent is given, it is given by an act that is minimally voluntary, and in this way voluntary action is a necessary condition of consenting. But if we do say this, it is important to remember that what voluntariness amounts to is contextually variable and is to be defined mainly by negation—by a range of possibilities that are excluded or ruled out—rather than standing for some uniform set of pro-attitudes or positive psychological states.[33]

Should We Strengthen Our Current Standards for Consent in Sexual Contexts?

In this section, I want to reflect on recent proposals to make the conditions of consent to sexual access more stringent than they now are. I will begin by outlining some general reasons for making our criteria for consent more demanding and then turn to some arguments specific to sexual access situations.

We know of a number of reasons for making the criteria for consent more strict or demanding in certain contexts than they are in others. One reason has to do with the seriousness of the physical, social, and psychological implications of the activity for the person whose consent is needed for its permissibility as well as for others who may be directly affected by permitting the activity. Stringent conditions for consent to access to nuclear power plants or to personal health care records are necessary if public safety and personal privacy are to be protected. Another reason is the need to offset the relative vulnerability or disadvantage (physical, psychological, social, financial) of one party in relation to another who is seeking consent, where that is a salient feature of the situation; here the more vulnerable can be protected from exploitation and illegitimate pressure by beefing up the requirements for consent. The use of proxy consent and living wills, restrictions on experimental subjects, and disallowing consent where persons are intoxicated or underage, illustrate this. A third reason is that in certain contexts, it is important to reinforce an emerging or newly emerged conception of the consenting party as an autonomous adult whose self-determination, including choices about what happens to his or her body, should be respected; a direct way of doing this is by seeing that the conditions for fully informed and autonomous consent are carefully specified and are upheld in practice. This reason applies especially to contemporary medical and sexual contexts. In the former, physician authority in medical decision making has been replaced by a more collaborative model in which patient autonomy is emphasized. And in the latter, equality gains for women have reduced their dependence on economic, emotional, and social supports from individual men. This increase in women's autonomy has been accompanied by a gradual transformation of models of sexual interaction from (male) pursuit based on conquest and seduction in the direction of models based on mutual attraction and respect.

All of these reasons apply in the case of sexual intercourse. Intercourse remains a profoundly intimate act that can have momentous consequences for women in particular. Many adult women continue to be economically vulnerable to men in positions of relatively greater influence and power, and very young and inexperienced women continue to be the targets of sexual exploitation and opportunism. More-stringent legal requirements for consent in sexual assault and rape have been introduced, but largely because women have fought vigorously for them. A major complaint of women continues to be that even where the law is theoretically respectful of the need for consent, its application draws on myths and suspicions about women that tend to erode the effectiveness of these legal provisions in practice. These reasons may explain recent support for a more affirmative or positive conception of consent to be used as the standard in conjunction with sexual offenses involving sexual intercourse.

What does a "more affirmative" idea of consent imply about the attitudes or psychological dispositions of one who gives consent? I shall assume for this discussion that we are talking only about adults whose competency and information is sufficient for consent. Even with this assumption, there are many questions about how an affirmative or positive conception of consent should be framed and understood. Does it mean that we should count as consent for purposes of sexual assault only those actions resulting from some more-positive desire or want than simply indifference or neutrality, or that only those who really want or desire to have sex should be held to consent to it? Does it mean that the law should emphasize willingness of the parties to participate, so that sexual contact without clear indications of willingness would be suspect?[34] Would it support an autonomy model of consent as developed by Stephen Schulhofer, which he illustrates with a medical example, whereby silence or absence of objection cannot be taken as consent to therapy, as it requires "an affirmative permission." Schulhofer thinks that on the autonomy model, nonconsent does not consist in a "purely crystallized negative attitude" but is "anything that is not an affirmative, crystallized expression of willingness."[35] Does it mean that the complainant's perceptions of and attitude toward the situation should be decisive, rather than the perceptions of the perpetrator or of a third party? This test is suggested by some judicial remarks in a United States sexual harassment case, *Meritor Savings Bank v. Vinson*, where the relevant question was posed as "whether [the victim] found particular sexual advances unwelcome."[36]

Until we get a clearer idea about what a more-positive conception of consent would entail, it will not be possible to assess its desirability for use in conjunction with serious sexual offenses. However, even at this stage, I want to raise a few cautions about this project and its potential uses.

First, it would be a mistake to define consent and nonconsent so that they jointly exhaust the possibilities. There are clear cases of consensual sexual contact, and there are clear cases of sexual contact without consent, but there is also an extensive set of reasons and motivations for sexual interaction whose effects on consent are uncertain, undetermined, and debatable. Boyle mentions a desire to avoid hurt feelings, to get a job, to avoid a deserved "F" in a course, to get medical treatment, to avoid rejection by one's therapist—and the list could go on. Deciding on such cases involves, if my earlier argument is right, both descriptive causal judgments about limits on choice and normative or moral judgments about what limits are permissible and what are not. And there may be cases, within the law and outside it, where the particular facts simply leave the question of consent indeterminate.

Second, while it is very important that the victim's perspective receives recognition in legal and extralegal determinations of consent, it would be a mistake to give some overriding standing to that perspective alone.[37] If consent is treated as a matter of one party's perception of the situation and mental/conative dispositions toward the act, then consent or its absence could exist without being expressed in that person's overt behavior. But a satisfactory measure of consent should draw on factors that can be, in principle, dispositive for both parties, or for an independent reasonable party, who is necessarily neither the "victim" nor the "perpetrator" and so must get evidence for consent from behavior in context. Putting this in other words, consent or its absence cannot exist entirely in the attitudes, desires, and beliefs of the victim, because it is given by certain communicative acts. It needs to be adequately communicated if the other party is to have a fair opportunity to recognize it.[38]

Women have objected to the view that consenting or nonconsenting to sexual contact should be determinable from a reasonable third-party perspective, because such a perspective has historically embodied male ideas about what conduct is reasonable and has shown little understanding of women's sexual priorities or sensibilities. Sexual contexts necessarily involve an interface between men's and women's views of sexuality and sexual messages, with men's views until recently being predominant in interpreting what is happening in sexual encounters. So although there has been relatively little gender bias in uses of consent in contract law and health care contexts, this is not true of consent in sexual contexts. What this shows, however, is not that the reasonable third-party perspective should be abandoned, but that its content has reflected a male bias that should be corrected. Since 1982 in Canada, women have had successes in incorporating their perspectives into what are accepted as standards for consent—by legislation clarifying the difference between submission and consent, recognizing abuse of authority, trust, or power as illegitimate grounds for consent, and upholding a woman's expression of lack of agreement as establishing no consent. This means in effect that the "reasonable third-party perspective" on sexual assault has become more gender-balanced as a result of the recent inclusion of more of women's perspectives.

Third, we need to be careful that the conception of consent that we adopt is suitable for a serious criminal offense like sexual assault (or rape). Individuals should not be liable for sexual assault for failing to meet certain ideal or desirable standards of sexual interaction or for failing to respect certain goals of full sexual equality. It is failure to meet certain minimally acceptable standards of conduct by doing something seriously wrong that attracts criminal penalties. The mere existence of a disparity in power or authority between parties having sexual relations should not in and of itself be sufficient to make one liable to a serious charge such as sexual assault or rape, although it might well be grounds for a lesser charge of improper sexual conduct or sexual exploitation. Similarly, making sexual overtures that are unwelcome to another scarcely seems enough to warrant a charge of sexual assault or rape. Finding conduct unwelcome is consistent with agreeing to tolerate it; it does not preclude the recipient from having a reasonable range of choice. If the initiative permits a woman to reject it without any prospect of harm or injury befalling her, and if there are known effective avenues for complaint that she can use, then acquiescence even to intercourse should probably not be held to vitiate consent or to warrant a sexual assault charge. Again, these improper interferences with sexual freedom should be covered by less-serious offenses. The imposition on choice posed by these kinds of sexual impropriety is less than that of intercourse secured by noncoercive but deceptive exploitation or abuse of trust of vulnerable young women and girls; this is a profound violation of sexual integrity and is clearly more culpable. The latter offenses are now included as sexual assault, and it can be argued that the major reason for including them is their seriousness as invasions of the sexual integrity and security of control that persons have over their sexuality.

Some feminists, such as Carole Pateman, think that the consent model is fundamentally flawed and cannot provide a sound basis for equal sexual relationships.[39] It is held to conceive women as reacting or responding to sexual initiatives always made by others. Although the model allows some exercise of individual choice by women, it is complained that the situations in which they exercise these choices are outside their control and are often imposed by social and economic disadvantage. As summarized by Chamallas, this view holds that consent has a social meaning that is "tied to a system of unequal sexual relationships in which the man actively initiates the sexual encounter and the woman is relegated to the more passive role of responding to initiatives."[40]

These claims highlight certain features of women's continuing social inequality that need to be addressed, but as claims about consent they are largely mistaken, I think. They overemphasize passivity as an element of consent and underestimate consent as an exercise of a right. There is nothing in the idea of consent that excludes mutual consent, and indeed the notion of consensual sex implies the idea of mutuality. Even if consent is consent to something proposed by another, the idea of there being an initiator and a recipient is fully compatible with sexual equality, since either sex can initiate on different occasions. The assumption that in sexual matters it is always or usually more desirable to be an initiator, or to be an equal initiator rather than to be a recipient, is also open to question. I have already argued that treating consent as crucial in cases of sexual assault has provided an avenue for women to get broader recognition for their sexual concerns into this part of the criminal law, and it is a promising vehicle for further progress in this direction.

What is important about these feminist criticisms of consent is their insistence that the consent model cannot begin to catch all of the social and political factors that continue to subordinate women's choices to men's in our social life. It is true that attending to consent makes us attend only to *some* of the factors limiting individual sexual choices. It takes particular contexts of choice as given and cannot itself ensure that the choice situations in which people find themselves will be fair or equal. For example, some women may find prostitution a choice open to them, but only because they are constrained by social inequalities to a very limited range of choices. But then, it is not the fault of consent that women's opportunities for choice are more limited than men's. We would be remiss if we never looked beyond consent to identify the larger sources of sexual inequality that limit the spheres and ranges of women's consent, but these sources of inequality need to be addressed by independent social initiatives. It is not reasonable to expect consent to do all the work needed for sexual equality in society.

Some have suggested that we should be moving toward a standard that requires overt positive expressions of interest from both parties for sexual interactions that are permissible. A model of mutuality, in which both parties welcome or are equally able to initiate sexual action, is suggested by Chamallas as a legal successor to consent.[41] For her, it is also an improved model for sexual activity, because it offers a more egalitarian basis for thinking about sexual relationships. The model sees both men and women as having similar motivations for sex (providing physical pleasure and emotional intimacy) and as being similarly able to control the situations in which sexual encounters take place.

I agree that this is a better model for social and educational initiatives about healthy sexual relations and one that could usefully guide reforms in family law and equity in employment. It also may be valuable in developing the offense of sexual harassment. However, it probably sets too high a level for the standard of conduct that needs to be met to avoid liability for sexual assault. And it is implausible to think that any single standard like this could be appropriate in all cases. We need to remember that what counts as acceptable consensual sexual interaction depends on the situation (e.g., is the encounter between strangers, mere acquaintances, or others) and is highly personal and extremely sensitive to the particular histories of sexual relations where they are relevant. For example, considerably less than "overt positive expressions of interest from both parties" might be the beginning of a satisfying consensual sexual interchange in a couple with a history of good mutual understanding and good sexual relations.

Canadian law now has in place many provisions designed to protect the use of a verbal standard of consent, enabling women to indicate their lack of consent by saying "no." What women need now is not so much that this standard be replaced by one that requires an affirmative "yes, by all means," but that continued efforts be made (in the form of judicial education, careful monitoring of cases, etc.) to ensure that this standard is really respected in practice.[42] The existing standard needs to be strengthened by being more thoroughly and conscientiously applied.[43] That means applying it with sensitivity to female (as well as male) views of sexuality and with careful attention to the subtleties of context, including larger social constraints on women's choices. This standard, *if* properly enforced, should give women a decent level of sexual control and security while providing a form of communication adequate to protect potential defendants.

Notes

I would like to thank Sheldon Wein, Eldon Soifer, and Joe Ellin for their valuable comments on this chapter at the 1998 meeting of the Canadian Section of The International Association for the Philosophy of Law and Social Philosophy.

1. Constitution Act, 1982. Anal intercourse without consent is therefore sexual assault, although the law has not been expanded to include attacks directed at a particular gender as sexual assaults, and thus sexual rather than gender integrity remains central to understanding the nature of the assaults covered. See Christine Boyle, "The Judicial Construction of Sexual Assault Offences," in *Confronting Sexual Assault: A Decade of Social Change*, ed. R. Mohr and J. Roberts (Toronto: University of Toronto Press, 1994), pp. 136–56.

2. Criminal law in Canada was codified as long ago as 1892. The Canadian Criminal Code (C.C.C.) incorporated a few common law offenses, and preserved the common law as a source for justifications and excuses, but otherwise marked a break with the common law. All criminal offenses are now held to derive from statute.

3. C.C.C. secs. 265(1) and 265(2). The Code definition of assault has amalgamated, while replacing, elements of the earlier common law offenses of assault and battery.

4. Subsections 273.1(2) and 273.1(3) were added in 1992 through enactment of Bill C-49 by the Canadian Parliament.

5. There are risks and drawbacks associated with these advantages, which are well pointed out by Stephen Schulhofer in a careful discussion of the complexities surrounding different ways to categorize serious sexual offenses. See his "Taking Sexual Autonomy Seriously: Rape Law and Beyond," *Law and Philosophy* 11 (1992):35–94. Schulhofer recognizes that attempts to expand/dilute "force" to cover implicit threats of harm or other sources coercing choice run the risk of becoming too inclusive and swallowing up acceptable consensual sexual relations in their nets. He argues that cases involving fraud and misrepresentation, as well as cases of abuse of authority and social power, are best considered as directed at the protection of sexual autonomy rather than protection from physical harm. This leads him to separate two distinguishable classes of offense(s), one centered around violent intercourse through physical force (rape) and the other around wrongful nonviolent interferences with sexual freedom or autonomy.

6. This line of reasoning agrees with that of J. H. Bogart in "Reconsidering Rape: Rethinking the Conceptual Foundations of Rape Law," *The Canadian Journal of Law & Jurisprudence* 8 (January 1995):159–82. Bogart compares two models for understanding rape, the voluntariness model and the consent model. My account targets analyses of consent, which regard it as consisting primarily in voluntary behavior expressing positive desires or favorable attitudes/dispositions of the one consenting and which underplay the normative importance of consent as a permission-giving act.

7. In the case of sexual access, consent works by giving a permission to another to act in a way that otherwise they would have an obligation not to act. This is one sort of case in

which the normative dimensions of our actions do not dovetail neatly into the more psychological and moral-psychological ways of describing them.

8. Nathan Brett, "Consent and Sexual Assault," paper delivered at the Canadian Section, International Association for the Philosophy of Law and Social Philosophy, Annual Meeting 1982; "Sexual Assault and the Concept of Consent," paper delivered at the Canadian Philosophical Association Annual Meeting 1994. This later paper shows that the normative act account need not treat "verbal consent" as either necessary or sufficient for actual consent and can explain why force or coercion eliminates consent. It also underlines the inadequacy of the attitudinal account in making changes in the rights and obligations of others depend on private inaccessible mental experiences. Brett's early views are outlined and discussed in my "Consent, Assault and Sexual Assault," in *Legal Theory Meets Legal Practice*, ed. Anne Bayefsky (Edmonton, Alberta: Academic Printing and Publishing, 1988), pp. 223–38. See also Brett's "Commentary," pp. 253–57, in that volume and Brett, "Sexual Offenses and Consent", *The Canadian Journal of Law and Jurisprudence* 11 (January 1998): 69–88. My thoughts about consent are heavily indebted to many discussions I have had with Brett on this topic during the past 15 years.

John Kleinig also emphasizes the importance for responsibility of consent as a public act rather than as a mental or psychological state, in "The Ethics of Consent," *Canadian Journal of Philosophy*, suppl. vol. 8 (1982):91–118. For a further discussion of these complexities of consent, see Joel Feinberg, *The Moral Limits of the Criminal Law*, vol. 3: *Harm to Self* (New York: Oxford University Press, 1986), especially chap. 22.

9. Consenting satisfies most of the features of a performative proposed by J. L. Austin in his "Performative Utterances," in *Philosophical Papers*, 3rd ed., ed. J. O. Urmson and G. J. Warnock (Oxford: Oxford University Press, 1979), pp. 233–52. It involves performing, in the appropriate circumstances, an action rather than merely saying something; it is felicitous or infelicitous rather than true or false, and it exhibits the performative's characteristic asymmetry between the first person singular present indicative active and other persons and tenses. The act of consenting, like promising, is not correctly viewed as "the outward and visible sign of the performance of some inward and spiritual act." Although it sometimes suggests or implies that the actor has certain beliefs or feelings or intentions, the performative act can be performed insincerely when there is an abuse of the procedure by someone who lacks the appropriate beliefs or feelings. The only feature of performatives that fits uneasily with consenting in sexual contexts is their reliance on what Austin calls a "conventional procedure." There are few settled conventions in the area of sex, which is by its nature highly personal and private. Sometimes talk of conventions seems quite out of place there. But sexual interactions and their interpretations do draw on a complex cultural set of social understandings and customary practices, and to this extent they do depend on a variety of conventions.

10. I promise something to someone else. When we "promise ourselves" we are speaking metaphorically, applying an interpersonal communication derivatively and imaginatively to ourselves as if we were two parties, one of which could hold the other part of us to the bargain. Similarly, consent is given to (or withheld from) another with respect to some proposed course of action. We cannot give consent to ourselves to do something. Consenting is an interpersonal communication, at least in *aim*. It may fail to be recognized or understood by the person to whom it is directed, however.

11. There are lots of questions that remain here. Consenting could be something that we do, while also being a mental act. Can't people consent to things without communicating

their consent—perhaps they can't communicate it because they are paralyzed or unable to communicate generally or refuse to do so? Should we say that John, suffering from ALS, consented to his daughter's plan to travel but couldn't communicate his consent to her? Or should we say that John agreed with or assented to or approved his daughter's plan, but he never gave his consent because he was unable to? We might say that his consent exists as a mental act, but only because he lacks the normal capacity to communicate; the natural expression of his consenting is in a communicative act, which he unfortunately cannot realize.

12. Attitudinal accounts of consent as consisting of one or more positive subjective mental dispositions had by one who consents to the act are to be found in "Forcible and Statutory Rape: An Exploration of the Operation and Objectives of the Consent Standard," *The Yale Law Journal* 62 (December 1952):55–83 and A. W. Bryant, "The Issue of Consent in the Crime of Sexual Assault," *Canadian Bar Review* 68 (1989):94. A defense of the position that any case of genuine consent requires a sympathetic or favorable disposition by an actor toward what he or she is consenting to was presented by Patricia Kazan to the 1995 meeting of the Canadian Section of the International Association for Philosophy of Law and Social Philosophy, in a paper entitled "Sexual Assault and Consent."

13. In addition to Aristotle's analysis briefly mentioned here, philosophical accounts of voluntary action are enormously diverse. The voluntary has been taken to refer to the normal agent's abilities or capacities to control behavior (in physiological, mental, informational, and other ways), a causal relation between selected mental antecedents and bodily movements, and a conscious making of a fair choice between envisaged alternatives, to mention only some proposals.

14. Still, even certain hard choices between undesirable alternatives are described by Aristotle as more like voluntary actions than not, insofar as they are "choiceworthy at the time they are done" though in general not choiceworthy.

15. The suggestion that my intentional and chosen actions are those thought to satisfy my strongest desires also ignores the role of evaluation in my practical reasoning of the worth of my desires. See R. A. Duff, *Intention, Agency and Criminal Liability* (Oxford: Basil Blackwell, 1990), p. 70.

16. Aristotle would likely have regarded such actions as not voluntary because they were done in ignorance. But neither ignorance of particulars nor ignorance of universals is well suited to cover this kind of case. By "ignorance of particulars," Aristotle had in mind an actor's lack of awareness of certain factual aspects of his action that were therefore done unintentionally or were not voluntary. But the lack of understanding had by children or noncompetent persons is not mere ignorance of particular facts, but is like ignorance of universals in being a failure to know what is right or wrong about the behavior engaged in. Aristotle discussed ignorance of universals in relation to competent adults, where he considered it a culpable failure to know what was morally required, which therefore could not excuse as involuntary (not voluntary) actions done out of such ignorance. He did not discuss moral ignorance arising from immature or arrested development, and while he would probably have regarded individuals as not responsible for conduct issuing from such ignorance, it is not clear what he would have said about its voluntary character.

17. Bogart, "Reconsidering Rape."

18. Ibid., p. 163.

19. Ibid., p. 165.

20. This is a major reason why many legal systems criminalize sexual intercourse when

one or both of the parties involved is below a certain age, in laws commonly called statutory rape laws. Possible normative frameworks for thinking about such laws are discussed by Keith Burgess-Jackson, "Statutory Rape: A Philosophical Analysis," *The Canadian Journal of Law & Jurisprudence* 8 (January 1995):139–58.

21. Don Stuart, *Canadian Criminal Law*, 3rd ed. (Toronto, Ont: Carswell, 1995), p. 521.

22. [1967] S.C.R. 677.

23. [1923] 1 K.B. 340 (C.C.A.).

24. It is significant that Canadian law recognizes this in relation to a number of less-serious sexual offenses (sexual interference, invitation to sexual touching, and sexual exploitation) by holding in sec. 150.1(1) that where the complainant is over 12 and not more than 14 years of age, it is not a defense that the complainant consented to the activity that forms the subject matter of the charge. The choice of legal language in this section of our Code is interesting, in that it allows that the complainant *consented* while withholding any permission-giving force from that consent. The fact that the word "consent" is used to describe the participation of normal 12- to 15-year-olds probably signals recognition of the fact that in relation to these sexual activities, these complainants may have a reasonably full grasp of their natures and consequences.

25. 464 F.2d 772 (D.C. Cir. 1972).

26. Ibid. It is possible in theory to draw the boundaries of consent in a different place than they are drawn here, by holding that what is wrong about this behavior is not the absence of consent, but the failure of the other party to respect some duty or rule forbidding a certain kind of action in this kind of situation. Such a prohibition might be regarded as not rescindable by any act of consent or expressed willingness to engage in such an action. There are some examples of this in the law, such as the provision that consent to be killed by another cannot serve as a defense to a charge of murder. But the clearest examples are also cases, like the murder example, where the conditions for consent are unequivocally satisfied. See Feinberg, *Harm to Self*, chaps. 22–26, for a sophisticated and thorough discussion of the role of consent in the criminal law.

27. Of course, it does not follow that every act of impermissible sexual intercourse should be regarded as unconsented to or as a case of sexual assault (or rape). Two individuals could engage in fully consensual sex impermissibly, as in the case of incest (or, in some societies, same-sex intercourse, etc.). This shows that other conditions than mutual consent may be needed for a sexual interaction to be permissible. Secondly, there could be cases of impermissible sexual intercourse which, while culpable enough to be prohibited, were not thought sufficiently grave to warrant a designation of sexual assault, as well as less-serious invasions of sexual security and self-determination rights than intercourse that, on grounds of lesser culpability, harm, or invasiveness are categorized as distinct offenses such as sexual interference, imposition, or exploitation.

28. Mich. Comp. Laws Ann. sec. 750.520 b–e, g.

29. This point is made by Boyle, "The Judicial Construction of Sexual Assault Offences," pp. 136–56. Remember, however, that the open-ended character of sec. 273.1 permits victims to introduce into assault trials (new) bases for nonconsent that have not been itemized in sec. 273.1(2).

30. It may be that, in practice, the Michigan statute and the Canadian sexual assault laws are less different than their formulations would suggest. Consent continues to be raised as a defense in Michigan, by way of arguing that because the complainant consented, force

(or threat of the use of weapons) was not in fact used to accomplish the act. Although issues of consent have therefore not been completely excluded by the Michigan statute, that statute appears to provide stronger protection for women in leaving the issue of consent as one that must be raised by the defense, rather than retaining it, as Canada does, as a defining element of sexual assault which must therefore be proven by the prosecution. However, once again, whether this amounts to more actual protection for victims of rape and assault will depend on other factors such as how easily the prosecutorial burden of "without consent" can be discharged in practice; it is likely that in both jurisdictions, evidence of consent falls mainly to the defense to determine.

31. Some important objections are detailed in Martha Chamallas, "Consent, Equality, and the Legal Control of Sexual Conduct," *Southern California Law Review* 61 (May 1988):777–862. A major objection is that the consent model emphasizes individual-to-individual interactions on an assumed footing of equality, ignoring the context of unequal social power and advantage between men and women that often structures their respective opportunities for choice unfairly.

32. Informal analogs of such "grudging consent" are common. When my neighbor asks to use my new lawnmower, I don't "want" him to use it but in order to be a good neighbor I grudgingly consent. My thanks to the editor for this example.

33. This point was first made by H. L. A. Hart in "The Ascription of Responsibility and Rights," *Proceedings of the Aristotelian Society* 49 (1948–49):171–94.

34. This formulation is based on an analysis entertained but not developed by Boyle in "The Judicial Construction of Sexual Assault Offences." It is interesting to note that Boyle takes "willingness" to focus on voluntariness and on a factual determination as to whether the victim's will was overborne in the particular circumstances.

35. Schulhofer, "Taking Sexual Autonomy Seriously," pp. 74–75. It is not always clear whether the autonomy model of consent is an attitude/internal sentiment model or whether it is a normatively significant act model. Schulhofer's talk of "crystallized negative decision" and "unambiguous positive permission" suggests acts, but his "affirmative expression of willingness" is ambivalent—Is it referring to an affirmative expression in action, words, or gestures, or is it the internal element of willingness that makes for the affirmative character of the expression? There is also uncertainty about what Schulhofer thinks is implied by the "positive permission" in the medical case he discusses; if it consists in the signing of a consent form, by someone competent and informed, then that does amount to an act of consent, but it need not express "a crystallized attitude of positive willingness."

36. 477 U.S. 57, 69–72 (1986). The case is discussed in Chamallas, "Consent, Equality, and the Legal Control of Sexual Conduct."

37. Bogart gives a very good criticism of analyses of rape that make central the experience of the victim of rape. See Bogart, "Reconsidering Rape," pp. 177–79. Several of his objections would also apply to similar analyses of sexual assault.

38. The court in *Vinson* also (not wholly consistently) said that the test of harassment was "whether the victim *by her conduct* indicated that the alleged sexual advances were unwelcome" (emphasis added) (*Vinson*, 477 U.S. at 69). Chamallas says that this "behavioral focus tends to support a standard under which the encounter is gauged from either the offender's perspective or the perspective of a third party." Chamallas, "Consent, Equality, and the Legal Control of Sexual Conduct," p. 806. But surely these perspectives, along with the consenter's own, are critical if consenting is an interpersonal action that affects the norma-

tive positions, with respect to the action consented to, of both the consenter and the one to whom consent is given.

39. Carole Pateman, "Women and Consent," *Political Theory* 8 (May 1980):149–68.

40. Chamallas, "Consent, Equality, and the Legal Control of Sexual Conduct," p. 814.

41. Ibid., p. 836.

42. This positive assessment omits one persisting problem in Canada's sexual assault law; namely, the difficulty of establishing limits to access to a victim's medical records in sexual assault cases. Canada's first "rape shield" legislation was struck down as violating the accused's rights under the Canadian Charter of Rights and Freedoms to a fair trial, and a second recently enacted and more qualified rape shield law (C.C.C. sec. 278) has now been challenged by several judges (both male and female) as weighing the complainant's privacy rights against the accused's rights to a fair trial in a way that violates the latter. These challenges have not yet reached the Supreme Court of Canada, but in another case that court recently upheld an appeal arguing that the shredding of files by a sexual assault crisis center compromised the right of an accused man to a fair trial; the court was split 5–4, with both women on the court belonging to the minority.

43. An important recent development is the case of rape victim Ms. Jane Doe, who successfully sued the Metro Toronto Board of Police Commissioners for negligent failure to warn possible victims (of which she was one) that a serial rapist was operating in a specific downtown area and was targeting women in certain kinds of situations.

4

JEFFREY A. GAUTHIER

Consent, Coercion, and Sexual Autonomy

Feminist theorists have faced a vexing dilemma in their attempts to formulate a conceptual basis for the reform of rape law. On the one hand, in an attempt to dispel the sexist ideology that has made it difficult for the legal system to find defendants guilty even where force and violence are clearly present, many prominent theorists have been at pains to describe a clear distinction between acts of sex and acts of violence.[1] On this account, the failure to distinguish rape from sex derives from a sexist point of view that fails to encompass the perspective of the victim for whom rape is a violent rather than a sexual act. On the other hand, in part to explain why such a distinction was not obvious in the first place, many theorists have situated rape as part of a system of violence that governs sexual relations more generally in a sexist social order.[2] Far from being a uniquely violent act in opposition to "normal" sexual encounters, rape stands at the end of a continuum of exploitative practices that permeate virtually all aspects of a woman's existence. While this has served to situate rape in a broader context of sexist acts against women, it has also posed a problem as concerns rape law. For if we lack a clear distinction between rape and sex, this would appear to imperil legal reforms predicated on that distinction. When institutionalized violence governs sexual practice in the bedroom, we lack the bright line needed to separate sexual violence from ordinary sexuality in the courtroom.

Nowhere are the ramifications of this dilemma more in evidence than in the discussion of nonconsent as a criterion for rape. For if consent is to be a meaningful expression of a person's interests and desires, then the consent must be granted under conditions in which that person was free from coercive pressures to grant or to withhold her consent. Under conditions in which sexualized violence is common, it is going to be difficult to determine whether or not a woman's consent is truly free. Moreover, making rape hinge on nonconsent, when many women know that they *did* consent, albeit under more or less coercive circumstances, will contribute to the underreporting of all rapes, acquaintance rape in particular. Partly in response to this state of affairs, a number of feminist reformers have called for moving the standard of noncoercive sex away from consent toward something approximating "mutuality" between the parties. In various ways, writers including Martha Chamallas, Lois Pineau, and Cynthia Wicktom have all called for reform that would redefine the place and the meaning of consent in rape law.[3] At the same time, however, others, both in the popular press and in the legal literature, have protested such a redefinition, arguing not only that it may move too far in the direction of helping the victim, but that it fails to respect the capacity of women to make their own sexual decisions and thereby infringes on their autonomy.[4]

In this chapter, I defend recent attempts to move away from consent as a criterion for rape by considering the nature of sexual relations under the coercive conditions of a sexist society. In the first section, I take up the relationship of sexual violence and sexuality in feminist discussions of rape and rape law, centering on the problems this relationship occasions for the consent criterion. Next, I describe some recent attempts to reform rape law, centering on the work of Martha Chamallas and Lois Pineau. I then turn to Donald Dripps's critique of Chamallas's mutuality account, critically assessing his alternative proposal for addressing feminist concerns about the present law of rape by appeal to a "commodity theory."[5] I go on to show that even if one accepts the basic premises of his exchange account of sexuality, his conclusion that all nonviolent sexual quid pro quo arrangements must be protected need not follow. Using regulations on market exchange in the capitalist workplace as a model, I argue that the state has an interest in restricting certain coercive proposals, and that this interest extends to "sexual bargaining" as well. Finally, I briefly examine objections to the use of labor market regulations as a justification for a mutuality criterion in rape law.

My central point is to establish that the law of rape and sexual assault is best understood as imposing prior constraints on proposed coercive exchanges between women and men. By protecting women from coercive exchanges to which they are vulnerable in a sexually exploitative system, the law can provide one of the means necessary for women to achieve the position of genuinely consenting agents within (and to some extent despite) that system. Moreover, to the extent that enabling women to achieve the status of fully consenting persons is a chief remedial goal of rape law reform, it is a mistake for the law to proceed on the assumption that women already have that status from the start. That assumption has occasioned a debilitating double-bind for plaintiffs in rape trials, one that has contributed to unacceptably low reporting rates for rape, especially acquaintance rape.[6]

Women, Rape, and Consent

Though various feminist theorists have highlighted the issue of consent in rape law, political criticisms of consent theory are not new. Specifically, the ways in which a conception of consent can serve to legitimate a coercive political order have been the subject of various radical critiques of liberalism, both feminist and nonfeminist.[7] These critics have charged that by conferring legitimacy to contractual agreements in which the parties consent to its terms, classical liberal theorists have not sufficiently attended to the initial conditions under which the parties consented to the contract. Crucially, consent theory assumes that each party possesses the requisite autonomy to reject the terms of contracts that are not in her best interest. By assuming that all human beings possess freedom and autonomy, however, consent theory ignores the fact that the concrete capacity to act responsibly and in one's self-interest depends critically on having that capacity respected in the institutions and practices of a society.[8] Problems arise when the law, the key institution in which the rights of persons must be publicly embodied, assumes that all persons are possessed of those rights already. Where institutional respect for the autonomy of members of a particular class is absent, members of that class will find themselves in a double-bind when the law expects them to act as if they were simply autonomous.

In the case of rape and other sexually motivated crimes against women, the law has implicitly assumed what I term the "sexual autonomy" of the victim.[9] For my purposes, sexual autonomy refers to the capacity of a person to act on the basis of her own sexual desires and interests. Under conditions of sexual exploitation, women's sexual autonomy, though it is assumed to exist in the abstract, fails to find recognition in the actual practices of the exploitative society.[10] Under such conditions, certain types of sexual "offers" may be coercive even when women, responding under conditions of generalized fear, consent to them.

The manner in which the fear of rape is an ever-present part of women's lives has long been a focal point for feminist social criticism.[11] Most importantly, feminist analysis has called attention to the fact that rape is not an "isolated occurrence" but part of an oppressive system in which the production of fear has served to maintain women in a condition of terror. This was perhaps best expressed in the opening words of Susan Griffin's now famous essay: "I have never been free of the fear of rape. From a very early age I, like most women, have thought of rape as a part of my natural environment—something to be feared and prayed against like fire or lightning. I never asked why men raped; I simply thought it was one of the many mysteries of human nature."[12]

More recently, Claudia Card has outlined the manner in which rape is part of a political practice of terrorism. As with other forms of terrorism, rape effectively disempowers its victims and potential victims by making all action against it appear useless.[13] As such, it occasions a situation in which consent to the demands of the rapist may be the only reasonable or acceptable alternative for the woman. It is also a power that divides the sexes into political classes as rape is an act that can be exercised by any man over any woman.[14] Finally, in distributing "roles and positions, powers and opportunities" to women and men, the practice of rape functions autonomously, with no need for a person or group to "supervise the operation as a whole."[15]

These conditions of fear and subordination brought about by the practice of rape extend into everyday heterosexual relations as well. In this context, it is generally taken for granted that the man will assume the role of sexual initiator and the woman that of the reluctant respondent. Here, too, a woman's refusal of a sexual overture has not been taken as worthy of respect in itself, but rather as an invitation for a more aggressive approach.[16] The insignificance of women's desires with regard to "ordinary" sex has been perhaps most apparent in the existence of the marital rape exemption that prevented husbands from being charged with the rape of their wives. The absence of a category of marital rape has meant that a woman's domain over the sexual use of her own body can legally be relinquished to a particular man.[17] Even though wife rape was a crime in all 50 states as of 1993, 33 states still have partial exemptions for husbands, with some extending limited exemptions to unmarried cohabitants and dates as well.[18] Clearly, if a woman's withholding of consent is not respected as such, her granting it is likewise of little significance. As Carole Pateman remarked: "[I]f 'no,' when uttered by a woman, is to be reinterpreted as 'yes,' then all the comfortable assumptions about her 'consent' are also thrown into disarray. Why should a woman's 'yes' be more privileged, be any the less open to invalidation, than her 'no'?"[19]

To the extent that women's experience is characterized by fear of rape, that fear raises problems that concern women's consent to sexual offers across the board. As Catharine MacKinnon has asked, "If you feel that you are going to be raped when you say no, how do you know that you really want sex when you say yes?"[20] Even the expressed sexual desire of a person who fears that she may be raped in any case may well reflect something less than consent.

Rather than offering an effective remedy to these conditions, the law of rape has historically served to institutionalize them within the state, further imperiling women's sexual autonomy. From their earliest considerations of the issue, feminists have called attention to the manner in which the psychological and sociological impediments to consent find institutional embodiment in the laws concerning rape and sexual assault. Though women could be held legally and morally responsible for their "consent" to violent sex, the extraordinary difficulties for the woman who would attempt to prosecute her assailant in rape and sexual assault cases revealed that the right of sexual consent functioned primarily to protect the rights of rapists. The manner in which rape trials involved a critical reversal of certain basic assumptions regarding the accuser and the accused, the virtual impossibility of obtaining convictions against any man with whom the survivor was acquainted, and the rigid requirements for proof of actual penetration and force all contributed to the realization among feminists that "Rape is only slightly forbidden fruit."[21] In contrast to other violent crimes, such as robbery, in which the question of the victim's consent to the assailant's directives is deemed irrelevant to the crime, in rape trials the focus has traditionally centered on how the survivor's behavior may have led the perpetrator to commit the crime.[22] In the practice of the rape trial, it is not the violation and humiliation suffered by the survivor that defines the crime, but the proof that the sexual access of the defendant was not one to which he was entitled.[23]

I return to the historical issues concerning the definition of the crime of rape in my discussion of specific reforms. The important political point to be taken from this discussion, however, is that under conditions of fear and a general lack of respect, a criterion of consent can scarcely be called upon to express the positive desire of women in matters of sexualized violence. In order to be a legitimate agent of sexual consent, a person must be recognized as a sexually autonomous agent.[24] The feminist critique of sexuality under patriarchy reveals that, under the laws and social practices of a sexist social order, a woman's possession of her body as a domain over which she can exercise consent lacks both social recognition and legal protection.[25] The fact that feminists have had to struggle to win recognition for the rights of women in decisions concerning their own bodies on issues as diverse as reproductive rights, eating disorders, occupational choice, and athletic participation, underlines the point that such autonomy cannot be taken for granted.[26] It is not legitimate for the law to expect a class of persons to behave in a manner befitting self-respecting agents possessed of sexual autonomy when that same law plays a central role in depriving that class of effective control over that domain. To do so is effectively to ignore the fact of oppression.

The blindness to oppression fostered by assuming that all agents simply are autonomous also encourages the illegitimate ascription of moral and legal responsibility to the oppressed for their oppression. Once again, this is well documented in typical rape trials. There it is assumed that if the complaining witness really did perceive an act as a violation of her person, it would be reasonable to expect her to display appropriate resistance to that act and not behave in such a manner that her resistance could be mistaken for consent.[27] Such expectations are reasonable, however, only if it can be assumed that the victim of a violent act is part of a social order in which she experiences herself as an agent worthy of respect, that is, one in which that agency is itself consistently respected. Among the minimal conditions for such a self-concept is that the agent not live in continuous fear of legally unactionable violation at the hands of members of a more powerful class. Under conditions of fear, domination, and inequality, agents *cannot* reasonably be expected to demonstrate the behaviors of "free and equal" human beings as those behaviors have been defined by the dominant classes. An agent under conditions of victimization will act, with more or less success, in such a manner as to survive those conditions.[28]

Here the law must confront a critical irony as concerns the abstract rights of members of historically oppressed groups of people. If women *were* respected as persons in the way that men are in actual social practice, then rape would not be the pervasive crime against women that it is. As Carolyn Shafer and Marilyn Frye observe, "Rape is the exposure of the public lie that women are respected persons."[29] To the extent that the fear of rape conditions women's sexual responses to men, it is unreasonable to expect a woman to behave as if she were an agent whose sexual autonomy really was protected, that is, to behave as if she were a man. As noted above, to the extent that actual rape and the fear of rape have conditioned women's sexual responses to men, it may not be an easy matter to distinguish between a woman's response to rape and her response to "consensual sex." Picking out the distinction may well require very special attention to, and even cultivation of, her own perspective of the rape scenario. If a generalized fear of rape serves to deprive members of the "rape-able" class of the social and psychological conditions necessary for genuine self-respect, holding members of that class up to the moral and legal standards that apply to autonomous persons runs the risk of blaming them for the violation they have suffered and thereby repeating the violation. Treating a person whose autonomy lacks social and legal recognition with the "respect" due a truly autonomous agent will help ensure that her true autonomy remains unrealized.[30]

Consent or Mutuality?

By revealing the forced nature of women's choices under sexism, the feminist critique of sexual exploitation of women shows how little women's consent amounts to under those conditions. If arriving at a theoretical account of the inadequacy of the consent criterion has been relatively simple, however, the common law's definition of rape as "carnal knowledge of a woman forcibly and against her will" has remained remarkably durable.[31] Michigan actually eliminated consent from its definition of criminal sexual conduct in 1974, focusing instead on the forceful nature of the offense.[32] Despite the removal of the word, however, defendants have successfully raised the issue of consent in order to defeat charges of force based on the presence of objective threats or weapons. This has meant, in effect, that consent gets raised later rather than earlier in the trial.[33] The consent criterion has lingered in the theoretical discussions of rape as well. In what has been described as "the most radical proposal to date in the literature,"[34] Cynthia Wicktom has called for "defining rape by the forceful nature of the offender's conduct."[35] Wicktom too, however, rejects the outright exclusion of consent as a criterion of rape in that "examining the victim's non-consent provides indirect information about whether force was used."[36] The fact that consent can be used, even indirectly, as a measure of force, however, places rape in a different category from other criminal acts involving force. A victim's consent under coercive conditions does not ordinarily vitiate the existence of force.

Reacting to the limitations of past attempts at reform, some theorists have called for more sweeping redefinitions or the outright elimination of the traditional notion of consent from the law. Martha Chamallas argues that mutuality rather than consent ought to be the measure of noncoercion in sexual relationships. Chamallas would define mutuality by a counterfactual test, asking "whether the target would have initiated the encounter if she had been given the choice."[37] On Chamallas's account, the central point of feminist criticisms of current conceptions of rape is the establishment of "welcomeness," whether or not the sex was desired by the victim, as the criterion of sexual assault. Citing the example of "a teenage girl whose boyfriend threatens to stop seeing her unless they have sex," Chamallas argues that although a girl's consent to such a quid pro quo might not be in question, coercion would also be present in that she would not initiate such a bargain were it hers to initiate.[38] In this as in many other instances in a woman's life, the girl finds herself in a situation where it is "advantageous" for her to bargain away her sexuality—the hallmark of a system of sexual exploitation.

Lois Pineau, while not eliminating consent from her account, argues that the absence or presence of consent should be measured by the absence or presence of an ongoing communication between the sexual partners. Acknowledging that under exploitative conditions, women may have reasons to consent to sex from which they derive little or no pleasure, Pineau argues that "if a man wants to be sure he is not forcing himself on a woman he has an obligation either to ensure that the encounter really is mutually enjoyable or to know the reasons why she would want to continue the encounter despite her lack of enjoyment."[39] For Pineau, bringing this information to light requires a kind of "communicative sexuality" in which the mutuality of the encounter is made clear throughout. This is especially important where the partners are not part of a long-standing professed relationship.[40] On her account, determining that the male partner in a sexual encounter has not bothered to establish the communicative dialog necessary to determine basic facts concerning the woman's reasons for consenting to the sexual encounter would be tantamount to establishing recklessness or willful ignorance on his part.[41]

As noted above, such sweeping reform proposals have occasioned a backlash of their own, though reform opponents have generally had little new to offer in addressing the problems that motivated the proposals in the first place. In his 1992 essay, "Beyond Rape," however, Donald Dripps proposed a sweeping reform of his own, one that ostensibly addressed the issues raised by feminist critics of rape law while not requiring mutuality as a standard for sexual encounters. Observing that it is unlikely that the same patriarchal tradition that has proven "wrong about all things sexual" could have managed to get "the basic idea right about rape," Dripps recommends reenvisioning rape as a violation of the property rights of an individual to her own body.[42] Taking the negative comparisons of how the law treats the robber as opposed to the rapist to their logical end, Dripps argues that the courts would do better to treat rape simply as the expropriation of a sexual commodity than to enter into the vagaries of what constitutes forceful and nonconsensual sex. Despite some important problems that I identify with his application of the model, Dripps's appeal to commodity exchange is not inconsistent with some radical feminist descriptions of rape as part of a system of sexual exploitation.[43] In the remainder of the chapter, I show that, contrary to Dripps's argument, legal recognition of the fact that a commodity exchange model of sexuality actually does govern a broad class of sexual relations in a sexist society does not entail the endorsement of such relations as a model for the law. I argue, moreover, that legal acknowledgment of the fact that women and men engage in exchanges in which sexuality is treated as an alienable commodity is not inconsistent with reform proposals aimed at replacing consent with mutuality as the norm in sexual encounters. In fact, embracing such reforms would be necessary to bring rape law into line with current thinking concerning "the labor market at large" that Dripps takes as the basis for his commodity model.[44]

Sexuality as a Commodity

Dripps's recommendations follow from what he argues is the failure of recent reforms to address the injustice built into the current legal requirement of a "conjunction" of force and nonconsent to establish rape. Accepting the feminist criticisms of this definition, Dripps observes that it results in a double-bind for the complaining witness in which "no matter how much force is used to obtain it, consent can still occur," and in which "no matter how non-consensual the sex may be, there is no crime without force."[45] By contrast, his commodity theory would predicate the wrongness of rape squarely on its violation of a basic property right. Starting from the Lockean premise that all persons "have a property right to the use of their own bodies," and a corresponding negative right to refuse others' use of them, Dripps argues that when another individual takes this property either through force (i.e., robbery) or without the proprietor's knowledge (i.e., burglary), it constitutes a violation of sexual autonomy.[46] Dripps claims that the commodity theory not only explains the moral wrongness of obvious cases of rape and sexual assault but also addresses further issues that neither current conceptions of the law nor adaptations designed to meet feminist criticisms of it do. By focusing on the unjust "taking" of sex as a commodity, the theory explains why we think sexual acts performed on unconscious victims are wrong. Because the "taking" from the unconscious victim requires no force and is not resisted, Dripps points out that the traditional requirement of a conjunction of force and nonconsent is not met. Moreover, Dripps argues that feminists who would redefine rape according to the "unwelcomeness" of the act are in no better position to explain the wrongness of sex acts on an unconscious victim inasmuch as she neither welcomes nor fails to welcome the act.[47]

Dripps further claims that his view recognizes the legitimacy of "complex relationships," in which women agree to quid pro quo arrangements to exchange otherwise unwelcome sex for nonsexual benefits offered by men. While such arrangements would not constitute rape on traditional accounts, feminist proposals such as those of Chamallas and Pineau that would restrict legitimate sex to exchanges where sex is mutually desired might so define it.[48] On Dripps's account, feminist calls for restrictions on this kind of sexual bargaining would violate the sexual autonomy of individuals who freely choose to engage in it. Dripps singles out Chamallas's insistence on "sex-for-sex" exchanges, arguing that such a demand is overly restrictive and that it fails to respect a woman's capacity to engage in complex quid pro quos in her life. Assuming that "baseline entitlements" to commodities, including sexual commodities, are equal, it is unjust for the state to preclude bargaining between parties for those goods. Anticipating the feminist objection that bargaining under conditions of sexual exploitation always leaves women in a disadvantaged position, Dripps counters that appeals to conditions of generalized sexual exploitation ultimately threaten protection against rape altogether: "[T]hose feminist accounts describing sex as inherently exploitative fail to justify a special law of sexual assault."[49] Indeed, Dripps suggests that women might well find themselves more "marginalized" in a society in which heterosexual men did not desire to bargain with them for rights to their "sexual assets." Under those conditions, men might find themselves with no incentive to exchange other goods in return for sex at all.[50]

Consistent with treating rape as a property crime, Dripps argues for a two-offense approach to rape law, distinguishing cases of "sexually motivated assault," where sexual expropriation was accomplished by violence, from those of mere "sexual expropriation" where the sexual taking required no violence. The burden would be on the prosecution to show "that the accused caused the victim's fear for the purpose of obtaining sex, and also that he knew he was causing fear at the time."[51] Even though, as under current law, the prosecution would have the burden of presenting evidence that the defendant was guilty of coercion, Dripps sees this burden as "hardly insurmountable."[52] Moreover, in contrast to the present patchwork of constitutionally dubious rape shield laws, Dripps claims that his proposal would permit a robust defense in keeping with the provisions of the Sixth Amendment.

I argue below that a more complex approach that begins with the recognition of the commodification of sex could substantiate feminist criticisms of rape law. It is far from clear, however, how Dripps's account can do that.[53] Strikingly, his commodity theory fails to eliminate either nonconsent or force as defining features of rape. In the more serious crime of sexually motivated assault, the prosecution must prove to the jury that the defendant knowingly used force (and thus did not believe that the plaintiff was consenting) in order for the charge to stick. As for the lesser charge of sexual expropriation, Dripps admits that the defense "cannot avoid inquiry into the complete relationship between the complaining witness and the defendant."[54] It is difficult to see precisely how this would improve the odds for survivors of acquaintance rape whose present access to rape shield laws provides at least some leverage to compel the defense to stick to the facts of the case at hand. Perhaps most important, Dripps's treatment of sex as the object of bargaining omits the fact that politically disadvantaged parties *consent* to *coercive* bargains all the time in various kinds of markets. In short, Dripps's analysis falters because, despite his acknowledgment of some of the shortcomings of the law's current treatment of the crime of rape, he fails to recognize either the crime or its treatment as symptomatic of a political system of sexual exploitation. By likening rape to property-based offenses such as mugging or robbery, Dripps obscures the political nature of the practice. As Rae Langton has remarked, "To call [sexual] violence simply 'crime' . . . without remarking upon the interesting fact that the perpetrators are nearly always members of one class of citizens, and the victims members of another, would be to disguise its systematically discriminatory nature."[55]

Suppose, however, that the law were to recognize the fact that, at least under conditions of sexual exploitation, women do in fact "bargain" with their sexuality, but that they do so in the context of a system in which they are the politically disadvantaged party. If, as Catharine MacKinnon has argued, the condition of women under sexism can, in some ways, be likened to that of workers under capitalism, then such bargaining under conditions of inequality would be typical.[56] In contrast to Dripps's libertarian legitimation of this condition, however, on this account the law would be obliged to recognize that women's exchange of their sexuality for other goods is at least partly caused by and serves to perpetuate their subordination as a class.[57] In other words, the legal recognition of the fact of the alienation of sexuality under sexism would not thereby legitimate that condition as morally neutral. As noted above, Dripps argues against such a possibility, claiming that acknowledgment of a generalized condition of sexual exploitation would delegitimize any sexual exchange and thus imperil any special protections against sexual assault.[58] A more careful examination of the protections offered under labor law reveals, however, that special protections are possible even where a generalized condition of exploitation is implicitly acknowledged. In fact, the inequalities of a bargaining situation can be taken into account in prohibiting certain kinds of exchanges in a market.

Markets and Protection from Unjust Offers

In exploring this issue, it is instructive to look to the labor market model from which Dripps developed his own analysis. In fact, the labor market offers an interesting and informative analog to the "sexual marketplace" of the commodity theory. There, too, one class of persons finds itself in the position of consenting to offers proffered by members of an advantaged class and consenting to some of them that, ceteris paribus, they would not welcome. Perhaps most interestingly, however, the capitalist workplace offers an informative example of a social situation with generalized conditions of exploitation, where the law provides special protections for members of the exploited class against certain kinds of exploitative offers. The logic and justification for these protections will be relevant for the law of sexual assault and rape as well.

The Occupational Safety and Health Act of 1970 (OSHA) required the setting of standards specifying permissible levels of exposure to certain hazardous materials and made it the legal responsibility of employers to see to it that exposure to workers did not exceed those levels.[59] Moreover, the Act forbids employers from making certain kinds of offers to workers, including "hazard pay," for consenting to exposure to technologically eliminable risks.[60] By making the employer liable for certain types of *proposals*, OSHA at least implicitly recognizes that workers might find it reasonable to consent to the risks in question. In effect, certain quid pro quo arrangements are proscribed for reasons of worker safety.

As might be expected, the primary theoretical opposition to OSHA has come from libertarian social theorists who defend a right to noninterference in forming contracts in the marketplace of labor.[61] As Tibor Machan has argued, the right of a prospective employee to choose dangerous work should be protected, and the regulation of this choice assumes a paternalistic vision of workers as "helpless, inefficacious, inept persons."[62] Interestingly, however, the view that the choices of institutionally disadvantaged parties are worthy of absolute protection has held considerably less force in the law of labor than in the law of rape.[63] As G. A. Cohen has argued in this regard, the fact that an action is chosen is no insurance that it is not also forced. To be forced to perform an action, that action must be one of a set of alternatives that is open to the agent. The agent must be "free" to perform it. Thus, the question of whether or not a worker is forced to accept a job turns not on his choice to perform it, "nor even that he had alternatives, but that he had an *acceptable* or *reasonable* alternative."[64] On this view, the restriction of workers' choices under OSHA is justifiable insofar as it recognizes that, under the threat of unemployment, workers' choices may often not reflect what workers would desire were they to choose their work setting under less-exploitative conditions.

Norman Daniels distinguishes between the social forces governing coercion in the institutional framework of the capitalist workplace and the standard examples of force usually assumed in the libertarian literature. While the situation of the worker does not limit alternatives in the same manner as the classic "Your money or your life!" scenario, it nevertheless compels the worker to accept and even to welcome certain choices that would be distinctly undesirable in the absence of the threat of unemployment. Daniels characterizes the typical context of the worker as "quasi-coercive":

> The intuition underlying calling unfair or unjust restrictions of options "quasi-coercive" is that they involve a diminished freedom of action of the same sort which is glaring in the central cases of coercion. A central difference may be in the mechanism through which freedom of action is diminished. We do not have the direct and invasive intrusion into the choice space of the individual which is present in the central cases of coercion, for example when the mugger exceeds his rights by pointing a gun at my head. Instead, we have an indirect, yet pervasive, erosion of that space as a result of unjust or unfair social practices and institutions.[65]

Because the restrictive force of quasi-coercion comes about as a result of the *institutional context*, it is distinct from both the direct coercive force that results from the restrictive acts of a particular individual and from the nonintentional forces of nature. First of all, this means that the liability of the employer for imposing the quasi-coercive force does not rest on her belief that she knowingly coerced the victim to perform the dangerous act in question. Thus, a conscious intention to violate worker autonomy need not be shown in order to establish that the worker's rights were violated. Second, the violation has no relation to the explicit unwelcomeness of the offer from the point of view of the worker, inasmuch as the conditions that define the baseline for workers may make such proposals desirable.[66] The fact that a worker consented to the act or even welcomed it has no bearing on its being an actionable violation of her rights.

Understood in this framework, the goal of OSHA is to "impose prior protective constraints" on the market exchanges of employers and workers, with the intent of preserving the autonomy of the workers.[67] While prior constraints of this kind do limit the choices of workers, Daniels argues that such limitations are necessary to curtail the risks to the life and health of workers that would result from their predictable acquiescence to quasi-coerced offers from profit-maximizing employers. These risks make the apparent enhancement of autonomy that would result from accepting the employer's offers entirely illusory: "Quasi-coercion undermines true autonomy in much the same way coercion does."[68] Nevertheless, because of the quasi-coercive conditions under which workers make their choices (i.e., under threat of unemployment), the change from the expected baseline may make dangerous offers welcome despite their costs. Accordingly, the justification for the constraints must make reference to a counterfactual condition in which workers' choices would be unconstrained. Because the risk to workers arises due to lack of information and the need for a job, a reasonable worker would contract to interventions that would protect her from making the harmful decisions that she would make because she is not "or cannot be adequately informed, competent, or free to make autonomous ones."[69] Under conditions of quasi-coercion, it is reasonable for a person to seek protection from having to make certain kinds of choices at all.

Daniels's account of quasi-coercive exchanges has important implications for the feminist discussion of rape, especially acquaintance rape. Much as the coercive nature of work under capitalism deviates from the standard "Your money or your life!" model of coercion, the coercive conditions operative in acquaintance rape deviate from the blatant force of what Susan Estrich has dubbed "real rape" scenarios.[70] Nevertheless, as previously discussed, the institutionally enforced conditions in which women are, and perceive themselves to be, economically dependent on, emotionally bonded to, and physically intimidated by men establish a social situation in which a typical woman is vulnerable to quasi-coercive pressures in her sexual decisions. Under these conditions, women may find it to their immediate advantage in a variety of social contexts to exchange their sexuality for benefits from men or to avoid costs imposed by men. Much as workers' autonomy is set at risk by the bargaining practices of an advantaged class aimed at procuring their labor, women's sexual autonomy is put at risk by the practices of powerful men, in which they are cast as sexual objects. If Dripps is right that women are less "marginalized" by being the object of men's sexual offers, it remains the case that the attention that men give to women in this context puts their sexual autonomy seriously at risk. Under the baseline conditions of a sexually exploitative system, women will be subject to sexual offers that threaten their integrity, their health, or their lives.

As noted above, the quasi-coercive situation of labor under capitalism requires that we appeal to a hypothetical condition in which workers' choices would be unconstrained in order to determine what kinds of workplace offers are truly legitimate. We cannot assume that a quid pro quo is legitimate merely because workers actually consent to or even welcome it under the coercive conditions. Similarly, to arrive at a just standard for sexual offers in a sexually exploitative system, we must look beyond the "complex relationships" that women accept. In the workplace scenario, OSHA assumes that a typical autonomous worker (i.e., of the sort not found under conditions of labor exploitation) would not consent to an offer that endangered her physical health if she had other alternatives. In the case of sexual exchanges, Chamallas's hypothetical condition in which an offer is legitimate only if "the target would have initiated the encounter had she been given the choice" suggests a standard for sexually autonomous choices.[71] Because respect for sexual autonomy consists of respect for the sexual desires and interests of the person, offers that would induce her to engage in sexual activities irrespective of her own desires for intimacy or pleasure fail to honor that autonomy. As Chamallas has argued, exchanges of sex for money, security, or other material goods not only unfairly advantage men (as men are typically the materially advantaged party), but reinforce the sexual objectification by which women are reduced to sexual commodities.[72]

If Chamallas's hypothetical question offers a means for arriving at a standard for legitimate sexual offers, Pineau's communicative sexuality suggests a mechanism for determining whether or not such a standard has actually been met in the sexual encounter. The man's responsibility for maintaining this communication derives from the place he occupies in the quasi-coercive situation. In the workplace scenario, an employer's ignorance of how plant conditions are affecting worker health is deemed reckless and culpable. A man's ignorance of how his behaviors are respecting or violating his partner's sexual autonomy are likewise reckless and culpable. In the absence of "an ongoing and encouraging response," the man who would continue the encounter displays willful indifference toward his partner's sexual autonomy.[73]

Taking OSHA as a model, it is clear that acknowledging the commodification of women's sexuality need not rule out restrictions against certain kinds of exploitative exchanges. Much as the restrictions of workplace law act as prior constraints against the worst of abuses in an exploitative marketplace for labor, the law of rape and sexual assault could function as a set of prior constraints on the worst of abuses in a sexually exploitative society.[74] Most important, just as the justification for OSHA implicitly acknowledges that an exploitative workplace exists, the law would be forced to acknowledge that protections against rape and sexual assault are necessary to protect women from the unjust offers that arise within a system of sexual exploitation. The issue to be decided would not be whether or not the survivor consented, but whether or not the offer was one to which a genuinely sexually autonomous person would have consented.

Objections and Limitations

Conceiving of rape law as offering protection against the worst abuses in an exploitative system gives rise to two competing sets of objections. On the one side, sexual libertarians such as Dripps may object that such protections are overly paternalistic in restricting women's choices to sex for sex exchanges. Because Dripps defines sexual autonomy negatively, that is, as consisting in "the freedom to refuse to have sex with any one for any reason," a decision to have sex, even if it is part of an otherwise unwelcome quid pro quo, is no threat to sexual autonomy.[75] The problem with this view, as with most libertarian accounts of autonomy, is that it fails to take account of the manner in which coerciveness can reside in the context in which decisions are made. As Daniels points out, the "autonomy" expressed in the acceptance of quasi-coercive proposals is entirely illusory. For this reason, most workers reasonably accept paternalistic interventions that protect them against harmful decisions that they would likely be compelled to make when they are not sufficiently free or informed to make autonomous ones.[76] Presumably, the typical reasonable woman would not find her autonomy threatened by laws restricting the ability of men to make otherwise attractive offers that violate her sexual desires and interests.

Putting aside the abstract libertarian objection, however, some feminists have objected to restricting women's sexuality to one of mutually desired encounters. Clearly, some women, perhaps most women at some times, make choices to exchange sex for other goods. Moreover, some women claim to enjoy forms of sexuality involving domination and seduction as opposed to the communicative and mutual sort endorsed here.[77] If sexual initiators are legally compelled to engage in communication with their sexual targets, such forms of sexuality will be effectively proscribed. This objection raises two distinct points that must be addressed in turn. In the first place, the objection itself conflates the *desire* for sex involving domination or seduction with simply *being* dominated or seduced, one's desire notwithstanding. These are not the same thing.[78] While the kind and the degree of communication may vary with different kinds of sexual encounters, respect for sexual autonomy will always involve careful attention to the desires of the other partner in the exchange.

Insofar as a criterion for mutuality makes proposals of sex for other goods illegal, however, it is true that it will not permit a woman's choice to engage in prostitution. Such a conclusion follows from the model outlined above, with the justification that sex for money exchanges under conditions of quasi-coercion cannot enhance women's autonomy. It is worth noting that a similar issue arises in the case of OSHA standards in restricting workers' choices to accept offers of hazard pay from employers. The argument here stands on the premise that if some willing workers are permitted to consent to proposals that endanger their health, this will exert a coercive force on all workers to accept such proposals whether they would welcome them or not. Similarly, if some willing women are permitted to consent to the commodification of their sexuality under conditions in which men hold economic, emotional, and physical power over them, this will make it more difficult for all women to lead sexual lives in accord with their own interests and desires.[79]

On the positive side, such a restriction might contribute to bettering the lives of the vast majority of prostituted women whose "choices" to remain in prostitution are far from uncoerced. Moreover, the model of OSHA would establish a legal basis for shifting liability onto the agents who make the quasi-coercive offers (i.e., pimps and johns), and away from the prostituted individual who accepts them.

While liberal critics might find the approach sketched in this chapter overly restrictive, other theorists may take it to task for being too modest in both its method and its goals. In the first place, from a legal perspective, the analogy between the law of sexual assault and that of occupational safety may seem to diminish the harm of rape. While rape and sexual assault are criminal offenses, legal actions under OSHA ordinarily involve monetary remedies. While this objection raises a set of issues that I cannot fully address here, two points are in order. First, it should be noted that some rape survivors have sought damages in civil court. Because the standard of proof in civil cases ("preponderance of evidence") is less than that of criminal cases ("beyond a reasonable doubt"), some complaining witnesses have found this to be a better setting for seeking redress, especially in cases of acquaintance rape.[80] Because rape shield laws apply only to criminal courts, however, fewer survivors have availed themselves of this venue than might have otherwise. Absent a consent criterion for rape, however, the complaining witness's sexual history would be irrelevant. At issue would be the coerciveness of the encounter in question, regardless of whether or not the survivor had consented to similarly coercive encounters in the past. Thus, the approach outlined here might facilitate civil remedies in a way that the present law does not.

Even if civil or tort remedies against acquaintance rape might be made easier, however, few feminist theorists would be satisfied with an approach that effectively decriminalized rape. It is not obvious, however, that criminal prosecution of the most egregious instances of exploitation is inconsistent with regulatory constraints on a marketplace. Under OSHA, some violations, for instance, willful violations of regulations resulting in death, are not considered to be compensable and are subject to criminal penalties under the Act.[81] Moreover, courts have found criminal willfulness to be present in cases of "indifference to the requirements of the law," even in the absence of a specific intention to cause harm.[82] Understanding rape to be at or near the end of a continuum of violence under conditions of sexual exploitation, it would be consistent to treat it as the kind of egregious violation that would warrant criminal prosecution. While less-serious violations (e.g., legally actionable instances of sexual harassment) could be compensated in civil court, rape might be judged noncompensable within the same regulatory framework.

In addition to legal objections to this account, however, its method for determining the presence of coercion also raises important philosophical questions. By relying on a hypothetical choice situation as the standard for whether or not an exchange meets the demands of sexual autonomy, the model may implicitly integrate elements of women's subordination into the standard. If women's choices are as constrained as the discussion at the chapter's outset suggested that they were, then any appeal to what women would choose or even welcome runs the risk of incorporating sexist elements into its criterion. While such a criticism has merit, it is important to note that for all its limitations, a criterion such as Chamallas's would take us much further in the direction of arriving at a just definition of rape than the current conjunction of force and lack of consent. Moreover, under global conditions of exploitation, it is impossible to arrive at normative standards apart from hypothetical appeals. While the abstract nature of those appeals always runs the risk of perpetuating the oppression that they seek to eliminate (and thus must always be open to revision), it is a risk that is impossible to wholly avoid when an oppressive system effectively defines the choice situation of the oppressed class.

Finally, the model proposed here may seem deficient not only in its method but in its goals as well. For rather than dismantling the exploitative conditions under which women's sexual choices are coerced, it merely offers redress against the worst abuses of the system. As in the case of OSHA, however, the beneficial effects on the autonomy of workers that follow from the enactment of restrictions on the worst abuses of an exploitative system may be a necessary condition for more sweeping change in the future. Until a definition of rape can permit the vast majority of rapes to be reported and effectively prosecuted, it is hard to see how women's overall situation will be improved.[83] While legal protections are only a starting point toward equality, they are no less indispensable on that account.

Notes

I am grateful to Keith Burgess-Jackson, Noelle Guest, Norah Martin, Cecelia Ober, and Lisa Schwartzman for discussion and critical comments on this essay.

1. Susan Brownmiller's classic study *Against Our Will: Men, Women and Rape* (New York: Simon and Schuster, 1975) emphasized this distinction. More recently, Lois Pineau's "Date Rape: A Feminist Analysis" (*Law and Philosophy* 8 (1989): 217–243, reprinted in Leslie Francis, ed., *Date Rape: Feminism, Philosophy, and the Law* [University Park: Pennsylvania State University Press, 1996]) linked sexist attitudes toward acquaintance rape to flawed models of sexuality that emphasize male aggressiveness rather than mutually communicative encounters.

2. In *Feminism Unmodified*, Catharine MacKinnon explicitly challenges Brownmiller's distinction between sex and violence, arguing that the merging of violence and sex in rape typifies sexist society. Claudia Card argues that rape is part of a terrorist system with ramifications for heterosexual relations throughout society (see "Rape as a Terrorist Institution," in *Violence, Terrorism, and Justice*, ed. R. G. Frey and Christopher Morris [New York: Cambridge University Press, 1992]. See also Larry May and Robert Strikwerda, "Men in Groups: Collective Responsibility for Rape," *Hypatia* 9 [1994]: 134–51).

3. See Pineau, "Date Rape: A Feminist Analysis;" Cynthia Wicktom, "Focusing on the Offender's Forceful Conduct: A Proposal for the Redefinition of Rape Laws," *The George Washington Law Review* 56 (1988): 399–430; Martha Chamallas, "Consent, Equality, and the Legal Control of Sexual Conduct," *Southern California Law Review* 61 (1988): 777–862. While Pineau and Wicktom would de-emphasize the place of consent without eliminating it altogether, Chamallas redefines the standard as mutuality.

4. For a popular expression of the latter point, see Katie Roiphe, *The Morning After: Sex, Fear, and Feminism on Campus* (New York: Little, Brown, 1993). For a legal perspective, see Drucilla Cornell's criticisms of MacKinnon in *Beyond Accommodation: Ethical Femi-*

nism, Deconstruction, and the Law (New York: Routledge, 1991) and *Transformations: Recollective Imagination and Sexual Difference* (New York: Routledge, 1993). For criticisms of Pineau's argument that focus on the defendant's rights, see Angela P. Harris, "Forcible Rape, Date Rape, and Communicative Sexuality: A Legal Perspective," in *Date Rape: Feminism, Philosophy, and the Law,* ed. Leslie Francis (University Park: Pennsylvania State University Press, 1996), pp. 51-61, and Catharine Pierce Wells, "Date Rape and the Law: Another Feminist View," in *Date Rape: Feminism,* ed. Leslie Francis, pp. 41–50.

5. Donald A. Dripps, "Beyond Rape: An Essay on the Difference Between the Presence of Force and the Absence of Consent," *Columbia Law Review* 92 (1992): 1780–1809.

6. In assuming that current changes to rape law have been insufficient, I am not claiming that recent reforms to the law of rape have been insignificant or without effects in their own right. In particular, they have made some important strides toward making convictions easier when charges have been filed. In one study on marital rape carried out by the National Clearinghouse on Marital and Date Rape between 1978 and 1985, 88% of the cases under study resulted in conviction (see Vernon K. Wiehe and Ann L. Richards, *Intimate Betrayal: Understanding and Responding to the Trauma of Rape* [Thousand Oaks, CA: Sage, 1995], p. 97). Even if this percentage is representative, however, it probably reflects results only for the most violent cases of marital rape, i.e., those with the greatest likelihood of ending in a conviction (see Diana Russell, "Date Rape" in *Acquaintance Rape: The Hidden Crime,* ed. Andrea Parrot and Laurie Bechhofer (New York: Wiley, 1991), pp. 129–39). It remains the case that the crime of rape most often goes unreported, and that most of these unreported crimes are committed by men who are acquainted with the women who are the victims.

7. For further discussion, see Carole Pateman, "Women and Consent," *Political Theory* 8 (1980): 149–168.

8. Libertarian theorists take this a step further, insisting that respect for consent simply is respect for autonomy (ignoring altogether the conditions under which consent is granted). Yet, as Robin West has observed: "People consent to changes in the world that involve a wide range of market choices, risk pools, and apparent authorities. Wives submit to abusive husbands; employees consent to exploitative and humiliating work environments; consumers consent to the sales of defective, dangerous, and overpriced merchandise; women consent to 'date rape' and to sexual harassment on the street and on the job . . ." ("Authority, Autonomy, and Choice: The Role of Consent in the Moral and Political Visions of Franz Kafka and Richard Posner," *Harvard Law Review* 99 [1985]: 427).

9. I use the term "survivor" to refer to the complaining witness in legal cases of sexualized violence. I reserve the term "victim" to refer to the recipient of sexual violence where it remains unclear whether the recipient survived the violence or not.

10. For the purposes of this paper, I shall use the term "sexual exploitation" to refer to a state of affairs in which women are variously required to alienate their sexuality to men in order to cope and ultimately to survive. For further discussion of sexual exploitation as a system, see MacKinnon, "Feminism, Marxism, Method, and the State: An Agenda for Theory," in *Feminist Theory: A Critique of Ideology,* ed. N. O. Keohane, M. Z. Rosaldo, and B. C. Gelpi (Chicago: University of Chicago Press, 1982).

11. See Ingrid Bengis, *Combat in the Erogenous Zone: Writings on Love, Hate, and Sex* (New York: Knopf, 1973); Brownmiller, *Against Our Will;* Lorenne M. G. Clark and Debra

Lewis, *Rape: The Price of Coercive Sexuality* (Toronto: Women's Press, 1977); Pamela Foa, "What's Wrong with Rape?" in *Feminism and Philosophy*, ed. Mary Vetterling-Braggin, Frederick Elliston, and Jane English (Totowa, NJ: Rowman and Allenheld, 1977); Andrea Medea and Kathleen Thompson, eds., *Against Rape* (New York: Farrar, Strauss, and Giroux, 1974); Susan Rae Peterson, "Coercion and Rape: The State As a Male Protection Racket" in *Feminism and Philosophy*, ed. Vetterling-Braggin, Elliston, and English; Diana E. H. Russell, *The Politics of Rape: The Victim's Perspective* (New York: Stein and Day, 1977) and *Rape in Marriage* (New York: Macmillan, 1982); and Carolyn Shafer and Marilyn Frye, "Rape and Respect," Meredith Tax, "Woman and Her Mind: The Story of Everyday Life," in *Radical Feminism*, ed., Ann Koedt, Ellen Levine, and Anita Rapone (New York: Quadrangle, 1973).

12. Susan Griffin, "Rape: The All-American Crime," in Vetterling-Braggin, Elliston, and English, eds., *Feminism and Philosophy*, p. 313. See also Robin Morgan, *The Demon Lover: On the Sexuality of Terrorism* (New York: Norton, 1989), pp. 23–24; and May and Strikwerda, "Men in Groups."

13. For an interesting discussion of terrorism that is informed by women's experience of the threat of rape, see Bat-Ami Bar On, "Why Terrorism Is Morally Problematic" in Frey and Morris, *Violence, Terrorism, and Justice*.

14. As Barbara Mehrhof and Pamela Kearon wrote in their early essay: "There are no actions or forms of behavior sufficient to avoid its danger. There is no sign that designates a rapist since each male is potentially one. . . . It is primarily a lesson for the whole class of women—a strange lesson in that it does not teach a form of behavior which will save women from it. *Rape teaches instead the objective, innate and unchanging subordination of women relative to men*" ("Rape: An Act of Terror," in Koedt, Levine, and Rapone, *Radical Feminism*, p. 230).

15. See Card, "Rape as a Terrorist Institution," pp. 297–98.

16. "What she may see as a refusal he may see as socially appropriate coyness. In such a situation he may go ahead and press her further. The outcome, sexual intercourse, which she considers forced, may be viewed by him—and participants in the courtroom who share his cultural attitudes—as consensual sex" (Carol Bohmer, "Acquaintance Rape and the Law," in Parrot and Bechhofer, *Acquaintance Rape*, pp. 321–22).

17. As Matthew Hale observed with regard to the wife's loss of the ability to claim rape by her husband, "by their mutual matrimonial consent and contract the wife hath given up herself in this kind unto the husband which she cannot retract" (cited by Gary Paquin, "The Legal Aspects of Acquaintance Rape," in Wiehe and Richards, eds., *Intimate Betrayal*).

18. Rachel Kennedy Bergen, *Wife Rape: Understanding the Response of Survivors and Service Providers* (Thousand Oaks, CA: Sage, 1995), p. 150.

19. Pateman, "Women and Consent", p. 162.

20. MacKinnon, *Feminism Unmodified*, p. 83.

21. Mehrhof and Kearon, "Rape: An Act of Terror," p. 232. See also Foa, "What's Wrong with Rape?" p. 356, and MacKinnon, *Toward a Feminist Theory of the State* (Cambridge, MA: Harvard University Press, 1989), pp. 172–183.

22. See Bohmer, "Acquaintance Rape and the Law," p. 321.

23. As MacKinnon notes, "From women's point of view, rape is not prohibited; it is regulated," *Toward a Feminist Theory of the State*, p. 179.

24. "The proper scope of one's power of consent depends upon one's *domain,* and the notion of domain is inextricably linked with that of personhood, for it is as a person that one has a domain" (Shafer and Frye, "Rape and Respect," p. 336).

25. As MacKinnon states, "To be rapable, a position that is social not biological, defines what a woman is," *Toward a Feminist Theory of the State,* p. 178. See also Shafer and Frye, "Rape and Respect," p. 334.

26. See, for example: Barbara Ehrenreich and Deirdre English, *For Her Own Good: 150 Years of the Experts' Advice to Women* (New York: Anchor, 1978); Kim Chernin, *The Hungry Self: Women, Eating, and Identity* (New York: Harper and Row, 1985); MacKinnon, *Feminism Unmodified,* pp. 117–124.

27. MacKinnon sees this problem in criminal prosecutions of both rape and sexual harassment: "[A] victim who resists is more likely to be killed, but unless she fights back, it is not rape, because she cannot prove coercion. With sexual harassment, rejection proves that the advance is unwanted, but also is likely to call forth retaliation, thus forcing the victim to bring intensified injury upon herself in order to demonstrate that she is injured at all," *Sexual Harassment of Working Women: A Case of Sex Discrimination* (New Haven, NJ: Yale University Press, 1979), p. 44.

28. See MacKinnon, *Toward a Feminist Theory of the State,* p. 177.

29. Shafer and Frye, "Rape and Respect," p. 343.

30. This is the sense of MacKinnon's criticism of abstract equality as a means of bringing about genuinely equal relations: "Abstract equality undermines substantive inequality, but it reinforces it at the same time," *Feminism Unmodified,* p. 14. To the extent that unequals are treated as equals, the effects of the initial inequality remain in force.

31. William Blackstone, *Commentaries* 4, *210. For discussion of the consent standard in contemporary state laws, see L. R. Harris, "Toward a Consent Standard in the Law of Rape," *University of Chicago Law Review* 43 (1976): 613–45, and Bohmer, "Acquaintance Rape and the Law," p. 318.

32. See Chamallas, "Consent, Equality," p. 799.

33. *People v. Hearn* 100 Mi. App., *People v. Thompson* 117 Mi. App., cited in Wicktom, "Focusing on the Offender's," pp. 419–20. See also Jeanne C. Marsh, Allison Geist, and Nathan Caplan, *Rape and the Limits of Law Reform* (Boston: Auburn House, 1982), p. 32.

34. Dripps, "Beyond Rape," p. 1785.

35. Wicktom, "Focusing on the Offender's," p. 425.

36. Ibid., p. 426.

37. Chamallas, "Consent, Equality," p. 836.

38. Ibid., pp. 837–38.

39. Pineau, "Date Rape," pp. 17–18.

40. Ibid., pp. 65–67.

41. Ibid., p. 23.

42. Dripps, "Beyond Rape," p. 1785. Dripps's argument from property rights is based on libertarian premises similar to those developed by Richard A. Posner in *Sex and Reason* (Cambridge, MA: Harvard University Press, 1992).

43. Such a view is most clearly articulated in MacKinnon's comparison of the expropriation of women's sexuality under sexism to that of workers' labor power under capitalism. See "Feminism, Marxism, Method, and the State: An Agenda for Theory" in Keohane, Rosaldo, and Gelpi, eds., *Feminist Theory,* and "Feminism, Marxism, Method, and the State: To-

ward Feminist Jurisprudence," in *Critical Legal Studies*, ed. Allan C. Hutchinson (Totowa, NJ: Rowman and Littlefield, 1989).

44. Dripps, "Beyond Rape," p. 1786.

45. Ibid., pp. 1793, 1794. For further discussion of how the absence of force has been taken as evidence of consent, see Lee Madigan and Nancy Gamble, *The Second Rape: Society's Continued Betrayal of the Victim* (New York: Macmillan, 1989), p. 103.

46. Dripps, "Beyond Rape," p. 1786.

47. Ibid., pp. 1788–89.

48. Whether or not all nonmutually desired sex would be rape would depend on the precise mechanisms by which moral illegitimacy would establish legal liability.

49. Ibid., p. 1791.

50. "The employer can almost always hire a man in preference to a woman, but a man can engage in vaginal intercourse only with a woman. Suppose . . . that a celibate or homosexual male elite governed society without the need for sexual bargaining with women. In such a world, would not women as a class be more, rather than less, marginalized?" (Ibid. pp. 1791–92).

51. Ibid., p. 1798.

52. Ibid.

53. For further discussion and criticism of Dripps's specific proposals, see Robin L. West, "Legitimating the Illegitimate: A Comment on *Beyond Rape*," *Columbia Law Review* 93 (1993): 1442–1459.

54. Dripps, "Beyond Rape," pp. 1801–2.

55. Rae Langton, "Whose Right?: Ronald Dworkin, Women, and Pornographers," *Philosophy and Public Affairs* 19 (1990): 334–335.

56. MacKinnon, "Feminism, Marxism, Method, and the State."

57. For a discussion of how the legal recognition of the commodification of sexuality serves to legitimate sexually exploitative bargaining, see West, "Legitimating the Illegitimate." For further criticism of the commodity model as a morally acceptable one for sexual relations, see Elizabeth Anderson, *Value in Ethics and Economics* (Cambridge, MA: Harvard University Press, 1993), pp. 143–150; and Margaret Radin, "Market Inalienability," *Harvard Law Review* 100 (1987): 1849–1937.

58. Cf., Dripps, "Beyond Rape," p. 1791.

59, The Occupational Safety and Health Act of 1970, Public Law No. 91-596, 84 Stat. 1590, codified at 27 U.S.C. 651–78 (1976).

60. Norman Daniels, "Does OSHA Protect Too Much?" in *Moral Rights in the Workplace*, ed. Gertrude Ezorsky (Albany: State University of New York Press, 1987), p. 51.

61. See, e.g., Peter Huber, "Exorcists vs. Gatekeepers in Risk Regulation," *Regulation* 23 (1983); Tibor R. Machan, "Human Rights, Workers' Rights, and the 'Right' to Occupational Safety," in Ezorsky, ed., pp. 45–50; Robert Nozick *Anarchy, State, and Utopia* (New York: Harper, 1975), p. 262. For replies to the libertarian attack on workplace safety legislation, see Nicholas Ashford, *Crisis in the Workplace* (Cambridge, MA: MIT Press, 1976); G. A. Cohen, "The Structure of Proletarian Unfreedom," *Philosophy and Public Affairs* 12, 1983: 3–33; "Are Disadvantaged Workers Who Take Hazardous Jobs Forced to Take Hazardous Jobs?" in Ezorsky, ed., pp. 61–80; Steven Kelman, "Regulation and Paternalism," in *Rights and Regulations*, eds. T. R. Machan and M. B. Johnson (Cambridge, MA: Ballinger, 1983), pp. 217–48.

62. Machan, "Human Rights," p. 49.

63. This is evidenced by the fact that the debate is over regulations already in force as opposed to the debate over rape legislation that has yet to come into being.

64. Cohen, "The Structure of Proleterian Unfreedom," p. 68. Onora O'Neill makes a similar point with reference to integrity of the chooser in her discussion of the unacceptable offers made by terrorists: "An 'offer' is made unrefusable when noncompliance is connected to 'consequences' that cannot be accepted by the victim: 'consequences' are unacceptable by the victim if their acceptance destroys that victim's very integrity or sense of self" ("Which Are the Offers *You* Can't Refuse?" in Frey and Morris, eds., *Violence, Terrorism, and Justice,* p. 186).

65. Daniels, "Does OSHA Protect Too Much?," p. 54.

66. Ibid., pp. 53, 55.

67. Ibid., p. 56.

68. Ibid., p. 69.

69. Ibid., p. 56.

70. Susan Estrich, *Real Rape* (Cambridge, MA: Harvard University Press, 1987).

71. Chamallas, "Consent, Equality," p. 836.

72. Ibid., p. 839.

73. Pineau, "Date Rape," p. 23.

74. Daniels, "Does OSHA Protect Too Much?," p. 57.

75. Dripps, "Beyond Rape," p. 1785.

76. Daniels, "Does OSHA Protect Too Much?," p. 56.

77. As Catharine Pierce Wells writes in reply to Pineau's proposal: "There are, in fact, many women who share a 'masterful seduction' view of sex and romance. There are women who support themselves by prostitution or by marriage to wealthy men. There are lesbians who enjoy patterns of domination and subordination. . . . In short, there are millions of women who do not seek—and may not want—the kind of communicative sexual relations that Pineau describes" (p. 48).

78. As Pineau herself points out, consensual sadomasochistic sex requires communication and should not be confused with simple brutality (p. 25).

79. As Elizabeth Anderson has argued: "If women's sexuality is legally valued as a commodity anywhere in society, it would be even more difficult than it already is to establish insulated social spheres where it can be exclusively and fully valued as a genuinely shared and personal good, where women themselves can be sexually valued in ways fully consonant with their own dignity" (*Value in Ethics and Economics,* p. 155). For further discussion of the relationship between individual and group risk scenarios, see Mark McCarthy, "A Review of Some Normative and Conceptual Issues in Occupational Safety and Health," *Boston College Environmental Affairs Law Review* 9 (1981–1982): 773–814.

80. For a discussion, see Paquin, "The Legal Aspects of Acquaintance Rape," pp. 102–104.

81. See *The Job Safety and Health Act of 1970: Text, Analysis, and Legislative History* (Washington, DC: Bureau of National Affairs, 1971), p. 54. For further discussion of court decisions regarding the relationship between civil and criminal penalties in the Act, see Mark A. Rothstein, *Occupational Safety and Health Law* (St. Paul: West, 1990), secs. 339, 503.

82. See Baruch A. Fellner and Donald Sarelson, *Occupational Safety and Health—Law and Practice* (New York: Practising Law Institute, 1976), p. 98.

83. As MacKinnon has written: "Marxism teaches that exploitation and degradation

somehow produce resistance and revolution. It's been hard to say why. What I've learned from women's experience with sexuality is that exploitation and degradation produce grateful complicity in exchange for survival. They produce self-loathing to the point of extinction of self, and it is respect for self that makes resistance conceivable. The issue is not why women acquiesce but why we ever do anything but" (*Feminism Unmodified*, p. 61).

5

KEITH BURGESS-JACKSON

A Theory of Rape

The law has said that lack of consent is the distinguishing feature of rape, but this is surely to miss the obvious. It is not the absence of consent, but the presence of physical coercion, which makes rape fundamentally different from "normal" acts of sexual intercourse. In a situation where a woman has no real choice, the question of her consent becomes patently irrelevant.[1]

Rape should be defined as sex by compulsion, of which physical force is one form. Lack of consent is redundant and should not be a separate element of the crime.[2]

What is rape? This may seem an odd question to ask for at least two reasons. First, scientists are busy investigating the causes and consequences of rape, hoping thereby to gain a better understanding of it as a biological, psychological, and social phenomenon.[3] Much of this work is conducted with an air of urgency because of the assumption (which I share) that rape is seriously wrong. It is thought that the more thoroughly rape is understood, the more amenable it will be to individual and social control.[4] Second, our legal system tries, convicts, and punishes individuals—sometimes quite harshly—for committing rape. The assumption is that rapists, no less than murderers or thieves, are free, responsible agents. The punishment is designed to pay them back for their misdeeds, incapacitate them, and deter others from engaging in similar conduct. Neither the scientist nor the lawyer pauses for very long (if at all) to inquire into the nature of rape.

But that is as it should be. Scientists, lawyers, and other practitioners *use* the concept of rape. Their aim is either to acquire knowledge (science) or to change the world in various ways (law, social work, therapy). The task of *investigating* the concept—marking out its contours, showing how it is related to other concepts, delineating its presuppositions, and situating it in a larger framework of thought—is a philosophical task calling for a different type of study. The philosopher qua philosopher is interested in such things as how rape differs (if it does) from battery, sexual harassment, incest ("daughter rape"),[5] seduction, prostitution, and so-called normal heterosexual intercourse. What exactly is the harm of rape, and how serious a harm is it? How severely should rape be punished, and why? Is rape best conceived as sex or as violence? Is it possible for rape to be both sex *and* violence? Why, in short, is rape wrong (assuming, as most people do, that it is)?

Answering these questions in anything but a haphazard, superficial way requires a theory. Not a scientific or a legal theory, which, as we saw, takes the nature of rape for granted, but a *philosophical* theory, which makes the nature of rape its focus. My aim in this chapter is to propound such a theory, one that I hope will be illuminating to philosophers as well as useful to scientific, legal, and other practitioners. Before doing so, however, I want to say a few words about what I take a philosophical theory (of rape or anything else) to be. This will forestall confusion about what I am doing.

First, I do not believe that philosophical theories are either true or false in the way that a proposition (say) is true or false. There is a sense in which *all* theories—descriptive or evaluative, philosophical or nonphilosophical, scientific or nonscientific—are *false*, for they abstract from reality. To abstract is to take out, separate, or remove, which destroys the agreement or correspondence that is necessary for truth. For this reason, the language of truth and falsity is best set aside when discussing theories.[6] The aim of a theory, in my view, is to pick out certain features of a situation as the most salient or illuminating. It is to carve reality in a particular—and one hopes a particularly *fruitful*—way. Theories are means of focusing attention on certain aspects of experience, which implies that attention is drawn *away* from other aspects that are just as much real or present. Rather than say that theories are true or false, therefore, we should say that they are more or less illuminating (the cognitive aspect) and more or less useful (the practical aspect). A good theory shows us something that we may otherwise have missed.

Second, different people find different theories attractive. Why? Because people begin in different places. If I disbelieve in God, for example, I will find any theory that presupposes the existence of God unattractive (although perhaps worth embracing, all things considered). It will not make sense of my beliefs, values, ideals, and commitments. On the other hand, I may come to *believe* in the existence of God precisely because a particular theory that is otherwise attractive to me—that makes sense of many of my beliefs, values, ideals, and commitments—presupposes or implies the existence of God. Theories, in my view, are systematizers of belief and value. Which theory of a given set of data one adopts depends, ultimately, on how well it accomplishes that systematizing task.

My theory, baldly stated, is that rape is coercion (more accurately, *coerced sex*). I believe that conceiving of rape in this way makes more sense than any alternative, of which there are many. My aim will be to show this by appealing to judgments that I believe most of my readers make. In the course of stating and elaborating my theory I will have occasion to discuss and evaluate (some of) its competitors. This will assist the reader in making an informed decision. I do not expect any reader to agree with every judgment I make. My aim is more modest: to show that conceiving of rape as coerced sex (in a sense to be specified and elaborated) accounts for more of the data than any alternative. I should also point out that the theory, once adopted, can be used as the basis for forming beliefs and making judgments about particular cases. It is, in short, both positive and normative.

Let me first situate the theory. One of the oldest debates among feminists (and others) is whether rape is a crime of sex or a crime of violence. Those (such as Susan Brownmiller) who urge that rape be conceived as a crime of violence do so for intelligible and laudable reasons.[7] Thinking of rape as sex, which for many people is an enjoyable and fulfilling experience, tends to trivialize and normalize rape. Rape becomes sex with something missing. If that something—consent, desire, will, or whatever—can only be supplied, the objectionableness of the act disappears. The movement to conceive of rape as violence was designed in part to change this way of thinking. Rape is not sex, the argument went; it is an act of violence perpetrated by a man against a woman. Rape is about force, compulsion, and domination, not desire. Perhaps *men* experience rape as sex, but women do not. Women are as traumatized by rape as they are by battery, robbery, and other violent crimes.[8]

Without disparaging this debate, which opened a needed dialog among feminists and others concerning the nature of rape,[9] it must be said that it had at least one unfortunate effect. It glossed over the distinction between force and coercion, both of which are subsumed under the term "violence." When one thinks of force, one pictures an individual physically overwhelmed by another. In the case of rape, one thinks of a man (the most common perpetrator) applying force to a woman's body so as to prevent her from resisting his sexual advances. The act of penetration, which has long been an element of the crime of rape,[10] is just one aspect of this force. The individual being forced (in the case of rape this is most often a woman) has no choice in the matter. Indeed, we would say that she has not *acted* at all. What we typically say is that somebody *did* something *to* her. She was acted *upon*. The force employed by the perpetrator undermined her volition, her choice, and her agency.[11]

The problem with understanding rape as forcible intercourse is that it accounts for only a subset (perhaps a numerically small subset) of the acts to which we would like to affix the label. Not all rapes are forcible in the sense that they leave the victim no choice. In many cases of rape, probably the vast majority of them, the victim is *given* a choice by the rapist. She is presented with two or more options, one of which is submission to sexual intercourse.[12] Unfortunately for her, the alternative to submission—death or physical injury, for example—is less desirable from her point of view, so she does as the rapist wishes. This phenomenon, which, following others, I call "coercion,"[13] lies at the heart of rape. It turns out that conceiving of rape as coercion (i.e., as coerced sex) has a number of theoretical and practical advantages over accounts that emphasize lack of consent, not least of which is that it makes sense of the feminist claim that rape is an act or practice of sexist domination. It also takes the focus in a rape case off the victim, which means it is no longer a defense to a rape charge that the accused *believed*, however reasonably, that she consented.[14] To bring these advantages to the fore, we need to give a clearer and more detailed account of coercion.

The verb "coerce," like most words used to describe socially significant states, events, actions, practices, and institutions, is ambiguous.[15] In the broadest, most generic sense it means "To constrain or restrain (a voluntary or moral agent) by the application of superior force, or by authority resting on force."[16] The *Oxford American Dictionary* defines the verb more succinctly as "to compel by threats or force."[17] If one were to provide a synonym for "coerce," it would be "compel." Coercion is compulsion. But as the second of these definitions suggests, there are two types of compulsion, one physical and one (for lack of a better word) psychological. I can compel you by physically moving your body (if I am strong enough) or by making it in your interest to move your body. The latter but not the former of these works through your will. In effect, *you* become the instrument of *my* will.

Let us call the first of these methods of compulsion—namely, physical compulsion—"force." Coercion in the broad sense, which I will call "coercion$_b$," comprises both (1) force and (2) coercion in the narrow sense, or "coercion$_n$." This reflects the generic-specific ambiguity of the term. To coerce$_n$ is to compel by threat; it is what I called "psychological" compulsion. To illustrate, suppose I want V to mow my lawn.[18] One way to achieve this is by threatening V with dire consequences should V *not* mow my lawn. I may say, for example, "Mow the lawn or I will break your arm." Note that I have not applied force to V. Indeed, I need not touch V in any way to achieve my objective of getting the lawn mowed. What I do instead is rearrange V's options in such a way that it is in V's *interest* to mow my lawn. V, who by hypothesis finds my threat credible, would rather mow the lawn than have his or her arm broken; so V mows the lawn.

Coercion so understood works through the victim's cognitive and conative faculties, which is why I called it "psychological." By definition, one cannot coerce$_n$ someone who either has no interests or is incapable of engaging in practical reasoning regarding those interests. Coercion$_n$, in other words, requires a witting, rational, self-interested victim.[19] Marilyn Frye's analysis brings out all the salient elements of the concept:

> The structure of coercion . . . is this: to coerce someone into doing something, one has to manipulate the situation so that the world as perceived by the victim presents the victim with a range of options the least unattractive of which (or the most attractive of which) in the judgment of the victim is the act one wants the victim to do.[20]

Note the expressions "perceived by" and "in the judgment of." The coercer *wants* the victim to choose. Indeed, the coercer wants the victim to make a *rational* choice. Where a person is threatened with death, serious bodily injury, or some other calamity, submission to sexual intercourse may be the rational choice.

Up to this point, I have urged that rape be conceived as coercion. I have distinguished broad and narrow senses of the term "coerce," one physical and the other psychological. Let me return for a moment to the feminist debate about whether rape is sex or violence, for we are in a position now to understand where the problem lies. Those (such as Brownmiller) who maintain that rape is violence intend, quite laudably, to draw attention away from the fact that rape involves sexual intercourse, for that, as we have seen, has unacceptable implications and associations. In doing so, unfortunately, they introduce a term, "violence," that connotes or suggests physical force. Some rapes do indeed involve physical force, so to that extent the maneuver has been beneficial and enlightening. It drew attention to the fact that sexual penetration is sometimes accomplished through physical compulsion rooted in superior strength.

But some (perhaps many or most) rapes are coercive in the narrow sense—that is, they involve an imposed ("forced") *choice*. The proposed definition of rape as violence has the unfortunate effect of obliterating (or at least camouflaging) this category. Conceiving of rape as coercion$_b$, as I propose, brings both types of rape into focus. Moreover, we can retain the term "violence" (if we wish), provided that we realize (and point out to all concerned) that it, too, is ambiguous. Rape is violence in the generic sense of violating its victim. It can do this *either* through the application of (physical) force *or* through the imposition of choice. So rape is violence, but the word "violence" itself has broad and narrow meanings, just like "coerce." The problem arose because many people heard "violence" as "physical force," which led them to limit rape to forcible invasions. This had the obnoxious effect of turning submission based on fear into consent; and since consent has long been viewed as a defense to rape, there was no rape in such cases.

Recent critics of feminist analyses of rape have alleged that the crime of rape has been defined so broadly, so promiscuously, so *vaguely,* that acts ordinarily described as seduction, fraud, or just plain bad or undesirable sex have been labeled "rape." Katie Roiphe, for instance, claims that "Today's definition [of 'rape'] has stretched beyond bruises and knives, threats of death or violence to include emotional pressure and the influence of alcohol."[21] David Carlin, another critic of feminism, elaborates:

> While "rape" used to mean coerced, nonconsensual sex, it now also includes having sex when you'd really rather not but you've been talked into it by a partner who has utilized any of a large number of items in the seducer's classical bag of tricks, e.g., flattery, promises, arguments, appeals to pity, reminders of past promises, threats to break off the relationship, etc. In other words, rape occurs even when consent is given, provided this consent is influenced by external pressure and is not simply the result of internal desire.[22]

These allegations, if true, are disturbing, for the consequences of labeling an act "rape" are severe indeed. We must not lose sight of that fact. In most states, rape is a felony calling for significant punishment. Do we wish our theory of rape to have the implication that one who uses "emotional pressure" (Roiphe) or "flattery" (Carlin) to induce submission to sexual intercourse is a *rapist?*[23] What about cases in which the "victim" (I use quotation marks to leave victimhood status open) engages in intercourse only because she is intoxicated, whether or not the intoxication was voluntary? If we wish to exclude such cases from the category of rape, as I do, our theory must give a principled reason for doing so.[24]

Let me be more specific about the contours of coercion$_n$,[25] for that is the heart of my theory. Fortunately there is a vast and sophisticated body of philosophical literature on the subject. Most theorists of coercion begin by distinguishing offers and threats. Offers are said to expand the range of options open to one's interlocutor (I use "interlocutor" rather than "victim," which would beg the question of the act's wrongfulness), whereas threats are said to contract the range. Stated differently, in the case of an offer, the interlocutor prefers the *post*proposal situation to the *pre*proposal situation.[26] In the case of a threat, the interlocutor prefers the *pre*proposal situation to the *post*proposal situation.[27] The distinction presupposes a baseline or starting point from which to determine whether there has been an expansion or a contraction of options. How one characterizes the baseline, and therefore how one characterizes deviations from it (as offers or as threats), is a matter of debate among theorists.

It is useful to begin with clear cases. Suppose P wishes to obtain some act (understood broadly to include inaction, compliance, acquiescence, or submission) from V. The act can be anything from delivering an object to P to remaining silent to submitting to a bodily intrusion. One thing P might do in order to achieve his or her ends is to make V an offer. "If you do X," P might say, "I will give you Y" (where Y is something P believes V desires). P's proposal may be rude or tactless, even exploitative, even seriously wrong, but P has not *threatened* V in any way. What P has done is make V an offer. As such, V can take it or leave it. Before P came on the scene, V had a certain range of options; once P made the offer (assuming it is genuine), V has an *additional* option. Since V is not being imposed upon in the sense of having his or her options limited or paths closed, it would be a mistake to say that V is coerced by P. In fact, as Robert Nozick points out, if V is rational, V will *welcome* the new option.[28] This makes sense. V is no worse off as a result of P's offer and may, depending on its content and on V's desires and preferences, be better off.[29] That is the sense in which recipients of offers prefer the postproposal situation to the preproposal situation.

Now suppose that P, who desires the same act by V, says "Do X or I'll harm you." Unlike before, P has closed off at least one option that was available to V, namely, *neither* doing X *nor* being harmed. P has restructured V's options by assigning a consequence to one action that did not previously exist. Here P has threatened V, not made V an offer. If rational, V will prefer the preproposal situation to the postproposal situation. Has P coerced V? Here is where theorists of coercion diverge. Some—the empirical or descriptive theorists—maintain that the mere making of a threat, as P has done, constitutes coercion. Others—the normative or evaluative theorists—say that something *else* is needed in order for a threat to constitute coercion, namely, a norm or value about what P may or should do.[30] Suppose the harm threatened by P is something that P is legally or morally entitled to do (for example, notify the police of V's criminal activity). Those who would limit coercion to threats to do what one is not entitled to do would say that this is not a case of coercion. The empirical theorists, however, would say that it is. Normative theorists differ in which norms or values they think are determinative.

Let me recapitulate and elaborate these points. First, we have distinguished offers and threats. The difference concerns the effect of one's action on another's options or choices. It is structural, not substantive. Hence, there is no implication that all offers are morally acceptable. Some, it seems to me, are not. If, knowing that V is starving, I offer V a can of beans in exchange for all of V's worldly goods, I make an unconscionable offer. If V accepts it—and, given the situation, V may—V is under no moral obligation to follow through by delivering the goods. Perhaps the law should act accordingly by refusing to enforce V's promise, but that is a separate question.[31] The point is that the difference between offers and threats is *not* the difference between that which is morally acceptable and that which is not. Some offers are immoral, either because they are exploitative or for some other reason.

Let us pursue this suggestion. The class of offers can be divided for analytic purposes into those that exploit and those that do not. Exploitation consists in taking advantage of another person's vulnerability or weakness. The vulnerability in question can have many sources, including the perpetrator's own actions. If I steal all of your money, then offer you $20 for a family heirloom, I not only *create* your vulnerability; I proceed to *exploit* it. I wrong you twice. But if someone *else* steals your money and I make my offer, I do no more than exploit your poverty (which is not to say that my act is morally defensible). What distinguishes exploitation from coercion is that the former is an offer (albeit one made under conditions of unequal bargaining power), whereas the latter is a threat. No acts, on this understanding, are *both* exploitative and coercive. The categories are mutually exclusive (although not, fortunately, exhaustive). As for which offers exploit and which do not, that depends on one's view of what constitutes vulnerability, weakness, or unequal bargaining power. I do not take a position on that issue since, with one exception (to be noted), my theory implies that exploited sex is not rape. Rape, I maintain, is *coerced* sex, and no coerced acts are exploitative in the strict sense.

I have suggested that not all offers are morally permissible; those that exploit others are arguably wrong. By the same token, not all threats are morally *im*permissible. If I have a right to do X, where X adversely affects some person V, is it not plausible that morally speaking I may *threaten* to do X unless V complies with my demand? This is not to say that it is always morally permissible to threaten to do what one has a right to do, for that may be too strong; it is to say that this is *sometimes* the case. Consider the following example. Assuming that I have a right to install a floodlight on my property (for security purposes, say), I have a right to threaten my neighbor, V, to install the floodlight unless V pays me a sum of money. We must not be thrown off by various negative connotations of the word "threaten." Some threats, such as this one, are to do what one is legally and morally entitled to do. Threatening V to install a floodlight is simply *informing* V of what I will do *unless* V acts in a certain way. I am communicating my intentions. V can pay me, as it were, to relinquish or forbear exercising my right. What makes my act a threat rather than an offer is that one of V's options—namely, neither paying me *nor* experiencing the adverse effects of the floodlight—is foreclosed by my action.

Thus far we have analyzed and distinguished force, coercion, and exploitation. There is one other category that needs to be mentioned before we apply these concepts to the case of rape, and that is mutual exchange. Here each party offers something to the other under conditions of equal, or roughly equal, bargaining power. Because of the (rough) equality, neither party is in a position to exploit the other's vulnerability or weakness. Indeed, there *is* no vulnerability or weakness. For obvious reasons, this category generates the fewest moral problems. We might even consider it the ideal of interpersonal (or at least market) relations. The following chart summarizes the distinctive features of each of the four concepts I have distinguished:

Feature/Concept	Force	Coercion	Exploitation	Mutual Exchange
Choice		X	X	X
Threat	X			
Offer			X	X
Vulnerability			X	

We might say that force, coercion, exploitation, and mutual exchange are different forms, types, or manifestations of power.[32] If I want something from someone, I can, in principle, obtain it in any of the following ways: by physical compulsion (i.e., force), by threat (i.e., coercion), or by offer, and if by offer then under conditions of (rough) equality (i.e., mutual exchange) or vulnerability (i.e., exploitation). This is not to say that these methods have the same costs, for they may not. As Thomas Wartenberg points out, "Force is uneconomic" compared to other types of power (such as coercion) in that it "requires that the dominant agent make some physical effort in order to keep the subordinate agent from doing what she would otherwise do."[33] The rational dominator, therefore, has reason to prefer coercion to force; it can produce the same benefits with fewer costs.

Just to be clear about what has and has not been done, I have not discussed variations within each category. Two acts that are equally coercive (i.e., equally cases of coercion) can differ with respect to what is threatened (death, physical injury, property damage, and the like), what is demanded (money, sexual submission), how many choices are given the victim, and so forth.[34] Prima facie, threatening to kill V is worse, morally speaking, than threatening to cut off V's hand, which is worse than threatening to destroy V's property. Two acts that are equally exploitative (i.e., equally cases of exploitation) can differ with respect to what is offered V (money, companionship, silence, forbearance, and the like), what is asked of V (money, sexual intercourse), and how unequal the bargaining positions are. Prima facie, taking advantage of someone's vulnerability to death or suffering is worse, morally speaking, than taking advantage of someone's need for employment, which is worse than taking advantage of someone's craving for (or addiction to) chocolate. What I have identified are four *types* of power, within each of which there is a continuum of actual and possible cases arranged by moral status (which is *not* to say that everyone will agree about how the cases are to be arranged).

It bears mentioning that however odious a case of $coercion_n$ may be, it *never* shades off into force. As the chart shows, the difference between force and $coercion_n$ is a difference of kind, not degree. The same is true of $coercion_n$ and exploitation. The least objectionable case of $coercion_n$—for example, "Give me a stick of gum or I'll tell Mom on you"—is not thereby rendered exploitative. It lacks the structure of exploitation, which requires an offer, which consists of an expansion rather than a contraction of options. Regrettably, much of the literature on rape, even some of that produced by philosophers, fails to make these basic and important distinctions. Terms such as "force," "coercion," and "exploitation" are either not defined at all or used in more than one sense. They *must* be defined, since each term is multiply ambiguous as well as vague. A topic as important as rape requires attention to the terminology in which it is discussed.[35]

If rape is to be conceived as coerced sex, as I propose, then several theoretical decisions must be made and defended. First, I must show why rape should be limited to cases of force and threat (i.e., to coercion$_b$) and *not* extended to offers. This may seem an arbitrary limitation given that (1) some offers are exploitative, (2) some offers generate hard choices, and (3) some offers are *experienced* as pressure by those to whom they are made. Second, we must decide whether to adopt an empirical or a normative baseline for purposes of characterizing threats. Does one coerce another whenever one limits the other's options (the empirical theory) or only when one does this without having a *right* to do so (the normative theory)? Finally, are we talking about legal or moral entitlement? My view is that rape should be conceived as a threat to do something *illegal* (more precisely, something that one has no legal right to do) in order to secure another person's sexual compliance, acquiescence, or submission. I also think that one class of offers is sufficiently analogous to threats to fall under the category of rape, hence to be punished as such.

As indicated at the outset, my argument for conceiving of rape as coerced sex appeals to the reader's intuitions about particular cases. I will also appeal to considerations of consistency in the law. As to the question whether rape should include offers, the main problem is marking off a category of offers that should be criminalized, for surely not all should be. Should it be a punishable offense to exploit a person's vulnerability even if one has played no role in creating it? If so, then many transactions that we now accept as legally permissible would be punishable as criminal offenses. For example, it would be a crime to offer a minimum-wage job to a person who has lost his or her property in a natural catastrophe. I assume that this result is unacceptable. Note, however, that if we decide *against* punishing egregious or unconscionable acts of exploitation, it does not follow that the law may not become involved in the matter; there are, at a minimum, good reasons for the law not to enforce promises made under such conditions. There is a difference, and an important one, between (1) criminalizing and punishing the *making* of an exploitative offer (which is what would occur if rape were to include such offers) and (2) not allowing the offerer to *benefit* from acceptance of such an offer.

It seems to me that the consequences of prohibiting and punishing all acts of exploitation, or even all acts of egregious/unconscionable exploitation, are unacceptable. Unless we are prepared to punish the water vendor who extracts a prohibitive price from the thirsty hiker, the employer who takes advantage of a worker's need, or those who offer money for blood, we should refuse to prohibit and punish those who take advantage of others' predicaments by offering incentives for sexual intercourse. In each case the offer is exploitative, odious, immoral, even despicable; but this in itself is no reason to make it a criminal offense. We must resist the temptation to criminalize all wrongful acts.[36] That way lies legal moralism.[37]

What about the second question? In conceiving of rape as coercion, should we adopt an empirical or a normative baseline? For the reasons given, I think we must adopt a normative baseline. The empirical baseline allows far too much to count as coercion, which, on the assumption that coercion is punishable, would criminalize far too much behavior. Here is why. The law as a whole, and the criminal law in particular, creates a space or field of action. Legally speaking, there are acts that one must perform (the obligatory), acts that one may but need not perform (the discretionary), and acts that one may not perform (the forbidden). Reasonable people can disagree as to which acts fall into which categories, of course, but anyone who values individual autonomy, understood as self-determination or self-governance, must view law in essentially this way. There must be ample room for individual discretion. Let us call the space "entitlement space," within which one is allowed by law to act.

The empirical theory of coercion says that it is always coercive to impose choices on others. In saying this it refuses to inquire into whether the "coercer" is entitled to do what he or she threatens to do. But what is the point of giving me an entitlement (i.e., discretion) to do X if I may not use it as a bargaining chip in my dealings with others? To use an earlier example, of what value is the right to install a floodlight on my property if I may not use that right in negotiations with my neighbor? To be sure, my neighbor would be happier *without* the floodlight (which we assume is a nuisance to him or her). But my neighbor might also be happier if I gave him or her a sum of money, and I have no obligation to do that. My legal right to install a floodlight, if it means anything, means that I can make the installation *unless and until* someone persuades me otherwise (as by paying me not to). Why should it matter if I advertise that I am persuadable by announcing my intentions to the neighbor? That, despite the ominous name, is the function of a threat. It starts a bargaining process.

I submit that the law would be inconsistent if it conferred rights but precluded rightholders from bargaining them away. To treat all threats as criminal acts, independently of whether the act in question is something one is legally entitled to do, would be absurd.[38] The relevant question is not whether a threat is *made*, much less how unsettling it is to the recipient, but whether the course of action threatened falls within one's legally recognized rights. I emphasize that we are talking about *legal* rights, not moral rights or moral permissibility. There is no inconsistency in having a legal right to do something that one has no moral right to do (lie to one's child, for example). Nor is there an inconsistency in having a legal right to do something that is, all things considered, wrong (same example with appropriate details added).[39] Depending on one's theory of morality, it may be wrong for me to install a floodlight on my property (because it would reduce overall happiness, say) *even though* I have a legal right to do so. Since my argument appeals solely to inconsistency, the question is what the *law*, not morality, entitles one to do.[40]

But this is still not specific enough for our needs. Suppose an employer makes the following threat to an employee: "Have sex with me or I'll fire you (or demote you, or deny you some benefit to which you are entitled)"—and that, to avoid being harmed, the employee engages in or submits to intercourse. What makes this a threat rather than an offer is that the employer closes off one of the employee's options, namely, not having sex while retaining her job.[41] The employee, if rational, prefers the preproposal situation to the postproposal situation. Is the employer legally entitled to fire (demote, deny benefits to) the employee? If so, then this would not constitute rape under the present theory.

The general rule in common-law jurisdictions is that one may hire and fire at will.[42] This rule can be supplanted by contract, of course, but let us suppose that there is no contract here, either individually or through a labor union. What complicates the matter is that there are laws against sex discrimination in the work-place,[43] and this sort of quid pro quo sexual harassment has been held to be action-able sex discrimination. It is not a *crime* to sexually harass, but one who engages in such conduct (as well as the person's employer in certain cases) can be held liable for damages.[44] Harassment, in other words, is a civil wrong rather than a crime.

The theoretical question we need to answer is this: Should the legal entitle-ment that makes a threat permissible (i.e., not a case of punishable coercion) be in-terpreted broadly to include criminal *and* civil law or narrowly to include only criminal law? If the former, then quid pro quo sexual harassment is rape, since one has no right under the Civil Rights Act (as construed by courts) to condition em-ployment on participation in or submission to sex.[45] I believe the legal entitlement should be interpreted narrowly. The reason is that we are trying to make the *crimi-nal* law consistent. If the criminal law creates entitlement space to do X, then one should be able to threaten to do X as a means of inducing others to act in certain ways. This does not mean, as I have indicated, that X is morally permissible or that doing or threatening X has no civil-law repercussions. The law can make doing X a tort or a violation of civil rights without making it a crime. Therefore, as long as it is no *crime* to fire (demote, deny benefits to) an employee, it is not *rape* to threaten to fire (demote, deny benefits to) an employee who refuses to comply with one's sexual demands.

This may sound harsh and counterintuitive, but three points should soften the conclusion. First, saying that quid pro quo sexual harassment is not rape does not imply that it is acceptable, even in the eyes of the law. It says that rape and sexual harassment are different.[46] Civil liability for sexual harassment in the workplace (as well as in educational institutions) is and should be substantial. Such behavior is unacceptable. Second, no other theory of rape of which I am aware, including con-sent theories, counts quid pro quo sexual harassment as rape. So if the conclusion just drawn strikes the reader as counterintuitive, it counts against *every* theory of rape, not just mine. Third, my theory, which distinguishes rape and sexual harass-ment, has the virtue of explaining *why* they are objectionable. This gives it the ad-vantage of simplicity. In both cases—rape and quid pro quo sexual harassment— one person imposes his will on another, which treats the other as a mere means to his ends. In doing so, he sets himself up as an authority-in-fact over the other, thereby implying that the other is his moral and social inferior. Where the other is chosen on the basis of her sex, he further implies that women *as a class* are inferior to men as a class, thus perpetuating and reinforcing patriarchy.

An incidental benefit of this analysis is that it makes sense of the feminist claim that rape, sexual harassment, and domestic battering are but different manifesta-tions of the same power dynamic. All are forms of sexist domination whereby one person (a male) subjugates another (a female). The difference between the acts is contextual. Sexual harassment (quid pro quo and otherwise) occurs in educational, employment, and other contexts in which men have traditionally wielded power over women. It is a way of policing both sex and sexuality. Domestic battering oc-curs in intimate relationships in which men have had, and unfortunately continue to have, de facto power over women and children. Rape, as I have explained, is a subset of sexual coercion in which one threatens to do what one has no right *under the criminal law* to do. I do not claim that rape is more serious than sexual harassment or battering (or that it is less serious). I claim that it is different—and that the difference should be marked both in our thinking and in our language.

I mentioned that there is a troublesome case lying near the border between coercion$_n$ and exploitation. This is the case of what I call "manipulated vulnerability."[47] Suppose I manipulate V's environment in such a way that V is vulnerable to a certain harm (starvation, for example). This may make V especially eager, and not just willing, to accept my offer of food. Strictly speaking I have not coerced$_n$ V since I have not threatened V with any harm. My proposal has the form, "If you want food, do X" rather than, "Do X or I will starve you." What I have done is exploit V's vulnerability. But the fact that I *created* the vulnerability gives this example a different moral complexion. Manipulating circumstances so as to gain assent to an offer is not far removed, theoretically, from imposing a choice through reduction of options. To see this, compare the case in which I threaten you with harm should you not give me your bicycle (a case of coercion$_n$) with the case in which, having stolen your other property, I offer you a nominal sum of money (say, five dollars) for your bicycle (a case of exploitation). By hypothesis, my objective is the same (namely, acquiring the bicycle), and you may experience the choices as equally onerous; the question is whether the cases should be treated alike or differently by the criminal law.

I believe they should be treated alike. If the criminal law were to allow manipulated vulnerability followed by exploitation, but *not* coercion$_n$, it would, in effect, be encouraging the former. Those bent on mischief but interested in avoiding criminal liability would first alter the circumstances in such a way as to make a particular offer attractive to a victim; then they would make an offer and await the expected result. Manipulated vulnerability is a drawn-out kind of coercion$_n$, a two-step rather than a one-step process. If the law has reason to criminalize coercion$_n$, and I shall argue that it does, then it has reason to criminalize manipulated-and-exploited vulnerability.

There are reasons of consistency, if nothing else, for adopting this position. It is a fundamental (and worthy) principle of law that a person may not profit or benefit from his or her wrongful conduct,[48] and surely it is wrongful to intentionally create and then exploit a vulnerability. I believe it is perfectly consistent for the criminal law to allow exploitation where the vulnerability is not created by the exploiter but to disallow such exploitation where the vulnerability is created. This is the one exception to the rule against criminalizing exploitation, and it is justified by its affinity to coercion$_n$.[49] There will be hard cases, to be sure—for example, where the exploiter *together with others* creates the vulnerability; but the fact that there are hard cases does not mean that there are no easy cases or that the underlying distinction is unsound.

To this point I have been engaged mainly in the clarification and elaboration of concepts that are central to the theory of rape I am propounding. It is time to draw the various strands of the essay together. What is the rationale for criminalizing sexual intercourse (using that term to include submission) accomplished by force or coercion$_n$ (the latter now being understood to include cases of manipulated-and-exploited vulnerability)? I have two types of argument for this conclusion, the first analogical and the second direct. The first argument rests on a structural similarity between rape and another crime, robbery, which has long been a felony and about which there is little or no debate concerning its status as a crime. My argument is that if robbery ought to be a criminal offense—and all but anarchists believe it should be—then, given its relevant similarity to rape (which I will bring out), so should rape.[50] One incidental benefit of the comparison is that it shows the respects in which rape has been treated differently by the law, a point feminists have been eager to make.

Robbery is a compound or nested crime. At its heart is larceny: the taking and carrying away of the personal property of another with the intent to permanently deprive the owner thereof.[51] Every robbery is a larceny, but not every larceny is a robbery. The additional elements for robbery are (1) "that the property be taken from the person or presence of the other" and (2) "that the taking be accomplished by means of force or putting in fear."[52] While robbery has a property offense at its center, it is best conceived as an offense against the person.[53] This explains why robbery is a statutory felony in every jurisdiction regardless of the amount taken.[54] Putting a person in fear of death or bodily injury sets back his or her interest both in autonomy and in personal security whether the amount extracted is a thousand dollars or ten cents.

Robbery can be accomplished either forcibly or by threat. The same is true of rape as I have conceived it. Both the rapist and the robber can physically overcome a victim *or* coerce$_n$ the victim into complying.[55] The force prong of robbery is satisfied in various ways, including cognitive disablement. According to legal scholars LaFave and Scott,

> One may commit robbery by striking his victim with fist or weapon and then, having thus rendered the victim unconscious or dazed or unwilling to risk another blow, taking his property away from him. One may also render one's victim helpless by more subtle means, as by administering intoxicating liquors or drugs in order to produce a state of unconsciousness or stupefaction; to act in this way is to use force for purposes of robbery.[56]

The *Model Penal Code* adopts this approach by counting as rape cases in which a male "has substantially impaired [a female's] power to appraise or control her conduct by administering or employing without her knowledge drugs, intoxicants or other means for the purpose of preventing resistance."[57]

This raises a question. What about cases in which the helplessness or disability of the victim is *not* brought about by the thief? It has been held that this does not constitute robbery,[58] which seems correct, since the gravamen of the offense of robbery (unlike larceny) is the use of force or putting another in fear. Should the same conclusion be drawn with respect to rape? Suppose R happens upon an unconscious V and sexually penetrates her; is he a rapist? According to consent theorists (and some courts),[59] the answer is "Yes," since the intercourse is without V's consent. Intuitively, this is the correct result, but it is not the result given by my theory of rape as coercion. One solution is to count such cases as forcible even though the perpetrator has not created the victim's helplessness; but this seems ad hoc and unacceptable. Another solution is to bite the bullet and deny that rape occurs in such cases. There is a battery, to be sure,[60] and perhaps also gross sexual imposition (if we wish to create a lesser offense than rape),[61] but there is no rape. I am inclined to keep the theory pure and not count this as rape.

In robbery, significantly, consent is not inferred from submission. That I deliver my wallet to the robber who threatens me in no way signals my consent to the transaction. Nor is resistance required—no matter how strong, agile, or courageous I may be. The mere making of a threat creates a presumption of lack of consent.[62] Moreover, robbery can be accomplished without a weapon (such as a gun or a knife) and without the use of any words. (That is, the threat can be nonverbal.) All that is required is that the robber *put the victim into a state of fear* and that the fear *induce the victim to part with his or her property.*[63] As LaFave and Scott put it, "if the victim is actually frightened by the defendant into parting with his property, the defendant's crime, on principle, is robbery, even though an ordinary person, with more fortitude than the victim, would not have been thus frightened."[64]

In robbery trials, unlike in rape trials, no inquiry is made—or allowed—into the alleged victim's charitable past. Defense attorneys do not suggest that because the robbery victim freely gave property in the past, he or she probably freely gave property to the robber on the occasion in question. If this rule were followed in rape cases, there would be no inquiry into a victim's sexual history, including her sexual history (if any) with the defendant. It is also significant that in robbery cases, there is no presumption, de jure or de facto, that philanthropists or entrepreneurs cannot be robbed. People who make gifts of property (sporadically or regularly) or who exchange property in the marketplace are just as capable of being robbed as anyone else. If this rule were applied in rape cases, it would undercut the inference, long drawn by juries and incorporated in various evidentiary rules, that some women (prostitutes and wives, for example) cannot be or are unlikely to be raped.[65] That a woman voluntarily engages in sex or that she exchanges sex for money on some occasions does not mean that she cannot be forced or coerced into sex on other occasions. What we see when we compare rape and robbery is a flagrant and objectionable double standard.[66] My theory of rape as coerced sex has the merit of bringing this out.

Another interesting feature of the law of robbery that bears on the subject of rape is that one can be robbed by friends or acquaintances as well as by strangers. That one associates with or knows another does not prevent the other from committing robbery against one. By the same token, that one associates with or knows another does not prevent the other from committing rape against one. Both property and submission to sexual intercourse can be extracted either forcibly or coercively[n] by those with whom one is acquainted—by coworkers, employers, friends, family members, teammates, ministers, physicians, and the like. Nothing in principle or practice precludes this. And yet, the law has long treated rape by friends and acquaintances differently from rape by strangers.[67]

As mentioned, much recent scholarly work on rape has centered on the concept of consent.[68] Indeed, some scholars argue that what distinguishes rape from unobjectionable (hetero)sexual intercourse is the absence of consent.[69] Let us explore this. Is consent a defense to robbery? If so, then, given the analogical nature of my argument, it should also be a defense to rape. In fact, consent is *not* a defense to robbery, although it *is* a defense to the embedded crime of larceny.[70] It is important to see why this is so. As a general proposition, consent is not legally effective when it is given or obtained under duress.[71] But the coercion employed by the robber *by definition* creates a situation in which the victim acts under duress. The robber, in robbing, forces a choice between unacceptable alternatives. This makes any expression of consent by the victim ineffective as a matter of law. The upshot is that, legally speaking, one charged with robbery cannot plead consent as a defense.

The same reasoning applies, mutatis mutandis, in the case of coerced sexual intercourse. If force is employed, the question of consent obviously does not arise. But what if R threatens V with harm should V not submit to his sexual advances — that is, what if R coerces V? Is it possible for V to consent under such conditions? If the law is to be consistent across crimes, the answer must be "No." To be sure, V may *choose* to submit to R; indeed, that is precisely what R desires. But choice under coercive conditions is not, in and of itself, consent.[72] It does not constitute consent in cases of robbery, so why should it constitute consent in cases of rape? Put differently, if consent is rendered legally ineffective in one area of the law (robbery), then it should be rendered legally ineffective in every area, including rape.[73] Thus, the emphasis on consent displayed in much current rape literature is misplaced. This is the point made by Clark, Lewis, and MacKinnon in the introductory quotations.[74]

Turning to another issue, what sorts of threat are necessary and sufficient for robbery? The *Model Penal Code* requires that the robber's threat be to inflict "serious bodily injury" on the victim,[75] but that view is rejected as too narrow in most modern jurisdictions (which require only fear of bodily injury).[76] Some statutes go further and allow threats of property damage or theft to suffice. In the case of rape, as opposed to robbery, the *Model Penal Code* requires that the threat be of "imminent death, serious bodily injury, extreme pain or kidnapping, to be inflicted on anyone."[77] In light of the theory presented in this chapter, this list is too narrow. I have argued that sexual intercourse accomplished by threat to do what one has no legal right to do constitutes rape. Therefore, since battery (nonconsensual touching), trespass, and larceny are crimes, a threat to inflict *any* sort of bodily injury (not just "severe" injury) or *any* pain (not just "extreme" pain) or even damage to property suffices.

The *Model Penal Code* goes some way toward expanding the list of threatened harms in its separate (and lesser) offense of "gross sexual imposition," which is a felony of the third degree. (Rape is either a crime of the first degree or a crime of the second degree, depending on whether serious bodily injury was actually inflicted on anyone and whether the victim was a "voluntary social companion" of the actor at the time of the alleged offense. First-degree felonies are punished more severely than second-degree felonies, which are in turn punished more severely than third-degree felonies.)[78] Here, unlike in the case of rape, there is no mention of bodily injury or death. One commits the crime of gross sexual imposition if one "compels [the victim] to submit by any threat that would prevent resistance by a woman of ordinary resolution."[79]

This provision, judged by the theoretical standard I have advanced, is both too broad and too narrow. It is too broad because it draws no distinction between threats to do what one is legally entitled to do and threats to do what one is not legally entitled to do. It would count as gross sexual imposition a threat to break off a relation-ship with V unless V submitted to R's sexual advances—provided this threat would have prevented resistance by a "woman of ordinary resolution." It is too narrow be-cause it fails to include victims whose resistance is less than that of the "ordinary" woman. To see this, suppose V is more timid than the ordinary woman. R says to her "Submit sexually or I will twist your arm until it hurts." I assume that this threat would *not* prevent resistance by a woman of ordinary resolution. (If you believe it would, then substitute another harm.) That is, a woman of ordinary resolution would resist the threatener *despite* the threatened pain. Therefore, according to the *Model Penal Code*, R's intercourse with V does not constitute gross sexual imposi-tion (*or* rape, since the threat is not to inflict "serious bodily injury" or "extreme pain"). But this seems wrong. Why should V be held to a higher standard of "reso-lution" than she actually has in order to have her assault considered a crime? She is just as much coerced into intercourse as the woman threatened with serious bodily injury or extreme pain; and isn't *that*—the fact of coercion—the gravamen of the offense?

This raises a general question about the use of objective standards in the law. When, if ever, should the law *impose* a standard of belief or behavior on an indi-vidual instead of accepting the belief/behavior he or she actually has/exhibits (a subjective standard)? Joel Feinberg makes a distinction that applies here and that seems right. Whether the law may impose an objective standard depends on whether others besides the agent are affected by the agent's behavior. The law rightly (according to Feinberg) imposes an objective standard when A coerces B into harming C (who is assumed to be innocent). Should B be allowed to plead in his or her defense that the act was performed under duress? Only if a reasonable person in the circumstances would have so acted. The law expects B to be as firm and as resolute as an idealized ("reasonable") person where the welfare of others is concerned, even if, in fact, B is not that resolute.

But in the case of rape there is, by hypothesis, no third party, let alone an inno-cent third party. R coerces V. The consequences of submission or resistance to R fall on V alone. Should V have to exhibit the firmness and resolution of an ideal-ized ("reasonable") person? The answer would seem to be "No." R has no right to coerce V. The only relevant inquiry is whether V *in fact* submitted as a result of R's threat.[80] How others similarly situated might have responded in these circum-stances is neither here nor there. So the *Model Penal Code* approach to gross sexual imposition is doubly defective. It counts as victims those who are threatened with acts that the threatener is legally entitled to perform; and it fails to count as victims those who do not resist where a woman "of ordinary resolution" would have.

The second argument for criminalizing coerced sexual intercourse is direct rather than analogical. I begin with the assumption, which even extreme liberals (although not anarchists) share, that

> It is always a good reason in support of penal legislation that it would probably be effective in preventing (eliminating, reducing) harm to persons other than the actor (the one prohibited from acting) *and* there is no other means that is equally effective at no greater cost to other values.[81]

In cases where a person is coerced$_b$ into engaging in sexual intercourse, the harm, understood as a wrongful (i.e., right-violating) setback to interest,[82] is clear. Every person has an interest in, and a corresponding negative right to, physical and psychological health, bodily integrity, security, liberty, and autonomy. The coercer$_b$ sets back each of these interests and violates each of these rights. In doing so, the coercer$_b$ "inflict[s] damage on the whole network of [the victim's] interests."[83]

These harms, while real, and while more than sufficient to support the criminalization of coercive sex, do not tell the whole story. The fact that rape, with few exceptions, is perpetrated by men against women suggests that there is more going on than individual transgression. Rape, unlike robbery and other crimes, is *gendered*. Feminists such as Catharine MacKinnon maintain that rape, like sexual harassment, battery, and pornography, is a practice of male domination—or, to appropriate the language of Katherine Franke, a "technology of sexism."[84] To view rape as something that one individual does to another is, while correct, to miss its class aspect. Viewed in class terms, rape appears as an act of domination. By disregarding the victim's autonomy, the rapist makes himself an authority-in-fact over her. He presumes to impose a choice: "Submit to me or else." This imposition renders her, the victim, a second-class citizen. To the extent that rape is not vigorously prosecuted and punished, the state itself is complicitous in enforcing sex-based inequality.[85]

One virtue of the theory of rape as coercion, therefore, is that it makes *intelligible*, in a way that consent theories (for example) do not, the feminist claim that rape violates women's right to equality. Rape, paradoxically, is both an individual transgression (a point conceded by the consent theorist) *and* a sexist practice or institution. It is an affront to both autonomy and equality. It is not just something a man does to a woman (although it *is* that); it is something men do to women. The liberal, unfortunately, sees only the former of these affronts; the radical, and in particular the radical feminist, sees both—and insists that the law do the same. MacKinnon eloquently captures this dual aspect of rape:

> If a woman has ever been raped, does she ever fully regain the feeling of physical integrity, of self-respect, of having what she wants count somewhere, of being able to make herself clear to those who have not gone through what she has gone through, of living in a fair society, of equality?[86]

As I said at the outset, a theory of any kind is acceptable to the extent—and only to the extent—that it (1) makes sense of our preexisting values and beliefs, (2) shows us something we may otherwise have missed about the data within its scope, and (3) is useful for various theoretical and practical purposes. I submit that conceiving of rape as coerced sex has all of these virtues, and that it has them to a greater degree than any competing conception.

Notes

1. Lorenne M. G. Clark and Debra J. Lewis, *Rape: The Price of Coercive Sexuality* (Toronto: The Women's Press, 1977), p. 163.

2. Catharine A. MacKinnon, *Toward a Feminist Theory of the State* (Cambridge: Harvard University Press, 1989), p. 245 (citation omitted).

3. See, e.g., Larry Baron and Murray A. Straus, *Four Theories of Rape in American Society: A State-Level Analysis* (New Haven, CT: Yale University Press, 1989); Lee Ellis, *Theories of Rape: Inquiries into the Causes of Sexual Aggression* (New York: Hemisphere, 1989); Randy Thornhill and Nancy Wilmsen Thornhill, "Human Rape: An Evolutionary Analysis," *Ethology and Sociobiology* 4 (1983):137–73. It is estimated that there are "as many as 1,000 new studies [of sexual coercion] published each year in reputable journals." Del Thiessen and Robert K. Young, "Investigating Sexual Coercion," *Society* 31 (March/April 1994):60. The reference section of Ellis's book (cited above) occupies 55 single-spaced pages.

4. Not everyone believes that the studies are worthwhile, however. Psychologists Thiessen and Young, for example, conclude that "the studies of [sexual] coercion [published between 1982 and 1992] lack rigor, reflect experimenter biases, and provide almost no insights into the causal mechanisms of coercive behaviors." Thiessen and Young, "Investigating Sexual Coercion," p. 60. The result, they say, is that "there has been little progress in understanding [sexual] coercion during the past ten years." Ibid., p. 61. As for who is to blame for this state of affairs, the authors single out "the feminist lobby." Ibid., p. 63. "The work as a whole," they write, "defines the female view of coercion and reflects the political perspectives of its advocates." Ibid. The authors do not address the question whether the previous *dearth* of work on sexual coercion, or their own work, is attributable to "the patriarchalist lobby" or to "the male view of coercion."

5. Sarah Lucia Hoagland, *Lesbian Ethics: Toward New Value* (Palo Alto, CA: Institute of Lesbian Studies, 1988), p. 31.

6. A less sweeping claim, inspired by the work of Karl Popper, is that only the language of *truth* should be avoided. In this view, theories can be shown to be false, but not true. Sandra Harding extends this idea, claiming that among the false theories, some are more false than others. See Sandra Harding, "Comment on Hekman's 'Truth and Method: Feminist Standpoint Theory Revisited': Whose Standpoint Needs the Regimes of Truth and Reality?," *Signs* 22 (Winter 1997):387–88.

7. See Susan Brownmiller, *Against Our Will: Men, Women and Rape* (New York: Simon and Schuster, 1975).

8. One explanation of the emphasis on violence is that it put women's experience of rape in the foreground. This was a radical idea in that it implied a sex-based divergence in the way rape is experienced. Many commentators think that rape is unique as a crime because of its sex-linked nature. See, e.g., Deborah W. Denno, "Introduction: Why Rape Is Different," *Fordham Law Review* 63 (October 1994):127 ("Rape is different because it overwhelmingly involves male perpetrators and female victims" [citation omitted]). See also MacKinnon, *Toward a Feminist Theory of the State*, p. 245 ("Rape is a sex-specific violation").

9. See, e.g., Catharine MacKinnon's critique of Brownmiller. Catharine A. MacKinnon, *Feminism Unmodified: Discourses on Life and Law* (Cambridge: Harvard University Press, 1987), pp. 6, 85–86, 92; see also MacKinnon, *Toward a Feminist Theory of the State*, pp. 134–35.

10. The penetration requirement goes back at least to the seventeenth century. See Sir Matthew Hale, *Historia Placitorum Coronæ* [*The History of the Pleas of the Crown*], 2 vols., with an introduction by P. R. Glazebrook (London: Professional Books Limited, 1971), vol. 1, chap. 58, p. *628 ("To make a rape there must be an actual penetration or *res in re*" [italics in

original]) (first published posthumously in 1736). (The asterisk before a numeral indicates original pagination.) See also *Model Penal Code*, sec. 213.0(2) ("'Sexual intercourse' includes intercourse per os or per anum, with some penetration however slight; emission is not required"). MacKinnon, for one, finds this requirement interesting. Men, she says, define rape in terms of how they define sex: as penile insertion. This supports her view that under conditions of inequality, rape and "normal" heterosexual intercourse are difficult, if not impossible, to distinguish. See MacKinnon, *Toward a Feminist Theory of the State*, p. 172.

11. See, e.g., Joel Feinberg, *The Moral Limits of the Criminal Law*, vol. 3: *Harm to Self* (New York: Oxford University Press, 1986), p. 190.

12. Other terms that I shall use to describe the victim's actions are "succumbing to," "complying with," "acquiescing in," and "acceding to."

13. My main influences, in chronological order, have been Robert Nozick, "Coercion," in *Philosophy, Science, and Method: Essays in Honor of Ernest Nagel*, ed. Sidney Morgenbesser, Patrick Suppes, and Morton White (New York: St. Martin's Press, 1969), pp. 440–72; Alan Wertheimer, *Coercion* (Princeton, NJ: Princeton University Press, 1987); and Onora O'Neill, "Which Are the Offers *You* Can't Refuse?," in *Violence, Terrorism, and Justice*, ed. R. G. Frey and Christopher W. Morris (Cambridge: Cambridge University Press, 1991), pp. 170–95. This is not to say that I agree with these theorists in every particular. Some of my differences with them will come out in the discussion.

14. See Dana Berliner, "Rethinking the Reasonable Belief Defense to Rape," *The Yale Law Journal* 100 (June 1991):2687–706. The reasonable-belief defense has been criticized by, inter alia, Catharine MacKinnon. MacKinnon's argument is that sexual intercourse has different meanings for men and women in our patriarchal culture. What a man experiences as "normal" intercourse may be experienced by his female "partner" as violation. When the law asks, as it traditionally has, what the man believed about the woman's consent, and whether it was reasonable for him to believe it, it adopts the man's point of view. This, MacKinnon says, is "one-sided: male-sided." MacKinnon, *Toward a Feminist Theory of the State*, p. 183. The solution is not, as one might think, to search for an "objective" understanding of what occurred, a "view from nowhere," for there is no such thing. There are two subjective experiences, two "views from somewhere," one of which reflects male experience and the other of which reflects female experience (as both are constructed by patriarchy). Conceiving of rape as coerced sex rather than as nonconsensual sex, as I propose, eliminates the need to ask what the man *believed*. It focuses instead of what he *did*.

15. See, e.g., Jeffrie G. Murphy, "Consent, Coercion, and Hard Choices," *Virginia Law Review* 67 (February 1981):79–95. For other uses of the term, see Elizabeth Grauerholz and Mary A. Koralewski, "What Is Known and Not Known About Sexual Coercion," in *Sexual Coercion: A Sourcebook on Its Nature, Causes, and Prevention*, ed. Elizabeth Grauerholz and Mary A. Koralewski (Lexington, MA: Lexington Books, 1991), p. 187 (sexual coercion is "The act of forcing, pressuring, or tricking another individual into engaging in a sexual act"; "The means used to coerce may be physical, financial, or psychological"); Charlene L. Muehlenhard and Jennifer L. Schrag, "Nonviolent Sexual Coercion," in *Acquaintance Rape: The Hidden Crime*, ed. Andrea Parrot and Laurie Bechhofer (New York: Wiley, 1991), p. 116 (direct sexual coercion "involves specific pressures to engage in unwanted sexual activity within a relationship").

16. *The Compact Edition of the Oxford English Dictionary* (Oxford, England: Oxford University Press, 1971), vol. 1, p. 457 (s.v. "Coerce").

17. Eugene Ehrlich et al., *Oxford American Dictionary* (New York: Oxford University Press, 1980), p. 120 (s.v. "coerce").

18. Throughout the essay, I use "V" as the name of the victim and "P" as the name of the perpetrator. This should not be allowed to obscure the fact that in the vast majority of rapes the perpetrator is a man and the victim a woman.

19. See O'Neill, "Which Are the Offers You Can't Refuse?," p. 174 ("Coercers fail unless their intended victim grasps *what* it is *that is demanded*, and that it is demanded" [italics in original]). O'Neill's discussion is highly illuminating (and highly recommended).

20. Marilyn Frye, *The Politics of Reality: Essays in Feminist Theory* (Trumansburg, NY: Crossing Press, 1983), pp. 56–57. See also Joel Feinberg, *Social Philosophy* (Englewood Cliffs, NJ: Prentice-Hall, 1973), pp. 7–8 ("In cases of coercion via threat, there is a sense in which the victim is left with a choice. He can comply or he can suffer the (probable) consequences. But if the alternative to compliance is some unthinkable disaster—such as the death of a child—then there is really no choice but to comply. In intermediate cases, between the extremes of overwhelmingly coercive threats and mere attractive offers, the threat, in effect, puts a price tag on noncompliance and leaves it up to the threatened person to decide whether the price is worth paying. The higher the price of noncompliance, the less eligible it will seem for his choice"). For a detailed discussion of coercion (both broad and narrow senses), see Feinberg, *Harm to Self*, chaps. 23 and 24.

21. Katie Roiphe, *The Morning After: Sex, Fear, and Feminism on Campus* (Boston: Little, Brown, 1993), p. 52 (quoted in Paula Kamen, "Acquaintance Rape: Revolution and Reaction," in *"Bad Girls"/"Good Girls": Women, Sex, and Power in the Nineties,* ed. Nan Bauer Maglin and Donna Perry [New Brunswick, NJ: Rutgers University Press, 1996], p. 142).

22. David R. Carlin, Jr., "Date Rape Fallacies," *Commonweal* 121 (25 February 1994):12. See also Margaret D. Bonilla, "Cultural Assault: What Feminists Are Doing to Rape Ought to Be a Crime," *Policy Review* (Fall 1993):26 ("Over the last few years, . . . a movement has developed aimed at expanding the definition of rape to include the use of verbal intimidation, coercion, or manipulation—rather than physical force—and to suggest that a woman who has been given alcohol or other drugs by a man is not responsible for the sex that may follow").

23. Psychologists Muehlenhard and Schrag describe a number of other cases. They say that "Men use many types of verbal coercion to obtain sex: threatening to end the relationship or to find someone else to satisfy their sexual needs; telling a woman that her refusal to have sex was changing the way they felt about her; asserting that 'everybody does it' or questioning the woman's sexuality (e.g., implying that she is 'frigid'); making the woman feel guilty; falsely promising love or marriage or using other lies; telling a woman with whom they were petting that she could not stop and leave them with 'blue balls' (an uncomfortable condition involving testicular congestion resulting from sexual arousal without orgasm); calling a woman a name angrily and pushing her away when she would not have sex; and threatening to do bodily self-harm." Muehlenhard and Schrag, "Nonviolent Sexual Coercion," p. 122 (citations omitted).

24. I am *not* saying (or implying) that the acts just described are morally permissible. That is another question altogether. Nor am I saying (or implying) that they should not be punishable by law. Rape, after all, is not the only actual or possible sexual offense. Put differently, I am propounding a theory of *rape,* not of sexual offense or immorality.

25. From this point forward, unless the context indicates otherwise, I use "coerce" (and its cognates) in the narrow sense. Subscripts will be omitted.

26. The term "proposal" is admittedly odd in this context. It should be understood to include both offers and threats.

27. Here I follow David Zimmerman and Lawrence (Larry) Alexander. See David Zimmerman, "Coercive Wage Offers," *Philosophy & Public Affairs* 10 (Spring 1981):133; Lawrence A. Alexander, "Zimmerman on Coercive Wage Offers," *Philosophy & Public Affairs* 12 (Spring 1983):161.

28. Nozick, "Coercion," p. 460 ("The Rational Man, being able to resist those temptations which he thinks he should resist, will normally welcome credible offers, or at any rate not be unwilling to have them be made" [citation omitted]). Threats, in contrast, are "normally not welcome," even by "the Rational Man," who by definition "is able to resist going along with them." Ibid.

29. The situation is analogous to Pareto superiority. I say "analogous" because Pareto superiority, strictly speaking, is a measure of *collective* rather than individual welfare (even though collective welfare is a *function* of individual welfare). State S_1 is Pareto superior to state S_2 if and only if at least one individual prefers S_1 to S_2 and no individual prefers S_2 to S_1. For a discussion of this and related concepts (such as Pareto optimality), see Jules L. Coleman, *Markets, Morals and the Law* (Cambridge: Cambridge University Press, 1988), pp. 71–76.

30. Normative theorists include Robert Nozick (see his seminal essay, "Coercion"), Alan Wertheimer (see his monograph, *Coercion*), and Jennifer Hankinson, "The Normative Nature of Coercion," *Southwest Philosophy Review* 11 (January 1995):49-57.

31. The law has developed a doctrine of unconscionability to handle cases such as this. See, e.g., John D. Calamari and Joseph M. Perillo, *The Law of Contracts*, 2nd ed. (St. Paul, MN: West, 1977), pp. 316–28.

32. For an elaboration of this point, see Steven Lukes, *Power: A Radical View* (London: Macmillan, 1974) and Thomas E. Wartenberg, *The Forms of Power: From Domination to Transformation* (Philadelphia, PA: Temple University Press, 1990).

33. Wartenberg, *The Forms of Power*, p. 95.

34. See Feinberg, *Harm to Self*, chap. 23, for a discussion.

35. Part of the problem is that the law uses so many terms without carefully defining them. "Rape" has been defined variously as forcible intercourse, as intercourse against a woman's will, and as intercourse without a woman's consent.

36. Since my argument appeals to consistency in the law, changes in the law can lead to changes in how sexual exploitation is dealt with. Suppose, as improbable as it sounds, that the law comes to prohibit and punish (and not just refuse to enforce contracts concerning) egregious acts of exploitation. Then consistency would require that egregious acts of exploitative sex be punished. I consider this empirical flexibility a virtue rather than a vice of my account.

37. Joel Feinberg defines "legal moralism" as the view (i.e., the principle) that "It can be morally legitimate to prohibit conduct on the ground that it is inherently immoral, even though it causes neither harm nor offense to the actor or to others." Joel Feinberg, *The Moral Limits of the Criminal Law*, vol. 1: *Harm to Others* (New York: Oxford University Press, 1984), p. 27. Later in his tetralogy, Feinberg redefines "legal moralism" as "the principle that *it is always a good reason* in support of criminalization that it prevents non-grievance evils or harmless immoralities." Joel Feinberg, *The Moral Limits of the Criminal Law*, vol. 4: *Harmless*

Wrongdoing (New York: Oxford University Press, 1988), p. 324 (italics in original). Feinberg ultimately rejects both principles.

38. I no sooner say this than I think of the law of blackmail, which criminalizes (certain) threats to do that which one has a legal right to do (such as publish private information) unless a sum of money is paid. See Wayne R. LaFave and Austin W. Scott, Jr., *Substantive Criminal Law*, 2 vols. (St. Paul, MN: West, 1986), vol. 2, sec. 8.12. But other threats (for example, to turn someone in for illegal behavior) are allowed by law. I believe the law of blackmail is an arbitrary exception to the general rule that one may threaten to do whatever one has a legal right to do. I am therefore prepared to count the law of blackmail as a *mistake*, hence not a counterexample to my theory. In this I side with the libertarians. For a brief discussion of blackmail (also known as extortion) and for references to the legal and philosophical literature, see Kent Greenawalt, *Speech, Crime, and the Uses of Language* (New York: Oxford University Press, 1989), pp. 93–94. For a liberal defense of the criminalization of (most) acts of informational blackmail, in which the threat is to reveal information, see Feinberg, *Harmless Wrongdoing*, pp. 238–76.

39. This point is well made in Alan Wertheimer, "Consent and Sexual Relations," *Legal Theory* 2 (June 1996):108 ("[T]here is no reason to think that the justified legal demands on our behavior are coextensive with the moral demands on our behavior"). Consider the case in which A says to B, "Have sexual relations with me or I will dissolve our dating relationship." Ibid., p. 103. This is a threat, according to my analysis, because A narrows B's options. Specifically, A rules out the option of B's not having sexual relations while remaining in the relationship. But by hypothesis, A has a legal right to dissolve the dating relationship. (Put differently, "B has no right that A continue his relationship with B on her preferred terms." Ibid., p. 104 [italics omitted].) So if B submits to sexual relations with A as a result of his threat (i.e., in order to sustain the relationship), it is not rape on my account. It may well be wrong of A, all things considered, to make such a threat. It may even be morally reprehensible of him to do so, but that is another issue. As I said earlier, I am providing a theory of *rape*, not of wrongful, unfair, or infelicitous sex.

40. There are, it would appear, as many ways to carve the class of threats as there are theorists. See, e.g., Greenawalt, *Speech, Crime, and the Uses of Language*, chap. 5 ("Threats") (distinguishing "manipulative" and "warning" threats and arguing that only—but not all of—the former may be criminalized); and C. Edwin Baker, *Human Liberty and Freedom of Speech* (New York: Oxford University Press, 1989), p. 58 (arguing that only speech that "is inconsistent with another's autonomy or is not intrinsic to the speakers's [sic] autonomy" may be criminalized). I do not have the space to criticize these or other theories.

41. I use sex-specific pronouns here because that reflects the reality of such threats.

42. See, e.g., Charles L. Knapp, *Problems in Contract Law: Cases and Materials* (Boston: Little, Brown, 1976), pp. 791–92 ("[I]t has long been considered as settled law in the United States that where an employment contract is 'at will,' with no fixed period of duration, either party may terminate at any time, for any reason—or, indeed, for no reason at all. In practice this has meant that a non-union employee can be discharged (or otherwise coerced by the threat of loss of employment) for any reason the employer may choose, whether or not related in any way to her performance on the job" [citation omitted]).

43. The main law, of course, is Title VII of the Civil Rights Act of 1964, 42 U.S.C. sec. 2000e (1994). See Katherine M. Franke, "What's Wrong With Sexual Harassment?," *Stanford Law Review* 49 (April 1997):691–772.

44. See Susan Estrich, "Sex at Work," *Stanford Law Review* 43 (April 1991):813-61; Franke, "What's Wrong With Sexual Harassment?"

45. See Franke, "What's Wrong With Sexual Harassment?"

46. Martha Chamallas uses the term "economically coerced sex" to describe cases in which A threatens B with economic harm (loss of a job, for example) unless B submits to sexual intercourse with A. This would include, although not be limited to, quid pro quo sexual harassment. See Martha Chamallas, "Consent, Equality, and the Legal Control of Sexual Conduct," *Southern California Law Review* 61 (May 1988):821. Chamallas says that "There have been some initiatives to change the law of rape to encompass economically coerced sex," ibid., but that they "are not likely to be adopted, in part because it is difficult to draft a precise statute that captures the many unacceptable forms of economic and psychological coercion without prohibiting what many perceive as less culpable conduct." Ibid., p. 823.

47. See Keith Burgess-Jackson, *Rape: A Philosophical Investigation* (Aldershot, England: Dartmouth, 1996), chap. 6.

48. See, e.g., *Riggs v. Palmer*, 115 N.Y. 506, 22 N.E. 188 (1889) (discussed in Ronald Dworkin, *Law's Empire* [Cambridge: Harvard University Press, 1986], pp. 15–20).

49. Joel Feinberg appears to share this view, although he casts his discussion in terms of the voluntariness of consent and uses the incongruous (to me) term "coercive offer." He writes: "[I]f A happens upon B in a condition of vulnerability and asks his consent to the terms of an exploitative 'coercive offer,' B's acceptance, while short of perfect voluntariness, will usually be voluntary enough to relieve A or [sic] *criminal* responsibility. But if A forcibly intervenes in B's affairs to create the conditions of vulnerability and then deliberately exploits those conditions with a coercive offer, B's consent so extracted will usually not be voluntary enough to provide A with a defense, and *a fortiori* consent produced by a credible *threat* of harm will have no legal force in any court, civil or criminal." Feinberg, *Harm to Self*, p. 263 (italics in original).

50. Rape has been assimilated to many different acts and crimes over the years—for example, murder, lynching, trespass, larceny (theft), assault, and battery. I think the parallel with robbery is most instructive. Some rapes—the forcible ones—are analogous to murder, lynching, and battery, since they give the victim no choice; but others—those that are coercive$_n$—are analogous to robbery. I know of no other theorist who has drawn this comparison.

51. See, e.g., LaFave and Scott, *Substantive Criminal Law*, vol. 2, p. 438.

52. Ibid.

53. I say "best conceived" rather than "conceived" because the *Model Penal Code* (to name just one code) classifies robbery with arson, burglary, theft, and forgery as "Offenses Against Property." See *Model Penal Code*, Article 222. Rape, on the other hand, is one of several "Sexual Offenses" that, together with criminal homicide, assault, and kidnapping, constitute "Offenses Involving Danger to the Person." See ibid., Article 213. LaFave and Scott say that "The modern trend is to consider robbery as an offense against the person rather than against property." LaFave and Scott, *Substantive Criminal Law*, vol. 2, p. 437 n. 3. This seems to me to be a good trend.

54. See LaFave and Scott, *Substantive Criminal Law*, vol. 2, pp. 437, 455.

55. In both cases, in addition, the coercer can fail to achieve his or her purpose, in which case there is an attempt but not a completed crime. The robbery victim may elect to

suffer the threatened injury rather than transfer the property; the rape victim may resist (and perhaps escape) rather than submit. For a discussion of attempt, which is classified as an "inchoate" or "anticipatory" offense, see, e.g., ibid., pp. 18–60.

56. Ibid., p. 447 (citations omitted).

57. *Model Penal Code*, sec. 213.1(1)(b).

58. *Hall v. People*, 171 Ill. 540, 49 N.E. 495 (1898) (victim voluntarily drunk).

59. See *Commonwealth v. Burke*, 105 Mass. 376 (1870) (conviction upheld where victim, at time of intercourse, was "so drunk as to be utterly senseless and incapable of consenting").

60. Criminal (as opposed to tortious) battery is traditionally defined as "the unlawful application of force to the person of another." LaFave and Scott, *Substantive Criminal Law*, vol. 2, p. 301.

61. See *Model Penal Code*, sec. 213.1(2)(c), which covers cases in which a male "knows that [the female] is unaware that a sexual act is being committed upon her."

62. See, e.g., *State v. Reinhold*, 123 Ariz. 50, 597 P.2d 532 (1979).

63. See LaFave and Scott, *Substantive Criminal Law*, vol. 2, p. 450.

64 Ibid., p. 451.

65. For prostitutes, see *People v. Abbot*, 13 N.Y. 576, 19 Wend. 192 (Sup. Ct. 1838) (evidence of complaining witness's "connection with other men," of intercourse with defendant on previous occasions, and of her "character as a common strumpet" ruled admissible as tending to show "assent" to intercourse with defendant on occasion in question). For wives, see Keith Burgess-Jackson, "Wife Rape," *Public Affairs Quarterly* 12 (January 1998):1–22, and references cited therein.

66. For a general discussion of this phenomenon, see Keith Thomas, "The Double Standard," *Journal of the History of Ideas* 20 (April 1959):195–216.

67. See, e.g., Susan Estrich, *Real Rape* (Cambridge: Harvard University Press, 1987); see also *Model Penal Code*, sec. 213.1(1) (reducing rape from first- to second-degree felony if the victim was "a voluntary social companion of the actor upon the occasion of the crime" and had "previously permitted him sexual liberties").

68. See, e.g., the June 1996 and September 1996 issues of the journal *Legal Theory*, which contain nine essays on "Sex and Consent." See also the new book by David Archard, *Sexual Consent* (Boulder, CO: Westview Press, 1998).

69. See, e.g., Richard A. Posner, *Sex and Reason* (Cambridge: Harvard University Press, 1992), p. 388 ("[A]ll that distinguishes [rape] from ordinary sexual intercourse is lack of consent"); cf. Feinberg, *Harmless Wrongdoing*, p. 168 ("Take away the victim's unwillingness in rape, and you have no victim and no harm, but only a sexual act which cannot be thought of as an evil or a harm in itself").

70. "There is, of course, no trespass in the taking, and hence no larceny, if the owner of property actually consents to the defendant's taking his property." LaFave and Scott, *Substantive Criminal Law*, vol. 2, p. 334 (citation omitted).

71. See Paul H. Robinson, *Criminal Law Defenses*, 2 vols. (St. Paul, MN: West, 1984), vol. 1, p. 316; see also *Model Penal Code*, sec. 2.11(3)(d) ("assent does not constitute consent if . . . it is induced by force, duress or deception of a kind sought to be prevented by the law defining the offense"). Whether we say there is no consent or that the consent is ineffective seems merely terminological.

72. As Joel Feinberg puts it in his discussion of the volenti-non-fit-injuria maxim, "Vo-

lenti is most plausible when it denies title to complain only to him whose consent was *fully voluntary,* and a person's consent is fully voluntary only when he is a competent and unimpaired adult who has not been *threatened,* misled, or lied to about relevant facts, nor manipulated by subtle forms of conditioning." Feinberg, *Harm to Others,* p. 116 (all but the last set of italics in original).

73. My argument depends on the analogy with robbery, but there is independent reason (of a Kantian sort) to maintain that coercion undermines or precludes consent. For an argument along these lines, see Onora O'Neill, "Between Consenting Adults," *Philosophy & Public Affairs* 14 (Summer 1985):259 ("[I]f we coerce or deceive others, their dissent, and so their genuine consent, is in principle *ruled out.* Here we do indeed use others, treating them as mere props or tools in our own projects. Even the most autonomous cannot genuinely consent to proposals about which they are deceived or with which they are compelled to comply" [emphasis added]).

74. See also MacKinnon, *Toward a Feminist Theory of the State,* p. 150 ("'[C]onsent' is supposed to be the crucial line between rape and intercourse, but the legal standard for it is so passive, so acquiescent, that a woman can be dead and have consented under it").

75. *Model Penal Code,* sec. 222.1(1)(b).

76. LaFave and Scott, *Substantive Criminal Law,* vol. 2, p. 448 n. 62.

77. *Model Penal Code,* sec. 213.1(1)(a).

78. See ibid., secs. 6.01, 6.06.

79. Ibid., sec. 213.1(2)(a).

80. See, e.g., Vivian Berger, "Not So Simple Rape," review of *Real Rape,* by Susan Estrich, in *Criminal Justice Ethics* 7 (Winter/Spring 1988):73 ("While one might properly question why the law should concern itself with the reasonableness of honest fear on the part of the woman that the man has intentionally or recklessly caused (legal prohibitions are frequently aimed at protecting the timorous and the gullible), in real life the difficulty with the requirement [that fear be reasonable] stems less from theory than application").

81. Feinberg, *Harm to Others,* p. 26 (italics in original).

82. See ibid., pp. 36, 105, 215.

83. Ibid., p. 37. Donald Dripps has recently argued that "legislatures should replace the independent crime of rape with a variety of new statutory offenses that would more clearly and more justly define criminal liability for culpable conduct aimed at causing other individuals to engage in sexual acts." Donald A. Dripps, "Beyond Rape: An Essay on the Difference Between the Presence of Force and the Absence of Consent," *Columbia Law Review* 92 (November 1992):1780. The new offenses, which Dripps denominates "sexually motivated assault" and "sexual expropriation," are designed to vindicate, respectively, the interests in "freedom from injury" and "exclusive control of one's body for sexual purposes." Ibid., p. 1797.

Dripps's offense of "sexually motivated assault" has affinities to what I am calling "coerced sex," except that he includes only threats of "physical injury." Ibid., p. 1807. My theory encompasses any threat to do what one has no legal right to do. Thus, my theory, but not Dripps's, would prohibit and punish threats to destroy or appropriate the victim's property should she not submit to sexual intercourse. As for Dripps's second offense, the acts that fall under "sexual expropriation" are already punishable as battery, and should remain so. Perhaps there should be a new offense called "sexual battery" in which the unlawful touching is sexual in nature, and perhaps it should be punished more severely than nonsexual battery.

This would not constitute *rape* on my theory, but as I said earlier, rape is not the only actual or possible sexual offense.

One virtue of Dripps's offense of "sexually motivated assault" is that it obviates inquiry into the victim's mental state. As he puts it, "By asking only whether the defendant threatened the victim for the purpose of causing sex, the proposed sexually motivated assault statute makes the victim's psychology irrelevant." Ibid., p. 1798. As for the *defendant's* mental state, "the government would bear the burden of convincing the jury that the accused caused the victim's fear for the purpose of obtaining sex, and also that he knew that he was causing her fear at the time." Ibid. These are factual questions for the jury. The *mens rea* for rape would no longer be belief in (knowledge of) nonconsent but *intention to secure sexual submission by means of threat*. Thus, while I reject the specifics of Dripps's proposal, I believe that he has advanced the theoretical debate concerning the nature and wrongfulness of rape. For a critique of Dripps, see Robin L. West, "Legitimating the Illegitimate: A Comment on *Beyond Rape*," *Columbia Law Review* 93 (October 1993):1442-59. For Dripps's reply, see Donald A. Dripps, "More on Distinguishing Sex, Sexual Expropriation, and Sexual Assault: A Reply to Professor West," *Columbia Law Review* 93 (October 1993):1460–72.

84. Franke, "What's Wrong With Sexual Harassment?," p. 693.

85. For an argument along these lines, see Catharine A. MacKinnon, "Reflections on Sex Equality Under Law," *The Yale Law Journal* 100 (March 1991):1281–1328.

86. MacKinnon, *Toward a Feminist Theory of the State*, p. 150.

6

JEAN HAMPTON

Defining Wrong and Defining Rape

Many wrongful acts against women, which in our time have finally been crimi-nalized, were not until rather recently perceived as wrong by the larger society. For example, rape by a husband of a wife, and battery of wives generally, have histori-cally been seen as legally and (by some) even morally permissible (as permissible as a farmer's beating his stubborn mule) and thus as legally permissible. In our own time, the idea that such behavior can be justified still clings to our criminal law and crimi-nal practices despite heavy attack. In part, this is reflected in the legal definition of rape, which in various criminal codes is generally understood as intercourse with a woman—normally understood to be someone other than the man's wife—by force or threat of force, against her will and without her consent.[1] It is hard to shake the thought embedded in this society that you can't be raped by your husband.

It also turns out to be hard to shake the thought that you can't be raped by your boyfriend or by someone with whom you have at least a temporary sexual relation-ship. Feminists who condemn what has come to be called "date rape" have met with both success and resistance in persuading our legal system to prosecute it. But recently, some of that resistance has come from women who are committed to fem-inist political goals but who oppose "establishment feminism": They have accused feminists who maintain that there is a high incidence of date rape in our society and who condemn what they take to be our "rape culture," of being guilty of dan-gerous hyperbole, hysteria, or retrograde views about the vulnerability of women and the wolfishness of men.[2]

To determine if there is anything to these charges, we need a way to think about what I will call "morally wrongful sex." It is, I suspect, a common assumption in our society that the only kind of morally wrongful sex between a man and a woman is rape, as the law understands it. On this view, as long as one is not raped in *this* sense, the sex one experiences, while perhaps not "good," cannot be "wrong." Such an assumption would explain why critics of feminist concern over date rape see that concern as exaggerated: If one's only "picture" of wrongful sex is the violent and coercive experience characteristic of felony rape (and generally performed by a person who is a stranger to the woman), one will resist the idea that *this* experience is as ubiquitous as certain feminists claim. But I shall argue in this chapter that there is a lot wrong with this picture.

The way to argue against it is not, however, to stay focused on the legal definition of rape. Not all wrongs are crimes, and not all acts of morally wrongful sex are rapes. In each case, the latter is a subset of the former. Determining the boundaries of the subset of rape therefore requires understanding the set of which it is a part. And once this understanding is achieved, I will argue that concern not only about date rape, but also about the way in which heterosexual intercourse is often practiced in this society, is highly justified.

Note that because this chapter starts and ends with the issue of rape, its focus is primarily on heterosexual intercourse, but as we will see, some of its arguments are also relevant to the moral evaluation of homosexual acts.

What Is a Wrong?

In order to define morally wrongful sex, we must begin by understanding the characteristics of wrongful action in general. This may not seem to be hard, particularly if one is a moral consequentialist. To put it simply (and a little crudely): On a moral consequentialist view, an act is right if and only if it leads to the maximization of (or achievement of) good consequences. According to this view, an act is wrong if it leads (in some way) to bad consequences or if it fails to maximize or achieve good consequences.

There are a number of problems with this view. There is the obvious problem of developing a compelling theory of what is to count as a good or a bad consequence. Apart from this, however, consequentialist moral theories are generally criticized for failing to capture our intuitions about what constitutes right action; actions that we normally commend, such as being honest or generous, only count as good in this view if they produce good consequences, despite the fact that we intuitively think that these actions have a "rightness" to them, regardless of how advantageous they are. This point can be made just as well with respect to wrong actions: On the consequentialist view, an action is wrong if it leads to bad consequences. Yet we can imagine situations in which what we intuitively regard as a wrongful action (e.g., lying, cheating) turns out to be advantageous, and that fact doesn't redeem the action and make it morally permissible.

Nonconsequentialist moral theories are committed to the idea that there are actions that are "intrinsically" wrong or right, regardless of the consequences they cause. But in what are these intuitions about intrinsic rightness or wrongness grounded? Why aren't these intuitions simply a function of our upbringing, education, and the conditioning of our society? Why should we regard them as reliable? Such questions are particularly compelling in light of charges raised by feminists and other "outsiders" that there are wrongs that our intuitions have "missed" or misunderstood or misgauged with respect to their seriousness. Such charges are not informed by "commonsense" intuition, since commonsense intuition is what they challenge. So what informs them? What are the ideas which the critics are using to make their challenges? How can we evaluate their soundness?

It might seem that nonconsequentialists can answer some of these questions by linking wrongdoing with harming (although that linkage must not be a consequentialist one if they are going to retain a nonconsequentialist theory). However, even if wrongful action has *something* to do with harm, the connection is not direct or straightforward because actual harm is not necessary for a wrong to exist; for example, an attempt at murder that fails and does no harm to the intended victim is still a (highly) wrongful act. Moreover, we (and the law) distinguish between harms and wrongs: Not all harms are morally wrong, and not all morally wrong actions produce harm. Nonetheless, by reflecting on the nature of harm in the next section, I will attempt to distinguish harm from that which is "in" a wrongful action that makes it wrong.

Harm and Wrong[3]

Harms are the concern of tort law, so it makes sense to begin the task of distinguishing wrongs from harms by looking at the difference between crimes and torts. Tort law is a complicated legal practice that, in the eyes of many, cannot be unified by a single, overarching moral or conceptual goal. But legal theorists such as Jules Coleman have argued that a central concern of most tort cases is the desire to administer what they call "corrective justice." Coleman understands corrective justice as follows: "Corrective justice imposes on wrongdoers the duty to repair their wrongs and the wrongful losses their wrongdoing occasions."[4]

Coleman insists that it is with the *losses* that corrective justice is concerned, not with the wrongful actions themselves:

> Annulling moral wrongs is a matter of justice: retributive, not corrective, justice. There is a legal institution that, in some accounts anyway, is designed to do retributive justice, namely, punishment. The bulk of cases in which claims in corrective justice are valid do not involve wrongs in this sense. If we abandon the view that corrective justice requires annulling wrongs as such, we are left with the claim that corrective justice imposes the duty on wrongdoers to annul the wrongful losses their conduct occasions.[5]

This way of dividing up the concerns of tort law and criminal law seems plausible. But whether or not it is right depends on what Coleman understands as a wrongful loss.

According to Coleman, a wrongful loss is a loss that results from wrongful conduct. Although he never offers an explicit definition of "loss," he seems to mean by that term roughly what many would understand as "harm." Henceforth, to clarify matters, I will use "loss" and "harm" interchangeably, and I will define them as follows:

> A harm or loss is a disruption of or interference in a person's well-being, including damage to that person's body, psychological state, capacities to function, life plans, or resources over which we take this person to have an entitlement.

Harms or losses therefore extend over everything we are prepared to consider to "belong" to a person.[6] Henceforth, when I speak of "correcting" or "rectifying a loss" I will mean the same thing as "repairing a harm."

Not all harms or losses are wrongful. "Innocent" sources, such as natural disasters or animals, can cause harms but not wrongful harms. A new business competitor can harm one's business (and damage one's life plans), but again, we do not think of this kind of harm as wrongful. A wrongful harm or loss only comes from wrongful conduct by an agent thought to be culpable. Tort law is only concerned with a wrongful harm or loss.

Like Coleman, I would argue that tort law is concerned, not with the wrongs or the wrongful conduct that causes these harms or losses, but with the harms or losses themselves (insofar as they are caused by such wrongful actions). And it is concerned with them in a particular way: It insists not only that such losses must be repaired, but also that they must be repaired *by the one who caused them*. We do not ask a wealthy Rockefeller to repair the loss that I have caused by my wrongful conduct, even if that Rockefeller is vastly richer than I am. Instead, *I* must cover it to the extent that I am able, since I am the one who caused it:

> [Corrective justice] provides wrongdoers with reasons for action that are peculiar to them—agent relative reasons in that sense—to annul losses they are responsible for. [W]rongdoing changes the nature of the relationship between the parties; it creates duties where none had previously existed. It gives agents reasons for acting that they did not previously have.[7]

Hence, corrective justice is that branch of justice that requires that those who cause losses by acting in wrongful ways are required to repair, correct, or annul such losses. *So corrective justice is not a branch of justice that is concerned with the wrongdoing itself.*[8]

In contrast, whereas corrective justice is concerned with wrongful harms, retributive justice is concerned with wrongful *actions* from which such harms result. Although a punishment may sometimes involve the wrongdoer compensating her victim in some way, the purpose of punishment is not to compensate the person for the harm suffered, but "to right the wrong." Retributive justice, which is (at least in part) the concern of the criminal law, is that branch of justice that is concerned with the actual wrongdoing.

What does "righting a wrong" involve? To answer this question, we need to appreciate that only a certain kind of wrong needs righting.[9] There are two categories of wrongful action:

(1)   A wrongful action (that can result in a wrongful loss) that requires a retributive response, and the losses of which require compensation.

(2)   A wrongful action (that can result in a wrongful loss) that does not require a retributive response, but the losses of which (still) require compensation.

Whereas wrongful losses (or harms) that arise from actions falling into either of the two categories require correction according to corrective justice and can thus be torts, only wrongful actions of the first sort are the appropriate concern of the criminal law. Now, not all torts are the result of wrongful action (so that not all torts are the subject of corrective justice).[10] But for those that are, not all of them are the result of wrongful actions falling into the first category. The second category of wrongful action recognizes the possibility that there can be a wrongful action that is not the appropriate subject of retribution and thus not the appropriate concern of criminal law, but which is wrongful nonetheless and which can cause harms that corrective justice requires the wrongdoer to repair. If we can better understand the nature of this second category, then we are in a position to isolate the element in the first category of wrongful conduct that makes a retributive response to it—and thus a response in criminal law—appropriate.

Let me give two examples of tortious action that fall into the second category, such that they do not require a retributive response. The first is the well-known case of *Vincent v. Lake Erie*. In this case, a shipowner tied his ship to a dock in order to avoid the virtual certainty of shipwreck by an approaching storm, despite the fact that the dockowner refused permission for him to do so. During the storm, the ship did considerable damage to the dock. The dock owner sued, and the court decided that the ship owner was liable for the damages, but was in no way legally punishable for having tied his ship to the dock given the circumstances. Like the court, our overall moral assessment of what the shipowner did is positive, but like the court, we agree that there is still a component of what he did—tying up his ship at another person's dock without permission—that is wrong in the sense that it violated a right. Because our overall assessment of the shipowner's conduct is positive, we do not think that he should be the subject of retributive punishment. Indeed, any attempt by the dock owner to have him convicted of trespassing or some other criminal offense would have been (rightly) rejected by the court. Nonetheless, something wrongful persists within his action; namely, making use of the dockowner's property without his permission. Because the loss suffered by the dockowner was the causal result of this wrongful conduct, it counts as a wrongful loss and thus one which the shipowner must rectify.

This case fits within the second category because the overall assessment of the injurer's action is morally positive, even though there is a component of wrongfulness within it. However, there are also cases in which the overall assessment of the injurer's action is morally negative but which nonetheless also fit within the second category. Consider, as an example, losses that result from noncriminal negligence: These are losses that result from wrongful conduct; but, nonetheless, such conduct does not merit a retributive response. Suppose Mary is taking her two kids to school on a wet day in her Honda, and after rounding a turn, is unable to avoid hitting Susan's car, which is stopped in preparation to make a left turn after the oncoming traffic clears. Moreover, to make this a clear instance of wrongful act in the second category, let us suppose that while not perfect, Mary's driving was not grossly negligent; e.g., suppose she was going no faster than the speed limit but rain water on the road made the surface slick in a way that she should have (but did not) notice. Mary has done something wrong; she has driven negligently in a way that has resulted in a loss to Susan (and perhaps also to her own kids in the back seat). So to say that she has done something wrong is to say that she has failed to conform to the norms appropriate for good driving in those weather conditions, norms that we believe she does (and should) know. Still, it seems deeply inappropriate to haul her in front of a judge in a criminal courtroom and demand that she be punished for what she has done. The wrongfulness of her conduct is not the *right kind* of wrongfulness to merit such a response. Instead, it is the sort of wrongfulness to which we think a court has completely and adequately responded when it requires her to repair the losses she caused.

We also think it deeply inappropriate to inflict a retributive response on some-one who has wronged herself: Most liberals—myself included—reject the criminal-ization of this sort of wrong, and even those who don't are usually reluctant to insist on any sort of criminal penalty for the crime of, say, attempting to commit suicide. In contrast, if someone has defrauded you of your life savings, we do not think that a court has completely and adequately responded to this wrongful action simply by requiring that this person return your money to you. So what is the difference be-tween the wrongfulness of the defrauder's action and the wrongfulness of the ac-tions of the negligent driver, the ship owner, or the suicide attempter?

Wrongfulness and Intrinsic Value

All wrongful actions are actions that violate a moral standard applicable in the cir-cumstances. But I will say that some moral actions violate those standards in a par-ticular way insofar as they are also *an affront to the victim's value or dignity.* Call such an affront a *moral injury:* In this section, I want to clarify the nature of a moral injury.

A moral injury is not the same as a wrongful loss or harm. The latter concept, as I have defined it above, involves material or psychological damage to that over which a person has a right (e.g., her possessions, her body, her psychological well-being), and comes about because of a wrongful action. In contrast, a moral injury is an injury to what I will call the "realization and acknowledgment of the victim's value." Hence, the idea assumes first a certain conception of value and assumes second a certain understanding of how actions can affect that value. Let me de-velop each of these ideas in turn.

To say that someone has value is to invoke a certain conception of human worth.[11] To hold a conception of human worth is to hold beliefs about how human beings are to be valued and how to appraise each individual's value. There are many possible theories of human worth, and philosophers have varied in how they have understood the nature of human value. For example, Hobbes regards human value as no different from the value of any commodity: "The value of each person," he insists, "is his price."[12] So on his view our value is entirely instrumental: We are worth only what someone would give to make use of our skills, labor, or other char-acteristics. Naturally, such a position is going to accord people different values, de-pending on the marketability of their various traits.

There are also noninstrumental conceptions of human worth, which grant people "inherent" or "intrinsic" worth on the basis of one or more characteristics. Many such conceptions are inegalitarian, granting human beings unequal value depending on their sex, race, caste, or alternatively, on the basis of how intelligent, accomplished, or morally worthy they are. Other such conceptions are egalitarian, insisting that people are equal in worth insofar as they all share certain critical, worth-defining characteristics. One popular egalitarian theory is that of Kant, which grants each of us equal worth insofar as we are all rational and autonomous.

All these theories of worth are substantive normative theories, not metaethical theories. I take no stand on the question of whether any of them attributes to people what seem to be nonnatural properties in a way that makes them implausible or nonscientific; nor will I discuss whether or not they can be interpreted such that they yield genuine (moral) knowledge. To what extent rational people should be committed to any of them is an issue I leave for another day. My only claim here is that such conceptions are a normal part of a culture's normative practices, animating its ethics and its punitive system.[13]

Because Kant's theory will be very important in what follows, I want to take some time here to explicate it. In a way, Kant has *two* theories of worth, only one of which will be important to us: First, Kant grants us worth insofar as we are "morally worthy," and when we evaluate one another's moral worth, Kant grants that—in this sense—we will likely be unequal in value. After all, some of us are vastly better from a moral point of view than are others of us. Second, Kant says we have worth simply insofar as we are human beings and calls each of us an "end-in-himself." In this second sense, we are all equal in value. Only this second conception of value is relevant to defining the kind of moral respect a person deserves. On this view (which has its roots in Judeo-Christian religious teaching),[14] our moral obligations to people don't increase with, say, their moral virtue; instead we are obliged to respect our fellow human beings *equally*, no matter the state of their moral character, insofar as each human being is an autonomous, rational being (although Kant would certainly maintain that how this respect should be demonstrated can vary depending on the state of a person's moral character.)[15] So Kant's second way of defining human worth is egalitarian—and critical to the concept of moral respect. All of us must be valued as equal insofar as we all have the same value as "ends in ourselves." This "democratic" conception of value has been popular, albeit not universally accepted, in the modern world.

It is this *second* sense of value that is fundamental to the account of moral wrongfulness that has come to animate our intuitions and the practice of the criminal law. Curiously, one critic of my view took it that by speaking of the "value of the victim," I meant moral worth in Kant's first sense.[16] But neither I nor Kant (nor anyone else I know) would maintain that we should respect people only to the extent that they are moral people! The Kantian view explicitly denies the idea that moral respect is based on a hierarchy of moral merit. Instead, this view maintains that moral respect is based on our intrinsic value as ends, which all of us have equally, and which is not straightforwardly capable of aggregation in the way that some utilitarian doctrines characterize it as being. On this view, morality demands of each of us that we respect the dignity of others and of ourselves, and thus reject the way that, for example, a white supremacist would insist on his own superiority over other racial groups or the way in which a male might relish the idea that he is the intrinsic superior of all women. Interestingly, it also demands that we reject the idea that any of us "good" people is the superior of any wrongdoers—a thought that, as I have argued elsewhere, is important to understanding how to define appropriate retributive punishment.[17]

In a way, it is misleading to call this the "Kantian" conception of value, insofar as it is a way of regarding people, the foundations of which can be found in Christianity and Judaism, although I cannot pursue those foundations here.[18] It has been more because of these religious connections, and not any substantial influence that

Kant had, that this conception of value has been enormously influential in modern Western societies and has therefore played a role in setting the normative standards for acceptable treatment of people in these societies. To see how (and the extent to which) it has done so, we must appreciate the way in which *human behavior is expressive,* and that what behavior expresses is partly a matter of cultural convention. The redoubtable Judith Martin, the expert on etiquette, has defended this idea in the context of arguing for the importance of manners as modes of behavior that constitute a language for conveying respect:

> The idea that people can behave naturally, without resorting to an artificial code tacitly agreed upon by their society, is as silly as the idea that they can communicate by a spoken language without commonly accepted semantic and grammatical rules. Like language, a code of manners can be used with more or less skill, for laudable or for evil purposes, to express a variety of ideas and emotions. In itself, it carries no moral value, but ignorance in use of this tool is not a sign of virtue. Inarticulateness should not be mistaken for guilelessness.
>
> Like language, manners pertain to a particular society at a particular time. If they were "just common sense" as is often claimed by critics of the field, why should Japanese behavior be any different from American, or medieval from modern? Like language, manners continually undergo slow changes and adaptations, but these changes have to be global, and not atomic. For if everyone improvises his own manners, no one will understand the meaning of anyone else's behavior, and the result will be social chaos and the end of civilization.[19]

So Martin sees manners as defined by convention (in the way that word meaning is conventional). But she neglects to note that conventions about manners will differ not only because societies use different behaviors to convey respect, but also because they have different conceptions of the kind of respect various kinds of human beings are owed. Inegalitarian hierarchical conceptions of value have been commonplace throughout human history, whereas egalitarian conceptions have only gained popularity in modern times. Moreover, the "official" or most popular theory of worth in a society may not always be embraced by all sectors of the society: For example, the Kantian, egalitarian theory of worth, implicit in American political values, has always been rejected by white racists and has been dismissed by sexists (whose egalitarianism is limited to evaluating the worth of males). In any pluralist society, just as there are a variety of spoken languages and/or varieties of one dominant spoken language, there are also varieties of value-expressive behavioral language that are "spoken" by different sectors of the society.

As we grow up in a certain sector of society, we do not merely learn the language expressing the "right" ways to behave; we also figure out the wrong ways. Moreover, we learn not only certain conventional behavioral formulas (e.g., shaking hands as a sign of respect, eating in ways that are deemed socially inoffensive) but also the behavioral ingredients for expressing messages about value in convention-flouting ways. So when we behave "wrongfully," we fail to conform to what our society would recognize as acceptable behavior, either by doing things that are conventionally understood to be wrong, or by inventing from conventional behavioral material novel ways of expressing our defiance of what society understands as respectful behavior.

Such defiance is not always understood by us to be *morally* wrong; when Rosa Parks refused to sit at the back of the bus, she was defying the manners of her sector of society in a way that we think was morally right. Yet note that her defiance of those manners was a defiance of a conception of the unequal worth of human beings based on race, a conception that we, along with Parks, reject as wrong. In contrast, those whose behavior defies what we take to be the *correct* theory of worth are people whom we regard as, to some degree, morally criticizable.

It is because behavior can carry meaning with regard to human value that it can be wrongful. The analogies between the meaningfulness of language and the meaningfulness of behavior are striking enough that one can use the Gricean theory of linguistic meaning to distinguish different ways in which human conduct can be meaningful, and in what follows, I will employ Gricean categories in the course of explaining how wrongful conduct is meaningful (although I cannot give any kind of complete Gricean analysis here).[20] Having done that, I will explain how that meaning is related to the moral injuries that wrongdoing effects. In brief, I shall argue that a person is morally injured when she is the target of behavior whose meaning, appropriately understood by members of the cultural community in which the behavior occurs, represents her value as less than the value she should be accorded. However, the insulting meaning of this behavior does not, by itself, *constitute* the moral injury. As I shall explain, the insulting meaning *inflicts* the injury in one of two possible ways.

Behavioral Meaning and Moral Injury

It isn't always true that when we fail to conform to the standards of acceptable behavior, we are thereby engaging in behavior that should be interpreted as defying or taking exception to the theory of worth motivating these standards. There are other explanations of our failure. When Mary ran into Susan's car, she may have been appalled at what she did and explain her conduct by saying that she had been distracted, inexperienced, or overconfident of her ability to control the car. So while she might heartily agree that she ought not to have driven the way she did, she might also insist that her careless driving conveyed no message of disrespect for anyone on the road. Given our reluctance to see her as a suitable target of punishment we tend to agree with this account of her behavior's "meaning."

The preceding example shows we cannot maintain that an agent inflicts a moral injury whenever her conduct (for which we hold her responsible) fails to conform to certain moral standards. Moreover, because, as I noted above, a moral injury can be inflicted by an action even when there is no actual harm done to the agent, a moral injury cannot be identified with the harm inflicted by the wrongful action. Indeed, a moral injury cannot even be identified with the psychological experience of pain following the wrong, since such pain is neither a necessary nor a sufficient condition for the existence of a moral injury. First, it is not necessary because there can be victims who for one reason or another fail to experience such pain but are nonetheless wrongfully treated; for example, an elderly man in failing health who, unbeknownst to him, is having his life savings slowly filched by his financial advisor, or a rape victim whose sense of self-worth is so low that she is unable to recognize the rape as wrong, mistaking it for an action permissible for someone as "low" as her. The first victim fails to recognize the wrong because he fails to recognize the action; the second victim recognizes the action, but fails to understand it as wrong. Nonetheless, both are victims of wrongful action. Second, psychological pain is not a sufficient condition for the existence of moral injury because there are people who experience such pain who are not wrongfully treated. White supremacists "brought low" by the actions of people such as Rosa Parks are, we believe, right to be lowered, because they claimed a position for themselves, relative to others, that we believe is too high; hence we do not take seriously the psychological pain they experience as a result of such actions.

Often, perhaps even usually, our sense of being wronged tracks genuine wrongful treatment, but this is not always so, as these examples demonstrate. Hence, these examples show that a moral injury is an "objective" and not a subjective injury. By this I merely mean that the existence of the moral injury does not depend on whether or not the agent *believes* she has received dishonoring treatment.

So if moral injury is not harm, and if it is not the psychological pain one might feel after the wrongful treatment, then what is it? In particular, what is it an injury *to?* As I shall now explain, it is a particular kind of injury to the person's value. In this section, I will argue that wrongful actions that merit retributive punishment carry meanings that effect injuries to a person's value in one of two ways: Either they can damage what I will call that person's "realization of his value," or they can damage "the acknowledgment of his value." In what follows, I want to explain more precisely the nature of the two forms of damage to value effected by wrongful actions, distinguishing, as I do so, between the value-denigrating meaning of a wrongful action and the injury that the action inflicts by virtue of its denigrating meaning.

Exactly how one conceives of a wrongdoing as injuring value depends on the theory of value that one accepts. A Kantian theory of value insists that human beings *never* lose value as ends-in-themselves, no matter what kind of treatment they receive. Hence, it is initially hard to see how such a theory of value could generate *any* conception of a wrongful action as an injury to the victim's value. Nonetheless, it can, as I shall now explain. As I will understand the phrase "Kantian theory of value," it is really a genus term, including a number of different species of theories of value. What all of them have in common is the belief that human value is intrinsic, equal, and "permanent" in the sense that our value cannot be degraded or lowered by any kind of action. But they differ with regard to what it is about human beings that explains why they are valuable, and they differ with regard to why human value is permanent in this sense. For example, one instance of such a theory (and the likely source of Kant's own views) is the Christian conception of human beings as intrinsically, equally, and permanently valuable insofar as each of us is the child of God, made in His image. Degradation is impossible on this view because nothing that any human being could do to another can remove this value: Indeed, not even killing a human being could do so, because death is not understood to kill off the person, who persists in an afterlife. Hence, this view posits what I'll call "strong permanence," that is, the idea that human value can be neither degraded nor destroyed. A different Kantian view understands human beings as valuable in virtue of their capacities for rationality and autonomy—although note that to remain

Kantian, such a view must understand value to be present equally in all of us after a certain threshold of these capacities is reached and thus not to vary depending on the extent to which our capacities to be rational and autonomous vary. This view recognizes that the characteristics that give us value can be damaged or extinguished by an immoral action (e.g., by murdering us or destroying our brains). But it would also hold that if this is done, our status as persons is destroyed; which would mean that although immoral actions could destroy our personhood and thus our value, such actions could not *lower* or degrade our value for as long as we remain persons. Such a view therefore posits "weak permanence," that is, the idea that human value can be destroyed but never degraded by immoral actions: The most such actions can do is to extinguish our personhood, in which case *we* are not lowered by such actions, because *we* cease to exist. Or to put it another way, even if we are murdered, that action cannot lower us in value (as if we remained behind in the corpse), but only extinguish that which *was* valuable. So whereas the first Kantian view holds that both degradation and extinction are impossible, the second grants the possibility of the latter but not the former.

So in different ways, both sorts of views reject the idea that our human value can be literally degraded for as long as we remain persons. However, both theories allow that there can be the *appearance of degradation,* which I will call *diminishment.* I will argue that diminishment is the normal result of an immoral action and that which constitutes the moral injury inflicted by a wrongdoing. It is therefore the damage or "loss of value" that wrongdoing inflicts.

To see what I mean, consider what we might say about the marring of some kind of valuable artistic object.[21] Let's say someone spray painted over the pages of the Book of Kells. We would be furious about the damage this person had done, and that is because we take the book's value to be such that many kinds of treatment with respect to this object—including anything that would mar the art work, are precluded. So our view of the value of this object implies that only certain kinds of treatment are appropriate for it. Let us say, therefore, that its *value generates certain entitlements.* For as long as the Book of Kells has that value, it has these entitlements, which include being preserved, treated with care, and so forth. (One might also want to call those entitlements "rights," but I shall not pursue here the question of whether or not this term is appropriate.)

Therefore, someone who intentionally does not give the valuable object that to which it is entitled can be said to flout its value. And by flouting it, this person is in effect denying that the object really has that value, because he is denying the entitlements that value generates. So by marring it, the person says by his action that the value is not what is being represented. (Suppose an art expert slit the canvas of a painting with his pen knife—those watching would be horrified unless he explained that the painting was a worthless fake). In this way, the person's actions diminish the value of the object.

Marring of valuable objects can do more than merely diminish them; marring can actually decrease their value. But as I discussed above, Kantian theories of human worth deny that crimes can ever lower human value (although, as I noted, one kind of Kantian will admit that such actions can certainly destroy a human being and, thereby, her value). Such views therefore insist that only diminishment, and never degradation, can be the result of wrongdoings. They are actions that say, and attempt to represent, the person as having some value less than that which the Kantian theory of value would attribute to them.

Diminishment is an "objective" phenomenon, by which I merely mean (as I noted above) that it is not something that can be identified with any psychological experience of victimization. Instead, it is something that we "read off of" the effects of immoral behavior. As I will now explain, diminishment is effected by the meaning of the immoral behavior and perhaps also by how others respond to the harm that the behavior may inflict. And as I will go on to explain, it is diminishment that causes moral injury, in one of two ways.

To see further how diminishment works, let me give a heinous example of it. The example comes from a story told by the modern dancer Bill T. Jones, who said it was originally related to him by his mother.[22] In her youth, Jones's mother knew a white farmer who had a black farmhand with four sons working for him. One day the farmhand did something that enraged the white farmer, and so he apprehended the hand and his four sons, put them in large burlap bags, hung the bags with the men inside them from a tree, and began burning each of them. Before he was burned, one of the men asked for a cigarette. The farmer answered him by using a knife to slit the bag holding him, cutting off the man's penis, and then sticking it in his mouth, saying "Here, smoke that." The message conveyed by the farmer's behavior in this incident is one that not only denies *all* of the humanity these men possess, *all* of their manhood, and *all* of their rights as sentient creatures, but also any part or feature of them that could be thought to make them worthy of any degree of respect. Even mere objects can be taken by us to have worth; this farmer denied that these men had anything that one should respect. By constructing an event that represented the people he killed as degraded and worthless, burning them to death seemed no more significant than burning a pile of trash. Note how many details of the entire event accomplish this diminishment: not only the killing but also the containment of bags; not only the castration, but the mocking reference to the penis as a cigar. From the Kantian point of view, the difference between the value that these people actually had and the (almost nonexistent) value he represented them as having is what makes his action so horrendous.

We can use a Gricean analysis of the meaningfulness of the farmer's various acts to show the variety of ways in which the farmer diminished the farmhands' value. Grice has distinguished four different ways in which conduct can be meaningful.[23] There is, first of all, "natural" meaning, as when we say "Smoke means fire." Note that this use of "means" is not really a linguistic one, for what we are really saying is "Smoke is evidence for fire." And with respect to behavior, if we said, "The fact that the art expert slit the canvas of that painting means that it is worthless," we would really be saying, "His action is evidence for its worthlessness." Nonetheless, a person can say or do something as a way of intending a person to draw a certain evidentiary conclusion, in which case, even if the natural meaning isn't itself linguistic, it is the object of a linguistic expression. Thus, the farmer intended anyone present at the killing of the farmhands to infer from the fact that he was killing them that they were, indeed, worthless. His deed was intended as evidence of their lack of value (and *not* merely as symptomatic of his belief in their lack of value).

The second Gricean category of meaning is word meaning. In any language, there are linguistic conventions defining the meanings of words, and these conventional meanings, in certain contexts, will prevail regardless of what one might intend to say when one uses them. Similarly, certain behaviors have fixed conventional meanings, so that, for example, blowing a raspberry will be taken to convey disrespect in this society, even if one intended it as a compliment.[24] The farmer's treatment of his farmhands involved using conventionally defined behaviors to convey deep disrespect, not only when he burned them alive, but also when he castrated one of them.

However, this farmer used more than just the behavioral conventions to hand in order to diminish the farmhands. Consider that the third Gricean category of "speaker meaning" (or nonnatural meaning) refers to occasions when a speaker accomplishes something meaningful, not through the use of convention, but by making clear in other ways what it is he intends to convey. To be momentarily at a loss for words in trying to describe what it is one wants to eat, and then pointing to a chocolate bar, is to convey meaning through one's intentions; and similarly, to attempt to blow a raspberry to convey one's disrespect, but fail in a way that, nonetheless, makes one's intentions clear, is also to convey meaning through one's intentions. While the story of the farmer gives no clear example of this form of meaning in his behavior, nonetheless, it does show that he made novel uses of conventional behavioral material to diminish the farmhands more thoroughly than if he had relied solely on the behavioral conventions themselves. For example, he didn't merely kill the men, but burned them alive in bags (as if they were, quite literally, bags of trash). And he didn't merely castrate the men, but did so in a way that denied that their penises could have had anything to do with their manhood. One might even say that the farmer made metaphoric use of the behavioral conventions of his culture in order to convey his intentions regarding these men's worth.

Grice's final category is that of "conversational implicature."[25] To respond to a rude store clerk by acidly thanking him for his help is to convey meaning outside of the conventions attached to one's words. The farmer's cutting off the men's penises and treating them as cigarettes in response to their requests to smoke was a reaction to them that, while in the form of an answer to a request, is about as denigrating to human worth as one could imagine.

However, as I shall now explain, the meaning of a wrongdoing involves not only the victim's worth, but also the worth of the wrongdoer himself. Consider once again the farmer's murder: We do not merely "read off" from his actions an expression of the farmhands' worthlessness, but also an expression of the farmer's vast superiority relative to them. He represented himself as, quite literally, the master of the men he murdered. He conveyed to them through his actions that he had the power as well as the authority to recognize their worthlessness and to decide their fate to the point of destroying them. So his treatment is intended to "mean" (i.e., to be evidence of) his superiority. They are his to own and to destroy, and thus they are no different from any other relatively worthless possession. Our fury at his murderous actions is connected with our disgust at his representation of his own value relative to them. Hence, the moral injury inflicted by wrongdoers such as this farmer involves more than the misrepresentation of the victim's value, but also the misrepresentation of the wrongdoers' own value.

So a wrongful action that produces moral injury and which is therefore a candidate for a response by the criminal law is an action that has a certain kind of meaning, which I will define as follows:

> A person behaves wrongfully in a way that effects a moral injury to another when she treats that person in a way that is precluded by that person's value, and/or by representing him as worth far less that his actual value; or, in a word, when the meaning of her action is such that she *diminishes* him, and by doing so, represents herself as elevated with respect to him, thereby according herself a value that she does not have.

Note that the example of the farmer shows us there are two potential "carriers" of diminishment in a wrongdoing: the act itself, and the harm (if any) that the act effects. Either (or both) can be the object of our moral anger, in virtue of the way each of them presents the victim and his wrongdoer. Consider, first, the harm: We will be upset about a harm effected by a wrongdoing, just as we would be upset about the same harm effected by a natural disaster. However, what makes the harm effected by a wrongdoing "worse" for us, and hence the target of a special kind of anger in us, is the way it constitutes a treatment of the victim that violates the entitlements that her value requires other human beings to respect. When a wrongdoing effects a state of affairs in which the victim is unable to secure that to which her value entitles her, where that can include her autonomy, her bodily integrity, the possession of property, and even her life, then insofar as we care about this person's value, we object, perhaps violently, to actions that violate those entitlements (and hence that value).

So harms anger us, not merely because they cause suffering we hate to see in others, but also because we see their infliction as *violative of the victim's entitlements given her value.* Hence, one way in which diminishment accomplished by an immoral action morally injures the victim is that it *damages the realization of her value.* That is, the false message about value carried in the action explains why the victim's entitlements aren't respected. Indeed, that false message can be taken to license quite ghastly treatments, as the farmer understood when he killed his farmhands in the most humiliating way possible.

Second, even when a wrongful action does not inflict a harm, it angers us simply in virtue of what the action says about the person. We care about what people say by their actions because we care about whether our own value, and the value of others, will continue to be respected in our society. The misrepresentation of value implicit in moral injuries not only violates the entitlements generated by their value, but also threatens to reinforce belief in the wrong theory of value by the community. Our views about human value are more or less secure, and we are more or less committed to them. Fearful that we are worth less than we wish (or perhaps less than others think we are worth) is a common human phenomenon, particularly in societies in which non-Kantian inegalitarian theories of worth have currency. A value-denying act can therefore be frightening to the victim (and others like him) insofar as it plays into those fears. However, perhaps more importantly, it can encourage the infliction of similar injuries by people who find appealing the apparent diminishment of the victim and the relative elevation effected by the wrongdoing. For many, the longing to be better is a lure to behave in ways that diminish another and elevate oneself. Call this damage to the *acknowledgment of the victim's value*.

So I will define a *moral injury* as *damage to the realization of a victim's value*, or *damage to the acknowledgment of the victim's value, accomplished through behavior whose meaning is such that the victim is diminished in value*.

The more a wrongdoing inflicts damage to value in either way, the more we object to it. If there is minimal damage, we generally find the act minimally immoral; indeed, we might not even bother to respond to it at all. Merely publishing a book proclaiming that, say, men are better than women, or whites are better than blacks,[26] is to deny value and thereby do something morally offensive, but unless other people respond to the book in some way, that damage is negligible and society does not bother to respond. If people take them seriously, and come to believe these assertions of superiority, the books become much more dangerous, because such beliefs can prompt people to interfere with the entitlements of these "inferiors" (to the point of inciting violent acts against them) and propagate the view that they are not valuable enough to be accorded these entitlements. So, in a way, such books morally injure not one individual, but a whole class of individuals, leaving them sitting ducks for treatment lower (perhaps much lower) than that which they deserve. And when such literature leads to damage to the realization and/or acknowledgment of some human being's value, then societal action against those who write it may be justified. Think of anti-Semitic Nazi literature in the 1920s and 1930s; or consider the prohibition by cities such as Los Angeles of racist or sexist video arcade games in public places or the argument by feminists such as Catharine MacKinnon for prohibiting pornography not only because of its alleged connection with sexual assault, but also because of the role it plays in encouraging a demeaning view of women.[27] So on this view, not only the actions that such books and visual material cause, but also their own *content*, is morally injurious. Such materials denigrate people, not only by causing others to inflict harm on them, but simply by representing them as inferior. It is a contested question whether this morally injurious character is, by itself, sufficient to justify their prohibition, since freedom of speech might be thought to be threatened were such censorship permitted. My point is that not only acts but also words and pictures can do moral injury to others and thus be morally wrongful.[28]

Some immoral actions are immoral only because of what they express, not because of any concrete damage they inflict. Again, think of attempted murder. If the attempt fails but is discovered, the behavior is sufficiently alarming in what it conveys about the intended victim's perceived worth that we seek to answer it with punishment, even though no damage has been done to that person's realization of value in the world. (And this is mainly because no harm has been done.) There are some actions, just as there are some words, that are intrinsically and deeply disrespectful, such that there is no way anyone could even attempt or intend them without understanding and intending that deep disrespect. There are also many actions—and the harm that resulted from them—whose meaning is more ambiguous, and an investigation of the wrongdoer's motives is necessary in order to uncover the existence and nature of disrespect: For example, an air traffic controller's failure to separate aircraft sufficiently to prevent a midair collision might be a function of his inability to handle the demands of his job (in which case, he is merely incompetent); or it might be a function of a cavalier and reckless attitude on the job, in which case we are angry at him for failing to appreciate the value of the people whose lives were endangered by his behavior, and thus find him criminally negligent; or it might be a function of a deliberate desire to murder someone on the plane, in which case we condemn him severely for having so little regard not only for the person he wanted to murder, but for those whom he murdered along with them.

So why do we care about these denials of value? Why should we take moral injuries to be objectionable? This question has been asked of me by readers of my work, puzzled about why anyone should care so much about the *appearance* of loss of value. Doesn't my Kantian analysis suggest that we should simply take a Nietzschean approach to wrongdoing and thus shrug off crimes merely as nuisances with respect to our value, ineffective in what they seek to establish given the permanence and equality of our worth as persons?

This question is actually a bundle of questions. I have defined wrongdoing in an objective way, as behavior that denies the value that a human being has. There is nothing subjective about this definition. So what can the theory tell us about why we subjects do care, or ought to care, about denials of value?

The answer to the "ought" question is straightforward: To be valuable is to be something about which human beings should care and something *for* which they should care. To witness the value of someone being misrepresented is to witness behavior that ought to violate one's sense of what is appropriate for this person and prompt a reaction that attempts to stop, and repudiate, that misrepresentation. Of course, the fact that people ought to care about the value of others is not to say that they do. The psychological requirements for being able to care in the right way are not something I can pursue here; suffice it to say that if someone is unable to respond to this value at all, we have reason to question their sanity and perhaps their very humanity. Nor does a Nietzschean attitude on the part of the victim suffice to answer the value-denial, because regardless of whether or not an immoral action shakes a victim's confidence in her worth, if it has damaged the realization or the acknowledgment of her value, it is morally offensive, and the representation of her diminishment is unacceptable. I cannot explain that offensiveness by appealing to something else, because it is the foundation of our objection to wrongdoing: It is part of what it means to say that something is valuable that we ought to care about preserving and acknowledging that value. Indeed, a Nietzschean self-confidence is useful not so much as an answer, by itself, to the diminishment accomplished by the wrongdoing, but as a psychological attitude that makes it *easier* for a victim to object to a wrongdoing. Consider the way in which many feminists want rape victims to come forward openly to accuse their attackers (and, for example, allow their names to be published), throwing off the mantle of shame and degradation that has traditionally been placed on rape victims, thereby becoming more effective in securing the conviction of those who wronged them.

Rape and Wrongful Sex

Those who reject my analysis of wrongdoing might claim that it is not so much in-correct as unnecessary. For what do we need to say about the wrongfulness of crimes such as rape except that it is "wrong in itself"—an intrinsically bad act, end of story? Why do we need to have an analysis of its wrongness? What does it add, that we don't already know?

Those who make this criticism are wedded to the standard deontological ap-proach to wrongdoing, which assumes that wrongness is some kind of property (one that seems nonnatural) that we can intuitively perceive, that applies to certain ac-tions. But what is striking to me and others who look at the history of crimes against women is that they were *not* perceived as wrong until quite recently, and that the failure of people to understand them as wrong was intimately connected to a view of women as lower, inferior, lesser in value. The idea that "we all know what is wrong" has been proved over and over not to be so. And establishing the wrongful-ness of certain forms of behavior has required revolutionizing the way people in a society think about the importance of one another, and in the case of crimes against women, how they look at the value of women.

Indeed, I would contend that the smug deontological belief that we can "in-tuitively see wrongness" makes it particularly difficult for people in a society who accept this way of thinking to "see" how their assumptions about what behavior is wrongful might be inadequate, or incorrect, or even abusive. We need a way to think about wrongfulness that will allow us to appraise the moral adequacy of our intuitions about wrongness. And this is, I think, particularly clear in the case of our intuitions about sex. I once heard a law professor say that "consent turns an act of rape into an act of lovemaking." Such a remark shows the extent to which this pro-fessor's intuitions about the wrongfulness of sex were informed by the legal defini-tion of rape, which makes consent the marker of the morality of the experience. But to take this focus as intuitively natural gives one no way to question whether con-sent should be understood as the *only* marker of the moral (and not merely the legal) acceptability of the sexual experience, and thus whether there can be wrong-ful sex even in cases where the legal definition of rape is not satisfied. We need a way of *reasoning* our way toward an understanding of what sexual behavior is morally wrong, and in what follows I shall aim to use my analysis of wrongdoing to provide one.

Although all wrongful actions are "disrespectful of value," exactly *how* they deny value differs: What they all have in common is the fact that they convey—and work to effect—the wrongdoer's elevation relative to the victim (understood as an individual or as a class of individuals).[29] But the nature of the diminished status that their actions give to their victims can differ radically. A thief who sneaks books from the library strikes us as departing only mildly from our egalitarian standards: His ac-tions represent him as only a little more important than others (so he will steal the book, but he would not, say, kill for it).

In contrast, the husband who persistently abuses his wife "in order to put her in her place" gives her the sort of treatment standardly given to sentient chattel such as animals, which not only conveys to her that this is all the value she has, but also makes that standing a fact of her everyday life (even if it is also a denial of her true standing as a person). Or consider the following description by a former athlete of what he took to be many male athletes' attitudes toward women, which he believed encouraged some of them to rape:

> The view is that women are "its," that women are objects, that women should be attracted to athletes. There's a male machismo there that they can take what they want and society will overlook their transgressions.[30]

Whereas a wife-beating husband's behavior conveys the idea that his wife is mere chattel, a rapist whose rape conveys this attitude expresses the idea that women are even lower than chattel—mere "objects" who are there to be used whenever the male feels the need to do so. And if he succeeds in raping her, not only is that the message one "reads off of" the rape, more distressingly, the rape is a kind of event that seeks to make that diminished status a reality. The woman is used as though she is an object, and so she is thought to be one.

The moral injury experienced by such a rape victim is *objective* on this view: That is, regardless of her psychological response to it, she has been wronged. This is because the message of the action and the actuality of what it accomplishes are not only capable of being understood apart from the victim's reaction to them, but also things that we read off of the action regardless of the psychological peculiarities of a wrongdoer's psychology that led him to commit the wrong. For example, a psychologist's explanation of the rapist's behavior might point to the way in which it arises from a poor sense of self, which the rapist tries to bolster through an action of mastery. But that explanation is irrelevant to the way in which the action is wrongful; it is the expressive content of the action—in both its commission and its results—representing the rapist as master and the victim as inferior object, and not the causal story we tell to explain why it was performed, that accounts for its being wrongful. While there may be times when that causal story is relevant to our determination of an action's expressive content (as in the air traffic controller case discussed above), nonetheless it is the former, and not the latter, which determines wrongfulness.

One of the most important aspects of rape as it occurs in our society is the way in which it is a moral injury to all women, not merely to the woman who experiences it, insofar as it is part of a pattern of response of many men toward many women that aims to establish their mastery *qua male* over a woman *qua female*.[31] Compare the persistent refusal of white apartment owners to rent apartments to prospective minority tenants; such discrimination is not just an injury to the particular people who are denied apartments, but also an injury to all members of the race being discriminated against. It is not merely that the owners are saying "You aren't my equal in worth"; they are saying "Your kind isn't the equal in worth of my kind." Similarly, the action of a rapist is not merely diminishing the worth of his victim; his action also diminishes all women insofar as its message is: "As a woman, you are the kind of human being who is subject to the mastery of people of my kind." Rape confirms that women are "for" men: to be used, dominated, treated as objects.[32] In our society, to know that it *can* happen to you, is to know that you are the sort of person for whom this confirmation is possible; it is to hear the following message implicit in the rape of any woman: "You are the sort of creature who is for me, and who will be used by me if I choose to do so."

But is the rapist's message only an extreme version of the same message that is conveyed in what we regard as "ordinary" and "acceptable" acts of heterosexual intercourse? Is rape a subcategory of a larger class of sexual acts that are wrongful insofar as they are diminishing? It is to the larger issue of what constitutes morally wrongful sex, and of how rape is a subcategory of morally wrongful sex, that I now turn.

One critic who is convinced that feminists have grossly exaggerated the dangers of rape and its occurrence in our society is Camille Paglia. Paglia insists that she is opposed to (what she calls) "real rape," but dismisses the idea that date rape is "real" in the same way. As a way of making this point, she maintains that "the sexual impulse is egotistical and dominating, and therefore I have no problem understanding rape."[33] She goes on to maintain that part of the thrill of sex for a woman is the danger of it—the fact that she is risking rape. The male, in Paglia's world, is represented as possessed of a sex drive that can rather easily get out of control, prompting sexual aggression and causing him to behave in an animal-like way. Rape is (merely) the result of this out-of-control sexual appetite, and while she maintains that "ethical men" don't rape, she insists that the potential power of the male sexual appetite—and the danger that it will result in their being raped—is part of the reason women are sexually attracted to men. Women therefore ought to be on their guard against rape, but acknowledge that the risk of it is part of the fun of sex: "I'm encouraging women: *accept* the adventure, *accept* the danger," says Paglia.[34]

Paglia's views are not unusual in our culture, but they are highly problematic for two reasons. First, such views make it extremely difficult to establish that any form of date rape or spousal rape is morally wrong. Paglia fails to see any *qualitative* difference between the rapist and the "normal" heterosexual male; the rapist is just more "extreme" in his sexual desire, and more aggressive in his pursuit of its satisfaction, than the average male. Moreover, "good sex" for a woman, according to Paglia, is connected with the risk that her male partner might have an out-of-control sexual appetite that causes him to rape her. But this means that if a woman ends up getting raped by a man she dates, she has, in a sense, brought it on herself, because she presumably associated with him in part because of the thrill that, in their intimacy, she was "risking rape." Paglia claims she is opposed to what she calls "real rape"—which presumably means stranger rape in a situation where the woman is in no way associating with or inviting the man to become intimate with her. But we can see why she has trouble understanding all the "fuss" about date rape: If women are supposed to like the "danger" of sex and the fact that they might be risking rape, then this force is itself intrinsic to the desirability of sex with a man and not antithetical to it. Paglia claims that, "You have to accept the fact that part of the sizzle of sex comes from the danger of sex. You can be overpowered."[35] But if risking rape is part of what makes sex with a man *good*, then just as many skiers regard crashing on a downhill skiing course as intrinsic to the fun of skiing (insofar as the fear of crashing contributes to the excitement and exhilaration of the experience), so too women, on this view, regard rape by their date or male partner as intrinsic to the fun of sex, although bad when it happens. So while this view can perhaps explain why women don't *like* to be raped (in the same way that skiers don't like to crash), it is hard-pressed to explain why there is anything *wrong* with date rape or spousal rape, even from the woman's point of view, since a woman's risking rape is intrinsic to her enjoying sex. But this view not only presupposes what I regard as a dubious (and unsupported) psychological theory of the female reaction to sex; more disturbingly, it makes date rape or spousal rape something to which any woman explicitly consents when she begins an association with any man. Paglia's message to women is: "You know what men are like—they're wolves, and any one of them might try to get you. So if you associate with them in any sort of intimate way, remember that you asked for it if they raped you." I find it difficult not to react to such a view as morally bankrupt. To be forced to have sex, and then be told that such a force was "part of what you risked" is not only to absolve men of responsibility for that force (and any act of violence accompanying it), but to deprive women of the moral ground necessary to insist that, in their company, only certain kinds of behavior toward them is acceptable. And it is to make the sexual appetites of women depend on the possibility of their being raped—representing them as feeding off the possibility of their own degradation. It is therefore a view that (deeply) dishonors women.

Second, it also dishonors men. It represents all of them as wolves or potential wolves. Her message is: We all know what they're like, and what we're risking if we associate with them. All men are either monsters or have the potential to be monsters on this view; so watch out! Moreover, Paglia's portrait of the rapist as no different from any man, with the exception that his appetites are less in control and more "animal-like" than the appetites of men who do not rape, flies in the face of the fact that, almost without exception, male members of animal species other than our own do not rape.[36] Rape is a human phenomenon and not a phenomenon common to animals who lack the rational capacity to control their appetites. So the evidence points to rape as deriving from something other than a voracious, animal-like sexual appetite. Paglia's portrait of the male is so crude that it gives us no way to locate what that "something" is.

On the other hand, there may be an idea animating Paglia's view of rape that is worth taking seriously.[37] Paglia tells the story of a woman she knew who got raped and afterward got counseling. Here is how she describes the experience:

> She said it was awful, that the minute she arrived there, the rape counsellors were saying, "You will never recover from this, what's happened to you is so terrible." She said, what the hell, it was a terrible experience, but she was going to pick herself up, and it wasn't that big a deal. The whole system now is designed to make you feel that you are maimed and mutilated forever if something like that happens. She said it made her feel worse.[38]

These remarks suggest to me that Paglia, at some level, understands the way in which rape is supposed to be something "maiming and mutilating," and she is attacking feminist rape counselors of the sort this rape victim encountered for inadvertently affirming that *real* degradation has taken place after a rape. Perhaps in the process of trying to protest the message of degradation implicit in rape, certain feminists start to talk as if the degradation attempted by the rape has actually occurred—insofar as that would make the act of rape all the more terrifying, all the more awful. But Paglia is right, on my view, to protest this way of viewing what rape accomplishes, particularly if a Kantian view of worth is the only sound foundation for understanding wrong. For on any version of the Kantian view, there is *nothing* that someone can do to you that literally lowers or degrades you in value. And it is very important for society to respond to a wrongdoing in a way that affirms this nor-mative fact—both for the sake of the victim's psychological health and for the sake of the rest of society, which one wants to hold a certain view about her value and about human value generally. We do not—and should not—want rape victims, and the larger society generally, going around believing that rape actually succeeds in making rape victims inferior in value or succeeds in transforming them into mere sexual objects. Perhaps Paglia's reluctance in the passage above to see even stranger rape as all that "wrong" is a way of trying to make compelling the idea that there is no way that rape, or any kind of sex, can really lower your value, and no way that you are precluded from recovering from the experience as long as you understand your enduring importance as a person.

Alas, her way of trying to make that point works to destroy the wrongfulness of rape altogether. We need a way of understanding when sex can be wrong, even while holding to the idea that its wrongfulness is never something that can lessen a woman's worth as a person, no matter what her society (or her psychologists) might tell her (or do to her) in the aftermath of the experience.[39] The point of distinguish-ing between diminishment (the mere portrayal of someone as lower) and degrada-tion (the actual lowering of a person's value), then linking wrongdoing only with di-minishment, is that we are able to affirm that the value of the victim always persists after the crime.

If the Kantian view of worth is essential to a sound view of moral wrongfulness, what does Kant himself say about rape and sex in general? Recently, the philoso-pher Barbara Herman has discussed Kant's views, noting that these days most of us will find them highly implausible.[40] Nonetheless, because Kant's remarks engage what I regard as the right theory of wrongfulness, examining them is a way to make progress toward a more successful view.

Consider the following passage from Kant's *Lectures on Ethics*, which Herman cites:

> Taken by itself [sexual love] is a degradation of human nature; for as soon as a per-son becomes an Object of appetite for another, all motives of moral relationship cease to function, because as an Object of appetite for another a person becomes a thing and can be treated and used as such by every one. . . . If then a man wishes to satisfy his desire, and a woman hers, they stimulate each other's desire; their in-clinations meet, but their object is not human nature but sex, and each of them dishonors the human nature of the other. (55)

One of Kant's maxims is "Never treat a person solely as a means," and his argument in this passage is that in a sexual relationship, each person is responding to the other solely as a means to the satisfaction of his or her sexual appetite—and nothing more. Note that Kant's argument applies just as much to homosexual acts as to het-erosexual acts and just as much to men as to women. Kant claims that the only way sex can be morally redeemed is through the legal institution of marriage, which establishes that each person in the marriage has a legal right, analogous to a property right, in the body of the other. The idea seems to be that by owning the other, who in turn owns you, each of you "wins back" your own personhood in a condition of unity with the will of another.[41] Again, note that Kant's argument that legal marriage can redeem sex can be used to provide a foundation for homosexual marriage just as much as for heterosexual marriage, although he could hardly have intended this.

I don't see how Kant's legal remedy can work. The fact that we jointly own one another doesn't seem to remedy what he claims is the fact that in the sexual act each of us is responding to the other as a mere "thing," useful as a tool for the satisfaction of a desire. But more fundamentally, not merely this remedy but also the whole Kantian diagnosis of the problem of sex seems implausible. I shall have a great deal to say on this topic later, but for now I simply want to note that it goes wrong by obliterating the distinction between morally right and morally wrong sex by making all sex (outside of marriage) wrong, for both male and female. While Kant would likely recognize degrees of wrongness, with rape a particularly extreme example of how sex wrongs someone, he nonetheless seems to regard all sex as analogous to rape in the way that it invariably involves the use of another for one's own pleasure. Those of us convinced that there is a difference between morally good and morally bad sex need another way to understand sex so as to make that distinction.

In thinking about this issue, I became intrigued by Andrea Dworkin's view of heterosexual intercourse, which, as Herman notes, has interesting affinities to Kant's view of sex. At times in her discussions, Dworkin suggests Kant's analysis of wrongfulness, for example, when she quotes from Leo Tolstoy's *The Kreutzer Sonata*, in which a man who ultimately killed his wife describes their sexual intercourse:

> Amorousness was exhausted by the satisfaction of sensuality and we were left confronting one another in our true relation . . . as two egotists quite alien to each other who wished to get as much pleasure as possible from each other.[42]

But in the main, Dworkin is inclined to see all heterosexual acts as morally wrong, not because it involves wronging both partners, as Kant argues, but because of what this sort of act does, and says, only about the woman. So unlike Kant, Dworkin does not condemn intercourse insofar as it involves using one's partner (whether male or female) for the mere satisfaction of desire—that makes intercourse seem equal, and for Dworkin, heterosexual intercourse is about destroying the idea that women are the equal of men. It is about establishing women as—indeed, *rendering* them—inferior: "[I]ntercourse distorts and ultimately destroys any potential human equality between men and women by turning women into objects and men into exploiters".[43]

And later she elaborates this idea:

> There is a deep recognition in culture and in experience that intercourse is the normal use of a woman, her human potentiality affirmed by it, and a violative abuse, her privacy irredeemably compromised, her selfhood changed in a way that is irrevocable, unrecoverable. And it is recognized that the use and abuse are not distinct phenomena but somehow a synthesized reality: both are true at the same

time as if they were one harmonious truth instead of mutually exclusive contradictions. . . . By definition, she [has] a lesser privacy, a lesser integrity of the body, a lesser sense of self, since her body can be physically occupied and in the occupation taken over. By definition . . . , this lesser privacy, this lesser integrity, this lesser self, establishes her lesser significance. She is defined by how she is made, that hole, which is synonymous with entry; and intercourse the act fundamental to existence, has consequences to her being that may be intrinsic, not socially imposed.[44]

What I like about these passages is the way that they capture the (Kantian) idea that sex goes wrong insofar as it comes to *mean* something about one's value—in particular, insofar as it is objectifying, a way of saying that a someone is really a something. Dworkin brutally but brilliantly cites literature, myth, and history to establish the extent to which not merely rape but the very act of intercourse has been intended as a means of lowering and rendering inferior any woman subject to it. Even the meaning of the word "vagina" suggests her analysis: It means "sheath," implying that the penis is a sword slicing the woman, destroying her bodily integrity and thereby her sense of her autonomy as an individual.

Moreover, Dworkin argues that men's sexual desire for women has everything to do with the male interest in subordinating them: The very nature of sexual desire, for Dworkin, is intimately connected with seeing, and wanting to confirm, women's status as lower than, and "for," men. To want a woman is therefore to see her as lower, as the subject of male master:

> [E]quality is the antithesis of sensuality when the sensuality is intercourse per se. The woman must be reduced to being this sexual object to be pleasing to men who will then, and only then, want to fuck her; once she is made inferior in this way, she is sensual to men and attracts them to her, and a man's desire for her—to use her—is experienced by him as her power over him.[45]

Note how (remarkably) little distance there is between this passage and the remarks of Camille Paglia that sex is egotistical and dominating—both Paglia and Dworkin see sexual attraction of men to women as bound up with their desire to master the women; the only difference is that what Paglia relishes, Dworkin despises. (One wonders which of them would be the more alarmed by their similar understanding of the nature of eroticism.) Note also that if the pleasure women derive from intercourse is a function of their acceptance of the subordinating message in the act, that pleasure is a by-product of the degradation the act effects. For those of us women committed to opposing such degradation, it would seem that we should give up heterosexual intercourse if, as Dworkin seems to believe, it is true that its pleasure can only be purchased at the price of accepting our own subordination.

Dworkin believes it is intrinsic to the experience of intercourse in any society, at any time, that women will feel inferior and dominated by men. Hence this message of intercourse is for her not something that is a product of a sexist society, although she is a little hesitant on this point—note that when she says that, for a woman, intercourse has "consequences to her being that may be intrinsic, not socially imposed" in the passage cited above, she uses the word "may." Nonetheless, the thrust of the passage is that the metaphysical lowering of women is what intercourse *naturally* brings. And this idea is repeatedly suggested in *Intercourse*, where, at best, Dworkin only raises the possibility that intercourse could exist "without objectification".[46] At one point she asks: "Would intercourse without objectification, if it could exist, be compatible with women's equality—even an expression of it—or would it still be stubbornly antagonistic to it? . . . Can intercourse exist without a woman herself turning herself into a thing, which she must do because men cannot fuck equals and men must fuck: because one price of dominance is that one is impotent in the face of equality?"[47] The reader gets the distinct impression that Dworkin's own answer to these questions is "No."

Note also that on Dworkin's analysis, sex can go wrong even when there is no force—even when there is "consent" of the sort the law would recognize. In a way, consent is irrelevant to the wrongfulness of the experience. Although force will likely make the experience particularly diminishing, force needn't be present in order for the sexual act to go wrong, because the act of penetration itself can be diminishing to the woman. Rape, on this view, is only an extreme example of wrongful sex: It is particularly degrading and particularly destructive of a woman's sense of self and value. But the same destructiveness can be present in sexual intercourse that meets the consent test required by law.

What makes Dworkin's analysis so interesting, in my view, is the way that she deepens the Kantian objection to sex. It is not merely the satisfaction of desire, but what the act of penetration *means* for men and women, that is the basis of the objectification of women. Kant sees sex as demeaning because of the way it treats human beings as instrumentally valuable only by virtue of their body parts; so on Kant's view our humanity is "put aside" when we have sex. But Dworkin sees sex as demeaning for the woman because of the way in which women's humanity is not so much put aside as denied altogether, such that she is literally degraded and transformed into something less than human. For Kant, sex is a kind of interaction that fails to engage the humanity of either party and therefore fails to be a respectful and morally permissible interaction. For Dworkin, sex is an interaction that does not merely fail to engage the woman's humanity, but actively seeks to destroy it.

Before elaborating on the way in which Dworkin's analysis of sexual intercourse goes right, I want to pursue certain important ways in which it goes badly wrong. Consider, first of all, the fact that Dworkin persistently talks as if women are permanently "ruined" by sexual intercourse. In one striking passage, she insists:

> What is lost for the woman when she becomes a sexual object, and when she is confirmed in the status of being fucked, is not recoverable. Just as the man is depraved, that is, an exploiter, so too the woman is depraved, that is, an object.[48]

This point is put even stronger later in the book:

> It is especially in the acceptance of the object status that her humanity is hurt: it is a metaphysical acceptance of lower status in sex and in society; an implicit acceptance of less freedom, less privacy, less integrity. In becoming an object so that he can objectify her so that he can fuck her, she begins a political collaboration with his dominance, and then when he enters her, he confirms for himself and for her what she is: that she is something, not someone; certainly not someone equal.[49]

So in Dworkin's view, either women insist on their bodily integrity and risk being punished for their rebellion against a social system that insists on this act as a way of establishing their inferiority (her discussion of the punishment of Joan of Arc for rebelling in this way is instructive);[50] or they give in and allow themselves to be "fucked" and then they are destroyed as persons — either becoming "mad" (as Sophie Tolstoy was said to have been)[51] or slavish and complicitous in their subordination.

However, there is something horrible and deeply violative of the Kantian view of the permanence of human value implicit in Dworkin's way of understanding victimization. Dworkin is admitting that men actually *win* in patriarchal society, so that women in these societies are *actually* inferior, *actually* slave-like in their natures. Like the sexist men she bitterly attacks, she holds a view of women as beings who are capable of being "broke," capable of being tamed to the mastery of men in such a way that they literally lose their status and value as human beings and are thus no longer the equals of the men who break them.

How different is this from the vision of those who would defend patriarchy? And in particular, how much is Dworkin really disagreeing with the patriarchal view that men are born to mastery and women are born to submission, unable to fight back (either individually or as a group) when men attack? Perhaps the only difference is that Dworkin condemns what her sexist opponents celebrate. Consider the following passage:

> There is the initial complicity, the acts of self-mutilation, self-diminishment, self-reconstruction, until there is no self, only the diminished, mutilated reconstruction. It is all superficial and unimportant, except what it costs the human in her to do it: except for the fact that it is submissive, conforming, giving up an individuality that would withstand object status or defy it. Something happens inside; a human forgets freedom; a human learns obedience; a human, this time a woman, learns how to goose-step the female way.[52]

Sometimes I wonder whether Dworkin's work should be read as lamentations on the success of patriarchy, not only in the oppression it has achieved, but in the way it has remade female nature into something that supports that oppression.

I find Dworkin's view of women not only upsetting but destructive. While it is surely right that sexual intercourse has been used by men to *hurt* women in all kinds of ways, Dworkin turns these harms into real degradations of the spirit. In her world, most women *really are not* the equals of men anymore: indeed, their very humanity is minimal. For how can we respect those women who have become the sort of persons who are goose-stepping, slavish collaborators of their male masters? Like the rape counselors in Paglia's story, Dworkin accepts that rape, and more generally demeaning intercourse, quite literally ruins the women who are victimized by it. But if this is so, then how can any of us treat these ruined women as fully human, or equals of those who have escaped such ruin, much less the equals of men? If their degradation is real, equal respect seems no longer appropriate for them. The best we can do, Dworkin suggests, is to work to save future females from their fate.

In my view, Dworkin's perspective goes badly wrong, mistaking the (very real) social degradation and inferiority that women must endure in a sexist society with their real and equal value as people—a value that is objective and something that society has an obligation to acknowledge, and a value that can never be degraded and that ought always to be acknowledged no matter what wrongs have been inflicted on them. I find Dworkin's way of thinking about what happens to women in wrongful sexual intercourse a way of tearing apart women even further—a feminist betrayal of the idea that, no matter what evil people try to inflict on women, their equal value as human beings endures, so that it never *becomes* right to treat them as inferiors.

Once again, a distinction between degradation and diminishment would make Dworkin's analysis sounder. Dworkin is right, I believe, to the extent that her analysis correctly isolates what intercourse (often) *says*: It conveys the appearance of degradation, which I have called diminishment. But I would submit that we must resist the idea that it succeeds in realizing what it says is the truth—that is, that it succeeds in degrading the individual. Whatever it might accomplish with respect to women's standing and opportunities in a social hierarchy, there is no way, on my view, that it can affect what any woman is owed or what any woman ought to think about herself and her honor as a person. The importance of this point is critical if the demeaning messages communicated to, and about, women are to be fought, and it is critical if feminists want to have a foundation for establishing what the right messages ought to be in sex, or in any other human behavior.

If Dworkin is right that intercourse "says" women are inferior, is she also right that the demeaning nature of intercourse is somehow "natural"—so that no matter what society or background a person is reared in, if she experiences the act of intercourse, she will understand it to communicate and ultimately effect her diminishment?[53] I find this idea hard to accept. On the Gricean analysis of meaning discussed above, the only nonsocially constructed natural sense of meaning is evidentiary, as in "smoke means (is evidence for) fire." And Dworkin does not argue that intercourse provides (natural) evidence of women's inferiority; instead, she sees it as a transformative experience, one that both communicates and effects women's inferiority. So, her analysis really suggests that this event has "word meaning," in the sense that the one who uses it intends it to convey a message and understands himself to be doing so using behavior that is conventionally understood to convey the victim's inferiority. The meaning of the behavior is therefore very much a function of social convention, established by a patriarchal society that controls not only the spoken language but the meaning of certain kinds of behavior, including sexual intercourse. So it cannot be "naturally" true that intercourse "means" bodily "invasion" and the destruction of bodily integrity. Such a meaning is a particular human response to the act, and it is not the only kind of symbolization it could receive.

Still, Dworkin might insist that, even if the meaning of intercourse is a social construction, nonetheless, given human psychology, the kind of degrading meaning that comes to be attached to it is, in some way, "psychologically inevitable" for men and women. Consider the following passage: "Women are unspeakably vulnerable in intercourse because of the nature of the act—entry, penetration, occupation."[54] She also speaks of the "devastating consequences of being powerless and occupied,"[55] suggesting that there is something innately disturbing and violative of bodily integrity about sexual intercourse for women, but not for men, such that it is easily used to convey and effect a degrading message about women's standing.

Dworkin may well be right that for women, the experience is naturally "uncomfortable" in the psychological sense and one that puts them in a psychologically vulnerable position that has moral implications. This is an issue that psychologists should pursue. But even if this is so, this is a long way from having an understanding of the experience as degrading—to have *that* understanding is only possible if one invests the experience with that meaning. And given the way that the meaning of intercourse is subject to social construction, we can hope that even if Dworkin correctly identifies the meaning that intercourse can and often does have in our society now, she is wrong that it *has* to have this demeaning message. And if it can have other meanings, why might it not be possible that in our pluralist society intercourse can have one of these meanings *now*, rather that the diminishing message Dworkin describes?

To pursue this point is to pursue the possibility that heterosexual intercourse is compatible with the equality of men and women. If such sex is possible, then it would seem that it would count as "morally right" sex, in contrast to the demeaning and wrongful sex that Dworkin describes.

But is the idea of "moral sex" worthy of ridicule? Some might claim that to insist that sexuality must affirm the partners' equality is the sort of talk that robs sexuality of its pleasure—a way of insisting that it should be "tame" and passionless.[56] Paglia sneers at the "warm, fuzzy, genteel thinking about sex that has been emanating for twenty years from privileged, white, middle-class feminists,"[57] and complains that in their vision of good sex, "[e]verything is so damn Mary Poppins and sanitized."[58] These remarks suggest that for Paglia and others who share her view of sex, the pleasure that is derived from the domination in sex is also what (in some way) "redeems" that dominating element in the experience. The idea is that both partners want it, even if it is an experience in which he (more or less) subordinates her, because of the pleasure both derive from his mastery—and so we are supposed to think it's okay (maybe not morally okay, but a good thing anyway).

Now if it were true that the pleasure of sex is necessarily connected to its being a dominating experience, then Paglia (and for that matter Dworkin) would be right to dismiss the idea that there could be "moral sex," although Paglia and Dworkin would disagree about whether the pleasure connected to this domination was sufficient to make the experience "okay." (It would surely be relevant to this quarrel that we don't think that if pleasure is involved in other wrongful actions, that pleasure redeems them morally.) But why should we think sexual pleasure has to be connected to domination? Note that the fact that pleasure *might* be connected to domination for *some* sexual partners is not the issue. That doesn't threaten the idea that moral (i.e., nondominating) sex is possible. What threatens its possibility is the claim that the pleasure of *all* heterosexual sex for *all* parties is so intimately connected to its subordination of the woman, that to imagine heterosexual intercourse without subordination is to imagine it without its fun, its "sizzle," its point.

I have a hard time believing this is right. Indeed, even Kant's analysis of sex presupposes that it isn't. Consider that on Kant's view, sexual pleasure *itself* is pure of degradation; the diminishment of sex in his view comes from using the other person to get it. Thus Kant had a sense of the pleasure of sex as separate from any moral consequences of the act—as something desirable and interesting in itself, connected to our biological nature as a species just as surely as the pleasure we derive from eating and sleeping. In this view, sexual desire can be understood as a raw bodily longing, and the pleasure derived in satisfying can be understood as pure of import about value. Such understandings make the desire and the pleasure free of meaning. But once human beings invest meaning in their experiences, responding in a particular way to the desire for and the pleasure of sex, it becomes something we can morally evaluate.

Contrary to Dworkin and Kant, I would suggest that there are all sorts of ways that human beings can invest sex with meaning, depending, in part, on how they are raised, what culture they are reared in, what experiences they have, and what kind of personality they have. Consider Toni Morrison's account in her novel *Sula* of the way in which a young girl named Sula learned to think about sex by watching her mother Hannah's encounters with men:

> Hannah simply refused to live without the attentions of a man, and after Rekus' [her husband's] death had a steady sequence of lovers, mostly the husbands of her friends and neighbors. Her flirting was sweet, low and guileless. Without ever a pat of the hair, a rush to change clothes or a quick application of paint, with no gesture whatsoever, she rippled with sex. . . . Hannah rubbed no edges, made no demands, made the man feel as though he were complete and wonderful just as he was—he didn't need fixing—and so he relaxed and swooned in the Hannah-light that shone on him simply because he was. . . .
>
> [S]ince in that crowded house there were no places for private and spontaneous lovemaking, Hannah would take the man down into the cellar in the summer where it was cool back behind the coal bin and the newspapers, or in the winter they would step into the pantry and stand up against the shelves she had filled with canned goods, or lie on the flour sack just under the rows of tiny green peppers. . . .
>
> Seeing her step so easily into the pantry and emerge looking precisely as she did when she entered, only happier, taught Sula that sex was pleasant and frequent, but otherwise unremarkable. Outside the house, where children giggled about underwear, the message was different. So she watched her mother's face and the face of the men when they opened the pantry door and made up her own mind.[59]

The child's lesson was that sex was enjoyable, easy, natural, unremarkable, something one pursues often for the pleasure of it. There are many other (often darker) messages sent about sex to children in other types of homes. While Dworkin is surely right that one (especially common) message about sex in our sexist society involves the idea of the woman's degradation, that is only one of many ways in which the experience can be given meaning.

If we accept that sexual desire and pleasure can be understood as biological experiences that are meaningful only if human beings invest them with meaning, then is it possible to figure out a way of constructing the experience so as to keep the pleasure, but, contra Dworkin, place it within the context of intercourse between a man and a woman regarding themselves as equals? And contra Kant, can we understand sex as an experience that engages not only the other's bodily organs but also their humanity? (One might worry, for example, that Hannah's and Sula's understanding of sex does not do this sufficiently.) If this is possible, then both Dworkin and Kant would be wrong to say that intercourse cannot be morally redeemed.

Let us begin by answering Kant's worries first. Unlike Dworkin, Kant doesn't make the investment of meaning in the sexual experience something that invariably degrades women; both parties are demeaned by the way they use the other to get pleasure. So note that he does not take the meaning of sex to be connected to its source in the social constructions of a sexist society, but in (what he seems to regard as) the inevitable response human beings have to this bodily experience. But consider that there are a variety of ways in which we do—and need to—"use" other people in order to satisfy our desires: for example, to eat, to find shelter, to perform all sorts of everyday tasks necessary to accomplish in order to assure survival. The Kantian thesis that we should never use someone as a mere means should not be understood to mean that we cannot use human beings as means to satisfy our desires, but rather that we cannot use human beings *solely* as a means to satisfy our desires. And why should sex be an experience in which either partner is used solely as a means? We can certainly imagine that this can happen, but why *must* it happen? Why is it inevitable? Why should the satisfaction of that desire preclude one from behaving respectfully toward the person whose aid is instrumental in our satisfying it? In the satisfaction of every other desire, we can engage the help of human beings to satisfy it, but still receive that help in the context of respecting them as persons. Why is the satisfaction of the sexual appetite any different?

One possible answer Kant might give is this: Personhood is lost in the sexual experience—in two ways. First, whereas what you need to satisfy other desires is some physical object (for example, food items, housing) that the aid of another human being might be necessary to supply, what you need to satisfy the sexual desire is the body part of another human being. Hence the process of satisfying it means responding to a person as valuable only insofar as he/she has body parts which you need. His or her humanity seems irrelevant to your bodily satisfaction. Having sex with another human would appear, for Kant, given these remarks, to be no different *in kind* from having sex with a physical object, although for various reasons it might be perceived as more pleasurable. Second, Kant might believe that your behavior as you satisfy your sexual desire involves no thought or rationality on your part; in the sexual experience you literally lose your mind and thus your nature as a human. It is as if Kant sees human beings who have sex as descending into an animal state and becoming human again only after it is all over.

But is sex just about using body parts to mindlessly "scratch" a certain kind of "sexual itch"? Even if it can be like this, need it be? And even if it can be like this, is such mindless mutual scratching really the essence of what we object to when we consider certain forms of sex, in particular rape, morally wrong? Consider that animals do not "use" one another when they mate; mindless mutual satisfaction of desire in the animal world is not the same as the "using" of another person for one's own gain in the human world. If the idea of "using" people is supposed to be a way of talking about wrongful behavior, then since animals cannot wrong one another, they cannot use one another either.

So it must be that sex goes wrong, in the Kantian view, precisely because human beings *do* have a conception of their partner in the sexual experience that animals do not (and cannot) have. It must be that, in the Kantian view, they see the other as a mere means for achieving their own pleasure—there is a perception of the partner as a tool for pleasure, not as having value in his/her own right. But even if some sex proceeds along these lines, why should we think that *all* sex does so? Consider Hobbes's very un-Kantian view of sex, which understands it as an experience that is, in part, about the *reciprocity* of pleasure-giving:

> The appetite which men call lust, is a sensual pleasure, but not only that; there is in it a delight of the mind: for it consisteth of two appetites together, to please and to be pleased; and the delight men take in delighting, is not sensual, but a pleasure or joy of the mind, consisting in the imagination of the power they have so much to please.[60]

For Hobbes, not only pleasure, but delight, characterizes sex, and that delight is as much about the fact that one has pleased the other as that one has been pleased oneself.[61] While Hobbes would surely admit that such reciprocity is not present all the time, his point, which many of us will find highly plausible, is that it can and often is present, in a way that makes the experience involve more than just a simple physiological experience. And when sex is as much about pleasing another as it is about pleasing oneself, it certainly doesn't involve using another as a means and actually incorporates the idea of respect and concern for the other's needs.

In the end, Kant's analysis not only fails to understand what sex can be like, but also fails to explore or even appreciate the way in which our humanity is deeply engaged in the sexual experience. Sexuality and humanity are deeply entangled, and how "good" one finds sex is in large part a function of the feelings connected to our sense of ourselves as persons that are engaged by the experience. Hobbes's definition of sex only scratches the surface: The range of emotions that sex can produce is very large. One can feel shame and feelings of degradation; elation and feelings of joy; keen affection for the other and a feeling of being loved oneself; or fear or humiliation or depression or even loneliness. But these emotions are elicited not by the sex act itself but by the nature of the relationship that holds between the partners as the sexual act is occurring—it is their relationship as human beings that generates these emotions, and thus, contra Kant, it is the fact that they are relating *as human beings*, rather than as mere objects of sexual satisfaction, that is fundamental to the experience. Indeed, I would argue that one's humanity is perhaps never more engaged than in the sexual act. But it is not only present in the experience; more important, it is "at stake," in the sense that each partner puts him/herself in a position where the behavior of the other can either confirm it or threaten it, celebrate it or abuse it.

If this is right, then I do not see how, for most normal human beings, sexual passion is heightened if one's sexual partner behaves in a way that one finds personally humiliating or that induces in one shame or self-hatred or that makes one feel like a "thing." Whatever sexual passion is, such emotions seem antithetical to it, and such emotions are markers of the disrespect that destroys the morality of the experience. Interestingly, Dworkin's own discussion, drawing from the descriptions of subordinating sex in literature and real life, seems to make that point. She quotes Sophie Tolstoy, used for years by her husband, describing sexual experience as "akin to suffering."[62] She describes Frida Kahlo's paintings as showing "the pain of inferiority delivered into your body—the violence of the contempt."[63] One of the most powerful messages emanating from Dworkin's prose is that sex in which your partner is making you "feel like shit" is not, for most human beings, fun.

Moreover, Dworkin's discussion also shows—in ways that are perhaps even more vivid—the way in which sex, for those who are making their partners "feel like shit," is also joyless. Dworkin quotes Leo Tolstoy as describing sex with his wife as "loathsome" and "a crime,"[64] experiencing it as ultimately deeply violative of *him*.[65] The murderous husband in Tolstoy's *Kreutzer Sonata* describes his first encounter with sex as "pathetic," making him want to "to cry,"[66] and he comes to see sex with his wife as shameful, disgusting, repulsive.[67]

Perhaps we are used to associating the concept of morality with monastic, passion-denying attitudes toward life in general, or with attitudes that are dismissive of the importance of feelings or the satisfaction of appetites, so that a call for "moral sex" seems to be a call for a pale imitation of the experience at its best. But that is not the sense of morality that underlies the analysis of the sexual experience in this chapter; in this view, what makes a sexual event morally right is also what provides the groundwork for the experience of emotions and pleasures that make for "good sex." At the bottom there needs to be—and should be—no opposition between our humanity and our sexual natures.

This thesis applies as much to men as it does to women. There is a good bit of literature suggesting how men can feel wronged through a sexual encounter with a woman. Consider an angry passage in *King Lear*, which some critics suggest was written after Shakespeare learned he had contracted syphilis, in which Lear says of women:

> Down from the waist they are Centaurs,
> Though women all above:
> But to the girdle do the Gods inherit,
> Beneath is all the fiend's: there's hell, there's darkness,
> There is the sulphurous pit—burning, scalding,
> Stench, consumption; fie, fie, fie! pah, pah![68]

Here the vagina is not a sheath to be entered by the male sword, but a consuming, castrating place, which brings about man's destruction. The passage is a counterpoint to Dworkin's stories, suggesting the way in which men can respond to the meaning of a sexual experience as victimizing, in a way that can make it personally awful for them. Presumably that victimization has the same structure that it has for women—it is an experience of being lowered and destroyed, "burned," and "scalded." And as this Shakespearean passage makes strikingly clear, when the sexual experience assumes this form, it becomes not merely wrongful but joyless.

What is sex like when it is joyful—not merely pleasurable but also affirming of the humanity of both parties? In her compelling book *Their Eyes Were Watching God*, Zora Neale Hurston uses an old, tired metaphor in a new way to try to convey how sex can be both affirming and satisfying for both parties. The protagonist of the novel, named Janie, has the following experience while a young girl:

> She was stretched on her back beneath the pear tree soaking in the alto chant of the visiting bees, the gold of the sun and the panting breath of the breeze when the inaudible voice of it all came to her. She saw a dust-bearing bee sink into the sanctum of a bloom; the thousand sister-calyxes arch to meet the love embrace and the ecstatic shiver of the tree from root to tiniest branch creaming in every blossom and frothing with delight. So this was a marriage! She had been summoned to behold a revelation. Then Janie felt a pain remorseless sweet that left her limp and languid.[69]

Hurston goes on to describe Janie's experiences through three marriages, two of which are deeply disappointing and hurtful to her, but the third of which is a *real* marriage, full of "remorseless sweetness" to a man named "Tea Cake" who becomes her deepest friend. Hurston's account of the sex between Janie and Tea Cake reflects her commitment to the possibility of pleasurable and satisfying sexual intercourse that is also morally sound. It is not an experience in which either degrades the other, or in which one becomes the master or conqueror of the other, but an experience between friends, whose sexual encounter affirms, and does not deny, their equal humanity; moreover, to believe, as Hurston does, in the idea of fulfilling and morally sound sex is a way of affirming the idea that women can be sexual beings, without being subordinated beings. Feminists have been accused of having as their ideal the "unsexed woman," but to be committed to the idea that sex need not and should not deny the equal value of both parties is fully compatible with a commitment to female sexual passion and its energetic fulfillment.

However, I see no reason to think that experiencing this kind of "good" sex is easy—nor does Hurston. Janie endures a great deal of bad sex before she discovers how it can be good. Some people, because of their personality or their life experiences, might be convinced that *for them* sex is too dangerous to risk often, or even at all. A woman who has been sexually abused as a child might decide that she is unable to experience sex without responding to it in a degrading way and so gives it up. Oliver Sacks describes a woman who is autistic, and whose inability to relate emotionally to other people has convinced her that, for her own well-being, she should remain celibate.[70] The way in which sex can engage our humanity is so various, and has so much to do with personality, culture, and life experiences, that there cannot be one set of rules about how often, with whom, or how it should occur. As I shall discuss in the next section, this is particularly true in our society, where I believe that a good deal of wariness about sex on the part of women is still warranted, in light of the fact that for many men, sex still remains an act of mastery.

Rape and Date Rape

I want to conclude by reconsidering the moral wrongfulness of rape. How, on this view, should we understand the role of consent in our evaluation of the morality of any particular sexual experience? Many feminists are ambivalent about the extent to which we can rely on consent to "redeem" a sexual act. To quote Susan Estrich:

Many feminists would argue that so long as women are powerless relative to men, viewing a "yes" as a sign of consent is misguided. For myself, I am quite sure that many women who say yes to men they know, whether on dates or on the job, would say no if they could. I have no doubt that women's silence sometimes is not the product of passion and desire but of pressure and fear.[71]

Is this sort of remark implicitly denying the maturity of women or their ability to take responsibility for their action? Is it the sort of attitude that leads to the advocacy of policies or laws that aim to "protect" women who are thought to be vulnerable to wolfish men—policies and laws of just the sort that the feminist movement has tried so hard to overthrow?

Answering such questions requires us to investigate why one should believe that consent is fundamental to making a sexual experience morally permissible. Consider the old maxim of the criminal law that "you can't consent to a crime." Presumably the idea behind the old maxim is that the authority of morality over you is not something you can alienate; so, for example, you can't alienate your right not to be murdered. The law also recognizes that you cannot alienate your right not to be raped, in the sense that consent to a situation in which rape is at risk is not construed by the criminal law as a consent that transforms it into a permissible sexual act. Nonetheless, it is the assumption of the law that you *can't* be raped (by definition) if you have explicitly consented to sex.

But while the law makes consent the marker of the permissibility of sex (and maybe, as I shall discuss later, it must do so in a liberal society), in my analysis one can be deeply and horribly wronged by sexual intercourse regardless of one's initial willingness to engage in it, and its abusiveness can occur in situations where a woman says nothing to protest it as it begins. Indeed, in my analysis, it is possible that you consent to sex, but experience something that is demeaning, damaging to your understanding of your worth as a human being, and an experience that is suffused with emotions that are responsive to the diminishment you feel. The point is this: If the wrongness of the act is a function of its diminishing nature, then that wrongness can be present even if, ex ante, each party consented to the sex. So even if consent is necessary and sufficient for legally permissible sex, consent is *never by itself* that which makes a sexual act morally right. It is at most a necessary condition of the moral rightness of a sexual experience, since consent is necessary in order for the experience to at least begin between regarding one another as autonomous equals. But it is not sufficient for moral rightness. Or, to put it another way, consent is not a decisive marker for a moral relationship in this experience; it is not what transforms rape into lovemaking. Lovemaking is a set of experiences of which consent is a necessary but not sufficient part, which includes attitudes and behaviors that are different in kind from the attitudes and behaviors involved in morally wrongful sex.

One of the reasons I was drawn to write on this topic was that I was convinced it was deeply unfair to charge feminists concerned about date rape with being "puritanical" about sex—that is, of subtly returning to the sort of view of women as in need of protection, a view which the feminist movement has done so much to overthrow. This analysis aims to show precisely in what way these charges are wrong. The traditional view of sex, often referred to—incorrectly—as "puritanical,"[72] and the view that some feminist critics have accused feminists of having, is not one that aims at affirming the equality of women; it is part of a view of sexuality that accepts a double standard for men and women. Men can do what they like but "respectable" women are supposed to keep themselves (or be kept) chaste for their future husband masters.[73] Such a view of sex saw it in terms of subordinating and controlling women, and it was integrated into social practices that expressed and (socially) accomplished this subordination and control.

But overthrowing such constraints on women's sexuality is not the same as overthrowing the attitudes about her subordinate status that sustained these constraints for so long. Even if the idea that women are subordinate is no longer expressed in a system that constrains their sexuality, it can still express itself within the sexual act itself: in the way that the act occurs, in the attitudes expressed, and, in particular, in the way it may involve force and physically harm the woman. Such force, however, while a sufficient condition of the wrongfulness of sex, is not a necessary condition. Diminishment can be expressed in other ways. I would defend feminist warnings to young women about date rape insofar as they are motivated in large part by the realization that the subordination that was part of the point of our past persists in an age of sexual freedom. It hardly strikes me as "hysterical" to note that males reared in a culture that encourages them to think and act in ways that express their superior standing may often engage in sexual behavior in a way that they take to *mean* their superior standing relative to women, making the experience for women (objectively and most likely subjectively) diminishing for them, such that they will find it miserable—perhaps extremely so.

Our sexuality is deeply important to each of us and in certain ways central to our sense of self. To express the subordination of another through the sexual act will therefore likely be wounding to that person in a profound way—not only psychologically but objectively, given the way in which the act will be powerfully expressive of the idea of inferiority. I do not see how it is "puritanical" to be concerned about that wounding, nor how it is "puritanical" to be concerned about the extent to which sexual experience in a variety of contexts in our sexist culture involves and expresses the same diminishment that is central to the experience of (what is generally recognized as) rape.

If this analysis of "morally wrongful sex" is right, it remains, nonetheless, a difficult issue distinguishing when the state should intervene to punish instances of it. It is not an issue that I can pursue here, in part because it involves coming to grips with the kinds of constraints on criminal legislation that many of us, who call ourselves "liberals," must accept in order to ensure a free society. Consider that the diminishment that is a hallmark of wrongful sex comes in degrees and occurs in the most intimate area of our lives. The extreme and unambiguous instances of it, especially those involving force, with an unwilling woman who has explicitly refused to consent to the experience, are obvious candidates for criminal legislation. But our general interest in keeping the state out of intimate affairs, an interest that feminists in particular have reason to take seriously in view of their opposition to laws controlling abortion, can make us leery of involving the state in cases where the diminishing aspects of the sexual experience are less severe or where the messages implicit in the experience are more mixed.

But perhaps the law can attack the subordinating use of sex indirectly, by prohibiting messages in the culture that encourage men to see and use sex as an experience expressive of the diminishment of women. The calls by feminists (such as Dworkin and MacKinnon) for prohibition of certain forms of pornography that are "subordinating" is one form of indirect attack. There may be others (for example, influencing the educational system or changing certain aspects of family law). How well any of these indirect methods of attack can work and how well they fit other aims of the liberal state are contested questions. But my point in this chapter is that it is deeply and importantly wrong to believe that such attacks must be understood as motivated by outdated "puritanical" attitudes, or the denial of women's sexuality, or some sort of retrograde view about the vulnerability of women or the importance of her chastity. I have argued that the wrongfulness such remedies attempt to address is very real, and unless this wrongfulness is addressed, it threatens the values of freedom and equality that are taken to be hallmarks of liberal states such as ours.

Notes

1. See Susan Estrich, *Real Rape* (Cambridge: Harvard University Press, 1987), p. 8.

2. Katie Roiphe, *The Morning After: Sex, Fear, and Feminism on Campus* (Boston: Little, Brown, 1993); Camille Paglia, *Sex, Art, and American Culture: Essays* (New York: Vintage Books, 1992); Jeffrie G. Murphy, "Some Ruminations on Women, Violence, and the Criminal Law," in *In Harm's Way: Essays in Honor of Joel Feinberg*, ed. Jules L. Coleman and Allen Buchanan (Cambridge: Cambridge University Press, 1994).

3. This section is adapted from a portion of my paper "Correcting Harms Versus Righting Wrongs: The Goal of Retribution," *UCLA Law Review* 39 (August 1992):1659–1702.

4. Jules L. Coleman, *Risks and Wrongs* (Cambridge: Cambridge University Press, 1992), p. 324.

5. Ibid., p. 325. Thus Coleman rejects (rightly, in my view) the view of Ernest Weinrib that tort law is concerned with answering the *wrong* rather than the harm. For Weinrib's views, see Ernest J. Weinrib, "Understanding Tort Law," *Valparaiso University Law Review* 23 (Spring 1989):485–526.

6. It is highly problematic whether or not children can be said to "belong" to their parents, such that a harm to the child is also a harm to the parent. In general, I want to avoid here the issues having to do with defining the right concept of ownership for tort purposes.

7. Coleman, *Risks and Wrongs*, p. 325. However, Coleman is prepared to entertain institutional mechanisms for implementing corrective justice that do not require the injurer to repair the loss entirely by himself. See ibid., chap. 18, for a discussion of the way in which corrective justice can be implemented successfully.

8. Thus, like Coleman, I am opposed to Weinrib's view of corrective justice, which sees tort law as concerned with the wrongful action rather than the loss. However, I do think, as I shall explain later in the chapter, sometimes correcting a loss can play a role in annulling the wrongdoing and is therefore a partial response to the wrongdoing.

9. So it is the product of what might be called a "moral agent." I do not have space here to develop a conception of moral agency, which would involve a complicated discussion of

autonomous action. Instead, I will focus on the nature of and conditions for culpability by such an agent.

10. Even if economic analysis of tort law is unpersuasive as an account of the operation of civil courts generally, it is certainly persuasive for some kinds of torts. Calabresi's idea that tort law operates such that people are allowed to perform certain actions on condition that they compensate those they may harm after the fact, if right, would show that some tort remedies are not responses to wrongful actions but are at most a kind of fine, the cost of doing business in a certain way. And Coleman argues that strict liability rules in tort law are actually a part of contract law, specifying the kind of liability that certain firms must undertake in their contractual dealings, and not rules that define, or are responsive to, harms caused by genuinely wrongful (and, in particular, culpable) action by those firms. See Guido Calabresi, *The Costs of Accidents: A Legal and Economic Analysis* (New Haven, CT: Yale University Press, 1970); and Coleman, *Risks and Wrongs*, chap. 18, sec. 5. Clearly, this chapter is interested only in those torts that are the result of wrongful action and hence are the subject of corrective justice.

11. I am only concentrating here on "human" worth to make my explanatory project more tractable. But I believe strongly that a certain kind of worth is possessed by animals, whose denial can also warrant retributive punishment.

12. Thomas Hobbes, *Leviathan: Or the Matter, Forme and Power of a Commonwealth Ecclesiasticall and Civil*, chap. 10, par. 16.

13. The reader may have recognized that a moral theory so conceived is not well described either as consequentialist or as deontological. The advantages of conceiving moral theory apart from these philosophical categories I will discuss in another section.

14. See Jeffrie G. Murphy, "Constitutionalism, Moral Skepticism, and Religious Belief," in *Constitutionalism: The Philosophical Dimension*, ed. Alan S. Rosenbaum (New York: Greenwood Press, 1988), pp. 239–49.

I was struck recently by how many people in American culture accept this view of worth when I read a letter written by parents of children in a Tucson-area elementary school, calling on the school to foster the idea that "all people are equal." In attempting to explain this equality, the authors of the letter noted that although each of us is different, our differences don't affect our equality: Just as 3 + 3 + 1 is different than but equal to 3 + 4, they explained, so, too, are we different than, but equal to, one another.

15. For example, Kant maintains that those who are morally bad can deserve punishment, but he is also well known for insisting that punishment is a way of respecting a person's autonomy and represents neither a violation, nor a suspension, of that autonomy.

16. See David Dolinko, "Some Thoughts About Retributivism," *Ethics* 101 (April 1991): 554. His confusion is betrayed by his use of the phrase "moral value." For Kant, we have value even when we are immoral, insofar as we are ends. Our moral worth is not the same as the value we have intrinsically, on which moral respect is based.

17. See Hampton, "Correcting Harms Versus Righting Wrongs."

18. See Murphy, "Constitutionalism, Moral Skepticism, and Religious Belief."

19. Judith Martin, *Common Courtesy: In Which Miss Manners Solves the Problem that Baffled Mr. Jefferson* (New York: Atheneum, 1985), pp. 14–15.

20. See Paul Grice, "Meaning," in *Studies in the Way of Words* (Cambridge: Harvard University Press, 1989), pp. 213–23. For the idea of using Gricean categories to make clearer my analysis of behavioral meaning, I am indebted to Gary Gleb.

21. I will leave aside here the issue of the source of the value of such objects; perhaps they have value only because human beings value them, or perhaps human beings value them because they have intrinsic value.

22. The story was told by Jones on a Public Broadcasting System television special about the artist, broadcast on 13 February 1992.

23. See Grice, "Meaning."

24. I am indebted to Gary Gleb for the example.

25. See Paul Grice, "Logic and Conversation," in *Studies in the Way of Words* (Cambridge: Harvard University Press, 1989), pp. 22–40.

26. The examples are due to Dolinko, "Some Thoughts About Retributivism."

27. See "Canada Court Says Pornography Harms Women and Can Be Barred," *New York Times*, 28 February 1992.

28. Liberals supportive of free speech are reluctant to grant this fact, fearing that to recognize the wrongfulness of certain forms of expression is prima facie to license their censorship. This is, however, not true; censorship might be precluded by moral concerns more important than the desire to deter the creation of such material, and, in any case, an effective retributive response to such material might be consistent with the permissibility of its publication.

Moreover, those who support the prohibition of such material, whether or not they are right, are nonetheless unwise, in my view, to think that the issue of prohibition turns on whether or not such material causes harmful actions: My point here is that even if it does not, such material is *already morally injurious* because of the fact that it diminishes the value of some human beings.

29. Immorality can also go in the other direction; I have argued elsewhere that there are people who respect themselves too little and others too much. Whether or not a retributive response is appropriate for such people is complicated and an issue I leave for another day.

30. Comment made by Jeffrey T. Sammons, professor of history at New York University and author of *Beyond the Ring: The Role of Boxing in American Society* (Urbana: University of Illinois Press, 1988). Sammons, who was quoted by the *New York Times* immediately following Mike Tyson's conviction for rape in February 1992, was trying to explain how the heavyweight boxer could have come to commit rape.

31. See Ann E. Cudd, "Enforced Pregnancy, Rape, and the Image of Woman," *Philosophical Studies* 60 (September-October 1990):47–59.

32. Cf. Andrea Dworkin, *Intercourse* (New York: Free Press, 1987), p. 45, and, more generally, chap. 3.

33. Paglia, *Sex, Art, and American Culture*, p. 59.

34. Ibid., p. 71.

35. Ibid., p. 57.

36. See Sarah Hrdy, *The Woman That Never Evolved* (Cambridge: Harvard University Press, 1981), p. 18. Hrdy says rape is unknown in all animal species except the orangutan. I assume that by "rape" she means "forced sexual intercourse"; on my analysis of rape, it is the message of domination it conveys (both to the victim and to all women) that makes it a distinctive wrong, and since no animal would seem to be able to engage in sexual behavior in order to *mean* something in this way, no animal could "rape" in the sense that human beings rape.

37. I am indebted to Julia Annas for encouraging me to think about this point.

38. Paglia, *Sex, Art, and American Culture*, pp. 62–63.

39. See Saint Augustine, *City of God*, bk. I (on the rape of the nuns in the sack of Rome).

40. Barbara Herman, "Could It Be Worth Thinking About Kant on Sex and Marriage?," in *A Mind of One's Own: Feminist Essays on Reason and Objectivity*, ed. Louise M. Antony and Charlotte Witt (Boulder, CO: Westview Press, 1993), pp. 49–67.

41. Ibid., pp. 60–61.

42. As quoted by Dworkin, *Intercourse*, p. 13 (from Leo Tolstoy, *The Kreutzer Sonata*, p. 380, in *Great Short Works of Leo Tolstoy*, trans. Louise and Aylmer Maude [New York: Perennial Library, 1967]).

43. Ibid., p. 10.

44. Ibid., pp. 122–23 (quoted in Herman, "Could It Be Worth Thinking About Kant on Sex and Marriage?," p. 56).

45. Ibid., p. 16.

46. Ibid., pp. 140–41.

47. Ibid.

48. Ibid., p. 16.

49. Ibid., pp. 140–41.

50. Ibid., pp. 83–106.

51. Ibid., chap. 1.

52. Ibid., p. 141.

53. See this idea suggested in ibid., pp. 138–42.

54. Ibid., p. 135.

55. Ibid.

56. So Roiphe suggests; see Roiphe, *The Morning After*, p. 60.

57. Paglia, *Sex, Art, and American Culture*, p. 56.

58. Ibid., p. 66.

59. Toni Morrison, *Sula* (New York: Alfred A. Knopf, 1974), pp. 42–44.

60. Thomas Hobbes, *Human Nature*, bk. ix, sec. 10 (quoted by Simon Blackburn under the entry "sex" in his *The Oxford Dictionary of Philosophy* [Oxford: Oxford University Press, 1994], p. 349).

61. Note, however, the vaguely egoistic spin of the last phrase; is Hobbes suggesting that the reason we are pleased at delighting the other is that we are pleased at the fact that we have the power to do so? If so, delight in pleasing another is derivative from pleasure at our own sexual prowess.

62. Dworkin, *Intercourse*, p. 6.

63. Ibid., p. 181.

64. Ibid., p. 7.

65. Ibid., p. 19.

66. Ibid., p. 12.

67. Ibid., p. 13.

68. William Shakespeare, *King Lear*, ed. Kenneth Muir, *The Arden Edition of the Works of William Shakespeare* (London and New York: Methuen, 1972), 166 (act 4, scene 6, lines 123–8).

69. Zora Neale Hurston, *Their Eyes Were Watching God: A Novel*, with a New Fore-

word by Mary Helen Washington (New York: Harper & Row, 1990; first published 1937), pp. 10–11.

70. See Oliver Sacks, "A Neurologist's Notebook: An Anthropologist on Mars," *The New Yorker* 69 (27 December 1993):106. The woman is Temple Grandin.

71. Estrich, *Real Rape*, p. 102.

72. For the real views held by puritans on sex, see, e.g., David Hackett Fischer, *Albion's Seed: Four British Folkways in America* (New York: Oxford University Press, 1989).

73. See, e.g., David Hume, A *Treatise of Human Nature*, bk. III, pt. II, sec. XII ("Of Chastity and Modesty").

PART III

SITUATING RAPE

7

LINDA LEMONCHECK

When Good Sex Turns Bad

Rethinking a Continuum Model of
Sexual Violence Against Women

[I]f one were to see sexual behavior as a continuum with rape at one end and sex liberated from sex-role stereotyping at the other, much of what passes as normal heterosexual intercourse would be seen as close to rape.

Diana E. H. Russell[1]

The point of view of men up to this time, called objective, has been to distinguish sharply between rape on the one hand and intercourse on the other; sexual harassment on the one hand and normal, ordinary sexual initiation on the other . . . [But] [w]hat women experience does not so clearly distinguish the normal, everyday things from those abuses from which they have been defined by distinction . . . What we are saying is that sexuality in exactly these normal forms often *does* violate us.

Catharine A. MacKinnon[2]

It may not be that rape is forced seduction but that seduction is a subtler form of rape.

Stevi Jackson[3]

An important part of radical feminist theorizing situates women's oppression along a continuum of sexual violence and victimization that maps the conceptual and normative connections among a wide variety of ostensibly unrelated types of violence against women. The elucidation of this continuum is meant to expose the normalization of violence in men's sexual behavior toward women by exposing the pervasive, systemic, and misogynistic nature of men's social control of women through sex. Whether heterosexual seduction, harassment, or rape, men's relationships with women situated on this continuum exemplify the sexual assault on, and control of, women that many radical feminists believe is at the heart of the institutionalized male dominance referred to as patriarchy.[4]

Feminists from a wide range of ideological perspectives have criticized this radical view for its reification of precisely the heterosexual stereotypes of women, men, and sex that radical feminists, among others, have long regarded as antithetical to women's sexual liberation. Critics charge, for example, that understanding sexual violence based on a continuum model reduces all heterosexual sex to sexual exploitation and abuse differentiated only by degrees of harm; and the model defines all men as sexual predators whose victims are vulnerable and sexually naive women unaware of the daily assaults they endure. It has been suggested that a continuum model blurs the distinctions among drastically different types of sexual offense so as to trivialize rape, equate a psychologically battered woman with a momentarily offended one, and turn a clumsy sexual overture into a criminal violation. Critics also contend that surveys used by feminists to affirm the accuracy of a continuum model are biased in their data collection and evaluation in order to "prove" the model's truth. Perhaps the most disturbing criticism asserts that by describing women's consent to sex as essentially coercive and coopted, a continuum model denies women's capacity for sexual agency and political resistance. In short, from this critical perspective, a radical continuum model fails the cause of women's sexual liberation by being antisex; condemns feminism's pursuit of gender equality by being antimale; and remains uncompromisingly deterministic in its victimizing and patronizing attitudes toward women.[5]

Such divisiveness among feminists has prompted those critical of feminism as a whole to castigate the movement as a disorganized and fragmented band of political extremists whose sympathies are appropriately rejected by contemporary women. I want to develop a new model for understanding sexual violence against women that can negotiate the tensions among a wide variety of feminists, thereby facilitating a continuing dialog on women, men, and sex. Such a model will be constructed in ways that can expose the pervasive and systemic character of men's sexual violence against women without implying, or appearing to imply, that women are the perpetual victims of male sexual abuse. To this end, the model will be located within a larger philosophical framework for thinking and talking about women's sexuality, which recognizes both women's sexual oppression under patriarchy and women's capacity to resist and transcend that oppression.[6] Moreover, this model will reflect the culturally located and context-specific expression of particular acts of violence against women. In this way, the new model addresses both the personal injury to individual women and the social injustice to women as a class that such violence represents. This approach can then assist further discussion of individual responsibility, political resistance, and legal reform.

In order to justify this new model, some preliminary discussion is in order. In the section immediately following, I elucidate why a continuum model for understanding men's sexual violence against women might be considered by feminists to be an illustrative and strategic framework for understanding (1) the specific character of men's sexual violence against women and (2) the more general character of men's sexual behavior toward women. In the subsequent section, I outline some of the major criticisms lodged by other feminists against the radical view of sexual violence represented by a continuum. In doing so, I set the stage in the next section for showing how the model facilitates feminist criticism by its form and content. However, I also suggest that feminist critics make their own presumptions about women, men, and sex that give less credence to their complaints against a more radical reading of sexual violence against women. I offer my own criticisms of a continuum model in this section as an immediate preface to the introduction of a new model of culturally specific, overlapping conceptual and normative frames of sexual violation.[7] In the final section, I outline this alternative for understanding and combating men's sexual violence against women, which I believe retains many of the elements regarded as crucial to a radical understanding of sexual violence, but obviates many of the criticisms or misreadings I have enumerated. I argue that this new model for theorizing sexual violence against women can negotiate the tensions among a wide variety of feminists by providing a philosophical framework for conceptualizing women and men as culturally diverse sexual subjects within the objectifying constraints of patriarchal institutions and ideology.

Why a Continuum Model of Sexual Violence?

Proponents of a continuum model of sexual violence against women regard its structure as critical to its strategic function as a consciousness-raising tool for women's prevention of, and resistance to, men's violence against them. Feminists invoke this model in order to show that otherwise disparate sexual offenses ranging from wolf whistles to sexual battering to rape are not the random, isolated, or capricious acts of an abnormal male—the result of private demons or sexual misfits—but part of an institutionalized and pervasive system of social control that normalizes men's sexual violence against women. This seamless social structure represents what has often been referred to as a "rape culture," in which violence, sexuality, and gender combine to form social relations defined, not by aberrant psychopathology, but by class-based social injustice. A continuum model exposes men's sexual violence against women as a crime against women because they are women—what Lois Copeland and Leslie Wolfe have called a bias motivated hate crime specific to gender. From this point of view, victims of men's sexual violence become interchangeable and appropriable sexual commodities whose risk factor is being female.[8] Women learn that public space is alien, occupied, and dangerous to them, because all men are potential predators. This discourages women's social activity and encourages their isolation to a domesticity whose violence is legitimized behind closed doors. In a society that rewards men's assertiveness, self-confidence, and risk-taking, women's sense of freedom and security in either public or private life is effectively thwarted.[9]

Gendering men's violence toward women politicizes, and therefore publicizes, otherwise private acts of sexual violence between husband and wife or boyfriend and girlfriend. Proponents of a continuum model contend that it also exposes the elements of hostility, dominance, and control in acts many regard solely as crimes of uncontrollable lust. Mapping the politics of sexual violence onto a continuum exposes the social construction of the violence, so that what might be regarded as a "boys will be boys" biological inevitability is seen as a cultural contingency that can and must be changed. Claudia Card notes that this is not equivalent to saying that men who terrorize women gather in smoke-filled rooms in patriarchal conspiracy, but rather it describes individual men acting out of common interests whose collective actualization is the social control of women. A continuum model also reiterates the contention of Susan Brownmiller, Marilyn French, and others that despite the fact that not all men rape, the knowledge that some men rape suffices to threaten all women. Larry May and Robert Strikwerda have suggested that while not all men are sexual predators, all men are responsible for the prevalence of rape by participating in institutions and acting in accordance with sexual ideologies that encourage sexual violence against women.[10]

The structure of a continuum model allows feminists to mark degrees of severity of sexual violence by type: Seduction is less egregious than unwanted touching, which is less egregious than sexual battery, which is less egregious than rape. As Lois Pineau points out, because male aggression and female reluctance are both common and expected features of sexual seduction, a woman's reticence, protest, and even vigorous resistance can all be consistent with her consent to sex. Men leer, gape, whistle, chase, press, persist, and exhaust, all in the name of "normal" flirtation and seduction; but if the heterosexual norm recommends that men press and women submit, men's intimidation, dominance, and control of women will define not only what is common and expected in sex, but what is valuable about it. Moreover, when rape, sexual abuse, or spousal battery can involve a woman's (or girl's) sexual acquiescence out of fear, guilt, disgust, ambivalence, anxiety, obligation, or even love, and the very same types of acquiescence are common to so-called normal sex, then violent sex begins to resemble the purportedly more respectful variety. Catharine MacKinnon observes, "I think it's fairly common, and is increasingly known to be common, for men to seek sexual access to women in ways that we find coercive and unwanted. On those occasions the amount and kind of force are only matters of degree."[11] By exposing the politics of gender implicit in heterosexuality under patriarchy, a continuum model is designed to show how consent to sex, including knowledge of, and access to, real alternatives, is problematic under conditions of inequality.[12]

This description may at first appear too radical for many feminists who invoke a continuum model to explain sexual violence against women, since proponents like Robin Warshaw and Tim Beneke refer to a continuum more narrowly by linking "merely" offensive sexual behavior (like catcalls) with outright physical assault (like rape). Such a continuum does not refer explicitly to the gender politics of consent in more traditional sexual relationships. Indeed, consensual sex falls outside the narrower model as inoffensive and unobjectionable from a feminist point of view. Nevertheless, this continuum is designed to expose the pervasiveness and normalization of nonconsensual sex.[13] Other feminists, like Diana Russell and Catharine MacKinnon, are specifically interested in a continuum of sexual violence designed to show the linkages of the above model *and* to show how the elements of sexual violence referred to by sociologists and mental health professionals—status, hostility, dominance, control, and coercion—are consistent with, if not foundational to, the concept of "normal" heterosexual sex.[14] However, the latter model is meant to be a seamless extension of the former, a continuum of a continuum of sexual violence as it were, since both models are intended to express the proposition, in the words of Anne Edwards, "that violence and sexuality are socially constructed in ways that

serve the interests of male dominance."[15] Indeed, once the narrower model describes conditions of gender inequality from a radical perspective, any consent to
sex consistent with this model is not prima facie free and informed but prima facie
manipulated, pressured, or forced sex; that is, sex somewhere locatable on the narrower model. So while the more comprehensive model of sexual violence may appear to be more radical than its narrower counterpart, both models have come
under the same critical scrutiny, because both indict what many people think of as
acceptable, or at least, tolerable male sexual behavior and both see sexual violence
as gendered, pervasive, institutionalized, and normalized under patriarchy.

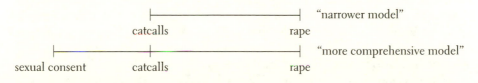

A continuum model is specifically structured to reveal conceptual and normative similarities among ostensibly different types of sexual offense, so that the pervasiveness of men's sexual violence against women is beyond doubt. The leering of an
ill-mannered waiter, the unwanted touching by a presumptuous employer, the in-
cestuous abuse by a domineering stepfather, or a boyfriend's date rape are all considered intrusive and manipulative appropriations of a woman's sexuality. Her sense
of violation, terrorization, exploitation, and dehumanization can thus be mapped
onto a continuum model as pervading the sexual victimization she experiences.[16]
Individual violations are also described as overlapping one another, as when the coercive threats of quid pro quo sexual harassment constitute what some victims refer
to as a "little rape," when rape is accompanied by sexual battery, or when harassing
language presages sexual abuse. Proponents of the model argue that sexual stereotypes of a woman as seductress, liar, and bitch permeate individual and institutional
attitudes about sexual violence toward women across the continuum. From sexual
ogling to rape, women are mythologized as provoking sex they secretly desire by
their dress, speech, or manner; yet these same women must purportedly preserve
their sexual "reputations" and so cannot admit to enjoying sex. Thus, women are
thought to put up a false fight, only pretending not to want the sex that inspires
men's uncontrollable desire. The stereotypical image of women as mendacious,
vindictive, and spiteful when they do not get what they want is especially damaging
to women's attempts to seek arrest and prosecution of perpetrators in a court of
law.[17]

Indeed, the accumulation of research by feminists like Linda Bird Francke,
Billie Dziech, Rosemarie Tong and others suggests that the institutionalization of
sexual violence against women repeats itself across the continuum: in the military,
where male officers exploit the credibility of their rank and gender to threaten female recruits with reprisal if they report their rape; in the economy, where breaking
a glass ceiling on wages or promotions may require suffering a male coworker's harassment; in academia, where student complainants go before sexual harassment
review boards whose members are colleagues of the accused, and where board
members' concerns for their campuses' reputations can hinder investigations; in

the law, where, despite recent changes in evidentiary and procedural rules that keep the focus on the defendant's conduct, investigating officers of the court may decide not to file charges if they believe that the victim is not sufficiently convincing; in the media, where feminists have charged that sexual violence against women is distorted by news organizations and endorsed by the entertainment industry; in the domestic sphere, where moral conservatives promote the maintenance of the two-parent patriarchal family without questioning whether male-dominated family hierarchies encourage the abuse of wives and daughters; and in a set of gender expectations that recommend women's deference to, nurturance of, and ultimate dependence on men.[18] Proponents of a continuum model point out that men who rape are no more abnormal or pathologically criminal than coworkers who doggedly press their colleagues for dates or fraternity brothers wanting to catch a glimpse of a sorority's new members' "tits and ass." Proponents also note that both victims and perpetrators are diverse in age, class, ethnicity, sexual orientation, and relationship to each other. Thus, it is argued that a continuum model can reinforce the fact that sexual violence is an entrenched part of the fabric of social life, that millions of women from different backgrounds are the daily victims of sexual violence and victimization, and that perpetrators are everywhere and invisible precisely because they are "normal."[19]

Women's reactions to men's sexual violence against them are also common across a continuum. Women who are harassed, battered, or raped can all suffer physical ailments such as nausea, sleep and eating disorders, and sexual dysfunction; posttraumatic stress disorder, including nightmares, depression, and paranoia; feelings of fear, anger, helplessness, vulnerability, guilt, self-blame, anxiety, low self-esteem, and a deep suspicion of men and sex, which only feeds the sexual myths about women cited above.[20] Failures to report the victimization women suffer commonly stem from fear of reprisal, fear of not being believed, shame at publicizing a sexual violation; ignoring, denying, or misunderstanding what is happening to them; or finding no institutional support for their complaints. Indeed, it is pointed out that the collection of U.S. crime statistics has only recently been improved to reflect instances of domestic violence other than homicide or multiple incidents by the same perpetrator.[21]

Proponents of a continuum model claim that the normalization of sexual violence, reinforced by its institutionalization, breeds the kind of invisibility and inevitability that inhibits women's resistance to the victimization they experience. Therefore, it is argued that a continuum model exposing the patriarchal bases of sexual violence is vital to the feminist organization and implementation of political change in individuals and institutions. Feminist researchers like Mary Koss contend that a continuum model encourages women to recognize and name the violence they experience and decreases the tendency in women to blame themselves for what has happened to them or to see themselves as alone in their suffering. This in turn produces better reporting and more accurate surveys on the types and incidence of violence, which increases public awareness of the many and varied sexual offenses perpetrated against women by men.[22] Feminists also argue that a continuum model can be used to show that institutionalized violence requires institutionalized reform, so that the rules and regulations that govern social life do not continue to legitimize violence against women. Thus, reform should not be limited to improved psychological counseling for women, but should require that educational, economic, military, and legal institutions, among others, examine how their traditions and bureaucracies support women's intimidation and abuse. Reforms would also include the kinds of support services for victims that would make women more economically and socially self-sufficient, so they are less vulnerable to male violence and male dependency. These services would offer better child care and health care for women and their families and improved access to affordable housing, education, and job training.[23] Feminizing such reforms would also require looking more closely at how stricter laws or stiffer penalties for perpetrators do not speak to the deeper problem of how female passivity and male dominance are encouraged by the gender expectations and sexual stereotypes of patriarchal culture. In this way, it is hoped that a continuum model may help both women and men appreciate how the demands of so-called normal heterosexual behavior threaten positive and pleasurable human relationships; thus, proponents argue that the model can encourage a cooperative effort among women and men to forge new links between sexuality, gender, and power.[24]

Opening the Door to Feminist Critics

> In the current feminist promotion of victim mythology, there is never anything "right" about sex.
>
> Rene Denfeld[25]

> The pivotal issue here is consent, and whether "real" consent is ever possible in patriarchal society.
>
> Margaret Hunt[26]

> What if sexual violence were argued to signify the limits of patriarchy, rather than to represent its totalizing authority or power over women as a system?
>
> Renee Heberle[27]

Many feminists have been openly critical of a continuum model of sexual violence against women for being antithetical to the cause of women's sexual liberation. Such critics variously argue that such a model mistakes the nature, misplaces the causes, and overestimates the extent of sexual violence against women; thus, the model misinforms at best and victimizes at worst, by bashing men and trashing sex with patronizing expressions of what women ought to think and do about their sexual lives. Critics contend that the result is an egregious overdetermination or "essentializing" of women, men, and sex:[28] If (1) all men are sexual predators, then (2) no sex is good for women, (3) any woman who thinks otherwise is suffering from false (patriarchal) consciousness, and (4) all women are victims, multiple victims, or soon-to-be victims, of male sexual violence. Such criticisms come from a surprising variety of feminist ideological perspectives despite the overlap in their complaints. I have grouped the critics into three general categories of "quasi-liberal," "sex radical," and "postmodern" feminists in order to consolidate discussion and isolate the unique character of each perspective.

Quasi-liberal feminists cover a wide range of political affinities, all affirming the necessity for gender equality under the law: moderate liberals or neo-liberals like Katie Roiphe, Rene Denfeld, and Christina Sommers, as well as self-described libertarians like Camille Paglia, have more conservative views than their radical sisters about the institutionalization and pervasiveness of men's sexual violence against women; while progressive liberals like Naomi Wolf share the radical view of a wide-ranging and systemic patriarchy but join more conservative feminists in charging that a continuum model characterizes women as incapable of overcoming their victimization by men. All such feminists share a common concern that a continuum model gives patriarchy a virtual lock on women and sex, thereby underestimating women's political, social, and sexual power to combat men's sexual violence against them.[29]

Katie Roiphe, Rene Denfeld, and Christina Sommers each express the view that a continuum model of sexual violence against women is fatalistic and overly pessimistic about women's sexual abuse at the hands of men. Roiphe contends that a continuum model encourages Take Back the Night marches, sexual harassment speak-outs, and campus rape brochures that celebrate an identity politics of victimization, engender false accusations by elevating the role of victim, and exaggerate the incidence of actual assault. All three critics believe that such exaggeration trivializes rape, making public support for, and credibility of, victims more difficult. As Roiphe remarks, "If we refer to a spectrum of behavior from emotional pressure to sexual harassment as rape, then the idea itself gets diluted."[30] Denfeld believes that a continuum model perpetuates a repressive antisex morality in which intercourse is painful and women are its reluctant participants. Moreover, Denfeld contends the model creates a "victim mythology" that paradoxically sells women's fear, passivity, and resignation, in tandem with relentless male-bashing.[31] Roiphe, too, wonders aloud at what she calls Andrea Dworkin's "vampire model" of male sexuality, in which Dworkin uncompromisingly states, "The annihilation of a woman's personality, individuality, will, character, is prerequisite to male sexuality." When Susan Brownmiller describes rape as something that defines relations between men and women, and Catharine MacKinnon observes that reports of rape and reports of normal sex "sound a lot alike," quasi-liberal feminists cringe.[32]

All three critics argue that such language is the rule and not the exception, when feminists believe rape has been "normalized" under patriarchy and sexual harassment is an everyday experience. It is charged that such beliefs invite a host of falsehoods: all heterosexual sex is rape; rape is no more than regrettable sex; uncoerced, consensual heterosexual sex is impossible; (therefore) any pleasurable sex women want with men is out of the question.[33] Moreover, Roiphe, Denfeld, and Sommers contend that, in a continuum model, women are also being sold a lack of self-confidence: Women are told that they cannot tell the difference between violent and pleasurable sex, having been socialized by a patriarchal ideology to believe that coercive and abusive sex is normal sex; however, this implies that women's first-person sexual experience is not to be trusted, so that the very experience women are supposed to "take back" from patriarchy is based on an irretrievably inauthentic or "false" consciousness.[34]

Such interpretations of women's sexual experience prompt all three critics to be suspicious of surveys by feminist researchers that purport to show the pervasiveness of men's sexual violence against women. Sommers argues that proponents of a continuum model conduct biased and unfounded "advocacy research" in the ways they word their questions, choose their respondents, and interpret their data, so that their surveys reflect information that would confirm their radical views. If an unwanted hug counts as an assault; if the population surveyed is small or self-selected; or if a rape is recorded despite the fact that the respondent did not believe she was raped, all three feminists contend that a continuum model is not, and cannot be, supported by the data collected.[35]

While Camille Paglia would agree with the charge that a continuum model inappropriately expands what counts as sexual violence against women, she differs from other quasi-liberal feminists in insisting that men are indeed sexual predators driven to prey on women by the compelling forces of biology. As Paglia contends, "Sex crime means back to nature."[36] Despite such forces, however, Paglia argues that women must take responsibility for bringing men to heel and men must take responsibility for learning how to behave. She objects to a continuum model that turns women into sexual naïfs, fragile flowers, or passive victims who are fearful, if not ignorant, of their own sexual power to tease, flirt, provoke, and ultimately seduce men. Paglia contends that men's fear and envy of this power combined with men's natural aggression results in their sexual abuse and exploitation of women. Thus, sexual violence against women is not a patriarchal social construction but a fact of life about two sexes "at war."[37] If women are to win any battles in this war, however, Paglia believes they must stop putting themselves in situations (like fraternity boys' bedrooms) where men can easily gain the upper hand; and women must start telling offensive men to back off instead of voicing weak-kneed whines about sexual harassment. Moreover, Paglia complains that the radical view on which a continuum model rests refuses to acknowledge that battered women "are exerting their own form of aggression" by manipulating their partners' feelings; and she observes that some women enjoy violent heterosexual sex, to which they freely consent as part of their autonomous pursuit of sexual pleasure.[38]

Naomi Wolf agrees with Sommers, Denfeld, and Roiphe that sexual violence against women produces a psychology of victimization that must be overcome but disagrees that the pervasiveness of such victimization is a fantasy to be debunked. Thus, she chastises fellow critic Roiphe for denying the epidemic proportions of sexual violence against women and for ignoring "the real differences in power that do exist between men and women."[39] Yet she agrees with Roiphe that feminists tend to publicize sexual violence against women in ways that are reactive and counterproductive. What Wolf fears are feminist theoretical models, of which she believes a continuum model is one, that mold women's victimization by men into an immutable identity, referred to by Wolf as "victim feminism." She wants women and men "to look clearly at the epidemic of crimes against women without building a too-schematic world view upon it." Wolf calls for "a [new] vocabulary for the relative nature of harm"[40] that would recognize the variability in men's sexual power and women's sexual vulnerability. Wolf's position means holding men accountable for their abuses without reducing all men to sexual predators; and she rejects any model that does not allow women to embrace lust—the sexual desire to take and be taken—without being able to resist rape. Wolf prefers what she calls "power feminism" in which women recognize, feel pride in, and take advantage of the power they do possess—as voters, consumers, income producers, networkers, grassroots organizers, protesters—to create even stronger financial and political power bases for themselves and each other. However, according to Wolf, when the victim feminism of a continuum model constructs power as inherently patriarchal, women will refrain from nurturing their own will to power.[41]

Sex radical feminists have not attacked a continuum model of sexual violence directly as much as they have challenged the patriarchal appropriation of dominant and submissive sexual roles that the model represents. From this point of view, a continuum model fails to afford women the sexual exploration, pleasure, and agency with which to transcend sexual violence against them, but not because, echoing a quasi-liberal complaint, the model repudiates noncoercive, traditional heterosexual sex. From a sex radical perspective, the model fails because it does not countenance women's consensual, self-conscious adoption of power-polarizing sexual or gender roles. These include the dominant and submissive sexual roles played in consensual lesbian sadomasochism (s/m) or butch-femme sex or the masculine personae taken up by transgendered females or female-to-male transsexuals.[42]

For example, Pat Califia calls on other radical feminists to regard consensual lesbian s/m as parody, catharsis, an erotic play at dominance and submission, an attempt to reconceptualize and recapture power in sex *for women*. Thus, Califia believes that lesbian s/m is poised to subvert patriarchal victimization of women, not reinstantiate it. Califia argues that even the most charitable reading of consent under a continuum model has so condemned sexual dominance and vulgarized masculinity that no power-polarizing or gender-bending roles for women are acceptable. According to such a model, s/m becomes confused with rape and other forms of sexual assault and reconfirms the mistaken but widespread belief that women, particularly "bottoms" who practice the "m" in lesbian s/m, are sexual masochists who secretly want to be raped. On the contrary, Califia and other sex radical feminists contend that by parodying male authority in mutually caring and careful erotic ways, lesbian s/m exposes the sexual nature of power and the possibility of power unconnected to male privilege.[43]

Califia is joined by Joan Nestle, Amber Hollibaugh, Cherríe Moraga, and others who challenge other radical feminists to rethink the strict dichotomy of gender that a continuum model represents. Sex radical feminists argue that like lesbian s/m, butch-femme sexual role playing may appear to do no more than recreate patriarchal stereotypes; but, unlike more traditional sex, butch-femme sex can parody, selectively appropriate, and subvert otherwise confining sexual stereotypes, thereby attaining meaningful, creative, and mutually satisfying sex. From this point of view, femmes are sexual agents who produce their own woman-identified version of femininity; and as Gayle Rubin points out, "[W]hen women appropriate masculine [butch] styles the element of travesty produces new significance and meaning."[44] Transgendered females or female-to-male transsexuals are similarly situated to demonstrate a self-conscious (re)construction of gender, not its incontestable biological imperative. But with the spectrum of acceptable sex and gender roles so narrow, sex radicals believe proponents of a continuum model advocate a politically correct sexuality that effectively inhibits women's sexual agency and self-definition. Amber Hollibaugh sums up the complaints of sex radical critics when she remarks, "I don't want to live outside of power in my sexuality, but I don't want to be trapped into a heterosexist concept of power either. But what I feel feminism asks of me is to throw the baby out with the bathwater."[45]

Like their sex radical counterparts, *postmodern feminist* critics acknowledge the existence of a pervasive and systemic patriarchy; and along with their quasi-liberal sisters, postmodern critics believe that a continuum model of sexual violence against women describes an identity politics of victimization that is detrimental to women's sexual liberation. But as postmodern feminists, such critics believe that the alternative is to provide women with a discursive model of sexual violence that encourages women to rewrite the narrative text of their sexual experience. From this view, by (re)describing their sexual lives in terms of agency instead of victimization, women can begin to deconstruct the patriarchal opposition of male aggressor/female victim that the language of a continuum model endorses.[46]

For example, Renee Heberle recommends that feminists aim for a "self-consciously performative and deconstructive approach to the political project of representing the experience of sexual violence."[47] Heberle notes that when men's sexual violence against women is represented in feminist discourse as a monolith of patriarchal dominance and control, attempting to break the cycle of sexual violence can only be understood in terms of rarity, desperation, and irrationality. However, when feminist narratives of sexual violence are read in terms of male fragility and patriarchal instability, women's resistance to the abuse they suffer is conceived as reasonable, possible, and necessary. Thus, Heberle believes that feminists should conceive of sexual violence as a trope for the fragmentation and destabilization of patriarchy, not its hegemonic power. In order to produce such a narrative, Heberle, like Katie Roiphe, would stress survival and prevention strategies like self-defense classes or alternative housing, as opposed to Take Back the Night marches or psychological counseling that tends to dwell on women's experience of victimization. Unlike traditional liberals, however, a postmodern feminist such as Heberle is suspicious of institutionally based forms of resistance, as she believes these rely too heavily on the prevailing phallogocentric discourse to be successful.[48]

Sharon Marcus also contends that the radical view represented by a continuum model describes sexual violence as an inevitable outcome of gender and not the socially constructed performance of it. Marcus contends that the purportedly linear progression of a continuum model is actually a fixed point in disguise, collapsing crude remarks and lewd gestures with rape. She argues that such a fixed point on which to locate sexual violence collapses the space and time in which women might prevent the violence directed against them. In such a model, women are "either already raped or already rapable."[49] Marcus disputes the claim by proponents of a continuum that women will be better able to resist abuse simply by identifying its incidence and perpetrators. According to Marcus, effective resistance to an experience like rape requires the production of a discourse describing prevention and sabotage whose text is a rescripting of patriarchal rape narratives. Such narratives are written by men but can be rewritten by women "to revise the grammar of violence," so that rape will be conceived as preventable, intervenable, and resistible. Marcus agrees with Heberle that a police or legal forum is not conducive for such rewriting, since such institutions have the patriarchal capacity "to exclude certain interpretations and perspectives and to privilege others."[50] Marcus wishes to focus on actual rape situations and individual rape prevention, scripting the female subject as "wounded inner space" instead of a violable and appropriable sexual object.[51]

The Need for Cultural Specificity and Moral Pluralism

While quasi-liberal, sex radical, and postmodern feminists have various complaints about the ways in which women's sexual oppression is characterized by a continuum model, they tend to underestimate how their own perspectives may essentialize women, men, and sex in ways antithetical to women's sexual liberation. Quasi-liberals, sex radicals, and postmodern feminists all talk about (re)empowering women by (re)naming and (re)claiming their own social, political, and sexual power; but this conversation often fails to consider that many women, particularly women of color and poor women of all colors, feel the real effects of cultural prejudice that preclude their participation in resisting men's sexual violence against themselves and other women. Quasi-liberals' demands for changes in legal institutions require the time, effort, and political savvy that women struggling to feed their families often lack. Moreover, entrenched institutional prejudices like racism or sexism tend to resist legal reform in the absence of a radical understanding of such prejudices' structure and function. Camille Paglia's ascription to battered women of personal responsibility for their abuse will ring a false note to poor women who have filed legal restraining orders and sought the safety of battered women's shelters, only to be stalked by their batterers when they leave. Moreover, Paglia's claims that "[w]omen will always be in sexual danger" and that the sexual impulse is "egotistical and dominating" sound no less continuum-based (and no less deterministic) than her radical counterparts.[52] Sex radicals' attempts to subvert patriarchal power through its erotic parody will seem disingenuous to lesbians of more conservative sexual tastes who must confront the daily harassment of their students, colleagues, or coworkers. Many heterosexual women will wonder why they should take up sex with other women that appears to be neither egalitarian nor erotic. Some black feminists have also looked with suspicion at white lesbians' eroticization of the roles of master and slave, questioning the politics of deriving pleasure from such repressive and colonizing symbols.[53] Postmodern feminists' call for the ex post facto rescripting of rape narratives requires that women exercise the kind of discursive power that can alter patriarchal texts. However, textual rereadings will not change how rape victims feel when they have no experience of themselves as vocal, articulate, or credible; nor does rescripting the event change the horror of what has happened. Moreover, creating new narratives of prevention and resistance will not translate into successful resisting, unless an entrenched phallogocentric culture can be made to accept, not just understand, a politically subversive language for thinking and talking about sexual violence against women.[54]

My own criticism of a continuum model reflects a desire to theorize sexual violence against women with a cultural specificity and moral pluralism that speaks to the sexual experiences of a wide variety of women. The continuum model under discussion represents a linear progression of degrees of severity of sexual violence by type: Consensual sex is less violent than sexual harassment, which is less violent than rape. Proponents of this model contend that a continuum is needed to expose the oppressively patriarchal character of violence against women, since so many women experience sexual violence against them as normal, if not unobjectionable. However, precisely because this model acts as a prescriptive, consciousness-raising tool, tokens of each type, that is, particular first-person accounts by women of sexual violence against them, are not individuated on the continuum. The model is not designed to *describe* what individual women experience—much of this would not show up on a continuum as "violence"—but rather to *prescribe* how women *should* think about the sexual violence against them. Consequently, the model begs the question of the pervasiveness of sexual violence against women by constructing a model that assumes it. A linear or progressive model moving from less- to more-severe types of violence cannot be used to describe what *different* women experience in any case, since such descriptions would overlap as well as contradict one another in nonlinear fashion. Moreover, a continuum model does not demarcate personal injuries done to individual women, precisely because it is designed to represent a type of social injustice done to women as a class.

In short, a continuum model can expose neither the pervasiveness nor the institutionalization of sexual violence against women, because it is a continuum that presupposes linkages between types of sexual violence without demarcating their actual incidence. Thus, ironically, the model cannot be used to show the normalization of sexual violence against women and so is self-defeating as a consciousness-raising tool. Moreover, the model's lack of representation of women's first-person experiences of sexual violence creates problems for a multicultural feminism interested in representing women's individual experiences of sexual violence differentiated by ethnicity, class, sexual orientation, age, nationality, religion, physical ability, and so on. Kimberlè Crenshaw, Valerie Smith, and others have pointed out that different women's multiple and overlapping oppressions give the sexual violence they experience a unique and complex character that is not reducible to gender politics alone.[55] Even if all women's cultural backgrounds were the same, their experience of sexual violence will still reflect their own traits of character and personality, so that what may be an embarrassing and hurtful experience of harassment for one woman may be easily ignored by another. Indeed, individual women's reactions to sexual violence may change over time. Thus, a continuum model's linearity by type will fail to reflect the complexity and diversity within and among women's sexual lives.

Moreover, because of its failure to demarcate the incidence of sexual violence against women, a continuum model cannot account for the severity of sexual violence due to a repetition or combination of violations. For example, while a woman might be able to put her boyfriend's rape behind her, she may become increasingly paralyzed by the constant and aggressive sexual harassment of her boss. Yet on a continuum model by type, sexual harassment is less severe than rape. Similarly, a female graduate student subjected to the leering, crude jokes, and pornographic posters of her male officemates may be more unnerved than when her roommate once threatened her with his fists. Yet on a continuum model, sexual harassment is less severe than assault. On the other hand, another graduate student might laugh off her officemates' antics and angrily demand that her roommate leave for good. Even if a continuum model were able to express particular incidents of violence, it is still unclear how its linearity could accommodate the variety in women's experiences of, and reactions to, sexual violence.[56]

A continuum of severity by type may appear useful nevertheless, because it can demarcate *specific types* of violence, such as date rape, stranger rape, spousal rape, workplace harassment, academic harassment, street harassment, and so on; thus, a continuum would appear to be capable of exposing the pervasiveness of sexual violence against women by exposing its variety of types, particularly if this variety incorporates multicultural diversity. However, this model still fails to demarcate individual women's first-person experiences of sexual violence; and naming a variety of types only further complicates their placement. Is date rape more, or less, severe than spousal rape? Is workplace harassment more, or less, severe than academic harassment? Which is more victimizing in the workplace, a pornographic poster or a crude and sexually explicit letter? If all consensual sex is suspect, is explicit verbal consent any less severe than ungrudging but nonverbal acquiescence? Where on a continuum do we place the so-called secondary victimization by police and state agencies of women reporting their abuse? How should *virtual* rape over the Internet be evaluated, where database subprograms can be manipulated to describe fellow users as targets of sexual violence?[57] Moreover, types of sexual violence can be constituted by repetition or combination: Where do we place the type of harassment in which both unwanted touching (hostile environment) and threats of demotion (quid pro quo) occur? What about a rape by a battering date? A repeated (gang) rape? And where do we situate the *threat* of rape or the *threat* of sexual harassment, especially when these may contribute to a climate of terrorization far more effectively than do the incidents themselves? Indeed, *who* is the "we" deciding the placement of a general type?

Such difficulties initially appear to be resolved by a dual continuum model proposed by social researcher Liz Kelly. With this model, Kelly proposes to show "that all women experience sexual violence at some point in their lives" and "[t]he fact that some women only experience violence at the more common, everyday end of the continuum is a difference in degree and not in kind."[58] One type of continuum describes the relative incidence of forms of sexual violence against women, from sexual harassment (more common) to incest (less common); the other type of continuum indicates women's experience of violence within each form, from consensual sex to pressure to force. Kelly affirms that this dual model is not linear, as it is designed to account for individual women's experiences of violence, singly, in repetition, or in combination, and how one woman's experience may change over time. However, Kelly has offered no guidelines as to how to integrate the two continua or how to identify linkages between incidents or experiences on a nonlinear model. Indeed, if neither continuum is linear in either incidence or experience, it is difficult to understand how a model that combines the two, in Kelly's words, "enables the linking of the more common, everyday abuses women experience with the less common experiences labeled as crimes."[59] Indeed, Kelly describes her dual continuum *as if it were linear*: Her continuum of incidence "moves *from* experiences which were *most* common in women's lives *to* those which were *least* common"; and her continuum of experience is "a continuum moving *from* choice *to* pressure *to* coercion *to* force"[60] (emphasis added). If linear, however, then Kelly's model will fall prey to the problems I have raised above about where to place different women's experiences on the continuum and how to justify placing them there. Moreover, her continuum will be subject to the essentializing charges of the feminist critics above for the ways it seeks to normalize sexual violence against women. In fact, her model cannot be used to show the pervasiveness of sexual violence against women as a class, since her continuum of incidence is explicitly based on a single survey of 60 women whose experiences are not meant by Kelly to be representative of all women.[61]

Without a way of exploring the actual incidence of sexual violence against women or a way of justifying the placement on a continuum of either tokens or types of violence, a continuum model inevitably presumes a universality of reaction to, and experience of, sexual violence across space and time that treats the sexual lives of a diverse group of women as if they were the same. This presumption has the unfortunate consequence of implying precisely the epistemological and moral imperialism that critics charge essentializes women, men, and sex. Such an approach also discourages women who are concerned about the pervasiveness of sexual violence against women from thinking of themselves as feminists ("I'm not a feminist, but . . ."), thus unnecessarily dividing political affinities among women. Moreover, this type of model does nothing to encourage police officers, attorneys, judges, or juries to question their own presumptions about what counts as genuine sexual violence against women. What I propose below is a model whose cultural specificity and moral pluralism can refine our understanding of sexual violence against women.

Overlapping Frames and Dialectical Discourses

Given the feminist impasse between proponents of a continuum model and its critics, I wish to outline a model for understanding sexual violence against women, which ranges over a broad political spectrum. This model is specifically designed to describe particular incidents of sexual violence against women on the basis of culture and context, so that incommensurable and contradictory experiences among diverse women coexist alongside commensurable ones. Thus, the model can speak to a wide variety of women whose moral evaluations of the relations between sex, gender, and power are specific to the context of their own lived experience.[62]

The model's cultural specificity and moral pluralism is grounded in a feminism that condemns sexual violence against women as both a personal injury to individual women and a social injustice to women as a class. Such a framework can accommodate a reading of sexual violence as both a repetitive but isolatable form of criminal behavior and a pervasive and normalized form of patriarchal social control. Thus, I contend that this broad feminist framework offers a context and legitimacy for making meaningful moral evaluations of sexual violence, without the necessity for moral consensus. Forcing such consensus, particularly concerning the sexual oppression of women, inevitably results in recreating precisely the patriarchal silencing of women's voices that feminists have long condemned. The relevant question this new model poses is not whether a given act is one of sexual violence but by whom and under what cultural constraints are the assessments of conduct being made. Using this more discursive and less oppositional approach, patriarchy is both overrated and ubiquitous, fragmented and monolithic, invisible and resistible, a complex set of institutions and ideologies that circumscribe sexual violence against women without determining women's lives. The cultural specificity of this approach ensures that the unempowered have a voice; its ascription of both oppression and agency to women recommends a dialectical dialog on sexual violence that acknowledges its pervasiveness without condemning women to it. In this model, women may variously succumb to, or resist, men's sexual violence against them, reflecting the unstable and dynamic relation between women's sexual oppression and women's sexual agency under patriarchy. By describing women as variously victimized or liberated, as sexual objects or sexual subjects—and often both at once—we can begin a conversation about sexual violence against women that appreciates the very different ways that women experience, and overcome, their victimization by men.[63]

I contend that such a conversation can be facilitated by a model of nonlinear, overlapping, and unstable conceptual and normative frames of sexual violation. The model's nonlinearity can expose the compounding, as well as the contradictory, experiences of sexual violence over a single life or over many different lives. Nonlinearity also allows women to talk about the ways in which being leered at is *not* like being battered, or the ways in which being emotionally abused is *not* like being raped. Most important, this feature facilitates making sense of sexual consent under patriarchy by marking disjuncts with, not merely similarities to, harassment, battering, and rape. The overlapping conceptual frames of the model capture the similarities (overlap) as well as the differences (contrast) in the concepts that different women use to think and talk about the violence they experience. Overlapping normative frames capture similarities and differences in how women evaluate their sexual experience. With overlap, the model reveals those similarities in experiences of sexual violence that expose its pervasiveness and normalization, such as similarities in women's physical and emotional reactions, in their fears of reprisal, in how myths and stereotypes wreak havoc on women's credibility, and in the institutionalization of the tolerance, if not the legitimacy, of men's sexual violence against women. Yet with contrast, the model avoids the appearance of an unassailable monolith of sexual violence in all women's lives. Thus, this model can serve as a consciousness-raising tool for prevention and resistance against sexual violence without presuming or implying an all-powerful patriarchy. Indeed, the overlapping of conceptual and normative frames is neither static nor stable, to account for repeat as well as novel experiences of sexual violence, to account for women's resignation as well as resistance to the violence they experience, and to account for changes in women's reactions over time. Such instability is consistent with the dialectical discourse on sexuality within which such frames are situated. Moreover, these are frames of *violation* to capture those experiences of sexual victimization that women regard as intimidating, manipulative, or degrading, as well as those that are expressly violent.

If a model of sexual violence against women is to avoid patronizing women with presumptions about what they "really" experience, and so give prima facie credibility to women's first-person accounts, then the model must, to paraphrase Katie Roiphe, find a place for that gray area in which one woman's rape may be another woman's bad night. So too, the model must reflect Naomi Wolf's concern that we make "more careful demarcations of harm that reflect the complexity of women's real experiences," without losing the important sense in which sexual violence against women is a powerful mechanism of patriarchal social control.[64] In short, if there is no single, canonical understanding of rape, then a feminist model of sexual violence that theorizes across a broad spectrum of women should reflect this.

Indeed, such a model can nuance conversations about women, men, and sex that a continuum model cannot. Sexual violence against women may be about male power, dominance, and control; but it is also about how *more* powerful white, affluent men can deny their responsibility for sexual violence by confining *less* powerful poor men or men of color to the role of sexual predator. Women of all cultural backgrounds must begin to understand what roles they may play in maintaining and reinforcing their own victimization, without succumbing to a univocal "blame the woman" syndrome. Many heterosexual men fully understand the patriarchal underpinnings of their sexual lives and work assiduously to overcome them; and lesbians are confronting women's sexual violence against women in their own communities. Moreover, making sense of sexual consent under patriarchy is essential not only to women's ability to undermine men's presumptions of sexual access, but also to heterosexual men's ability to avoid using coercion to have sex.[65] The ability to exercise consent is also essential for women who are convinced that they can use power-polarizing sexual roles in subversive and sexually liberating ways. In a society with entrenched sexual stereotypes of male dominance and female submission, heterosexual sex has features in common with rape, can look like rape, can be rape, but it need not be rape. In this way, a dialectical model that appreciates the different ways women experience their sexuality can avoid the essentializing features of a continuum.

Individuating experience within a patriarchal context also reflects the dual condemnation of sexual violence as both personal injury to individual women and social injustice to women as a class. As I mentioned above, this condemnation provides the normative baseline that grounds the dialectical model's moral pluralism. Thus, individual acts of sexual violence against women can be understood as not only, or primarily, examples of bias motivated hate crime, but also injuries by *this* man directed at *this* woman with *this* cultural history in *this* relationship. Date rape and spousal rape are often devastating precisely because of a woman's personal relationship with, and corresponding expectations of, her aggressor. Victims who refuse to accept their dehumanization by perpetrators can also improve their resistance to them: Victoria Davion describes how personalizing her connection to her attacker helped her escape his violence and helped him see his responsibility for what was happening.[66] Moreover, this dual reading marries the feminist goals of identifying men's individual responsibility for particular acts of violence and challenging men's collective participation in, and reinforcement of, the patriarchal institutions that normalize sexual violence against women.[67]

Both proponents and critics of a continuum model agree that the incidence of sexual violence against women, however it is to be characterized, is unconscionably high. They also agree that feminism can play an important role in raising public awareness of the necessity for increased prevention and resistance and in apprising both women and men of the roles that gender discrimination and sexual stereotypes play in the perpetuation of the sexual victimization of women. However, feminist presumptions about women's experience of violence or their abilities to liberate themselves from it can only alienate many women from feminism and reduce the credibility of feminists' fight against sexual violence. The model I have outlined in this section situates overlapping conceptual and normative frames of sexual viola-tion within a larger cultural discourse on women's sexuality that acknowledges the institutionalization of, and resistance to, men's sexual violence against women. Such a model encourages a nonmonolithic view of both feminism and patriarchy; and the model's cultural specificity and moral pluralism can appeal to a wide vari-ety of women without condoning the harm. My hope is that such a perspective en-courages negotiating, not reinvigorating, the tensions among feminists, so that we may work together toward ever more powerful and successful resistance against sexual violence.

Notes

1. Diana E. H. Russell, elucidating the thesis she states in *The Politics of Rape* (New York: Stein & Day, 1975), p. 261, in *Sexual Exploitation: Rape, Child Sexual Abuse, and Workplace Harassment* (Newbury Park, CA: Sage, 1984), p. 121.

2. Catharine A. MacKinnon, "Sex and Violence," in *Feminism Unmodified: Discourses on Life and Law* (Cambridge: Harvard University Press, 1987), p. 86.

3. Stevi Jackson, "The Social Context of Rape: Sexual Scripts and Motivation," in *Rape and Society: Readings on the Problem of Sexual Assault*, ed. Patricia Searles and Ronald J. Berger (Boulder, CO: Westview Press, 1995), p. 20.

4. For variations on this central theme, see MacKinnon, "Sex and Violence"; Catha-rine A. MacKinnon, "Rape: On Coercion and Consent," in *Toward a Feminist Theory of the State* (Cambridge: Harvard University Press, 1989), pp. 171–83, 295–99; Russell, *The Poli-tics of Rape*, and *Sexual Exploitation*; Jackson, "The Social Context of Rape"; Andrea Dworkin, *Intercourse* (New York: Free Press, 1987), and *Letters from a War Zone* (London: Secker and Warburg, 1988); Marilyn French, *The War Against Women* (New York: Ballantine Books, 1992); Susan Brownmiller, *Against Our Will: Men, Women and Rape* (New York: Ban-tam Books, 1975); Susan Griffin, *Rape: The Power of Consciousness* (San Francisco: Harper and Row, 1981); Diana Scully, *Understanding Sexual Violence* (Boston: Unwin Hyman, 1990); Lorenne M. G. Clark and Debra J. Lewis, *Rape: The Price of Coercive Sexuality* (Toronto: Women's Press, 1977); Judith Lewis Herman, *Trauma and Recovery* (New York: Basic Books, 1992); Susan Schechter, *Women and Male Violence: The Visions and Struggles of the Battered Women's Movement* (Boston: South End Press, 1982). Feminists like MacKin-

non analyze rape primarily as a crime of sex, in order to reveal the socially sanctioned relationship between sex and violence. Others like Brownmiller and Griffin emphasize that rape is a crime of violence (whose vehicle is sex), in order to show that the motivation for rape is not sexual passion but patriarchal dominance and control. For the purposes of this discussion, these are not irreconcilable differences, since all such feminists are committed to the view, reflected by a continuum model of sexual violence, that the construction of heterosexuality under patriarchy encourages and normalizes violence against women. However, there is a group of radical feminists who refer to themselves as sex radical feminists for whom this version of sexual violence against women is grossly misleading. I review some of these feminists' objections to a continuum model, along with objections from other feminist quarters, later in this chapter.

5. Critics who have garnered broad popular appeal include Christina Hoff Sommers, *Who Stole Feminism?: How Women Have Betrayed Women* (New York: Simon and Schuster, 1994); Katie Roiphe, *The Morning After: Sex, Fear, and Feminism on Campus* (Boston: Little, Brown, 1993); Rene Denfeld, *The New Victorians: A Young Woman's Challenge to the Old Feminist Order* (New York: Warner, 1995); Naomi Wolf, *Fire with Fire: The New Female Power and How to Use It* (New York: Ballantine Books, 1994); Camille Paglia, "The Strange Case of Anita Hill," "Rape and Modern Sex War," and "The Rape Debate, Continued," in *Sex, Art, and American Culture* (New York: Vintage Books, 1992), pp. 46–74, and "No Law in the Arena," in *Vamps and Tramps: New Essays* (New York: Vintage Books, 1994), pp. 24–56.

6. I argue for the usefulness of this framework to feminist theory and practice, in the context of women's sexual experience, in *Loose Women, Lecherous Men: A Feminist Philosophy of Sex* (New York: Oxford University Press, 1997). For further discussion of sexual violence analyzed from within this framework, see *Loose Women, Lecherous Men*, chap. 5.

7. I develop this model for a more complex and culturally diverse reading of sexual harassment, in Linda LeMoncheck, "Taunted and Tormented or Savvy and Seductive?: Feminist Discourses on Sexual Harassment," in *Sexual Harassment: A Debate*, Linda LeMoncheck and Mane Hajdin (Lanham, MD: Rowman & Littlefield, 1997), pp. 48–56.

8. Lois Copeland and Leslie R. Wolfe, *Violence Against Women as Bias Motivated Hate Crime: Defining the Issues* (Washington, DC: Center for Women Policy Studies, 1991); also see Jill Radford and Diana E. H. Russell, *Femicide: The Politics of Woman Hating* (New York: Macmillan, 1992); French, *The War Against Women*, pp. 192, 197; Charlotte Bunch, "Women's Rights as Human Rights," in *Gender Violence: A Development and Human Rights Issue*, Charlotte Bunch and Roxanne Carrillo (Dublin, Ireland: Attic Press, 1992), p. 8. Many political pundits do not regard hate crimes as gender specific, because women are not typically regarded as a separate minority group who suffer prejudice from the wider public. There is a double irony here, given that (1) feminists have fought vigorously to dispel the mistaken notion that rape is always, or even often, a public act committed by a stranger; and (2) legislators have recommended the exclusion of gender as a category of hate crime, as they believe the huge numbers of crimes committed against women would "overload the system." See Copeland and Wolfe, "Violence Against Women as Bias Motivated Hate Crime," pp. 12, 15.

9. See Jill Radford, "Policing Male Violence–Policing Women," Eileen Green, Sandra Hebron, and Diana Woodward, "Women, Leisure, and Social Control," and Elizabeth A. Stanko, "Typical Violence, Normal Precaution: Men, Women and Interpersonal Violence in England, Wales, Scotland and the USA," in *Women, Violence and Social Control*, ed. Jalna Hanmer and Mary Maynard (Atlantic Highlands, NJ: Humanities Press, 1987), pp. 30–45,

75–92, 122–34; Susan Rae Peterson, "Coercion and Rape: The State as a Male Protection Racket," in *Feminism and Philosophy*, ed. Mary Vetterling-Braggin, Frederick A. Elliston, and Jane English (Totowa, NJ: Littlefield, Adams, 1978), pp. 360–71; Copeland and Wolfe, "Violence Against Women as Bias Motivated Hate Crime," pp. 2, 11.

10. See Larry May and Robert Strikwerda, "Men in Groups: Collective Responsibility for Rape," *Hypatia* 9, no. 2 (Spring 1994): 134–51; Claudia Card, "Rape as a Weapon of War," *Hypatia* 11, no. 4 (Fall 1996): 9–10; Copeland and Wolfe, "Violence Against Women as Bias Motivated Hate Crime," pp. 3–4; Brownmiller, *Against Our Will*, p. 229; French, *The War Against Women*, p. 182.

11. MacKinnon, "Sex and Violence," p. 83; Lois Pineau, "Date Rape: A Feminist Analysis," in *Date Rape: Feminism, Philosophy, and the Law*, ed. Leslie Francis (University Park: Pennsylvania State University Press, 1996), pp. 6–10.

12. See MacKinnon, "Sexual Violence," and "Rape"; Jackson, "The Social Context of Rape"; Robert Rosenfeld, "The Burden of Initiation," paper presented at a symposium for the philosophy of sex and love at the Eastern Division meeting of the American Philosophical Association, Boston, MA, December 1994; also see Keith Burgess-Jackson, *Rape: A Philosophical Investigation* (Aldershot, England: Dartmouth, 1996), pp. 94–96, 99–102.

13. See Robin Warshaw, *I Never Called It Rape* (New York: HarperPerennial, 1994); Tim Beneke, *Men on Rape* (New York: St. Martin's Press, 1982); Copeland and Wolfe, "Violence Against Women as Bias Motivated Hate Crime," p. 8.

14. See Russell, *The Politics of Rape*, and *Sexual Exploitation*; MacKinnon, "Sex and Violence," and "Rape"; Pineau, "Date Rape"; Jackson, "The Social Context of Rape."

15. Anne Edwards, "Male Violence in Feminist Theory: An Analysis of the Changing Conceptions of Sex/Gender Violence and Male Dominance," in Hanmer and Maynard, *Women, Violence, and Social Control*, p. 27.

16. See LeMoncheck, *Loose Women, Lecherous Men*, pp. 164–91.

17. Julie A. Allison and Lawrence S. Wrightsman, *Rape: The Misunderstood Crime* (Newbury Park, CA: Sage, 1993), pp. 98–126; Warshaw, *I Never Called It Rape*, pp. 38–47; Pineau, "Date Rape," pp. 10–13; David M. Adams, "Date Rape and Erotic Discourse," in Francis, *Date Rape*, pp. 29–30; Brownmiller, *Against Our Will*, pp. 346–47.

18. See Linda Bird Francke, *Ground Zero: The Gender Wars in the Military* (New York: Simon and Schuster, 1997); Judith Hicks Stiehm, ed., *"It's Our Military Too": Women and the US Military* (Philadelphia, PA: Temple University Press, 1996); Billie Wright Dziech and Linda Weiner, *The Lecherous Professor*, 2d ed. (Urbana: University of Illinois Press, 1990); LeMoncheck, "Taunted and Tormented or Savvy and Seductive?" pp. 9–25; Warshaw, *I Never Called It Rape*, pp. 127–50; Linda A. Fairstein, *Sexual Violence: Our War Against Rape* (New York: Berkley Books, 1995), pp. 85–96, 121–28; Rosemarie Tong, *Women, Sex, and the Law* (Savage, MD: Rowman and Littlefield, 1984); Lisa Frohmann, "Discrediting Victims' Allegations of Sexual Assault: Prosecutorial Accounts of Case Rejections," in Searles and Berger, *Rape and Society*, pp. 199–214; Allison and Wrightsman, *Rape*, pp. 195–218, Susan Estrich, "Is It Rape?" in Searles and Berger, *Rape and Society*, pp. 183–93; Brownmiller, *Against Our Will*, pp. 374–86; Lisa M. Cuklanz, *Rape on Trial: How the Mass Media Construct Legal Reform and Social Change* (Philadelphia: University of Pennsylvania Press, 1996); Larry L. Tifft, *Battering of Women: The Failure of Intervention and the Case for Prevention* (Boulder, CO: Westview Press, 1993), esp. pp. 89–95.

19. Indeed, some feminists argue that the most predictable perpetrators are precisely

the men who meet their gender expectations best—the most normal of "normal" men. See Russell on the "overconforming" male, *Sexual Exploitation,* pp. 117–19, and Allison and Wrightsman on "hypermasculinity," *Rape,* pp. 12–13, 29–33, 77–84; also see Louise F. Fitzgerald and Lauren M. Weitzman, "Men Who Harass: Speculation and Data," in *Ivory Power: Sexual Harassment on Campus,* ed. Michele A. Paludi (Albany: State University Press of New York, 1990), pp. 125–40; Peggy Reeves Sanday, *Fraternity Gang Rape: Sex, Brotherhood, and Privilege on Campus* (New York: New York University Press, 1990); French, *The War Against Women,* pp. 194–96.

20. See Herman, *Trauma and Recovery,* pp. 33–73, 103–10; Warshaw, *I Never Called It Rape,* pp. 54–64; Mary Koss, "Changed Lives: The Psychological Impact of Sexual Harassment," in Paludi, *Ivory Power,* pp. 73–92; Sandra McNeill, "Flashing: Its Effects on Women," in Hanmer and Maynard, *Women, Violence, and Social Control,* pp. 102–5; Stanko, "Typical Violence, Normal Precaution."

21. See Warshaw, *I Never Called It Rape,* p. 50; Copeland and Wolfe, "Violence as Bias Motivated Hate Crime," pp. 6–7; Tifft, *Battering of Women,* pp. 39–56.

22. Mary P. Koss, "Hidden Rape: Sexual Aggression and Victimization in a National Sample of Students in Higher Education," in Searles and Berger, *Rape and Society,* pp. 35–49.

23. See Schechter, *Women and Male Violence,* pp. 287–91; note 18 above.

24. See Edwards, "Male Violence in Feminist Theory"; Pineau, "Date Rape."

25. Denfeld, *The New Victorians,* p. 78.

26. Margaret Hunt, "Report of a Conference on Feminism, Sexuality and Power: The Elect Clash with the Perverse," in *Coming to Power: Writings and Graphics on Lesbian S/M,* 3d ed., ed. SAMOIS (Boston: Alyson Publications, 1987), p. 87.

27. Renee Heberle, "Deconstructive Strategies and the Movement Against Sexual Violence," *Hypatia* 11, no. 4 (Fall 1996): 67.

28. For an extended discussion of essentialism/anti-essentialism debates within feminism, see Naomi Schor and Elizabeth Weed, eds., *the essential difference* (Bloomington: Indiana University Press, 1994).

29. See Sommers, *Who Stole Feminism?*; Roiphe, *The Morning After*; Denfeld, *The New Victorians*; Paglia, "The Strange Case of Anita Hill," "Rape and Modern Sex War," and "The Rape Debate, Continued," in *Sex, Art, and American Culture*; Paglia, "No Law in the Arena," in *Vamps and Tramps*; Wolf, *Fire with Fire.*

30. Roiphe, *The Morning After,* p. 81; also see op. cit., pp. 29–50, 59–60; Denfeld, *The New Victorians,* p. 89; Sommers, *Who Stole Feminism?,* pp. 208, 212–16, 218–22.

31. Denfeld, *The New Victorians,* pp. 59–88, 286–89.

32. Dworkin quoted in Roiphe, *The Morning After,* p. 46; Brownmiller quoted and paraphrased in Roiphe, pp. 55–56; MacKinnon quoted in Roiphe, p. 81; also see Sommers, *Who Stole Feminism?,* pp. 19–40, 44–45.

33. See Roiphe, *The Morning After,* pp. 56, 59–84, 85–113; Denfeld, *The New Victorians,* pp. 81–82; Sommers, *Who Stole Feminism?,* pp. 198–99.

34. See Sommers, *Who Stole Feminism?,* pp. 213–14, 223; Roiphe, *The Morning After,* pp. 68–69; Denfeld, *The New Victorians,* p. 73.

35. Sommers, *Who Stole Feminism?,* pp. 181–87, 189–226; also see Roiphe, *The Morning After,* pp. 51–55; Denfeld, *The New Victorians,* pp. 62–76.

36. Paglia, "No Law in the Arena," p. 26.

37. Paglia, "Rape and Modern Sex War," pp. 50–54; "The Strange Case of Anita Hill," pp. 46–49; "No Law in the Arena," pp. 24–38, 41–56.

38. Paglia, "No Law in the Arena," pp. 44, 45–46; "The Rape Debate, Continued," pp. 55–74.

39. Wolf, *Fire with Fire*, pp. 135–36.

40. Ibid., pp. 140, 196.

41. Ibid., pp. 135–51; 180–197; 215–32; 235–321.

42. See Pat Califia, "A Secret Side of Lesbian Sexuality," "Feminism and Sadomasochism," "Genderbending: Playing with Roles and Reversals," and "Love and the Perfect Sadist: Can S/M Work in the Context of an Ongoing Relationship?" in *Public Sex: The Culture of Radical Sex* (Pittsburgh, PA: Cleis Press, 1994), pp. 157–82, 222–30; SAMOIS, ed., *Coming to Power*; Joan Nestle, ed., *The Persistent Desire: A Femme-Butch Reader* (Boston: Alyson, 1992); Joan Nestle, "The Fem Question," in *Pleasure and Danger: Exploring Female Sexuality*, ed. Carole S. Vance (London: Pandora Press, 1989), pp. 232–41; Amber Hollibaugh and Cherríe Moraga, "What We're Rollin Around in Bed With: Sexual Silences in Feminism," in *Powers of Desire: The Politics of Sexuality*, ed. Ann Snitow, Christine Stansell, and Sharon Thompson (New York: Monthly Review Press, 1983), pp. 394–405.

43. Califia, "A Secret Side of Lesbian Sexuality," p. 164; "Feminism and Sadomasochism," pp. 167–69; Kitt, "Taking the Sting Out of S/M," Cynthia Astuto and Pat Califia, "Being Weird is Not Enough: How to Stay Healthy and Play Safe," and Susan Farr, "The Art of Discipline: Creating Erotic Dramas of Play and Power," in SAMOIS, ed., *Coming to Power*, pp. 60–63, 69–80, 183–91; also see Patrick Hopkins, "Rethinking Sadomasochism: Feminism, Interpretation, and Simulation," *Hypatia* 9, no. 1 (Winter 1994): 116–41.

44. Gayle Rubin, "Of Catamites and Kings," in Nestle, *The Persistent Desire*, p. 469; also see Ann Cvetkovich, "Recasting Receptivity: Femme Sexualities," in *Lesbian Erotics*, ed. Karla Jay (New York: New York University Press, 1995), pp. 125–46; Joan Nestle, "Flamboyance and Fortitude: An Introduction," in Nestle, *The Persistent Desire*, pp. 13–20; Nestle, "The Fem Question"; Hollibaugh and Moraga, "What We're Rollin Around in Bed With."

45. Amber Hollibaugh, in Hollibaugh and Moraga, "What We're Rollin Around in Bed With," p. 397; also see Muriel Dimen, "Politically Correct? Politically Incorrect?" in Vance, *Pleasure and Danger*, pp. 138–48; Califia, "Gender Bending."

46. See Heberle, "Deconstructive Strategies and the Movement Against Sexual Violence," pp. 63–76; Sharon Marcus, "Fighting Bodies, Fighting Words: A Theory and Politics of Rape Prevention," in *Feminists Theorize the Political*, ed. Judith Butler and Joan W. Scott (New York: Routledge, 1992), pp. 385–403; Kathleen J. Ferraro, "The Dance of Dependency: A Genealogy of Domestic Violence Discourse," *Hypatia* 11, no. 4 (Fall 1996): 77–91.

47. Heberle, "Deconstructive Strategies," p. 69.

48. Ibid., pp. 65, 67–72; also see Ferraro, who advocates moving from a "crime discourse" to a "liberation discourse" in narratives of domestic violence, in "The Dance of Dependency," pp. 85–89.

49. Marcus, "Fighting Bodies, Fighting Words," pp. 386, 389.

50. Ibid., pp. 387, 400.

51. Ibid., pp. 387, 398–401.

52. See Paglia, "The Strange Case of Anita Hill," p. 50, and "The Rape Debate, Continued," p. 59.

53. See Karen Sims and Rose Mason, with Darlene Pagano, "Racism and Sado-

masochism: A Conversation with Two Black Lesbians, in *Against Sadomasochism: A Radical Feminist Analysis*, ed. Robin Ruth Linden, Darlene R. Pagano, Diana E. H. Russell, and Susan Leigh Star (San Francisco: Frog in the Well, 1982), pp. 99–105; Melinda Vadas, "Reply to Patrick Hopkins," *Hypatia* 10, no. 2 (Spring 1995): pp. 159–61; Celia Kitzinger, "Anti-Lesbian Harassment," in *Rethinking Sexual Harassment*, ed. Clare Brant and Yun Lee Too (London: Pluto Press, 1994), pp. 125–47.

54. For further discussion of complaints against the critics of a radical model for under-standing sexual violence against women, see LeMoncheck, *Loose Women, Lecherous Men*, pp. 94–102, 200–10, and "Taunted and Tormented or Savvy and Seductive?," pp. 40–59.

55. See Kimberlè Crenshaw, "Mapping the Margins: Intersectionality, Identity Politics, and Violence Against Women of Color," *Stanford Law Review* 43 (1991): 1241–99; Valerie Smith, "Split Affinities: The Case of Interracial Rape," in *Conflicts in Feminism*, ed. Mari-anne Hirsch and Evelyn Fox Keller (New York: Routledge, 1990), pp. 271–87; Jennifer Wrig-gins, "Rape, Racism, and the Law," in Searles and Berger, *Rape and Society*, pp. 215–22; Geneva Smitherman, ed., *African American Women Speak Out on Anita Hill–Clarence Thomas* (Detroit: Wayne State University Press, 1995); Angela Davis, *Women, Race and Class* (New York: Vintage Books, 1981), pp. 172–201; Jacquelyn Dowd Hall, "'The Mind That Burns in Each Body': Women, Rape, and Racial Violence," in Snitow et al, *Powers of Desire*, pp. 328–49; W. Lawrence Neuman, "Gender, Race, and Age Differences in Student Defini-tions of Sexual Harassment," *Wisconsin Sociologist* 29 (1992): 63–75; Kitzinger, "Anti-Lesbian Harassment"; Radford, "Policing Male Violence–Policing Women," p. 44.

56. For further discussion of the problems of where and how to place experiences of sexual victimization on a continuum, see LeMoncheck, "Taunted and Tormented or Savvy and Seductive?" pp. 48–56. For how different women react to the same incident of violence, see McNeill, "Flashing," pp. 100–102; Linda Brookover Bourque, *Defining Rape* (Durham, NC: Duke University Press, 1989), pp. 131–70; Barbara Gutek, "How Subjective Is Sexual Harassment? An Examination of Rater Effects," *Basic and Applied Social Psychology* 17 (1995):447–67; note 55 above.

57. See Julian Dibbell, "A Rape in Cyberspace; or, How an Evil Clown, a Haitian Trickster Spirit, Two Wizards, and a Cast of Dozens Turned a Database into a Society," in *Flame Wars: The Discourse of Cyberculture*, ed. Mark Dery (Durham, NC, and London: Duke University Press, 1994), pp. 237–61; also see Frohmann, "Discrediting Victims' Allega-tions of Sexual Assault."

58. Liz Kelly, "The Continuum of Sexual Violence," in Hanmer and Maynard, *Women, Violence and Social Control*, p. 58.

59. Ibid., p. 59.

60. Ibid., pp. 52, 54.

61. Ibid., p. 52.

62. For more detailed discussion of a feminist moral pluralism, see Laurie Shrage, *Moral Dilemmas of Feminism: Prostitution, Adultery, and Abortion* (New York: Routledge, 1994), pp. 174–79; Raymond A. Bellioti, *Good Sex: Perspectives on Sexual Ethics* (Lawrence: University Press of Kansas, 1993), chap. 7; LeMoncheck, *Loose Women, Lecherous Men*, pp. 106, 216–19.

63. See LeMoncheck, "Taunted and Tormented or Savvy and Seductive?," pp. 55–59, 166–67; LeMoncheck, *Loose Women, Lecherous Men*, pp. 5–6, 22–26, 204–10, 216–19.

64. Wolf, *Fire with Fire*, p. 140; Roiphe, *The Morning After*, p. 54.

65. See LeMoncheck, *Loose Women, Lecherous Men*, pp. 59–60, 171, 210–15; also see Kenneth Clatterbaugh, *Contemporary Perspectives on Masculinity: Men, Women, and Politics in Modern Society*, 2d ed. (Boulder, CO: Westview Press, 1996); Larry May and Robert Strikwerda, eds., *Rethinking Masculinity: Philosophical Explorations in Light of Feminism*, 2d ed. (Lanham, MD: Rowman and Littlefield, 1997); Rosenfeld, "The Burden of Initiation"; Larry Lobel, ed., *Naming the Violence: Speaking Out about Lesbian Battering* (Seattle: Seal Press, 1986); Smith, "Split Affinities"; Wriggins, "Rape, Racism, and the Law."

66. Victoria Davion, "Rape, Group Responsibility, and Trust," *Hypatia* 10, no. 2 (Spring 1995): 153–54.

67. See Pauline Bart and Patricia O'Brien, *Stopping Rape: Successful Survival Strategies* (New York: Pergamon, 1985); May and Strikwerda, "Men in Groups."

8

LARRY MAY AND EDWARD SOULE

Sexual Harassment, Rape, and Criminal Sanctions

This chapter raises the question: How should various forms of sexual harassment, especially those that resemble cases of rape and battery, be treated in law? We do not argue for wholesale legal reform. Rather, we believe the present statutory framework is probably adequate if we properly frame what takes place in the context of sexual harassment offenses and if we are willing to include sexual harassment offenses in standard legal categories. We will argue that some forms of sexual harassment should be given the status of criminal offenses and treated like cases of rape, intimidation, attempted rape, and battery. And we will argue that the law should recognize and hold sexual harassers responsible for causing emotional distress and for creating harmful nuisances. At the moment, most sexual harassment is treated as sex discrimination. We do not think this is wrong but see it as overly broad. We believe that this "one treatment fits all cases" approach glosses over other crucial aspects of sexual harassment that might deserve more severe punishment. Indeed, it is surprising to us that there have been so few criminal legal remedies attempted in sexual harassment cases.

Initially, our attention will be on the coerciveness of sexual harassment. As the coerciveness gets more and more questionable, so the role of law is more and more difficult to work out. Beyond coercive behavior, we identify a range of actions that are overtly menacing and harmful, although they may not be intended to coerce any specific outcome from their victims. Some of this behavior is best treated in a court of law, but moral suasion or social pressure will best treat some of it. We need to think more creatively than we have, viewing the various types of sexual harassment as each calling for potentially different forms of legal, or extra-legal, action.

We begin by sketching a rough typology of forms of sexual harassment. First, there are various forms of sexual harassment that involve either coercion or unwanted physical contact. "Rape-like" harassment is that form of sexual harassment in which serious threats are used to extort unconsented sexual intercourse. "Seduction" harassment is that form of sexual harassment in which employment and educational relationships are exploited to *attempt* to gain unconsented sexual intercourse or where employment or educational relationships are exploited to gain unconsented forms of sexual intimacy short of intercourse. "Intimidation" is similar in form to "rape-like" harassment. However, we single it out as a different way to view coercion and thereby draw on a different legal remedy. "Sexual Battery" looks at familiar forms of physical "horseplay" from the legal framework of criminal battery. In our view, cases that share the properties of rape, attempted rape, intimidation, and battery should be the basis for criminal sanctions and not be limited to the civil sanctions currently employed in sexual harassment cases.

Second, there are various forms of sexual harassment that involve menacing and annoying behavior, not necessarily sexual, by men who exploit positions of power over women. These offenses have traditionally been conceived as forms of unwanted flirtation and are lumped together under the sex discrimination heading of "Hostile Work Environment." We revisit the hostile work environment offenses and suggest enlarging its scope. We suggest that this form of behavior could be significantly curtailed by seeking additional legal remedies. We believe that some of this behavior inflicts "mental or emotional distress" and should be treated accordingly. And other acts create a "nuisance" that, like other public nuisances, should be treated under tort law.

Rape and Sexual Harassment

Consider the following example of sexual harassment.[1]

> Joe is a manager of some 20 workers at a small manufacturing plant in a rural community. Jane has worked at the plant for several years and although she is uneducated and unskilled, her tenure and good performance have elevated her earnings to something in excess of minimum wage. She is a single mother and only survives at the slimmest of margins above the poverty line; living "check to check" and not always making ends meet. On several occasions, Joe has made romantic overtures to Jane who has consistently rebuked his advances. Her refusal was made in such a manner as to leave no doubt in Joe's mind that Jane is not interested in him.

> Recently, Joe received word from his superiors that it will be necessary to reduce by eight the number of workers in his area. Jane falls into a category of ten workers, any of whom could justifiably be terminated. That is, her performance, tenure, and skills make her indistinguishable from the other nine members of this group. Given Joe's long-standing attraction to Jane he confronts her with an offer; he intends to terminate her employment unless she will have sexual intercourse with him. Jane decides that she would rather have intercourse with Joe than suffer the harms of unemployment. Her decision is heavily influenced by the employment prospects in her small community where her only opportunities would mean decreased wages and severe financial hardship to her family. To save her job, Jane has intercourse with Joe.

It goes without saying that Joe's behavior is predatory, menacing, and obnoxious toward her. He clearly acts in a discriminatory way toward her. His actions also represent perhaps the clearest case of quid pro quo sexual harassment. However, we would like to push these facts further than normal to gain a more subtle understanding of the nature of this offense. We will contend that there is a criminal element in this behavior that may go unnoticed in part due to its classification as a variety of discriminatory sexual harassment. The present legal setting of sexual harassment omits crimes of a serious enough nature to warrant punishment as a criminal offense. We think this is a mistake that serves to diminish the seriousness of sexual harassment in general. If the worst possible case of sexual harassment lacks any possibility of criminal sanction, we fear that the milder cases may be viewed as trivial or at least less harmful than we think they actually are. Many categories of harm, such as libel or false imprisonment, run the gamut from criminal to simple civil torts. Sexual harassment would indeed be unusual if its most egregious interpretation lacks any behavior that is criminally sanctionable. We begin this chapter with an attempt to recalibrate the range of sexual harassment by characterizing its most egregious form as a variety of the crime of rape. To draw this conclusion out of Joe's behavior, it is first necessary to review in some detail the moral and legal underpinnings of rape itself.

The term "rape" refers, at a minimum, to nonconsensual or coerced sex. Rape is especially harmful because it assaults the bodily integrity of its victims. The seriousness of this harm is seen by the severe forms of punishment including long jail sentences that mark rape off as on a level with very serious forms of battery. But unlike other criminal offenses, the issue of what constitutes lack of consent can be highly problematic in the case of rape. Rarely is there any question about whether a form of taking is gift receiving or robbery, although whether one receives a gift or steals is ascertainable by consent or the lack thereof. It is an extremely audacious thief who would argue that her victim had registered consent. Normally, the circumstances surrounding the incident would provide an obvious refutation of such a claim. Whether an act is rape or mere consensual sex is not as clear-cut as whether something is robbery.

Only in the most egregious instances of rape can the victim's lack of consent be inferred from the physical circumstances of the case. If a stranger lurking in the bushes overpowers his victim by brutally assaulting her, there is not much question whether consent entered the equation. It is presumed that the level of force exerted by the rapist negated any genuine possibility of consent. Indeed, the *Model Penal Code* describes the paradigm case of rape in terms of forcible sexual intercourse or the threat thereof, which presumably negates any possibility of consent. Rape is defined in terms of compelling a woman "to submit [to sexual intercourse] by force or by threat of imminent death, serious bodily injury. . . ." First-degree rape is distinguished from second-degree rape by the presence of one of the following two factors: either the woman does in fact suffer serious bodily injury or the defendant and victim were strangers at the time of the incident. Absent these two qualifying ingredients, a second-degree rape may have still occurred but with significantly diminished penalties. In terms of our analysis, we think it is important to note the objective stance the law takes in determining the coercive nature of rape. That is, the behavior of the perpetrator is determinative of whether and what sort of crime has taken place.

The third category of rape, gross sexual imposition, applies to cases of nonviolent rape. This category of rape, punishable in many states by imprisonment of from one to five years, is defined as compelling a woman "to submit by any threat that would prevent resistance by a woman of ordinary resolution."[2] We believe that the most egregious instances of sexual harassment involve criminal behavior like that in rape. However, to support this belief we must overcome the murky language of gross sexual imposition. The phrase "resistance by a woman of ordinary resolution" deforms the objective standards for determining violent rape and almost ensures that the statute will be unworkable. Unlike threats of death, bodily injury, kidnapping, and so forth, the notions of "resistance" and "a woman of ordinary resolution" defy objective standards for interpretation. So our objective is to discern what this standard should be.

In what follows we will develop a workable interpretation of gross sexual misconduct that is in keeping with the other rape categories. In attempting to reform the definition of gross sexual misconduct, we will preserve the link between threatening a woman and having intercourse with her. Since we are now outside the domain of violent threats, we need to carefully circumscribe what counts as a legitimate threat. Only those threats of serious injury should qualify as a basis for this type of nonviolent rape. The standard for determining the seriousness of nonviolent rape should be consistent with the objective standard of criminal threats in general and not thrown back on the ability of the victim to resist. For instance, in robbery, we do not define this crime in terms of whether or to what extent the victim resisted or could have resisted the thief. If one is held up at gunpoint or if her house is burglarized, it is not normally relevant to wonder about her level of resistance. This is also true of cases where there is only an implied threat of violence for noncompliance. If a group of large menacing ruffians confronts us (two rather slight nonviolent sorts) in a dark alley and asks for our money, no one would construe our compliance as a contribution to their pension fund. It is clear that we are not responsible for resisting their "request" because of the risk of bodily harm to us implicit in the circumstances.

On the other hand, some threats would not be criminally sanctionable. For instance, panhandlers also ask for our money, but unlike the ruffians, the threat for noncompliance is not the same. At least in New York City, failure to comply with the panhandler's demand will often result in some deprecating comment about one's eleemosynary tendencies (e.g., "cheapskate!"). If we should succumb to this implied threat, the beggar does not become a thief, and likewise we are not victims of robbery but just begrudging donors. The key would seem to be that the panhandler's threat to mutter obscenities or disparage our characters is not a threat of serious injury; these threats are irritating, but clearly not criminal.

So, we would argue, in the case of nonviolent rape there is a sense in which the seriousness of the threat is relevant to whether the act is criminal or not. If a woman is threatened with some trivial consequence there is little justification for defining the act as criminal. Consider a woman on a date with a man she finds boorishly disagreeable, obstinate, and obnoxious. Driving in his car, he announces that unless she consents to have sex with him she will be driven home immediately or perhaps he will not ask her out again. Or he may announce that unless she has sex with him, he will hum religious hymns throughout the movie they plan to attend. Such threats simply do not involve serious risk of harm. The point is that the content of the threat matters.

Returning to our example, if Joe did not threaten to fire Jane, but only threatened to take away her close-in parking space, the coerciveness is diminished. That is, Jane could suffer the results of the threatened action without any serious injury. Although Joe's behavior may be inappropriate, immoral, and (as will be discussed in subsequent sections of this chapter) annoying, it is hardly criminal. But the threat of job loss is different. Jane's job is what stands between her family and poverty. We presume that she will suffer severe financial consequences for a lengthy period of time if she loses her job. In fact, we must presume that the reason Joe turns to this ploy is because he understands the nature of the threatened injury and how Jane will view it. Given his unsuccessful sexual overtures in the past, he tries to use the weapon of employment security to get what he has otherwise been denied.

Based on this reading, Joe has made a threat, the content of which involves significant harm to Jane.[3] If we stop there, we have a parallel case with that of rape. But when there is no violence, the *Model Penal Code* introduces a further burden by having us wonder whether Jane behaved in a manner consistent with the "woman of ordinary resolution." Whether Jane is a "woman of ordinary resolution" raises what we think is a loaded question that adds nothing to a fair characterization of Joe's behavior. It is loaded because the notion of Jane's resolution turns on unstable social standards infused with male concepts of female chastity. That is, Jane may be expected to resist sexual advances, even if doing so places her at bodily or significant economic risk. Moreover, it seems peculiar that the law would establish a criterion for a criminal offense based on the victim's character as opposed to the nature of the threatened harm. This would seem to establish a double standard between nonviolent rape and all other criminal behavior—rape in particular.

The question of a woman's resolution is reminiscent of a poignant scene from the movie *Forrest Gump* in which Sally Field, playing Forrest's mother, submits to sexual intercourse with a school principal in order to gain Forrest's admission into the school. As the principal leaves the school, wiping sweat from his brow, he encounters Forrest who sat outside listening to the whole ordeal. The principal looks down at Forrest and says something like, "Boy, your momma really cares about your education." How would a standard of ordinary resolution apply here? As the movie proceeds we come to know Forrest's mother as a woman of very strong character and extraordinary resolution. But if Forrest's mother were in Jane's circumstance with Joe, we presume that she would have submitted to his demands. If she was willing to have sex with the crusty principal in order to gain admission for her son, we presume she would do likewise to be able to continue basic economic support for her family. But why should strong character of the victim excuse the acts of the perpetrator?

Traditionally, the lack of resistance served as evidence for consent in violent rape cases. If a woman was *really* raped, or so the defendant would claim, there should be evidence of a physical struggle. Absent kicks, bites, scratches, and so forth, it was presumed that the woman consented to the attack. The value of this ploy has been discredited because it puts the victim in an untenable position. Resistance may lead to even more bodily injury, so it is not reasonable to conclude anything from its absence. Rather, consent (or the lack thereof) is based only on the nature of the threat.

This change is one of the successes of the legal reform movement in the criminal law of violent rape. It has the effect of focusing attention on the behavior of the perpetrator and his expressed or implied threats. This has been a reasonable strategy in sorting out the crime of violent rape from consensual "rough" sexual relations. In particular, this strategy makes rape consistent with other crimes, where it is possible to hold a defendant guilty of a crime in virtue of his threats; even though we may nonetheless believe that the victim could have resisted him. In general, the law treats threatening behavior of a sufficiently harmful nature as deserving of criminal sanction. The criminality of the conduct is not diminished by whether a victim could or should resist them. And so we believe it should be for threats of serious economic harm.

There is one final consideration of the quid pro quo case that argues for its consideration as a form of nonviolent rape. If we regard Jane and Joe's intercourse as a case of consensual sex we are hard put to square her feelings subsequent to the act. In many such cases, the woman may experience a sense of disgust, resentment, anger, and other feelings associated with having been sexually violated. If we are to grant any standing to these feelings, we are driven even further in the direction of coercion and nonconsent.

The project of fitting the quid pro quo case of sexual harassment into our interpretation of gross sexual imposition triggers the objection that we have misconstrued Joe's offer to Jane as a threat at all. This criticism emanates from the well-trodden coercion literature based in part on Robert Nozick's[4] distinction between offers and threats. Implicit in this literature is the idea that coercion is tied to threats but not offers. Offers are generally welcome since they increase one's options. Since Jane is already vulnerable to losing her job, Joe positively expands her options by giving her a way to secure her job. By this line of thought Jane previously had only one option but now is presented with two choices, each of which has a cost, and she chooses the one she considers more desirable. Because one of these choices has the possibility of improving her circumstances, Jane is thought to be better off in virtue of Joe's proposal. If the costs that Jane associates with Joe's proposal are allowed somehow to undermine her consent, then most commercial transactions are nonconsensual and most vendors are thieves.

Our response is twofold. First, it is unclear whether Jane is made worse or better off and hence unclear whether on this analysis quid pro quo sexual harassment is coercive or not. In this sense, we find the tools of Nozick's coercion analysis inadequate.[5] But secondly, we believe that a conclusion of coercion (or the lack thereof) based strictly on expanding or narrowing one's options is morally nearsighted—it overintellectualizes the moral issues attendant to sexually harassing behavior. Even Nozick recognizes that finding coercion, based on a parsing of offers and threats, will sometimes fail to draw the proper moral conclusion. This is so in cases where a proposer puts forth a proposal that, by Nozick's lights, is not coercive because it fails the technical definition of a threat.[6] But nonetheless, the of-feree cannot be considered as freely choosing between the alternatives. This notion is redolent of Mario Puzo's *offer he can't refuse*. Nozick defines coercion in such a way that unless one threatens another, one has not coerced her. However, he also recognizes that even in offer situations, a person may still be able to say, "I had no choice."[7]

We recognize that a case can be made that Joe is merely offering Jane the op-portunity to secure her job. This case rightly assumes that Jane has no moral or legal right to indefinite employment, so the proper reading of Joe's proposal is "if you will have sex with me, I will secure your job." And since the ordinary course of events was not "a secure job," Joe has offered to improve Jane's circumstance. By this reading, Jane's agreement to the proposal was not coerced because Joe did not lodge a threat. Even if this case is construed as an offer it does not follow that Jane's agreement to it is tantamount to consent unless we ignore the power that Joe wields over Jane. Joe has taken advantage of his role as Jane's boss to construct a circum-stance whereby, in Nozick's words, Jane "has no choice" but to have sex with him. And if that is the case, then we are hard put to believe that Jane's behavior is con-sensual. Nozick's analysis breaks down in the context of asymmetrical power rela-tionships such as those between bosses and workers.

The significance of this point can be brought into relief by recasting our exam-ple in a context outside that of power relationships. Suppose instead of Joe, Jane's friend, Frank, proposes she have sex in return for securing her job. Frank is Joe's friend and Joe owes Frank a favor. Frank proposes to call in his favor and secure Jane's job if she will have sex with him. By most analyses, Frank's proposal is an offer and Jane's agreement would be consensual. We would agree that Frank's be-havior is not coercive but not simply because Jane's options are increased or the consequences of her actions are improved. We also attach importance to the fact that Jane has a genuine choice in the following sense—unlike Joe's proposal, Jane is free to reject Frank's proposal without any untoward consequences. Her probability of job loss is unchanged by rejecting Frank's offer. In contrast, her probability of job loss increases when she rejects Joe's offer. It is that sense in which asymmetrical power relationships can contaminate the offer/threat calculus.

Defining consent in terms of threats, and threats in terms of the desirability of possible outcomes, naively ignores the importance of the context in which the pro-posal is made. If we take consent seriously we are obliged to consider whether the offeree is actually being asked to choose something or whether the context virtually forces a decision. If we only look to the form of the proposal and the characteristics of the various options, we risk losing sight of the core element in consent. If the power of the offeror and the context of the proposal give the offeree no genuine or legitimate choice in the matter, then it is fair to conclude that coercion is present. One of the assumptions of normal commercial transactions is that offerees are not under compulsion to decide. We take this to mean that they can walk away from proposals unscathed by the rejection of the offer.

In our example, Nozick's analysis forces us to ignore the context of Joe's "offer" and focus exclusively on his words. His position of power implies that Jane cannot simply reject it and return to "business as usual." Indeed, in most "offers" of this sort, the prospects for fair treatment subsequent to the "offer" being made are remote, and the offeree is sensitive to this inevitability. The terms of the relationship are changed by the "offer," and for that reason we think this scenario should not be evaluated strictly in terms of whether Jane's options are increased.

But, it might be said that our view misses the main point of Nozick's analysis — Joe's proposal has in fact done something good for Jane. That is, given her circumstances, she might indeed welcome it. Although his behavior has probably done irreparable harm to their working relationship, and although Jane must endure the indignity of having sex with him, and even though she feels she has no choice in the matter, she may prefer this outcome to loss of her job. We do not take issue with this consideration, but by the same token, we do not think it should be given any moral or legal weight in characterizing what Joe has done. This may seem paternalistic on our part, but it is in keeping with the analysis of most crimes where, owing to the peculiarities of the circumstance, the victim thinks she is better off. In these cases, the victim may be grateful that the crime took place but the perpetrator remains guilty of a criminal offense. It is partly as a result of these counterintuitive results that the determination of crimes focuses primarily on the objective behavior of the perpetrator and not on the feelings of the victim.

A few examples outside the realm of rape may be helpful. Consider the case where a burglar makes off with valuable jewelry or furs. Perhaps the owner has tired of the jewels and no longer finds it politically correct to wear the fur. Insurance proceeds put her in the happy position of replacing the stolen goods with more desirable things. But the fact that the victim is contented with her expanded options does not change the characterization of the thief's actions.

Also consider a thief who steals a motorcycle missing a cotter pin in its rear wheel. As the rider speeds away from the crime scene, the wheel disengages and the rider is thrown. But for the actions of the thief, the owner would have suffered a similar outcome. So the thief has actually done the owner a favor by stealing the bike. Why hold the thief liable for such helpful behavior? Of course, the answer is that the behavior is wrong, in and of itself, and considering the victim's preferences, is a needless distraction. Now, it may be argued that we have misinterpreted these cases because even though the victim is better off in a narrow sense, she is actually worse off in all these cases. That is, we have chosen odd situations where the victim's immediate interests are served although in a wider sense she has been harmed. Although her options are improved on, she has been harmed in virtue of having to live in a world where her property is not safe. Generally, victims are not better off and so it is incumbent on society to condemn all such cases, regardless of the victim's preferences.

Likewise, we believe that all cases of quid pro quo sexual harassment should be condemned regardless of the victim's preferences. There are good reasons that those in positions of authority should not be permitted to use their power for personal advantage. Only when we view the case of quid pro quo sexual harassment from a larger social context do we discern the true harm of this behavior. We have tried to show that analyzing this behavior in terms of offers versus threats does not get at the real problem. And the real problem we have in mind is the corruption of the workplace and the violation of women by those who would wield their powerful positions for personal enrichment. If we continue to talk only of the preferences of the victim we will never arrive at the problem created by the offending perpetrator.

This seems clear in cases involving pecuniary gain but is somehow obscured when it comes to sex. Consider the larcenous company buyer who insists on personal gifts before awarding contracts to a vendor. Some vendors may be happy to have the opportunity to give the buyer a vacation in return for a large contract. However, morally and legally, the preference of the buyer is irrelevant to our characterization of the buyer's behavior. It has long since been established that such behavior has a deleterious effect on the buying process and, depending on the circumstances (e.g., for government contractors), may be considered criminal behavior.

To sum up our first point, we hold that Jane's submission to Joe's proposal is nonconsensual because her acquiescence was not the result of her *choice* in any meaningful sense of the word. Joe's preferred weapon to overpower Jane is grave financial harm. But she is violated in a similar sense as a rape victim who is overcome by physical force. And the harm inflicted distinguishes this form of sexual harassment from the other varieties. Sexual harassment involving coerced sex in exchange for job security is like nonviolent rape in that there is a violation of the victim's physical person. At this end of the spectrum of sexual harassment we find criminal behavior, not merely sex discrimination.

Attempted Rape and Seduction

Another large category of sexual harassment is what we are calling "seduction harassment." This form of sexual harassment involves placing hurdles in the way of a woman student or employee as a way of coaxing her to have sex with her teacher or boss. Seduction harassment differs from the rape-like harassment we discussed above. Seduction harassment stops short of nonconsensual sexual intercourse; but there is a serious *attempt* to force a female employee or student to have sexual intercourse. Our own observations and the experiences of many we have talked to confirm that an attempt to obtain sex is often the motivation behind sexually harassing behavior.

Seduction harassment is morally problematic because of the attempt to obtain unconsented sexual intercourse. The term "seduction" is most often used for the attempt to obtain consented sexual intercourse. This is not what we are interested in here; but we will touch on this later when we take up "nuisance" harassment. What concerns us here is the way that men in positions of power use or abuse their power to try, but somehow fail, to get women, against their wills, to have sex with them. At present, such behavior might be treated as sex discrimination under the hostile workplace doctrine. However, in keeping with our characterization of some forms of sexual harassment as varieties of rape, we ask whether it is appropriate to carve out a special category for the failed quid pro quo harasser. Some crimes involve merely the "attempt" to do something wrong. "Attempt" crimes such as murder involve the intention to do wrong but the object of the intended behavior is not accomplished. One possibility would be to treat seduction harassment in the same way attempted rape is treated.

In the case of *Alexander v. Yale,* a male political science professor allegedly threatened to lower his female student's grade in his class (from a B to a C) if she did not sleep with him.[8] If the student had indeed been threatened with the lower grade, but had not acquiesced, then on our typology this would be a case of seduction harassment. Here the faculty member attempted to exploit the student-teacher relationship in order to obtain nonconsensual sexual intercourse.

Seduction harassment shares many morally salient features with attempted rape. In attempted rape, an attempt is made to coerce a woman into having sexual intercourse that she does not want. Similarly, the case of the student and professor mentioned above is also a case of attempted coercive nonconsensual sexual intercourse. It is attempted coercion in many of the same ways that attempted rapes in back alleys are coercive; namely, the woman's options are curtailed and she is pressured to acquiesce because she fears what will happen to her if she does not. In seduction harassment, the woman does not normally fear for her life, but her future prospects often do hang in the balance. As we discussed above, loss of job or poor grades can have permanent and quite detrimental effects on the future prospects of nearly all of us.

Typically, attempted rape is difficult to prove. *Black's Law Dictionary* indicates that attempt crimes generally require "more than mere preparation or planning for [something], which, if not prevented, would have resulted in the full consummation of the act attempted, but which, in fact, does not bring to pass the party's ultimate design."[9] The difficulty with cases of "seduction" harassment is that what prevents "the consummation of the act attempted" is the woman's unwillingness to acquiesce; the failure is not based on some factor external to the two parties involved. To prove that the seduction was like attempted rape one would need to show that what the employer or teacher did was more than mere preparation and planning, but involved something which would, under normal circumstances, bring about the result. Generally, in attempted rape cases, there would normally have to be evidence of a clear-cut serious threat of physical force, which would be strong enough in other contexts to lead to unconsented sexual intercourse.

Is the failure of the woman to acquiesce in the case of "seduction" harassment sufficiently like the failure of the woman to give in to the threat of physical force in the attempted rape case? The pressure that the employer or teacher brings down on the woman is meant to have the same effect that the threat of physical force would have, namely, that the woman has unconsented sexual intercourse with him. But in another sense these cases are not parallel, for the employer is not trying to gain acquiescence to sexual intercourse at any price—indeed, he might be repulsed by the idea of physically compelling the woman to have sex with him. What he wants is to have something approximating normal sex, not at knifepoint, but with her going along, based on the pressure he exerts on her.

The difficult question concerns what standards of evidence, and what legal sanctions, are morally appropriate in cases of "seduction" harassment. Here the problem is that the perpetrators of these acts are generally not physically menacing and may very well have become convinced that the women really were interested in forming sexual liaisons with them. If the man really does believe that the woman is in some sense consenting, then in criminal law the strongest of the *mens rea* criteria of criminal liability is undermined since it would not make sense to say that he intended to rape her if he did hold this belief. But the same can be said of attempted rape cases generally. Often potential rapists also believe that their victims really do like them. It may be, as some courts have held, that it was nonetheless negligent or reckless of him not to have realized that she was not really consenting.

As in the cases of attempted rape, we believe that seduction harassment will turn on the facts and circumstances of the case. One salient (but not controlling) consideration is the history of the relationship between the two parties. For instance, had the woman consistently rebuked the boss or the professor prior to his threatening proposal? If so, then any innocence he might attach to his threat is doubtful. However difficult some of these cases may be to adjudicate, we do not see this area as hopelessly mired in confusion. We believe that the norms and cues that underpin relationships between men and women are sufficiently clear-cut for most of us to distinguish a healthy romantic proposition from an extorting threat.

Intimidation and Sexual Harassment

Rape is but one way to conceive of the criminal element in sexual harassment. Employers or teachers can use their positions of power over female[10] subordinates or students so as to extract sexual or nonsexual favors not otherwise available. The use, or abuse, of power can often result in intimidation in which the subordinate fears reprisals if she does not acquiesce. In law, intimidation is defined in characteristically physical terms. *Black's Law Dictionary* says:

> To take, or attempt to take, "by intimidation" means willfully to take, or attempt to take, by putting in fear of bodily harm. Such fear must arise from the willful conduct of the accused, rather than from some mere temperamental timidity of the victim; however the fear of the victim need not be so great as to result in terror, panic, or hysteria.[11]

This narrow construal of intimidation means that few cases of sexual harassment strictly involve intimidation. Nonetheless, the parallels are rather striking between "putting one in fear of bodily harm" and "putting one in fear of loss of job," or "putting one in fear of receipt of a failing grade."

As we have intimated, loss of job or the receipt of a failing grade can be at least as devastating as a punch in the nose. For this reason, when one is put in fear of losing a job or receiving a failing grade the coercion can be at least as strong as in those cases where one is put in fear of being punched. If the coercion can be as strong in the nonphysical as in the physical intimidation cases, then there is no initial reason to think that the criminal law could not be used to adjudicate the nonphysical cases. In fact, this is just what we have seen in recent changes in the law of extortion and blackmail to include those cases where a defendant makes "a threat with the intent thereby to acquire the victim's property," but does not carry through with the threatened physical violence. LaFave and Scott say: "A number of statutes leave the realm of property altogether and cover threats made to induce the victim to do any act against his will." And the threat does not have to include physical violence, but can include a threat to "cause economic harm," or to ruin one's personal character or reputation.[12]

On the criminal level, it is criminal battery and assault that provides the basis for new legal avenues in sexual harassment cases involving intimidation. "Intimidation harassment" is often the sort that gets women subordinates to act against their will. When it is coupled with the sexual overlay we discussed above, sexual harassment as intimidation provides an example of one of the most odious forms of extortion. Sexual predators would be less likely to act on their impulses if they thought that their actions risked criminal sanctions in addition to the civil penalties currently used to deter their behavior. As we will argue at the end of our chapter, we need to pursue these criminal penalties as a way of indicating how serious the problem of sexual harassment is for the egalitarian functioning of our society.

Sexual harassment that takes the form of intimidation is especially problematical when it singles out women as a group for special, adverse treatment. In this sense, intimidation harassment is doubly harmful: It causes harm to the individual women in question and it discriminates against women as a group.[13] While in many cases the individual harm may appear to be too small for the law to concern itself with, the group-oriented effect is often quite large indeed. The civil law has become more and more involved in sexual harassment cases precisely because of the disparate impact that sexual harassment has on the employment and educational careers of women as compared with men.

Battery and Sexual Harassment

We now leave the more egregious forms of sexual harassment and consider those that lack coercive threats. Many critics of the expansion of the domain of sexual harassment refer to it as innocent horseplay or, at worst, annoying behavior. But there are bases in tort law for making some of the seemingly innocuous forms of sexual harassment actionable. In tort law, for instance, what counts as battery has been expanded to include any form of unwanted touching. Prosser and Keeton describe the state of tort law in this way:

> The defendant may be liable when intending only a joke, or even a compliment, as where an unappreciated kiss is bestowed without consent, or a misguided effort is made to render assistance. The plaintiff is entitled to protection according to the usages of a decent society, and offensive contacts, or those which are contrary to all good manners, need not be tolerated.[14]

In a note, Prosser and Keeton say: "Taking indecent liberties with a person without consent is of course battery."[15] Jokes and horseplay can sometimes amount to this kind of "taking indecent liberties." This characterization strikes us as fairly straightforward and would take in some of those seemingly innocent forms of sexual harassment.

Critics will argue that this is a perversion of the concept of battery, that we have confused hugs, kisses, caresses, and pats with slaps and punches. However, we do not think it so difficult to discern a difference between wanted and unwanted physical contact. Most importantly, we do not see those instances of unwanted physical contact as innocent expressions of affection. Rather, we believe that social convention is sufficiently determined to permit us to cull out the truly innocent and desirable cases from the obnoxious unwanted variety. And not to make this distinction is to ignore or trivialize the effects of offensive touching.

Two examples come to mind that illustrate this distinction. In one case, a jocular male worker grabs the buttocks of his female coworker, complimenting her on the results of her exercise regime. And in another, he hugs his female coworker and strokes her back as she struggles and squirms to be released from his grip. In both cases, the male worker would argue that he is simply expressing his affection or paying a well-deserved compliment. However, in both cases, the woman in question will often suffer the indignities associated with an invasion of her private, physical person. And social conventions are not so blurred that this behavior is condoned in any other but the most intimate of relationships. Social custom is clear that grabbing parts of a woman's anatomy is not acceptable behavior. For this reason, such behavior can be grounds for suit in tort law in most walks of life. And social cues are not so ambiguous that men are oblivious as to when it is appropriate to hug and caress women. Violating these norms is rightfully characterized as actionable outside the realm of the workplace and we do not see where the employment relationship changes the custom.

Sexual Harassment and Mental or Emotional Distress

Some other forms of sexual harassment are more like flirtation than like attempted rape. These forms of sexual harassment involve the use of sex appeal, or the attempt to exploit it, in the behavior of bosses or teachers toward their female workers or students, respectively. Such forms of sexual interaction have been going on in education and employment contexts probably since there have been such contexts. For many of these cases, the "flirtation" is relatively harmless. But in those cases where the flirtation is persistent and clearly indicated to be unwelcome, the employee or student might find it more difficult to pursue her job or studies than is true for her male colleagues. As with other forms of harassment, when such behavior interferes with how a person wishes to lead her life, there is the possibility of harm. And this harm becomes particularly pernicious when economic and educational opportunities are at stake.

Flirtation is relatively harmless and often desirable in those cases where it is mutually welcome. In such cases, people should be free to pursue their romantic interests as they see fit as long as others are not adversely affected. Many flirtatious encounters lead to relationships that are mutually beneficial. Yet, where flirtation is not welcome, especially in contexts of employment and education, it can become morally problematic by emotionally disturbing the women who are the focus of the flirtatious behavior.

American courts have increasingly seen sexual harassment as creating an unjustified burden on women of having to work or study in a hostile environment. But American courts have not approached sexual harassment as these courts have approached other forms of harassment that create hostile environments. One of the chief avenues that has not been sufficiently explored concerns the area of law involving the intentional infliction of mental or emotional distress. Courts have been willing to use this basis for holding liable telephone solicitation that occurs repeatedly and is clearly unwelcome or for holding private detectives liable for hounding people trying to get them to admit that they committed a certain act. As Prosser and Keeton put it:

> The extreme and outrageous nature of the conduct may arise not so much from what is done as from abuse by the defendant of some relation of or position which gives the defendant actual or apparent power to damage the plaintiff's interests. The result is something very like extortion. . . . It is seldom that any one such item of conduct is found alone in a case; and the liability usually has rested on a prolonged course of hounding by a variety of extreme methods. Similar outrageous bullying tactics on the part of insurance adjusters seeking to force a settlement, or evicting landlords seeking to harass unwanted tenants, have been subjected to the same liability.[16]

It is not clear to us why sexual harassment, which has already been held by the Supreme Court to create a hostile work environment, should not be treated as a form of intentional infliction of mental distress.

In a twist of fate reminiscent of Kafka, it is becoming increasingly popular for the alleged perpetrators of sexual harassment to sue their accusers on grounds of intentional infliction of mental distress.[17] If such cases are considered legitimate, why not suits by those sexually harassed? Indeed, there are many forms of nonsexual harassment that are considered legitimate bases of such legal suits. Even crank phone calls, obscene or not, which can be shown to harass and cause emotional distress are the subject of this type of tort action.[18] Ever since Prosser argued successfully that the intentional infliction of mental distress should be considered a "separate and independent tort," a wide range of types of harassment have been recognized to generate such complaints.[19] It seems to us time for sexual harassment victims to press these complaints as well, both against their employing institutions and against the individual sexual harassers.

Sexual Harassment as a Nuisance

There is also a well-established set of legal precedents against behavior that is a nuisance. Courts have ruled, for instance, that public profanity addressed at the plaintiff constituted a public nuisance that was actionable as a tort.[20] The key here is to show that the plaintiff did not take offense merely because she was overly sensitive, but that a reasonable person in these circumstances would also be offended. In establishing what is reasonably and what is not reasonably offensive, there has been quite a bit of controversy. In our context, one of the questions to ponder is whether we should appeal to a genderless reasonable person, or a reasonable woman, to determine what is overly sensitive "taking of offense" and what is reasonable "taking of offense."

If the harassing behavior is directed only at women, and takes the form of horseplay or low-grade annoyance, some men think of this behavior as innocent and will regard women who are offended by the behavior as overly sensitive. Nonetheless, many women regard such behavior as unwelcome, although some women will undoubtedly not mind the attention. If this is a correct assessment of a gender-gap in how sexual harassment as horseplay and annoying behavior is regarded, how should we determine what is "reasonable"? We are convinced that the best strategy is to ask how the average woman would respond, since women are the targets of this form of sexual harassment. The benefit of the doubt should go to the victims instead of the perpetrators of putatively offensive behavior.

This would seem to be a logical extension of how the law treats other forms of discriminatory behavior. For instance, certain behavior has been held to be actionable due to its symbolic harm. So if a vandal scrawls a Swastika on the home of a Jew, the crime is not just one of minor trespass or trivial destruction of property. And if a cross is burned in the yard of an African American homeowner, the offense is not simply one of illegally starting a fire. The point is that in these types of behavior, the standard for offensiveness is intelligible only from the standpoint of the intended victim. The defendants in these cases may argue that their actions were only "horseplay" and not intended to inflict serious harm. However, the law looks at how a Jew or an African American would feel under the circumstances. To do otherwise would miss the point of the discriminatory harmfulness of these acts.

But the cases are not completely parallel—gender and racial discrimination are not the same. We readily admit that the forms of sexual harassment that are more like horseplay and annoyance than like rape cannot be as easily dealt with in either the criminal or civil law. There are reasons for regarding most of this behavior as suspicious nonetheless, where legal remedies should be sought, but also where changes should be made in the way that we socialize boys or in the court of moral suasion and conscience. The main reason why some response is called for is that when female employees or students find themselves with lowered self-esteem or find it difficult to do their jobs, or perform their roles, unfairness has resulted. It is our belief that sexual harassment, in all of its forms, is inconsistent with the goals of a putatively egalitarian society.

Conclusion

Throughout this discussion it should be apparent that we believe that the pernicious nature of sexual harassment is often clear-cut. Individual women are victimized across a range of harms from humiliation and degradation to the invasion of their physical persons. The reason that sexual harassment is not taken more seriously is the tendency to trivialize the offence by characterizing any given victim as overly sensitive. Earlier we expressed our dismay at the lack of any criminal analog to the civil offense of sexual harassment. But our argument is from more than mere symmetry. We believe that criminalization of certain forms of sexual harassment is a necessary tool to reflect the seriousness of sexual harassment and to set the stage for its appropriate punishment.

Many forms of sexual harassment seem to us to call for a criminal remedy similar to other forms of harmful behavior that society wants and needs to eradicate. Consider the parallel case of tax fraud, where rules are established to maintain a voluntary system of self-assessment. Those who fail to comply with these rules are subject to a range of sanctions from monetary penalties to incarceration. Theoretically, there is a level at which fines could be levied that would discipline tax evaders to comply with the rules. However, in practice, compliance is not readily achieved through fines alone. The imposition of jail terms alters the stakes to a point where many potential tax evaders do not even consider cheating.

Likewise, deceit is recognized as morally reprehensible. And those who would defraud others are subjected to sanctions that, once again, range from forced restitution to criminal liability. The area of insider trading is illustrative of the power of criminal sanctions. Regulators and law enforcement officials have struggled to eradicate these activities from the securities markets. But their challenge is hobbled in part by the allure of quick, large profits. Absent the threat of incarceration, potential perpetrators would only consider their activities in terms of monetary risks and rewards. But when they see or read about a suspected colleague being escorted from her workplace in handcuffs, the nature of their calculations is fundamentally altered. When business students read about the excesses of the 1980s, it is not the enormous fine that Michael Milken was assessed but the jail term that impresses on them the seriousness of his crimes. Indeed, in this and many other cases, monetary fines have very small consequences on companies or their executives. Criminal liability changes the "rules of engagement." The potential for criminal sanctions changes the way the offense is regarded and significantly diminishes the potential for violations in a way that monetary penalties cannot.

We conclude that it is now time for the widespread recognition of a criminal sanction analog in the case of sexual harassment. Without such recognition, people are not led to view sexually harassing behavior in the same fashion as, for example, deceit or fraud. It is our view that if the more egregious forms of sexual harassment were given criminal standing, the entire category of crimes would be taken more seriously and attempted less frequently. If we genuinely believe that obtaining unconsented sex is socially pernicious behavior, then all forms of the behavior should be subject to similar legal sanctions.

Notes

1. Although we chose an example in the workplace, we believe the facts could be modified to accommodate a campus setting. Substitute professor and student for boss and worker, respectively, place at stake some vital good of the student such as continued status in a program, and a similar result could be obtained. But we recognize that this case is more difficult than the employment case, because there is normally no immediate harm such as that associated with financial ruin.

2. *Model Penal Code* Sec. 213(a).

3. It follows from our interpretation that not all instances of sex obtained by threatened job loss will be cases of gross sexual misconduct. The facts and circumstances of each case will be controlling because the extent of the threatened harm is what matters. But such advances may be sexual harassment of another nature as will be discussed.

4. R. Nozick, "Coercion," in *Socratic Puzzles* (Cambridge: Harvard University Press, 1997).

5. For Nozick, the crucial issue is how the proposal alters the course of events (see note 6). But in the case of sexual harassment, the course of events is either unknown or is subject

to manipulation by the harasser. It is not possible to say, with any degree of certainty, whether the quid pro quo harasser actually improves the victim's circumstances or not. Perhaps the victim would have kept her job anyway. In recognition of this problem, Nozick introduces the notion of the "morally expected" course of events. However, this qualifier adds little in our case, because the morally expected course of events is what we are trying to discern. If we make this a factor in determining the morality of the situation, we create a vicious circle. That is, we cannot base the morality of the harasser's behavior on the impact on a morally expected course of events until we determine if the course of action is moral. And finally, Nozick's analysis is problematic, because the harasser controls the outcome of events. That is, it seems bogus to say that Joe improves or worsens the ordinary course of events, since he can manipulate the outcome.

6. "As a first formulation, let us say that whether someone makes a threat against Q's doing an action or an offer to Q to do the action depends on how the consequences he says he will bring about change the consequences of Q's action from what they would have been in the normal or natural or expected course of events. If it makes the consequences of Q's action worse than they would have been in the normal and expected course of events, it is a threat; if a sanction makes the consequences better, it is an offer. The term *expected* is meant to shift between or straddle *predicted* or *morally required*" (p. 24).

7. Ibid.

8. This was the student's claim. The professor claimed that he merely offered to raise her grade from a D to a C, and that such an offer did not threaten her in any way. For analysis of this case, see John C. Hughes and Larry May, "Sexual Harassment," *Social Theory and Practice*, vol 6, no. 3 (Fall 1980): 249–280. On this point, also see Larry May and John C. Hughes, "Is Sexual Harassment Coercive?," in *Moral Rights in the Workplace* (Albany: State University of New York Press, 1987), pp. 115–122.

9. *Black's Law Dictionary*, 5th ed. (St. Paul: West, 1979), p. 116.

10. We will here ignore the cases where males, especially homosexual males, are similarly harassed. For more on this topic, see Larry May, *Masculinity and Morality* (Ithaca, NY: Cornell University Press, 1998), esp. chap. 6.

11. *Black's Law Dictionary*, p. 737.

12. Wayne R. LaFave and Austin W. Scott, Jr., *Criminal Law*, 2nd ed. (St. Paul, MN: West, 1986), pp. 790–791.

13. On this topic, see Marilyn Friedman and Larry May, "Harming Women as a Group," *Social Theory and Practice*, vol. 11, no. 2 (Summer 1985): 207–234.

14. W. Page Keeton, ed., *Prosser and Keeton on the Law of Torts* (St. Paul, MN: West, 1984), pp. 41–42.

15. Ibid., p. 42 n. 36.

16. Ibid., pp. 61–62.

17. Alba Conte, "When the Tables are Turned: Courts Consider Suits by Alleged Sexual Harassers," *Trial*, 32, no. 3 (March 1996): 30–36.

18. R. J. Cooper, "Grievous Bodily Harm by Telephone," *Journal of Criminal Law*, vol. 59, no. 4 (November 1995): 401–410.

19. William L. Prosser, "Intentional Infliction of Mental Suffering: A New Tort," *Michigan Law Review*, vol. 37 (1939): 874–892. Also see Calvert Magruder, "Mental and Emotional Disturbance in the Law of Torts," *Harvard Law Review*, vol. 49 (1936), esp. pp. 1033–1051.

20. Keeton, *Prosser and Keeton on the Law of Torts*, p. 648 n. 54.

9

BAT-AMI BAR ON

The "Scottsboro Case"

On Responsibility, Rape, Race, Gender, and Class

The "Scottsboro Case" is far from a single case in the legal sense.[1] Its name is derived from that of a town in Jackson County, Alabama, the county's seat in March 1931. This was where the legal proceedings began that revolved around the rape charges made by Roby Bates (17 years old) and her friend Victoria Price (21 years old or perhaps even 27 years old), both White, poor, and underemployed mill workers, against Olen Montgomery (18 years old), Clarence Norris (18 years old), Haywood Patterson (18 years old), Ozie Powell (16 years old), Willie Roberson (16 years old), Charlie Weems (20 years old), Andy Wright (19 years old), Roy Wright (14 years old), and Eugene Williams (15 years old), all temporary workers, African American, and poor. The proceedings ended in 1938 in Decatur, Alabama, where they were moved in 1933, following a request from the defense for a change of venue. This happened after Bates recanted her testimony while working with the defense team of 1933; two U.S. Supreme Court decisions that found for the defense, one in 1932 in *Powell v. Alabama* and the other in 1935 in *Norris v. Alabama*; a negotiated dropping of charges against Montgomery, Roberson, Williams, and Roy Wright in 1937; and the beginning of what were expected to be long-term incarcerations for Norris (sentenced to death but the sentence was commuted to life; he was paroled in 1944), Patterson (sentenced to 75 years but escaped in 1948), Weems (sentenced to 75 years and paroled in 1943), Andy Wright (sentenced to 90 years and paroled in 1944), and Powell (who would have been released with Montgomery, Roberson, Williams, and Roy Wright, following the negotiated agreement between the prosecution and the defense, but instead was sentenced to 20 years after pleading guilty to assaulting a sheriff; he was paroled in 1946).

In Scottsboro, there were four trials, the first for Norris and Weems, the second for Patterson, the third for Montgomery, Powell, Roberson, Williams, and Andy Wright, and the fourth for Roy Wright. All nine defendants were found guilty as charged and sentenced to death, though the prosecution asked for life imprisonment for Roy Wright, who had testified against all the others. Patterson testified against those who were not his friends: Montgomery, Norris, Powell, Roberson, and Weems. As a result of the more severe sentence handed down by the jury, Roy Wright's trial ended in a mistrial. He was reindicted but never tried again before his release from custody in 1937. Patterson, on the other hand, was tried four times and sentenced to death three out of the four times. Norris was tried three times and sentenced to death each time. It was following their second trials that Powell, Weems, and Andy Wright were sentenced to their respective prison terms. Like Roy Wright, Montgomery, Roberson, and Williams were tried only once.

The Alabama Supreme Court was appealed to three times, first in 1932, with regard to the Scottsboro trials, in 1934, in relation to the first Decatur trials, and in 1937, after the second Decatur trials. The Court found only once for any of the defendants: Eugene Williams, who should have been tried as a minor in 1931. The U.S. Supreme Court, despite the many ways it limited its discussions of its "Scottsboro Cases," excepting from consideration analysis of the far-from-neutral atmosphere in which the defendants were tried, and refusing to engage with a third "Scottsboro Case" in 1937, at least pointed out in both *Powell v. Alabama* and *Norris v. Alabama* that the trials did not meet some due process standards, either because of the lack of proper counsel for the defense or because of the unjustifiable exclusion of African Americans from the jury. Yet, the Alabama Supreme Court did not even see that these very narrowly specific and technical kinds of problems occurred in the Alabama lower courts.

One lower-court judge, James E. Horton, who presided over the first Decatur trials, was disturbed when the jury found Patterson guilty of rape with the sentence to death. Horton did not believe that the evidence warranted the jury's conclusion about the charge of rape and set both the verdict and the sentence aside. Yet, like the U.S. Supreme Court, Horton did not discuss the trial's atmosphere, which was questioned by the defense when it requested a new trial for Patterson. The defense lawyers, Samuel Leibowitz and Joseph Brodsky, contended that "religious prejudice" against them and efforts mounted in the North in defense of the "Scottsboro Boys" (presented by the prosecution as a form of Jewish intervention with justice), and "racial prejudice" against the defendants and African American witnesses for the defense, which was obvious by the disrespectful treatment shown to them by Thomas E. Knight, the Alabama Attorney General—let alone the general racist pressure on the court—made a fair trial quite impossible. What Horton preferred to focus on was the demonstrated lack of corroborating evidence for the charge of rape and the lack of credibility of the prosecution's most important witness, Price. She persisted in her claim that she was raped, this even after Bates said neither of them had been raped and that Price concocted the story, telling her to collaborate in its telling when they were apprehended with the "Scottsboro Boys," facing the possibility of vagrancy or prostitution charges.

Horton was but a typical (Southern) liberal projecting and deflecting white guilt feelings about and responsibility for race relations on what he took to be "a white woman of murky virtue," thereby absolving white men of their guilt, according to Brownmiller (1975), who introduced the "Scottsboro Case" into the U.S. second-wave feminist discourse of rape with its discussion in *Against Our Will*. Brownmiller claims that not only liberals but the Left, specifically the Communist Party of the time, also erred in its approach to the "Scottsboro Case" because, in addition to raising issues about Price's reputation, it construed the case "as symbolic of the perfidy of the American system" (p. 235). The "Scottsboro Case," Brownmiller believes, should be understood instead as "a white man's game that was played out in the Scottsboro trials, with black men and white women as moveable pawns" (pp. 232–233).

Brownmiller, who enters her discussion of the "Scottsboro Case" cautiously because she is convinced, and for quite good reasons,[2] that she is violating Leftist taboos, is at pains to point out that it is not a matter of a racist projection but rather a matter of fact that not only white-on-black but also black-on-white rapes occur and that some African American men indulge the fantasy of, and male privilege to, sexually harass and rape white women. She tries to discuss rape from its victims' perspective, and she takes this perspective to be exclusively that of women, specifically Price and Bates. Even though she believes that racial injustice occurred with regard to the "Scottsboro Case," it is not clear whether she is truly persuaded of the complete innocence of the "Scottsboro Boys" or whether she suspects that something did happen, even if not the rape that Price continued to assert took place despite Bates's changed testimony. Independently of her possible suspicions, though, Brownmiller does believe that, as Bates began saying in 1933, she and Price perjured themselves by pressing false rape charges against the "Scottsboro Boys," and they did so quite selfishly in order to avoid vagrancy or prostitution charges.

What for many would follow from this is some form of moral indignation and not merely at the South's racism in general, or the racism of Southern white men in particular. One would also be indignant, if not at both Bates and Price, then, at least, at Price. Yet, this is just what Brownmiller resists. She does so by equating the situation of the African American "Scottsboro Boys" with that of both white women. Appealing to what she takes as a shared perspective among women, she says,

> The singular opportunity afforded Bates and Price should be appreciated by every woman. From languishing in a jail cell as the lowest of low, vagrant women who stole rides on freight cars, it was a short step to the witness stand where dignity of a sort could be reclaimed by charging that they had been pathetic, innocent victims of rape. . . . Operating from precisely the same motivation—to save their own skin—some of the black defendants tried to exculpate themselves in court by saying they had seen the others do the raping. (pp. 231–232)

The response to Brownmiller's refusal of moral indignation at Bates and Price was angry and swift. According to Edwards, "Susan Brownmiller's analysis of the Scottsboro case is so outrageous it shocks the conscience. It is utterly and irredeemably obscene" (p. 8). And for Davis (1981),

> Susan Brownmiller's discussion on rape and race evinces an unthinking partisanship which borders on racism. In pretending to defend the cause of all women, she sometimes boxes herself into the position of defending the particular cause of *white* women, regardless of its implications. Her examination of the Scottsboro Nine case is a revealing example. As Brownmiller herself points out, these nine young men, charged and convicted of rape, spent long years of their lives in prison be-

cause two white women perjured themselves on the witness stand. Yet she has nothing but contempt for the Black men and their defense movement—and her sympathy for the two white women is glaring. . . . No one can deny that the women were manipulated by Alabama racists. However it is wrong to portray the women as innocent pawns, absolved of the responsibility of having collaborated with the forces of racism. In choosing to take sides with white women, regardless of the circumstances, Brownmiller herself capitulates to racism. (pp. 198–99)

Both Edwards and Davis believe that Brownmiller is seduced, possibly unintentionally, by her tendency toward a form of paradigmatic thinking that disregards racism in the "Scottsboro Case." They see Brownmiller as alarmingly mistaken for not assigning moral blame to the women, this mistake specifically resulting from the equation of the situation of the "Scottsboro Boys" with that of the women. The equation is wrong, according to them, because Bates and Price were white, and at the least this means that the "Scottsboro Boys" could not save themselves at the two women's expense, while the two women could benefit "from the privilege of being white in Southern society" and save themselves "at the expense of nine lives" (Edwards, p. 9).

Edwards's and Davis's responses to Brownmiller either presuppose or suggest three related theoretical claims about oppression:[3]

(1) There are several and distinct kinds of oppression in the United States.

(2) In any society in which there are several and distinct kinds of oppression, a person may be a member of one or more oppressed groups and, at the same time, also be a member of one or more dominant groups.

(3) While there may not be a hierarchy of oppressions among the several and distinct kinds of oppressions in force in a society, in at least some situations involving members of differently oppressed groups not all of the relevant oppressions are similarly salient for the dynamic unfolding of those situations.

It is about the third claim, insofar as it applies to the "Scottsboro Case," that Brownmiller, Edwards, and Davis disagree. All three seem to agree on the first, if not for every kind of oppression, then for class, race, and gender. They all also agree on the second, since according to all of them, the "Scottsboro Boys" are African American but also male, and Bates and Price are female but also White. For Brownmiller, race- and gender-based oppressions are similarly salient in the "Scottsboro Case," and, therefore, she sees no one as located in a more advantageous position. To Edwards and Davis, race-based oppression, thus racism, is more salient than gender-based oppression or sexism, in this case, and it does locate Bates and Price in a more advantageous position relative to that of the "Scottsboro Boys."

The disagreement between Brownmiller and Edwards and Davis is not merely that between observers with different partial perspectives. For all of them, both race-based oppression and sex-based oppression are relevant to an analysis of the "Scottsboro Case." When they disagree here about whether racism or sexism is more salient, what they disagree about is what each of them takes to be facts that the others should incorporate into their analysis. For Edwards and Davis, Brownmiller's failure to understand the salience of race-based oppression goes beyond her analysis of the "Scottsboro Case" and affects her very understanding of rape as a socio-historical phenomenon, which, as a result, is far from nuanced. Other Brownmiller antiracist critics have developed this theme too. Thus, between them, Hall (1983) and Wriggins (1983) point out the extent to which Brownmiller still operates within and contributes to a racist conceptual framework that portrays white women as innocent and black men as lustful. And hooks (1981) comments, in addition to and in a manner that foregrounds one of the crucial effects of this framework, that "Brownmiller further perpetuates the belief that the real danger to women of interracial sexual exploitation in American society is black male rape of white women" (p. 53).

Brownmiller's protective focus on white women is a point that Crenshaw (1989), too, picks as particularly significant. Like others of Brownmiller's antiracist critics, she first takes notice of Brownmiller's discussion of the rape of black women and her attempt to undercut the hysteria caused by the myth of the black rapist and even lauds it before turning to some of the shortcomings of Brownmiller's analysis. These, Crenshaw believes, are clearest in Brownmiller's treatment of the Emmet Till case.

According to Brownmiller, Till, a 14-year-old African American from Chicago, while visiting in Money, Mississippi, bragged about his sexual success with white women to other African American teenage boys who then wanted proof. He proceeded to sexually harass white Carolyn Bryant, who ran him off. He was later murdered by two white men, J. W. Millam and his half-brother and Carolyn Bryant's husband, Roy, who wanted to just rough him up but got angry at his continued bragging. When Brownmiller analyzes the case, she says

> Rarely has one single case exposed so clearly as Till's the underlying group-male antagonism over access to women, for what began in Bryant's store should not be misconstrued as an innocent flirtation. Till's action was more than a kid's brash prank and his murder was more than a husband's revenge. . . . Emmet Till was going to show his black buddies that he, and by inference they, could get a white woman . . . . In concrete terms the accessibility of all white women was on review. This is how it must have been perceived by Till's companions. . . . And we know this is how it was perceived by Millam and Bryant. (p. 247)

And Crenshaw remarks

> [Brownmiller's] analysis places the sexuality of white women, rather than racial terrorism, at center stage. . . . While [she] seems to categorize the case as one that evidences a conflict over possession, it is regarded in African American history as a tragic dramatization of the South's pathological hatred and fear of African Americans. (p. 159)

Brownmiller, of course, knows that she is centering the sexual harrasment of a White woman in her analysis of the Till case and not racial terrorism. But for her, to accept the African American perspective that Crenshaw uses to illuminate the Till case is to place men center-stage in a feminist antirape discourse. According to Brownmiller, what makes it possible for Till to harass Carolyn Bryant is the salience of sexism in U.S. culture, and what she believes Till's harassing of Carolyn Bryant does is to show how much more salient sexism is in comparison with racism. The African American perspective that Crenshaw deploys is, for Brownmiller, the very same one that she is resisting when she refuses to accept archival information about lynching as telling all there is to know about rape and race.

Brownmiller believes that the standard story of lynching, which provides the interpretive framework for Till's murder in the African American community and is the story that could and was used to provide a similar interpretive framework for the "Scottsboro Case," now reads as a case of "legal lynching," a story of race-based victimization, usually the victimization of men.[4] In this story, rape is indeed only a legitimizing ploy for morally unjustifiable white terrorism, even if it is actually used in approximately one quarter of the lynchings. Though rape appears in lynching, the standard story of lynching does not center on women. Since her interest is in theorizing rape from the experience of women and not men, Brownmiller holds that lynching cannot provide her with the material with which to make a feminist sense of rape.

Apthekar (1982), accepting both Brownmiller's characterization of the usual African American antiracist perspective as male-centered and the characterization of her own perspective as concerned with the centering of women, nonetheless tries to reconcile the two through the examination of lynching. Apthekar describes her own goal as that of assuming "a point of view that would resolve the apparent contradiction between being able to resist the racist use of the rape charge against Black men, and at the same time counter the pervasive violence and rape that affects women of all races and classes" (p. 53). For her, focusing on lynching is methodologically enlightening in this respect, particularly when lynching is understood from the perspective of the African American women's antilynching movement. This movement, according to Apthekar, was at the same time "a movement against rape" (p. 62).

Conceived from the perspective of the African American women's antilynching movement, Apthekar says, "The dialectics of the lynch mentality required the dehumanization of Black men (as rapists), Black women (as prostitutes), and white women (as property whose honor was avenged by the men who possessed them)" (p. 62). The implication of this for an attempt to make sense of rape and lynching together is that "the conventional categories of 'lynching' and 'rape'" have to be forgone (p. 54). Apthekar does not articulate the conceptual changes that took place for her once she let go of the "conventional categories" of "lynching" and "rape." Yet, her work and the work of other antiracist critics of Brownmiller, who also do not articulate the conceptual changes that they believe are needed in order to think differently about rape, suggest several possibilities for an enlarged conception of rape that is inclusive of, yet is much more expansive than, the one Brownmiller uses and develops. Like Brownmiller's conception, this one too is not an attempt to articulate which acts constitute rape but rather some of its social meanings and effects. Thus, according to this conception of rape,

(1) Rape is, among other things, a means of terror similar to lynching, but also to other means of terror intended to coerce a specific person or group and cause it to act in certain ways.[5]

(2) Rape does not merely presuppose but also enacts the distinction between "good" women, understood to be "rapeable," and "bad" women,
considered to be "unrapeable."[6]

> (a) In an anti-Black racist society like the United States, the good/bad
> and rapeable/unrapeable distinctions racialize women because of the
> clustering of goodness, rapeability and Whiteness on one side and bad-
> ness, unrapeability and Blackness on the other.[7]

> (b) A similar clustering occurs in the United States in relation to class
> with lower-class women being characterized as bad and unrapeable
> while middle- and upper-class women are characterized as good and
> rapeable.

> (c) Among the functions of the clustering is also the domestication of
> white and middle- and upper-class women.

(3) Rape victimizes directly and indirectly. Among rape's direct victims are
raped women but also lynched African American men who are accused of
rape.[8]

The anti-racist-feminist conception of rape that seems to be suggested by
Apthekar's and other antiracist critiques of Brownmiller's work, all of whom are
feminists, while attentive to women's experiences, is not women-centered in just
the ways that Brownmiller would have liked a conception of rape to be. Indeed, for
Brownmiller, centering on women is so important that she even understands men's
rape experiences, especially in jail, as modeled on the rape of women. She says

> Prison rape is seen today for what it is: an acting out of power roles within an all-
> male, authoritarian environment in which the younger, weaker inmate, usually a
> first offender, is forced to play the role that in the outside world is assigned to
> women. In a wicked twist of irony, it is often the avowedly homosexual youths, be-
> cause of their "feminine" mannerisms and pariah status, who fall victims to the
> most brutal of prison gang rapes. . . . The other favored category of inmate who
> is earmarked for prison rape—perhaps the favored victim—is the slight, sensitive
> young man, whatever his sexual persuasion, who cannot or does not wish to fight.
> (p. 258)

At the same time, though, the anti-racist-feminist conception of rape is not
men-centered in ways that would have necessarily alarmed Brownmiller since,
while it includes men's experiences, it does not prioritize them over the experiences of women. Still, because it includes men's experiences, this enlarged conception both affirms and undercuts some of the aspects of Brownmiller's analysis. It
does so in particularly revealing ways with respect to the cases that she uses to call
attention to the salience of sexism, even in racist contexts.

The enlarged conception of rape affirms some of Brownmiller's suggestions
with regard to the Till case. This conception confirms that, as Brownmiller insists,
Carolyn Bryant, though a victim of sexual harassment and not rape, has to be seen
as a victim in the case just as is Emmet Till, who was killed following the harass-

ment. Carolyn Bryant is not only a direct but also an indirect victim due to her do-mestication as a white woman constituted through her husband and his brother's actions as if needing their protection and as their property. Emmet Till is a direct victim, killed because he was an African American who dared to have a sexual interest in white women.

Looking back at the "Scottsboro Case" from the perspective afforded by the anti-racist-feminist conception of rape, one can see that Brownmiller's primary problem is that she fails to distinguish between direct and indirect victims when she asserts that the "Scottsboro Case" should be understood as "a white man's game that was played out in the Scottsboro trials, with black men and white women as moveable pawns." The "Scottsboro Case" had nine direct victims, all African American men, who while not extra-legally lynched, were "legally lynched" from the very start because they were tried and incarcerated for alleged rapes of white women. Bates and Price were not direct victims of rape in the "Scottsboro Case." They were, nonetheless, victimized by rape.

The categorization of Bates and Price as indirect victims of rape makes the moral evaluation of their responsibilities more complicated than it seems at first sight. The principle that Davis uses to hold Bates and Price morally blameworthy is that of intentionality. That is, according to Davis, if one intentionally engages in wrongdoing, one is morally culpable for one's actions. So, since Bates and Price were not "innocent pawns" and have chosen to "collaborate with the forces of racism," intentionally using their racial location as white women to their own advantage, they are morally reprehensible.

But, Davis's principle of intentionality does not distinguish between the intentionality of people who are differently affected when several kinds of oppression operate simultaneously, even if in some situations, one or another kind is more salient, as racism is in the "Scottsboro Case." From Davis's perspective, Bates and Price are morally guilty because they intentionally used their position as White to their advantage. Yet, Bates and Price were not simply white women. Bates and Price were poor, underemployed white women. The implication of their kind of indirect victimization by rape is that usually they were perceived as bad and un-rapeable. Thus, when they perjured themselves, they could only gamble, and with added risk to themselves if they were not to be believed, about the advantage that their racial position gave them.[9]

To intentionally bet on one's racial position is not the same as taking privilege for granted. When one takes privilege for granted, one is quite certain that certain things will or will not happen. One can be certain, for example, that one will be taken seriously as a credible witness. But, due to their specific class position, Bates and Price did not have the same kind of "white privileges" as white women of higher classes, and what they lacked, in particular, is witness credibility. They pre-tended and tried to "pass," and not being able to take privilege for granted, wagered on whether they could tap into "white rage." Even if their gamble implies a choice to "save themselves" at "another's expense," choices of this sort may carry the pre-sumption of moral culpability, but do not assign it absolutely and with full force, because there are conditions under which one has only bad choices to make.

Bates and Price would have been unique and admirable if in 1931 they would have chosen to be arrested and tried for prostitution and vagrancy rather than bet on the possibility of "saving themselves" at the "Scottsboro Boys" expense. They were racist and not antiracist, at least when the "Scottsboro Case" began and before Bates changed her testimony and started working for the defense and with the "Scottsboro Boys" defense committee. Yet they need not be judged against an abstract ideal of moral responsibility.[10] They need to be morally evaluated in their concrete situation, something that neither Brownmiller nor Brownmiller's antiracist critics seem to tend to do because each of them tries to claim salience for only one of two kinds of oppression—that based on sex or that based on race. One may note that in both cases, class-based oppression is mentioned and elided.

ACKNOWLEDGMENTS   I first learned about the "Scottsboro Case" when still a child and in Israel. It was among the cases my father brought to my attention when we discussed alternative political systems and compared socialist ones with that of the United States. I came back to it while active in the feminist anti-rape movement in the United States and the publication of Brownmiller's *Against Our Will* (1975). I began wanting to examine it more closely a few years ago as I was preparing for a course on feminist jurisprudence that centered on feminist critical race theory. I would like to thank everyone I had the chance to talk with about the "Scottsboro Case" during these different times and in these very different places. I would also like to thank Lisa Tessman for her thoughtful listening and insightful comments, Keith Burgess-Jackson for editorial help, and Mary Jane Treacy for additional suggestions.

Notes

1. There are a few historical accounts of the "Scottsboro Case." I am using Goodman's *Stories of Scottsboro* (New York: Pantheon, 1994). Goodman, who is convinced that the rape charges were fictitious and the "Scottsboro Case" could not even take an initial form but for the "poisonous . . . idea that black men are rapists," nonetheless, tries to understand the conflict over the facts from many perspectives, believing that no contestation can make sense unless "even as we evaluate and cast judgment upon competing points of view, and by those judgments live our lives," one approaches a struggle from the many points of view of those engaged in it, attentive to "how and why other people make sense of their experience the ways that they do" (p. xiii).

2. According to her own account, Brownmiller was a student of Aptheker and very aware of the Left's prioritization of antiracist over feminist politics. Her experience of the marginalization of women's issues on the Left was far from unique. See the accounts by Robin Morgan in "Goodbye to All That" (1970) and Marge Piercy in "The Grand Coolie Damn" (1970).

3. These three claims represent a current consensus achieved through the work of many, including, of course, Brownmiller, Edwards, and Davis. I would like to mention just a few of the other contributions to its formation, such as the 1977 Combahee River Collective's "A Black Feminist Statement," Moraga and Anzaldúa's *This Bridge Called My Back* (1981) and bell hooks's *Ain't I a Woman* from the same year, Lugones and Spelman's "Have We Got a Theory for You: Feminist Theory, Cultural Imperialism, and the Demand for 'The

Woman's Voice'" (1983), Young's "Five Faces of Oppression" (1988), and Spelman's *Inessential Woman,* also from 1988, as well as Collins's *Black Feminist Thought* (1990).

4. Gerda Lerner (1972) was the first to call second-wave feminist attention to lynching. Further discussions of lynching in second-wave feminist literature began with critiques of Brownmiller such as Hall's. The issue has been rebroached following the Anita Hill-Clarence Thomas hearings due to Thomas's claim that the hearings functioned like a lynching. Following that, more attention has been given to gender in the description of lynching by feminists as, e.g., in Brown's "Imaging Lynching: African American Women, Communities of Struggle, and Collective Memory" (1995).

5. For a discussion of terrorism see my "Why Terrorism is Morally Problematic," and for a discussion of the relationship between rape and terrorism, see Card, "Rape Terrorism" (1996). See also essays in my *Hypatia* special issue on women and violence.

6. The notion of "rapeability" as it is used here does not imply anything about any woman's real risks of rape. It is only intended to suggest how women are viewed culturally, which has implications for their credibility if and when they present themselves as having been attacked.

7. A similar claim can be made about other specific racisms since as Gilman notes in *Difference and Pathology* (1985), racism sexualizes in quite specific ways. See also James, *Resisting State Violence* (1996).

8. While I will not develop this theme here, I believe that it is important to further expand even this already expanded conception of rape. What it does not allow yet is thinking about white men who were lynched following rape accusation. Nor does it allow for differentiations that would make it possible to think more carefully about cases such as that of Leo Frank who was lynched following his murder conviction, which seemed to have depended on accepting an African American testimony only because he was Jewish and the murder victim was white and Christian. See the discussion in Lindeman's *The Jew Accused* (1991).

9. This is not just a theoretical implication. Brownmiller notes that exactly the kind of issues brought up by the defense in the "Scottsboro Case" have worked elsewhere and in other times to abate the "collective rage" of whites against African Americans accused of rape (p. 220).

10. The moral evaluation of choices under oppression is discussed in an interesting way by Frye in *The Politics of Reality* (1983).

References

Aptheker, Bettina. *Women's Legacy: Essays on Race, Sex, and Class in American History.* Amherst: University of Massachusetts, 1982.

Bar On, Bat-Ami. "Why Terrorism Is Morally Problematic." In *Feminist Ethics,* edited by Claudia Card. Lawrence: University of Kansas, 1991.

Bar On, Bat-Ami, ed. *Hypatia: Special Issue on Women and Violence* 11(4) (fall 1996).

Brown, Elsa Barkley. "Imaging Lynching: African American Women, Communities of Struggle, and Collective Memory." In *African-American Women Speak Out on Anita Hill-Clarence Thomas,* edited by Geneva Smitherman. Detroit, MI: Wayne State University, 1995, pp. 100–124.

Brownmiller, Susan. *Against Our Will: Men, Women and Rape.* New York: Simon and Schuster, 1975.

Card, Claudia. *The Unnatural Lottery: Character and Moral Luck.* Philadelphia, PA: Temple University Press, 1996.

Collins, Patricia Hill. *Black Feminist Thought.* Boston: Unwin Hyman, 1990.

The Combahee River Collective. [1977] "A Black Feminist Statement." Reprinted in *But Some of Us Are Brave: Black Women's Studies,* edited by Gloria T. Hull, Patricia Bell Scott, and Barbara Smith. New York: The Feminist Press, 1982, 13–22.

Crenshaw, Kimberlè. "Demarginalizing the Intersection of Race and Sex: A Black Feminist Critique of Antidiscrimination Doctrine, Feminist Theory, and Antiracist Politics." *The University of Chicago Legal Forum* 139 (1989): 139–167.

Davis, Angela Y. *Women, Race and Class.* New York: Random House, 1981.

Edwards, Susan. nd. *Rape, Racism, and the White Women's Movement: An Answer to Brownmiller.* Chicago: Sojourner Truth Organization.

Frye, Marilyn. *The Politics of Reality: Essays in Feminist Theory.* Trumansburg, NY: Crossing, 1983.

Gilman, Sander. *Difference and Pathology: Stereotypes of Sexuality, Race, and Madness.* Ithaca, NY: Cornell University, 1985.

Goodman, James. *Stories of Scottsboro.* New York: Pantheon, 1994.

Hall, Jacquelyn Dowd. "'The Mind That Burns in Each Body': Women, Rape, and Racial Violence." In *Power of Desire: The Politics of Sexuality,* edited by Ann Snitow, Christine Stansell, and Sharon Thompson. New York: Monthly Review, 1983: 328–349.

hooks, bell. *Ain't I a Woman: Black Women and Feminism.* Boston: South End, 1981.

James, Joy. *Resisting State Violence: Radicalism, Gender, and Race in US Culture.* Minneapolis: University of Minnesota, 1996.

Lerner, Gerda, ed. *Black Women in White America: A Documentary History.* New York: Pantheon, 1972.

Lindeman, Albert S. *The Jew Accused: Three Anti-Semitic Affairs (Dreyfus, Beilis, Frank) 1894–1915.* Cambridge: Cambridge University, 1991.

Lugones, María C. and Elizabeth V. Spelman. "Have We Got a Theory for You: Feminist Theory, Cultural Imperialism, and the Demand for 'The Woman's Voice'." *Women's Studies International Forum* 6(6)(1983): 573–581.

Moraga, Cherríe and Gloria Anzaldúa, eds. *This Bridge Called My Back: Writings by Radical Women of Color.* Watertown, MA: Persephone, 1981.

Morgan, Robin. 1970. "Goodbye to All That." In *Voices from Women's Liberation,* edited by Leslie Tanner. New York: The New American Library, 268–276.

Piercy, Marge. "The Grand Coolie Damn." In *Sisterhood is Powerful: An Anthology of Writings from the Women's Liberation Movement,* edited by Robin Morgan. New York: Random House, 1970, 421–438.

Spelman, Elizabeth V. *Inessential Woman: Problems of Exclusion in Feminist Thought.* Boston: Beacon, 1988.

Wriggins, Jennifer. "Rape, Racism, and the Law." *Harvard Women's Law Journal* 6 (1983): 103–141.

Young, Iris Marion. "Five Faces of Oppression." *Philosophical Forum* 19(4)(1988)270–290.

PART IV

EVALUATING RAPE LAW

10

DAVID ARCHARD

The *Mens Rea* of Rape

Reasonableness and Culpable Mistakes

An Honest but Unreasonable Mistake

The kind of case that I want to discuss in this chapter has the following features:

(1) Smith had sex with Jones.
(2) At the time of this sex, Jones did not consent to sex with Smith.
(3) Smith would not have had sex with Jones had he believed (2).
(4) At the time of this sex, Smith did not believe (2).
(5) In some sense, it may be appropriate to describe Smith's cognitive state as specified in (4) as unreasonable.

This is a rather formal way of describing the kind of case in which someone makes an honest but unreasonable mistake about the other person's giving of consent to sex. *Morgan* was such a case and the judgment made in that case by the British House of Lords—to the effect that an honest but unreasonable mistake as to consent may constitute a defense to the charge of rape—has figured prominently in subsequent discussions of rape and its *mens rea*.[1] Critics have argued strongly that a palpably unreasonable belief in the woman's consent should not excuse a man from the charge of rape. Against that it has been urged that rape is not the sort of crime for which negligence should constitute *mens rea*. And an honest failure to see what a reasonable prudent person would have seen is negligence.[2] Thus specific issues pertaining to the nature of rape as a crime, and general issues about whether guilt requires a person to be in a particular state of mind, have been raised by this kind of case. In what follows, I want to say something about the sort of mistake that is being made in this case and about the nature of the charge of unreasonableness being made with regard to this kind of mistake.

First let me say something about each of the case-defining statements listed above. Together, (1) and (2) define the *actus reus* of the crime of rape. The man, Smith, had sex with a woman, Jones, to which she did not, at the time of the sex, consent. The use of the phrase "Smith had sex with Jones" is deliberately imprecise. It allows us to say that rape can encompass more, and other than, penetrative intercourse. In talking of consent at the time of the sex, I mean to allow that, in some particular encounter with a man, a woman can consent to some forms of sexual intimacy but withdraw consent from subsequent more explicit sexual activity. It should also be possible that a woman may consent to penetration but not to completed coitus.[3] Consent to the former should not be taken as consent to complete sexual intercourse.[4] I want also to rule out a charge of rape that follows from a change of mind after the event. A woman may come to regret that sex has taken place but she cannot retrospectively withdraw her consent if that consent has already been given. Revoking consent during sex is distinct from retrospective withdrawal of consent after the event.

Statement (2) says merely that Jones did not consent to sex with Smith. In the past, the law—such as that which has operated in Britain, for instance—has spoken not simply of a lack of consent but of a lack of consent due to "force, fear or fraud." Feminists have, with justice, criticized this more stringent standard. For it has often required of the prosecution in a rape trial that they show evidence of "utmost resistance" by the victim to the alleged rapist; or that they prove that the victim submitted only in the face of superior force or credible threats of extreme violence. Susan Estrich notes, "rape is most assuredly not the only crime in which consent is a defense; but it is the only crime that has required the victim to resist physically in order to establish nonconsent."[5] The absence of consent should not be equated with resistance to overwhelming force.[6] Under British law, it is now accepted that the presence of force, fear, or fraud may be evidence for the lack of consent but are not criteria of its lack. In the case of *Olugboja* the British Court of Appeal firmly stated that "the question now is simply: 'At the time of sexual intercourse did the woman consent to it?' It is not necessary for the prosecution to prove that what might otherwise appear to have been consent was in reality merely submission induced by force, fear or fraud, although one or more of these factors will no doubt be present in the majority of cases of rape."[7]

Statement (3) is important for it allows us to say of Smith that he does not disregard the importance of Jones consenting to sex with him. It is not true of Smith that he knows Jones not to be consenting but is nevertheless determined to have sex with her regardless. Nor is it true that if he were to think about whether Jones is consenting, and conclude that she is not, he would continue to have sex with her. Smith does not discount her lack of consent as a reason not to have sex with her. If he did know her not to be consenting he would not continue. He does not, to use Lord Hailsham's memorable phrase in the *Morgan* judgment, proceed with the "intention of having intercourse willy-nilly not caring whether the victim consents or no."[8]

We can imagine other versions of (3), such as "Smith would not have had sex with Jones had he entertained any serious doubt that (2) might be true." According to this version of (3), Smith acknowledges that there may be a risk attached to having sex with Jones, and it is one that he is not prepared to run if it is possible that such sex is not consented to by Jones. Note further that Smith might not be prepared to run this risk out of regard for Jones—he does not want to risk harming her—or out of regard for himself—he does not want to risk being accused of rape and of suffering the possible consequences of such an accusation. In what follows, such alternative construals of (3) are understood to be possible. Furthermore, the two distinct reasons for avoiding the risks of unconsented sex should be borne in mind.

Statement (4) is a complex statement, and this is reflected in the use of the phrase, "cognitive state." This comprises two possibilities: that Smith had a belief; namely, that Jones was consenting, or that Smith lacked a belief; namely, that Jones was not consenting.[9] Clearly, if Smith believed Jones to be consenting, he also did not believe her not to be consenting. But the converse does not hold. Lacking a belief that someone is not consenting does not entail the holding of a belief that she is. Let me first take the case of lacking a belief in nonconsent. We might imagine that Smith has not given any thought to the question of consent ("His mind is a total blank on the subject."[10]). Or we might imagine that Smith has adverted to the issue of consent and its possible absence, only to quickly and immediately put it out of his mind. He is so determined to have sex with Jones that he refuses to have any belief about her consent (or nonconsent). He suppresses all such thoughts of consent or its absence. Remember that, according to (3), Smith would desist from sex if he thought Jones was not consenting. But he avoids having the thought that she is not consenting.

Let me now turn to the case of Smith believing that Jones is consenting. Here there are two broad possibilities. The first is that Smith should form such a belief by never even considering that she might not be consenting or by putting out of his mind any consideration that she might not be. He believes, positively, that she does consent by discounting the contrary possibility or evidence for such a possibility. A belief in consent conjoins with and is, in some sense, based on a lack of belief in nonconsent.

The second possible understanding of what it might be for Smith to believe that Jones is consenting is that Smith should think about the possibilities—of Jones consenting or not consenting—and should form the judgment that she is. He does not ignore the possibility of her not consenting. Nor does he simply suppress any thought that she is not. This is the understanding of (4) that I shall henceforth concentrate on. I do not mean to imply that the other understandings are not possible ones. Nor that they do not constitute important understandings. However, I think it valuable to concentrate on the case of "honest mistake," which is most favorable to the view that someone who makes such a mistake should not be held culpable. After all, it is relatively easy to see why someone who acts without even thinking whether in doing so he acts on a mistake, or who discounts the very possibility of making a mistake, may be described as acting culpably. But in the favored case, Smith does countenance the possibility of Jones's not consenting; he concludes, mistakenly by (2), that she is consenting. In the language of advertence that often figures in definitions of negligence and recklessness, Smith adverts to the risk of her nonconsent. He does not consciously disregard this risk or fail to see that there is such a risk.

Two last points about (4). First, Smith is honest in believing that Jones is consenting. Second, Smith honestly believes this at the time of having sex with Jones. I rule out any *post hoc* rationalization by Smith ("She must have been consenting"). I also rule out any simple inference from "There is reason to think Jones will consent to sex with me" to "There is reason to think that Jones is now consenting to sex with me." There are obviously behaviors by Jones that may make it reasonable for Smith to judge that she is likely to consent to sex. But these behaviors need not also constitute of themselves present consent or evidence that consent is presently forthcoming.

Making a Mistake

From the conjunction of (2) and (4), it follows that Smith made a mistake. We also allow that it is an honest mistake. Statements (1) and (2) together are sufficient for the *actus reus* of rape. Statement (3), however, gives us a reason to think that there is not the requisite *mens rea*. To see that (3) and (4) are not sufficient for *mens rea*, consider the case of the "Escaped Psychopath." Jones correctly believes that there is an escaped psychopath, Brown, who has committed many appalling acts of violence. He likes to rape women, but he most likes to secure sexual compliance that is behaviorally indistinguishable from pleasurable and consensual sex. Should a woman fail convincingly to act out the part of willing partner in a mutually enjoyable sexual encounter, Brown resorts to crude and brutal violence to get his way. Jones mistakenly believes that Smith is Brown and has sex with him. Smith believes that Jones really is consenting to sex with him, and he certainly would not have sex with her if he thought that she was not consenting. Jones does not consent to such sex at the time, because she is in a state of terrified acquiescence. But she successfully masks such terror, and her charade of pleasured compliance is convincing—she thinks it must be if she is to prevent "Brown" from detecting her real feelings and proceeding to awful violence against her.

In such a case, (1) to (4) are true, but it seems evident that Smith does not display the *mens rea* essential for him to be guilty of rape. We judge this to be so because we do not think that Smith, or any reasonable prudent person, could or should be expected to doubt that Jones's behavior was anything other than the giving of real consent. Should Smith have asked, "Are you only appearing to consent willingly because you think I am the psychopath Brown?" (And how should Jones answer if she really does think that Smith is Brown?) If we are not prepared then to think that (1) to (4) are jointly sufficient for the case to be one of rape, it is because we think that for Smith to be judged culpable, it is necessary also that his belief that Jones is consenting is, in some sense, unreasonable; that is, that Smith is properly accounted culpable for coming to believe as he does. For this reason, (5) must be added to the statements defining the case under discussion.

To make better sense of how we should estimate the reasonableness of the mistake involved in such a case, let us consider the various respects in which one or both parties might be mistaken about the character of a sexual encounter between them. It seems wrong to maintain that a man cannot unwittingly engage in sexual intercourse.[11] In the case of women, there are very rare cases of rape due to fraud in the *factum*, that is, where the sexual act itself is misrepresented as something else or is represented as being with someone else. A classic instance of the former would be a doctor having sexual intercourse with a patient but representing it as a vaginal examination or surgical procedure. Cases of the latter, impersonation, are more common.[12] We might regard women who are deceived in either fashion to be extraordinarily naive or even willfully ignorant. Yet there is no reason to think a very inexperienced man should not also fail to realize what it was he was doing when he had sex with someone. Moreover, there are surely conceivable cases of heavily drugged, semiconscious, hallucinating men who may not fully grasp what they are engaged in.

Let us concede that, normally, sexual intercourse for men is not unwitting. Is it possible to be mistaken as to the identity of one's sexual partner? Of course, there can be the failures of reference familiar to philosophers of language. Smith, the unwitting adulterer, may know that he is having sex with Carol Jones, or even just with *this* woman *here and now*, but not know that he is having sex with the wife of Charles Jones, because he does not know that Carol, or this woman here, is the wife of Charles. More interestingly, there is no reason not to conclude that men, like women, could be the victims of impersonation.

Normally, also, a man must be aware of the character of the sexual intercourse he is engaged in; that it is with a woman, that it is anal, vaginal, or oral sex, for instance. Nevertheless, it must be said that there have been celebrated instances of long-standing sexual relationships in which the man has failed to realize that his "female" partner was, in fact, a man.[13] Prostitutes are reported successfully to use interfemoral coitus as a convincing substitute for intravaginal sex. It needs hardly be added that men do frequently get it wrong about the pleasurability for their partners of any sexual encounter. Men are all too often unwilling to believe that displays of female "pleasure" could be anything other than genuine.[14]

All of the above goes to show that the character of any sexual intercourse—that it is sex, with whom it is sex, what kind of sex it is, and how pleasurable or not it is—are not evidently and infallibly self-intimating to its participants. Mistakes—occasionally of a very significant and substantial kind—can be and are made. But what of consent? Can parties be mistaken about the presence or absence of consent? The case under consideration allows that there can be such mistakes, and the case of the "Escaped Psychopath" allows that such a mistake could be an eminently reasonable one. Yet consider the following claim made by Antony Duff, "in ordinary sexual contexts there is no logical space for either doubt or mistake about the consent of either party: their consent, as actively interested participants in a mutually consensual activity, informs and structures their intercourse from the start."[15] Compare also the following claim by David Telling, "If a man is having, or is about to have, intercourse with a woman (unless he is completely or seriously intoxicated) it is virtually impossible for him to fail to appreciate whether or not she is consenting to what he is doing or is about to do by the very nature of the exercise."[16]

The claims being made here are possibly various and need to be carefully distinguished. The conceptual claim would be that sex is to be defined in terms of consent. Talk of sex as "structured" by consent or as a "mutually consensual activity"[17] appears to license that interpretation. But then the claim is that nonconsensual sex is inconceivable. And if it were, then there could not, logically, be such a crime as rape. Or, perhaps, the rapist is guilty of engaging in something that is reprehensible but that is other than sex. But not being allowed to say that it is bad for being unconsented *sex* makes it that much harder to see why it is reprehensible. The claim may be an evaluative one about what makes good sex "good."[18] It is plausible that consensuality is constitutive of good sex, though we should at least allow that an instance of unconsented sex is not, always and all things considered, a bad thing. However, it does not advance the argument to be told simply that persons who engage in nonconsensual sex do not engage in good sex because of the role that consent must play in the goodness of sex.

It is most likely that the claim is an epistemic or epistemic-evaluative one: It is about what parties to sex or parties to good sex must know if they are properly described as engaged in sex (or good sex). However, *pace* Telling, it is not "virtually impossible" for a man to appreciate whether a woman is not consenting to what, sexually, he is doing. It may seem evident that a man could not fail to see signs of dissent (struggling, clearly and loudly voiced protests, obvious distress, and so on). But he could mistake them. In *Morgan*, it was precisely conceded that several men could—sincerely if unreasonably—judge that such signs were not of dissent but rather of complicit pleasure in consensual sex.

Read as an epistemic-evaluative claim Duff's point that two people who engage, as they should, in sex only as an essentially consensual activity cannot entertain doubts about the other's consent. The "cannot" is not, however, logical; it is normative. If what matters to me about doing X with another is that she should consent to our together doing X, such that I cannot properly think of myself as conjointly doing X unless we do both consent, then I ought not to be in any doubt that the other is consenting. There is a logical but not a moral space for such doubt.

However, and crucially, I should reassure myself of the other's consent, not by denying that anything other than her consent is inconceivable, but precisely by reminding myself of how possible such a lack of consent is. The point can be made by means of imagining a man who, in his first sexual encounter with a woman, strives extremely hard to be sensitive to any possible hint that she does not consent. He treats even a verbal declaration of affirmative consent as open to possible suspicion of being an insincere declaration. He is motivated in his behavior toward her by the unconditional imperative not to engage in nonconsensual sex. It is in virtue of his feeling himself to be under such an imperative that he is led to entertain doubts that would not trouble less morally conscientious men. Of course, he will not proceed to have sex with the woman if he does, as a matter of fact, doubt her consent. But it is not the case that foreclosing the moral space thereby occludes the logical space for doubt. His certainty that she does consent, required by satisfaction of the moral imperative to have only consensual sex, is grounded on a recognition that lack of consent is always conceivable and all too possible.

Unreasonable Mistakes

The question then remains. Since it is possible to be mistaken about the other's consent, what warrants us in saying that certain kinds of mistake are unreasonable? Remember that the mistaken belief is an honest one, and that its unreasonableness is not being taken as grounds for thinking that it is not believed at all. The absence of reasonable grounds for someone to believe P may be taken as grounds for doubting that he does believe P.[19] But, once it is conceded that someone does sincerely believe P, it is a further possible question whether it is reasonable for them to hold that belief. It is also the case that a man might be more likely to hold an unreasonable belief in certain circumstances; for example, when intoxicated.[20] Yet while drunkenness may make the holding of an unreasonable belief more explicable, it does not render the belief itself any more reasonable.

In judging the reasonableness of holding a belief, one may evaluate both the reasons the individual has (or might have) for holding it and the consequences of acting on that belief if held. It is plausible to think that the more serious the likely effects of acting in the light of a belief are, the more well-grounded such a belief ought to be. In particular, action informed by a given belief may run certain risks that are greater the less well-grounded the belief in question is. Let me first spell out the various elements that are involved in an estimation of the reasonableness of a belief in terms of the riskiness of acting on it and do so by particular reference to the riskiness of believing that the other person is consenting to sex.[21]

There is, first, the likelihood that the belief is mistaken. Mistaken belief in another's consent is possible. One might think that the more concerned someone is to be sure that the other is consenting, the less likely he is to be mistaken in his beliefs that this is so. On the whole, conscientious truth-seekers are cognitively more-reliable belief-formers. Yet a concern to get it right must be yoked to a reliable set of belief-forming processes. In this sense, Duff's claim, above, might also be read as saying the following: Men who think of sex in consensual terms, and behave appropriately in sexual encounters, will both be more concerned to ensure that the other's consent is forthcoming and more sensitive to evidence in the other's behavior that such consent is or is not forthcoming.

Second, there is the value of that which is being exposed to risk by holding the belief. In the present case, this is the possible cost to the woman of sex obtained without her consent. That can be great and ought never be assumed to be inconsiderable. Having sex with a woman without her consent is of a different moral order than taking her car and driving it without her agreement. The former is a direct assault on her integrity as an incarnated will. For very many women, unconsented sex is a devastating event with seriously harmful effects on their physical and psychological health.

The third element at stake is the value of that which is being pursued at the risk of possible nonconsent by the women. This is the value to the man of having sex with this woman here and now. Two comments are in order. First, the failure to have sex with this woman here and now does not amount to a generalized failure to have sex with any women at any time. The risked loss is of a sexual gratification by means of and with a particular other, but not of other future gratifications of a comparable kind. Second, Hegel famously argued that the slave's compelled obeisance to the master is of no value to him because it is not that of a free will.[22] Similarly, it is to be hoped that unconsented sexual "service" is valueless for one who only values freely given sex. Of course, there are those, such as sadistic rapists,[23] who value sex only if it is compelled, who would not only not desist if they knew the other not to be consenting, but would see that fact as a compelling reason to persist. But, in the constructed case being considered, Smith does not wish to have sex with Jones if he knows her not to be consenting.

Fourth, there is the necessity of running the risk. Does Smith have to risk obtaining sex with Jones when Jones does not consent? Here there is available a forceful answer. It is always open to a man, at no great cost to himself, to gain assurance that a woman is consenting by seeking a verbal affirmation of consent. The case of the "Escaped Psychopath" demonstrates that such an affirmation is not always a guarantee of consent. But it does at least supply greater assurance than nonverbal behaviors whose meaning is open, reasonably, to ambiguous interpretation. There are those who have defended an affirmative verbal consent standard that holds that consent is given if and only if an explicit "yes" or its unambiguous verbal equivalent is uttered.[24] The presumption that consent needs to be given in each and every sexual encounter for that encounter legitimately to be accounted consensual seems to be insensitive to the different kinds of sexual relationship there can be. What is appropriate for a sexual encounter between strangers need not be that which is proper for lovers of long standing. It is important sometimes to ask for and require a "yes." It does not follow that everything on every occasion needs a "yes" in order to be permitted.[25]

A mistake as to the other's consent is unreasonable in as much as there is a risk of harming, possibly greatly harming, the other when little or nothing is gained for oneself by running this risk, and when the risk can always be avoided or greatly minimized at no significant cost to oneself by direct inquiry of the other. This discussion of the riskiness of believing that the other person is consenting to sex has limited itself to the case in which Smith risks acting on the mistaken belief that Jones is consenting. What of the contrary risk? What are the risks of Smith believing that Jones is *not* consenting when in fact she is? We need to consider these risks because a complete account of the harms that are risked by acting on the erroneous belief that Jones is consenting must balance these harms against those that are risked by mistakenly *not* acting on this belief when it is correct.[26] There are, in short, two possible errors associated with two sets of possible harms.

The most evidently risked harm in the second case is that Jones is deprived of the sex with Smith that she really wants. Since she could make her desire for such sex explicit, it needs to be shown why it is reasonable for her to risk a loss she could so easily avoid. According to a familiar traditional picture, women either lack sexual desires or are required not to make them explicit. Innate or socialized, such sexual passivity and demureness are essential to femininity.[27] In terms of such an understanding, women require and expect of men that they make the first move and that they persist even in the face of apparent initial unwillingness or ambiguous signals.[28] Jones may thus want sex with Smith even while she gives him seemingly good reasons to believe that she does not.

Such a picture is a justifiably criticized stereotype of women and of female sexuality. Moreover, in the present context, it is a dangerous stereotype. For, even if some women *do* intend their apparent "no" to mean "yes" (or at least not to signify "no"), the vast majority of women most definitely do not. And the risked harms of unconsented sex with them are far greater than the risked harms of denied gratification for a few. It remains true, even on balance, that unacceptable and needless risks are run, at no great possible gain, by acting on the possibly mistaken belief that another person is consenting.

Let me now turn to the epistemic reasonableness of the belief in consent by addressing the risk that is run by coming to believe that consent is given. That is, how and why does Smith go wrong when he makes the mistake of believing that Jones is consenting to sex with him? There are two possibilities. Smith comes to believe Jones is consenting in the face of evidence to the contrary or does so in the absence of any such evidence.

If Jones is displaying signs of dissent, there are two ways in which Smith might discount such signs. One is to believe that Jones is *ambivalent* or in two minds about sex with Smith. Part of her says "yes" while another part of her says "no," and Smith judges that the greater part of Jones says "yes." The other way to discount the signs of protest is to believe that they are *ambiguous* and may be read as indicating either consent or dissent. Smith interprets the signs as betokening agreement. It can go with either way of discounting signs of protest that behaviors that are neutral—being strictly behaviors signifying neither consent nor dissent—are read as consensual. For instance, a woman does not take an opportunity to escape the alleged rapist. This may be due to frozen fear or willing complicity. The man interprets it as signifying the latter. Thus we have a complex notion of "equivocal conduct": conduct that contains signs of both consent and dissent, "dissenting" conduct that can be reinterpreted as consensual and conduct interpretable as either consensual or dissenting that is taken as consensual.

It should be evident that employment of such a notion of "equivocal conduct" shifts the onus onto a woman to provide unequivocal evidence of dissent. And it does so in the same way that taking lack of resistance or submission as evidence of consent does.[29] Such a shift is unfavorable to victims and favorable to alleged perpetrators of rape. But there is a general failing detectable in this shift. This can properly be explained only once I have addressed the case in which Smith comes to believe Jones is consenting in the absence of any evidence to the contrary. Jones does not say "yes," but she does not say "no." What licenses Smith in thinking that her behavior signifies "yes"?

The most obvious manner of doing so is by reliance on rules or conventions that permit consent to be inferred from an action or actions that are not, in themselves, explicit declarations of consent. In an important article, Douglas Husak and George C. Thomas have argued that there are just such social conventions by which women express their agreement to sexual relations.[30] I have criticized their arguments at greater length elsewhere.[31] Here I wish only to summarize the main lines of my criticism. First, Husak and Thomas shift from the claim that there are conventions whereby women indicate that they might or will probably consent to the claim that such conventions are ones whereby women actually give their consent. Second, Husak and Thomas fail to acknowledge that men and women attribute different meanings to the same behavior. Further, there are no good reasons why women should adjust their behavior, and understandings of it, to male expectations. Third, Husak and Thomas rely on general conventions applicable to all possible relationships, when men should attend to the individual features of any particular encounter. Fourth, Husak and Thomas discount the responsibility that men have to seek to assure themselves that women are consenting, when exclusive reliance on a convention runs the risk of making a mistake.

Defying a Woman's Authority

I want now to suggest that when Smith goes wrong in thinking that Jones is consenting to sex with him—both when there is evidence of dissent by Jones and in the absence of such evidence—he behaves unreasonably insofar as there is a general explanation of why he goes wrong and that he does wrong in going wrong in this way. I want to borrow an insight of Jean Hampton's about what amounts to criminal culpability, though I intend to apply this insight in a way not licensed by her own use of the idea. Hampton suggests that someone acts culpably insofar as he *defies* what he knows to be the authoritative rule of his conduct. Culpability lies in "the choice to supplant what one knows to be an authoritative rule with a different authority that sanctions the act one wishes to take."[32]

Now, what is characteristic about Smith's coming to believe, mistakenly, that Jones is consenting? It is the supplanting of what would be an authoritative rule for determining whether she is consenting with a different authority, sanctioning the belief and the action that follow from it, which thus licenses Smith in his desired action. Smith defies the authority of Jones as the only legitimate source of the giving of her consent. How does he do this? When Jones's behavior protests against sex and indicates lack of consent, Smith substitutes the authoritative voice of the truly protesting Jones with that of another who permits such protest to be read as equivocal.

Such a substitution can be quite literal. In the case of *Morgan*, young men were invited by Morgan to have sex with his wife. He told them that his wife enjoyed forced sex, and that her struggles, protests, etc., should be understood as only "play acting." In proceeding to have sex with Morgan's wife, the men supplanted her as the authoritative source of her wishes with her husband. What *he* said she really wanted rather than what *she* said and did became their guide to her wishes. The fault of these men was not simply their credulity in believing what other more reasonable individuals would not have believed. It was that they gave credence to the testimony of someone other than the proper and authoritative source of the relevant belief.[33]

When there are no signs of protest or dissent, Smith relies on conventions under which Jones's behavior may be interpreted as indicating her consent. In doing so, Smith supplants the authoritative voice of Jones with the authority of a convention. This is unreasonable insofar as its authority is not or need not be one that is recognized or accorded it by Jones herself. She is not the "author" of that convention by which her own actions are seen as authorizing a belief in her consent.

Smith does Jones an injustice in getting it wrong about whether or not she consents, because he refuses to acknowledge the authoritative status of her own wishes as she expresses them. Smith acts wrongly, not in shutting his eyes to the possibility of getting it wrong, but in shutting his eyes to the most authoritative way of getting it right. His "wilful blindness" is not just to the facts that a reasonable, prudent person might see, but to the only authoritative source of illumination on those facts. The "wilful abstaining from knowing" is in fact a "purposely abstaining from ascertaining"; his "shutting his eyes to the obvious" is a shutting of his eyes to the obvious source of knowledge.[34]

The wrong that is done can be made clearer by distinguishing it from two related wrongs. Smith is not to be condemned merely for being credulous. It may be that credulity is vicious.[35] But the claim here is that Smith is more than simply credulous; that is, apt to believe in Jones's consent on weak or insufficient grounds. It is also that he refuses to acknowledge the source of stronger and sufficient grounds. For some, the wrong done in making an honest but unreasonable mistake is an indifference to the woman as an other, as possessed of a distinct integrity whose consent matters.[36] But the wrong done to Jones's integrity as a sexual agent is not at the level of being practically indifferent to the question of whether or not she consents. For Smith does care whether or not she consents. It is done at the level of being indifferent to her as a source of knowledge about whether or not she consents.[37]

Let me further reinforce the point about a woman as the authoritative source for a man's belief about her consent by comparing the crime of rape with those of bigamy and statutory rape. Someone is guilty of bigamy if, while married, they marry another person. Someone is guilty of the crime of statutory rape if they have even willing sex with someone who is below a specified age of majority. In both crimes, a defense of honest but reasonable mistake as to the pertinent facts is permitted. In the case of bigamy, the relevant cited British case is *Tolson*,[38] where the woman believed, on reasonable grounds, that her husband had been drowned at sea and, more than five years later, she married again. In the case of sex with a girl who is over 13 but under 16, it is a defense for the man that "he believes her to be of the age of sixteen or over, and has reasonable cause for the belief."[39]

In both cases, the reasonableness or unreasonableness of the honest mistake does not make essential reference, as it does in the case of rape, to the special authority of one party; that is, the person who is in fact still married or the person who is in fact below the age of majority. Whether someone is of the required age or is married is a pure question of fact about which the relevant person does not have a special authority.[40] Someone, ignorant or misled about the procedures for divorce, may not know that they are still married. Someone, having forgotten or misremembered their birthday, may not know that they are still short of their sixteenth birthday. In the case of rape, to repeat, the injured party *is* an authoritative source of knowledge about her consent.

The unreasonableness of even an honest mistake about another's consent lies in the fact of supplanting the woman as source of knowledge about her consent. Yet it might be said that it is surely sometimes reasonable to supplant one source of knowledge with another. A doctor who cannot directly consult his patient to ascertain her wishes may, under normal circumstances, reasonably trust to the declared wishes of the patient's relatives. However, it is reasonable to shift from one source of knowledge to another only if the following conditions are met. First, that the first source is unavailable; second, that there are no reasons to think that the second source is any less reliable than the first; and, third, that there are no compelling reasons not to proceed on the basis of a belief derived from this second source. Neither of the first two conditions is met. Jones can directly be invited to confirm her consent. While the case of the "Escaped Psychopath" shows even a "yes" to be possibly, if very rarely, misleading, there is every reason always to take "no!" as meaning no and no reason to take nonverbal behaviors as gainsaying such a firmly declared negative.[41]

What of the third condition? Are there compelling reasons not to proceed on the basis of a belief derived from a source other than the woman herself? Yes, because, to repeat an earlier point, unconsented sex is very probably harmful to her and can be desisted from at no great cost to the man. Compare here the case of a mistake-of-fact defense to murder.[42] A man who mistakenly believes that the other is threatening his life in a way that can be forestalled only by killing the other must act if he believes as he does. He risks his own death by failing to act. Further, he cannot wait or seek to confirm his belief in some other way. By comparison, however, Smith runs no risk to his own life or health by not acting on the mistaken belief that Jones consents to sex with him. Nor must he act immediately and without waiting to seek confirmation of his belief.

A Culpable Mistake?

Against all that has been said, it may be urged that someone should not be held culpable for holding an unreasonable belief. According to a familiar argument, beliefs are not the sorts of states of a person that they can choose to be in. One cannot will oneself to believe P or not to believe Q.[43] Employing familiar reasoning, since "ought" implies "can," and one cannot do other than believe as one does, someone cannot be subject to the moral requirement that they not form an unreasonable belief. A legal requirement of culpability might be thought to track the moral requirement in making the same presupposition that agents could have done other than they did. It might do so for two reasons. First, it will be said that a necessary condition of a crime's being committed is that the offender is at fault, and being unable to do otherwise negates fault. Or it will be said that the sanctions of the law are designed to change conduct by deterring the potential offender, and the man who can do no other than he does do cannot be deterred. For either reason, it is standardly argued that negligence should not amount to the *mens rea* that is a necessary condition of criminal culpability.[44]

The following is a sketch of a familiar argument in response. First, the central purpose of the law is to prevent significant harms to innocent persons. Second, such harms can result as much from carelessness as from deliberate intentions. When the harms are significant, there is, thus, a case for enforcing conformity to a duty of care. Moreover, when we enforce such a duty, we can reasonably hope thereby to change people's standards of behavior by making them more careful. A law that punished men for making mistakes about women's consent to have sex with them would encourage men "to take more care in forming their beliefs or in acting upon them."[45]

But we might argue that there is more than simply a deterrent reason for enforcing the duty of care. When, as in the present case, unreasonably mistaken beliefs are formed from which harmful actions follow, it may be proper to attribute the formation of such beliefs to defects of character for which the agent is to blame.[46] Such a defect of character may be regarded as morally wrong, since the individual bears primary responsibility for knowingly allowing it to have developed in this way.[47] In short, a person who believes something unreasonably may be unable to will himself to believe other than he does currently believe. But he comes to believe as he does because of a character that forms beliefs in an unreasonable way. The law has a reason—grounded both in moral fault and deterrence—to improve his character. It can do so by enforcing a duty of care in what one believes about, and consequently how one acts toward, the other.

The character of a man who allows the authoritative voice of a woman, with regard to her giving or not of consent, to be supplanted by other authorities (conventions, the testimony of others, etc.) is defective. From such a character spring unreasonably mistaken beliefs which, together with certain desires, produce harmful actions. Such a defective character is blameworthy and one that the law should seek to change.[48]

It will still be argued that all of this goes too far. The standard against which beliefs—and, indirectly, the characters that form beliefs—are being measured is one of "reasonableness." Yet such a standard is other than and considerably more stringent than the law's own standard of "reasonableness." If we wish to know what, in law, is a reasonable belief, we inquire as to what a reasonable man would believe in the relevant situation. The law's "reasonable man" is a fictive personality; he is the man of ordinary prudence, care, and foresight. He is the man in the street. The characteristics of such a man are objective and impersonal, deliberately abstracted and removed from the idiosyncratic and particular features of the individual defendant. Yet the reasonable man and his beliefs are what the law in practice determines to be the norm: "In truth the reasonable man is a personification of the court or jury's social judgment."[49]

By contrast, the standard of "reasonableness" by which defiance of the authoritative voice of a woman is accounted unreasonable is a normative one. It prescribes how beliefs should be formed; it does not describe how beliefs, as a normal rule, are formed. The law's reasonable man might well believe in some particular instance that a woman gave her consent even while defying her authoritative voice on the matter. It will be charged that the law should not abandon a standard rooted in how people ordinarily act and think for one that derives from principles directing how, ideally, they ought to do so. Nor, relatedly, should the law condemn and punish those who behave perfectly reasonably by the first standard, even if they do not do so by the second. Here we broach large and difficult issues—concerning legal criteria of reasonableness, the relevance to law of ideal standards of behavior, the propriety of legal compulsion as a means of character formation, and so on.

Let me offer some brief comments. It has long been charged by feminists that the law's standard of reasonableness is masculine, that it is precisely in terms of the beliefs of a reasonable *man* that a court measures those of actual individuals. In the present context, the standard of "reasonableness"—defiance of the authoritative voice of the relevant person—has, hopefully, great plausibility. It displays why a man may be said to behave unreasonably in ignoring the woman's authoritative voice concerning her wishes. But such defiance would be unreasonable if it were a woman who ignored the authoritative voice of a man. The criterion of reasonableness is not gender specific. As a standard, it may thus serve both to judge the behavior of ordinary men as "unreasonable," while not itself being open to the charge of merely being a woman's standard of reasonableness.

It may or may not be appropriate for the law to seek to enforce forms of behavior that go against the current grain of accepted, normal, everyday dispositions. However, this apart, individuals cannot complain if the law, in seeking to prevent evident harms, clearly communicates a standard of reasonableness in the formation of beliefs to which a body of case law conforms. Men can be made to be more careful in forming their beliefs and can know what is required of them if they are to be careful in this regard. The law should enforce a duty of care if it takes seriously the harms that are caused to women by failure to discharge this duty.

Smith does not directly intend to have unconsented sex with Jones. He does not fail to see that there might be a risk of unconsented sex with Jones. His mistake in thinking that she does consent is honest. But it is unreasonable for its defiance of her as the authoritative source of knowledge about her consent. And for having this defiant and defective character, Smith is culpable. He deserves the sanctions of the criminal law.[50]

ACKNOWLEDGMENTS   I am very grateful to Antony Duff, Keith Burgess-Jackson, and Marcia Baron for their helpful comments on an earlier draft of this chapter.

Notes

1. *Director of Public Prosecutions v. Morgan* [1975] 2 All E.R. 347. Among the more central philosophical discussions of the case and its implications are: E. M. Curley, "Excusing Rape," *Philosophy and Public Affairs*, 5 (1976): 325–360; Leigh Bienen, "Mistakes," *Philosophy and Public Affairs* 7 (1978): 224–245; M. T. Thornton, "Rape and *Mens Rea*," *Canadian Journal of Philosophy*, Suppl. Vol. VIII (1982): 119–146.

2. "Negligence, then, is failure to conform to the standard of care to which it is the defendant's duty to conform. It is failure to behave like a reasonable or prudent man, in circumstances where the law requires such reasonable behaviour." Glanville Williams, *Textbook of Criminal Law*, 2nd ed. (London: Stevens and Sons, 1983), p. 88.

3. It is generally true, both legally and morally, that consent has a definite and limited scope. Someone, for instance, who gives their consent to a particular medical procedure does not thereby consent to any medical outcome and may legitimately seek redress for actions that clearly go beyond the agreed procedure.

4. *Regina v. Kaitamaki* [1980] NZLR, 59 is a case in which this issue was central. For further details and discussion of the case, see Richard H. S. Tur, "Rape: Reasonableness and Time," *Oxford Journal of Legal Studies*, 1 (1981): 432–441.

5. Susan Estrich, "Rape,' *The Yale Law Journal*, 95 (1986): 1087–1184, at p. 1090. "No similar effort is required of victims of other crimes for which consent is a defense," p. 1125.

6. Donald A. Dripps, "Beyond Rape: An Essay on the Difference Between the Presence of Force and the Absence of Consent," *Columbia Law Review*, 92 (1992): 1780–1809; Lucy Reed Harris, "Towards a Consent Standard in the Law of Rape," *University of Chicago Law Review*, 43 (1975): 613–645; J. A. Scutt, "Consent Versus Submission: Threats and the Element of Fear in Rape," *University of Western Australia Law Review*, 13 (1977): 52–76; Robin D. Wiener, "Shifting the Communication Burden: A Meaningful Consent Standard in Rape," *Harvard Women's Law Journal*, 8 (1983): 143–161.

7. *Regina v. Olugboja* [1981] 73 Cr App Rep, 344, at p. 350.

8. *D.P.P. v. Morgan* [1975] 2 All E.R. 347, at p. 362.

9. Glanville Williams allows for culpable inadvertence to the risk of nonconsent only in the former case: "As applied to a charge of rape, the man is unaware of a risk that the woman is not consenting only if he believes that she consents." "The Unresolved Problem of Recklessness," *Legal Studies,* 8 (1988): 74–91, at p. 84.

10. Jennifer Temkin, "The Limits of Reckless Rape," *Criminal Law Review,* 1983: 5–16, at p. 6. Temkin usefully distinguishes the various possible states of mind of a defendant in a case of nonconsensual intercourse. See also the "Typology of Rape-Related Mental States" in Keith Burgess-Jackson, *Rape: A Philosophical Investigation* (Aldershot, England: Dartmouth, 1996), pp. 139–140.

11. As does Toni Pickard, "Culpable Mistakes and Rape: Relating *Mens Rea* to the Crime," *University of Toronto Law Journal,* 30 (1980): 75–98, at p. 76.

12. In *Regina v. Elbekkay* [1995] Crim L R 163, a woman "consented" to sexual intercourse in the false belief that it was her male partner who had got into bed with her.

13. This was the subject of the 1993 film, *M. Butterfly.*

14. It requires Sally's (Meg Ryan) celebrated public demonstration of a fake orgasm to convince Harry (Billy Crystal) otherwise in the film, *When Harry Met Sally* (1989).

15. Antony Duff, "Recklessness and Rape," *Liverpool Law Review,* 3 (1981): 49–64, at p. 58.

16. David Telling, "Rape—Consent and Belief," *Journal of Criminal Law,* 47 (1983): 129–139, at p. 138.

17. Compare Duff's *Intention, Agency and the Criminal Law: Philosophy of Action and the Criminal Law* (Oxford: Basil Blackwell, 1990), p. 169, where he describes sexual intercourse as "*essentially* a consensual activity between parties" (emphasis in original).

18. There is no reason why the "good" here should not describe both the moral and nonmoral—perhaps its pleasurability—features of the sex.

19. "If at a trial for a rape offence the jury has to consider whether a man believed a woman was consenting to sexual intercourse, the presence or absence of reasonable grounds for such a belief is a matter to which the jury is to have regard, in conjunction with any other relevant matters, in considering whether he so believed." Sec. 1(2) of the British 1976 *Sexual Offences (Amendment) Act.*

20. Drink was undoubtedly a factor in the behavior of the men in *Morgan,* and also in a similar British case, *Regina v. Cogan* [1976] QB, 217.

21. I follow here the useful analysis of Henry T. Terry, "Negligence," *Harvard Law Review,* XIX (1915): 45–50. Reprinted in Herbert Morris, ed., *Freedom and Responsibility: Readings in Philosophy and Law* (Stanford, CA: Stanford University Press, 1961): 243–246.

22. G. W. F. Hegel, *Phenomenology of Spirit,* trans. A. V. Miller with Analysis of the Text and Foreword by J. N. Findlay (Oxford: Clarendon Press, 1977), B. IV. A. "Independence and dependence of self-consciousness: Lordship and Bondage."

23. Burgess-Jackson, *Rape: A Philosophical Investigation,* p. 139, describes such rapists as "purposive rapists."

24. Lois Pineau, "Date Rape: A Feminist Analysis," *Law and Philosophy,* 8 (1989): 217–243; Lani Anne Remick, "Read Her Lips: An Argument for a Verbal Consent Standard in Rape," *University of Pennsylvania Law Review,* 141 (1993): 1103–1151; Stephen J. Schulhofer, "The Gender Question in Criminal Law," *Social Philosophy and Policy,* 7 (1990): 105–137.

25. I talk about the different presumptions appropriate to different kinds of sexual relationship in chap. 2, "Sexual Consent," of my *Sexual Consent* (Boulder, CO: Westview Press, 1998).

26. These risks are run if Smith acts on his mistaken belief that Jones is not consenting, and if Smith decides not to run the risk of acting on his true belief—that she is consenting—which he fears may be mistaken.

27. "Even if it could be denied that a special sentiment of chasteness was natural to women, would it be any the less true that in society . . . they ought to be raised in principles appropriate to it? If the timidity, chasteness, and modesty which are proper to them are social inventions, it is in society's interest that women acquire these qualities." Jean-Jacques Rousseau, *Politics and the Arts: A Letter to M. d'Alembert on the Theatre*, trans. A. Bloom (Ithaca, NY: Cornell University Press, 1968), p. 87. Quoted by Carole Pateman, "'The Disorder of Women': Women, Love, and the Sense of Justice," *Ethics* 91 (October 1980): 20–34, at p. 25.

28. Leslie Margolin, "Gender and the Stolen Kiss: The Social Support of Male and Female to Violate a Partner's Sexual Consent in a Noncoercive Situation," *Archives of Sexual Behavior* 19 (1990): 281–291.

29. Dana Berliner, "Rethinking the Reasonable Belief Defense to Rape," *Yale Law Journal*, 100 (1991): 2687–2706, criticizes the use of a concept of "equivocal conduct," first addressed in the case of *Mayberry*, in this fashion, pp. 2698–2699.

30. Douglas N. Husak and George C. Thomas III, "Date Rape, Social Convention and Reasonable Mistakes," *Law and Philosophy*, 11 (1992): 95–126.

31. "'A Nod's as Good as a Wink': Consent, Convention, and Reasonable Belief," *Legal Theory*, 3 (1997): 273–290.

32. Jean Hampton, "Mens Rea," *Social Philosophy and Policy*, 7 (1990): 1–28, at p. 16.

33. It is interesting to note that the young men, "who were complete strangers to Mrs. Morgan, were at first incredulous but were persuaded that Morgan's invitation was intended seriously when he told them stories of his wife's sexual aberrations and provided them with contraceptive sheaths to wear." (*D.P.P. v Morgan* [1975] 1 All ER 8, at p. 8) It would appear from this report that their incredulity was not that Mrs. Morgan should behave in this way but that Mr. Morgan should be serious in his invitation to them to have sex with his own wife. It is worth adding that the men's actual final defense was that Mrs. Morgan eventually, after an initial struggle, actively cooperated in and showed signs of enjoying the sex.

34. The quoted phrases are all formulations of culpable "connivance" or "constructive knowledge" in British law, discussed by J. Ll. J. Edwards, *Mens Rea in Statutory Offences* (London: Macmillan, 1955), pp. 199–202.

35. E. M. Curley, "Excusing Rape," pp. 346–7.

36. Jennifer Temkin, "The Limits of Reckless Rape," pp. 15–16; Antony Duff, *Intention, Agency and the Criminal Law*, p. 171.

37. Jeremy Horder, "Cognition, Emotion, and Criminal Culpability," *Law Quarterly Review*, 106 (1990): 469–486, argues that the fault of the *Morgan* defendants lay in the fact that their "leaping before looking" was explicable as due to a morally unwarranted prioritization of their own sexual satisfaction. One may act precipitately and on a mistaken belief, but this is only excusable where this is due to certain emotions, such as fear. My response is that the mistake would be unreasonable even if not precipitately made and from whatever emotion it sprang (fear of rejection, for instance). The unreasonableness of the mistake is not

simply that someone leaps before they looked, but that they failed to look in the obvious place.

38. *Tolson* [1893] 23 QBD 168, CCR.

39. Section 6(3) of 1956 *Sexual Offences Act.* This is not the case in many States of the United States, and the *Model Penal Code* allows this defense only when the minimum age is ten years. See MPC 213.6(1)

40. Leigh Bienen, "Mistakes," p. 241.

41. "Her lips said 'No!' but her eyes said 'Yes'" is the false and self-serving rationalization of many a rapist.

42. This comparison is due to Berliner, "Rethinking the Reasonable Belief Defense to Rape," pp. 2700–2701.

43. The *locus classicus* for a defense of this view is Bernard Williams, "Deciding to Believe," in his *Problems of the Self, Philosophical Papers 1956–1972* (Cambridge: Cambridge University Press, 1973): 136–151.

44. J. W. C. Turner, "The Mental Element in Crimes at Common Law," in *The Modern Approach to the Criminal Law* (London: Macmillan, 1945), pp. 208–9; Jerome Hall, *General Principles of Criminal Law,* 2nd ed. (Indianapolis/New York: Bobbs-Merill, 1960), pp. 136–7.

45. E. M. Curley, "Excusing Rape," p. 345.

46. Glanville Williams, *Textbook of Criminal Law,* 2nd ed. (London: Stevens and Sons, 1983), p. 91.

47. "But perhaps a man is the kind of man not to take care. Still they are themselves by their slack lives responsible for becoming men of that kind . . ." Aristotle, *Nicomachean Ethics,* 1114a 3–4.

48. He may display this defect of character in the way that he behaves toward the woman, so that we find evidence for the unreasonableness of his belief in such behavior toward her (Dana Berliner, "Rethinking the Reasonable Belief Defense to Rape," pp. 2703–5). But this behavior makes manifest and is evidence for his culpable fault. It is not the criterion of that fault. Similar remarks apply to suggestions offered as to when an honest but mistaken belief in consent should not be counted a defense in André Marin, "When Is an 'Honest But Mistaken Belief in Consent' NOT an 'Honest But Mistaken Belief in Consent,'" *Criminal Law Quarterly* 37 (1995): 451–460.

49. David M. Walker, *The Oxford Companion to Law* (Oxford: Clarendon Press, 1980), p. 1038.

50. Whether he is guilty of the crime of rape to which there is no defense of honest but unreasonable mistake or whether he is more appropriately thought of as guilty of a distinct and lesser crime of "negligent sexual invasion" [Celia Wells, "Swatting the Subjectivist Bug," *Criminal Law Review,* (1982): 209–219, at p. 213] is a further question, which cannot be addressed here.

11

VICTORIA DAVION

The Difference Debate
Rape and Moral Responsibility

Supposed differences between women and men have given rise to "the difference debate" in feminist jurisprudence. The debate concerns whether women's interests are better protected by laws adhering to a strict doctrine of formal equality, seen as gender neutrality, or by laws trying to take certain differences between men and women into account. It has centered around issues concerning divorce and pregnancy. However, it is also discussed in relation to laws governing sexual assault.[1] In a recent controversial article, "Date Rape: A Feminist Analysis," Lois Pineau has argued that the law can protect women better against nonaggravated date rape by regarding sex from "a woman's point of view" (1996). I shall examine her argument along with charges that her position is essentialist and should therefore be dismissed. I shall argue for the following conclusions: Pineau's position is essentialist, but this is not what is wrong with it. Some essentialist claims can be strategically appropriate, so noticing essentialism should not be grounds for automatic dismissal of positions, particularly ones aimed at public policy. However, I shall argue that Pineau's key insight, that we need a shift in attitudes so as to hold sexual aggressors responsible for *actively* ensuring that partners are consenting, is better achieved without appeals to "a woman's point of view." Hence, I shall offer an alternative argument for shifting attitudes based on a minimum standard of sexual decency and show how this approach is better able to handle some key objections that have been made against Pineau.

A Note on Language

Because Pineau wishes to acknowledge that date rape is a major problem for women, and that it is a crime almost exclusively committed by men, she uses sex-specific pronouns in her analysis. In discussing her argument, I shall follow this style. The issue of whether sex-specific pronouns are appropriate will be dealt with in later sections.

Pineau's Argument

Pineau is concerned with what she calls "date rape," nonaggravated sexual assault, nonconsensual sex that does not involve physical injury or the explicit threat of physical injury (p. 2). I object to Pineau's assumption that date rape is nonaggravated. Date rapes can be violent (Koss et al., 1993). I shall use the term "nonaggravated date rape" to discuss the crime that Pineau has in mind. Pineau rightly complains that because physical injury is often considered the only proof that sex was nonconsensual, victims of nonaggravated sexual assault are often left with no recourse. Pineau argues that the problem is an underlying belief that nonaggravated sexual assault is distinguished from normal sex only by the absence of consent. Hence, what is really sexual assault is often mistaken for seduction. This means that, in cases of nonaggravated sexual assault, the question of whether someone consented is central, and the criterion for determining consent is a major focus of discourse on sexual assault. A related problem that concerns Pineau involves the issue of *mens rea*. In order to obtain a conviction, the prosecution must establish that the defendant (who Pineau calls "the man"), has the necessary *mens rea*, the belief that the complainant was either not, or probably was not, consenting. The result is that in many jurisdictions a man who sincerely believes that a woman is consenting would be considered innocent, even if the woman did not consent and even if the belief that the woman consented is unreasonable, provided that it is sincere.

The so-called sincerity condition has been widely criticized. It has been argued that *mens rea* should only be defeated in cases where a man's belief that the woman consented is reasonable. According to Pineau, legislation requiring that the man's belief be reasonable can help provide women with greater protection against violence. This raises the crucial question of what counts as a reasonable belief. It is also worth noting that even if a sincere belief rather than a reasonable belief criterion is used, people will be less likely to believe that someone's belief is sincere, if it is unreasonable. Thus, the question of when it is reasonable for a man to think a woman is consenting arises even if the sincere belief criterion is operative.

Pineau maintains that under the present system, consent is taken as implied unless emphatic, episodic signs of resistance by the woman can be established. In addition, even in cases where resistance can be demonstrated, there is often a suspicion that it is merely a token act, and therefore, that it cannot be interpreted as lack of consent. This suspicion especially comes into play in situations where the man and woman know each other. In such cases, almost anything a woman does can be reasonably interpreted as merely token resistance.

Myths Underlying the Present Criterion

Pineau offers a fairly typical feminist analysis of the kinds of myths underlying the present model of aggressive sex as masterful seduction, which leads to the belief that the only thing distinguishing masterful seduction from sexual assault is the presence or absence of a woman's consent. Since her account is typical, I will just briefly sketch some major points before moving on. The myths are basically that

women are not free to express sexual desire in our society. Women are naturally passive while men are sexually aggressive. Good women will say no to sex even if they
really want it, they may even offer token struggles, because "good women" are not
supposed to be sexually active outside of marriage. On the "sex-as-masterful-seduc-
tion" model, male aggression and female reluctance are normal. Male aggression is
consistent with consent. And, if reluctance is normal for women, then reluctance
must be consistent with consent, if consent is possible at all under normal conditions.[2] Unfortunately, Pineau's discussion suffers from a lack of attention to ethnic,
racial, and class issues. The myth of the good woman as sexually pure has been primarily the myth of the pure, white, middle- to upper-middle-class woman. Other
groups of women, such as African and African American, have been stereotyped
as "loose" by nature and therefore basically unrapeable (Davis 1983; Griffin 1971;
hooks 1989, 1990). I shall return to this point.

Pineau believes that the key to protecting women better is to reformulate the
standard notion of consent from a woman's viewpoint. The central issue should be
what it is reasonable for a woman to consent to. Once this is determined, it can be
argued that if it is unreasonable to expect that a woman would consent to sex under
certain conditions, then it is unreasonable for a man to believe she has consented to
sex under those conditions, absent some additional evidence of consent. Pineau asserts that, under the present criteria, there is a belief that it is reasonable for women
to consent to the kind of sex that date rape involves, and that it is reasonable for
men to think that women have consented. However, according to Pineau,

> My argument is that it is not reasonable for women to consent to that kind of sex
> and that there is furthermore, no grounds for thinking that it is reasonable. Since
> what we want to know is when a woman has consented, and since the standards of
> consent are based on the presumed choices of reasonable agents, it is what is rea-
> sonable from a woman's point of view that must provide the principal delineation
> of a criterion of consent that is capable of representing a woman's willing behavior
> . . . I will argue that the kind of sex to which it would be reasonable for a woman
> to consent suggests a criterion of consent that would bring the kind of sex involved
> in date rape well within the realm of sexual assault. (p. 6)

An Alternative Model: Communicative Sexuality

Pineau offers an alternative model of women's sexuality, one that she believes is
more "biologically adequate," and argues that sexual relations that deviate from this
model should be presumed unreasonable from a woman's point of view. Pineau
combines a Kantian notion of autonomy with some data from sexologists about
what can be expected to be sexually satisfying for women. Applying a Kantian
model of autonomy, Pineau maintains that using another as a mere means to our
ends is to fail to respect the other's autonomy. The end of a sexual encounter, according to Pineau, is sexual pleasure. In order to respect the ends of another in a
sexual encounter, one must know what the ends of the other are, how they achieve
sexual pleasure, and how to help the other attain this end. An epistemic obligation
is involved. The only way to fulfill this epistemic obligation is to engage in ongoing
communication with the other about her/his wants and desires, which Pineau

refers to as "communicative sexuality." Because engaging in communicative sexuality is the only way to fulfill one's epistemic obligation to the other in a sexual encounter, it is morally required. Therefore, it should be the standard of what is reasonable for sexual encounters. The kind of sex involved in date rape is unreasonable for women to consent to, because no effort is made to see what women want or how to help them achieve it when high-pressure tactics are used.

Pineau draws on the research of sexologists to back her notion that noncommunicative sex is unlikely to bring sexual pleasure to women. She states:

> Sexologists are unanimous, moreover, in holding that mutual sexual enjoyment requires an atmosphere of comfort and communication, a minimum of pressure, and an ongoing checkup on one's partner's state. They maintain that different people have different predilections and that what is pleasurable for one person is very often an anathema to another. These findings show that the way to achieve sexual pleasure, at any time at all, let alone with a casual acquaintance, decidedly does not involve overriding the other person's express reservations and providing them with just any kind of sexual stimulus. And while we do not want to allow science and technology a voice in which the voices of particular women are drowned, in this case science seems to concur with women's perception that aggressive incommunicative sex is not what they want. But if science and the voice of women concur, if aggressive seduction does not lead to good sex, if women do not like it or want it, then it is not rational for them to agree to it. Where such sex takes place, it is therefore rational to presume that the sex was not consensual. (pp. 15–16)

Because the kind of sex involved in date rape should be presumed unreasonable from a woman's point of view, a defendant claiming reasonable belief that a woman consented should have to show evidence of consent to rebut the presumption of nonconsent, according to Pineau.

Pineau believes that this shift in perspective to a "woman's point of view" will encourage questions that attempt to ascertain whether, in the face of strong reasons to believe that the woman was not consenting, the man made sincere and reasonable efforts to be sure that she was. Questions might include: Did he ask her what she liked? If she was using contraceptives? If he should? What tone of voice did he use? How did she answer? Did she make any demands? Did she ask for penetration? How was that desire conveyed? Did he ever let up the pressure long enough to see if she was really interested? Did he ask her which position she preferred?

Essentialism in Feminist Theory

Before examining charges of essentialism with regard to Pineau's work, I shall make some comments about the charge of essentialism in feminist theory in general. Charges of essentialism usually point out that a view makes incorrect overgeneralizations about members of particular groups. What gets called essentialism is often really a matter of false universalization, which need not involve essentialism at all (Cuomo 1998). It is not a matter of the attribution of immutable essences to a particular group but rather of making false claims about members having traits in common. One can argue that women contingently have traits in common, but that these are mutable. It matters a great deal for those in the social-change business whether something is an essential characteristic. If it is, there is absolutely no point in trying to change it. However, a universal but contingent trait is changeable.

One major problem in making false universalizations is that the experiences of people who do not fit the generalizations are made invisible. A related problem is what I call the descriptive-normative slide, the unacknowledged slide from description to prescription. In discussing this problem, Bat-Ami Bar On has argued that those who claim to do theory that starts with the experiences and or practices of a particular group are usually doing normative work under the guise of description. For example, Sara Ruddick claims that her discussions of mothering come from the experiences and practices of actual mothers, yet she openly acknowledges that many mothers do not engage in these practices or have these experiences at all. Thus, what Ruddick is actually doing is creating a normative ideal of a "good mother," by including the experiences of *some* mothers and excluding the experiences of others and passing it off as a description of mothering as a practice. Bar On argues that this is typical of theorists who claim to theorize from the experiences of the members of a particular group (Bar On 1993).

Unfortunately, the charge of essentialism is often enough to cause complete dismissal of positions within current feminist theory. Yet, as many theorists have pointed out, simple dismissive antiessentialist critiques are problematic (De Lauretis 1989; Cuomo 1998). They stop the theoretical process too soon. To stop inquiry based on charges of either false universalization or false claims of essentialism is to fail to ask why some obviously problematic generalizations continue to be made within various social contexts. And, where there is a descriptive-normative slide, stopping analysis ceases to question whose interests the normative ideal that is constructed serves. For example, the idea of women as essentially nurturing seems to persist despite the fact that almost everyone is aware that not all women are nurturing. It is important to examine why such associations are incredibly persistent and what social functions they serve. Finally, for those who do political work, the question of the merits of strategic essentialism arises. Identity politics, often based on false universalizations or problematic appeals to essential characteristics, have often been successful in motivating people into political action despite theoretical limitations (Cuomo 1998).

Essentialism in Pineau's Work

The charge of essentialism comes from Pineau's assertion that there is really only one way that women can have "good sex," and therefore, only one kind of sex that it is reasonable for women to consent to, "communicative sex." To put it another way, only communicative sex can be reasonable from the woman's point of view. As Catharine Wells points out, there is no unifying "woman's experience" or "woman's point of view" (Wells 1996). Women consent to many different things in sex. Who is Pineau to argue that only one kind of sex is "good sex" for women or that it is in fact unreasonable for women to consent to anything other than communicative sex?

Pineau responds to charges of essentialism by insisting that she is not attributing any essential, immutable characteristics to women, and therefore is not being essentialist. Her response is inadequate. In asserting that there is a "woman's point of view" regarding sex and sexuality, she at least appears to be making a problematic false universalization. And, as far as I can see, this is what objectors find problematic. In addition, Pineau clearly makes a descriptive-normative slide. In addressing objections that her descriptions of women as wanting only communicative sex are based on false universalization, Pineau asserts that, while communicative sexuality is her ideal of "good sex," it is in fact merely that—an ideal.

> The ideal was not supposed to set the minimum standard of sexual exchange. Rather, it is intended to provide an effective illustration of what reciprocal sexual interest is like. To the extent that the illustration is successful, it enables us to picture things somewhat differently and to shift our expectations and our understanding accordingly. As such, it is intended to assist us in arriving at the required minimum standard of reciprocity. This minimum standard, as we shall see, does not entail that the highest level of intuitive understanding of where one's partner is to be exercised. It requires only that negative responses be given their ordinary meanings, that positive steps be taken to discover whether one's partner really consents, and the acknowledgment that consent may be withdrawn at any time. (p. 93)

In maintaining that it is merely an ideal, she implies that it is not a description of women's actual experiences and desires, but a prescription about what she believes women ought to desire, which is another issue entirely. In recognizing her construction of "a woman's point of view" as prescriptive rather than descriptive, she grants that, because it does not describe the way things currently are, it should not necessarily be imposed in rape cases. Hence, Pineau clearly makes a false universalization and engages in what I have called the descriptive-normative slide. I have argued that it is not enough to point these things out and abandon the discussion. The question of whether an appeal to "a woman's point of view" is somehow strategic in helping women fight back against the threat of rape needs to be answered. Answering this question requires exploration of whose interests are served by describing communicative sexuality as sexuality from "a woman's point of view," and whose interests are served by prescribing that communicative sexuality should be sexuality from "a woman's point of view," even if it is not. In what follows, I examine these questions.

Describing Women's Sexuality

Problematic descriptions of women's sexuality have been used to justify "no means yes" and "yes means yes" myths that allow almost anything a woman does to be interpreted as wanting sex. These myths in turn allow defendants in rape cases to claim innocence by using the sincere belief criterion that Pineau finds so problematic. By showing that the justifications of such defenses use problematic gender stereotyping, I hope to show why options that avoid such stereotypes will better promote Pineau's aim that people encounter each other as individuals to the greatest extent possible within sexual encounters.

According to Douglas Husak and George Thomas III, beliefs grounded in social convention (what I am calling stereotypes) are reasonable (1992, p. 109). If a defendant operated on accepted social conventions in forming his belief that a woman has consented, his belief is reasonable. Therefore, he is innocent of any wrongdoing. To be guilty, according to Husak and Thomas, the defendant must not only have done something illegal, but be culpable. Keith Burgess-Jackson (1996) summarizes the argument as follows:

1. Criminal punishment (perhaps limited to severe and stigmatic criminal punishment) is morally permissible only if the defendant is culpable/blameworthy/at fault.
2. If the defendant reasonably believes that the victim consents to sexual intercourse with him, then, even if the defendant is mistaken, he is not culpable/blameworthy/at fault.

Therefore,

3. If the defendant reasonably believes that the victim consents to sexual intercourse with him, then, even if the defendant is mistaken, criminal punishment of the defendant is morally impermissible. (Burgess-Jackson 1996, p. 144)

According to Husak and Thomas, reasonableness should be linked with social convention. If a man acts on the reigning social conventions regarding sex, then his belief is reasonable, even if it is mistaken. Although they admit that meaningful generalizations about social conventions are almost impossible to generate, that different conventions operate in different contexts, that there are circumstances in which the relevant conventions are unclear and still evolving, and that social conventions are contingent and subject to change, they maintain that, at any given moment, the question of whether a convention exists or obtains is a factual matter (1996, p. 149). I take this to mean that at any given moment, there is an objective discoverable truth to the matter. On this view, it is the job of those evaluating a reasonable-belief defense to ascertain the fact of what social conventions are in play and apply this fact in evaluating the defense. Husak and Thomas argue that in contemporary American society, "the empirical evidence suggests that the prevailing convention is that women do not specifically ask for sex when they want it" (Husak and Thomas 1992, p. 121) and that "women give nonexplicit consent to such courtship rituals as whether they want to be approached by a particular man" (1992, p. 114). The result of this approach is that, just as Pineau says, given the so-called conventions, it is almost always reasonable for a man to think that a woman may want to have sex with him, regardless of her behavior, unless her behavior is quite violent.

There are many kinds of objections that one might make against Husak and Thomas, but the key point for this discussion is that relying on stereotypes is used as an excuse for not treating individual potential partners as individuals. The so-called myths about women's sexuality, which Husak and Thomas call the prevailing social conventions, are themselves taken to represent a woman's point of view on sexuality. The defense that Husak and Thomas have in mind relies on stereotyping women's desires and expected behaviors. This is why it is highly problematic. The burden of determining whether someone has consented to sexual intercourse must involve interactions with the particular person rather than an imposition of some stereotype that might not apply. The cost of employing stereotypes is lack of attention to individuality, the very thing that Pineau seems to want us to attend to in communicative sexuality.

Saving the Burden of Determining Consent

I believe that the most compelling aspect of Pineau's analysis is her position that we need to hold defendants responsible, not only for being passively receptive to indications of lack of consent, but for taking more positive steps to insure that a potential partner is an enthusiastically willing participant. However, I believe that this is best argued for without problematic appeals to "a woman's point of view." I shall first examine Pineau's central arguments for a shift in moral responsibility and then present my own gender-neutral argument to the same conclusion.

Pineau offers two arguments in favor of her key insight about sexual responsibility. The first is what I call an "equal time" argument, based on an analogy with some arguments in favor of affirmative action. The second is that what Pineau is calling "a woman's point of view" is an ethically superior approach and should be adopted on these grounds. These arguments are not inconsistent, but different implications follow from whether both or only one of them holds true. For example, if one believes that affirmative action is needed because of past and present systematic injustices against certain groups of people, one may then argue that at some point when things are balanced out, affirmative action will no longer be necessary. Similarly, if turning to "a woman's point of view" is justified on the basis of the claim that the current system has been using "a man's point of view," this implies that at some point when the scales are better balanced, we should attempt to create a more sex-neutral approach, if possible. The second argument maintains that the "woman's point of view" is ethically better on other grounds. Pineau maintains that while the patriarchal view is unfair to women, what she calls the feminist view (meaning her alternative approach) is not unfair to men. She claims that if forceful seduction is not what women want, and if it is what men want, it is clear that a criterion that provides ready-made defenses for those engaging in forceful seduction benefits men at the expense of women. It serves men's interests at the expense of women's and is therefore unfair. Pineau offers an analogy with robbers and those who are robbed. Just as it would be unfair to protect the interests of thieves at the expense of their victims, it is unfair to protect the interests of those who desire to overpower those they have sex with into submission at the expense of those who do not wish to be overpowered.

In offering the above analogy, Pineau appears to be saying that something is wrong with overpowering someone into sexual submission just as something is wrong with robbery (other things being equal). Given this, Pineau seems to think that what she is referring to as "a woman's point of view" on good sex is ethically superior. Thus, it should be the standard not simply because another standard has prevailed as a matter of balancing the scales, but because it is a better norm, period.

A Gender-Neutral Approach to Sexual Decency

I agree with Pineau insofar as I accept the norm that one *should* make absolutely sure that another is consenting before engaging in sexual acts. I do not think this is because we have taken "a man's point of view" thus far, and so we now need to balance the scales. While I think that the system has been biased to benefit at least some men, the most important reason to change it is because the alternative is ethically better. Thus, I do not think that after a period of balancing things we need to move onto something else. In my view, it is a major mistake to characterize this minimum standard of sexual decency as "a woman's point of view." It is a standard of minimal sexual decency that should apply to everyone. If most women are socialized to understand this more than most men, it is the product of a system badly in need of reform. However, we do not have to promote the idea that being overpowered into sexual submission is wrong as a "woman's point of view"; we can promote is as a minimally decent approach to sex with others.

While Pineau is right to point out the gender-specific nature of date rape generally, men also rape other men and rape children of both sexes. And women can commit rape as well. The burden of making sure that another is consenting to any sexual activity taking place clearly remains regardless of the sex or sexual preference of those involved, and not simply from "a woman's point of view."

My suggestion encourages a focus on genuine communication. It acknowledges differences among women and puts the burden on everyone to ensure that sexual partners are not sexual victims. It discourages false universalization at the source. It also allows for individual reasons to choose or not to choose sex. Not all sexual encounters are chosen for sexual pleasure. This may seem unfortunate, but it may not always be. For example, I may choose to have sex with someone to comfort them, and this does not seem outright unreasonable to me. I believe that I could consent to this. There is no need to argue for a full-blown account of what it is reasonable for women to consent to in sex. What we need is to place the burden on each participant in sex to ascertain that the other or others are *really* consenting, and this needs to be done by paying attention to the individual, not by applying a stereotype.

A Critical Objection

Before going further, I want to deal with a possible objection to my approach that I consider critical to address at this juncture. As I write in favor of what might be called a gender-neutral approach to the problems under consideration, I am uneasy that my discussion will be taken to imply that issues of gender are irrelevant to rape. Nothing could be further from the truth. Issues of gender, race, class, ethnicity, and sexual preference are all relevant and will be specifically addressed in other sections of this chapter. The fact that almost all rapes are perpetrated by men is a crucial one. The fact that most of those victimized by rape are women and children, coupled with the fact that women are still saddled with primary responsible for the well-being of children, makes rape an issue of enormous concern for women—a feminist issue. Promoting a gender-neutral standard in no way implies that we should ignore issues of gender with regard to rape. I believe that while the problem involves gender socialization to a major degree, the answer is not to further entrench gender-specific norms with regard to sexuality.

Specific Advantages of a Gender-Neutral Approach

Aside from the fact that a communicative approach to sexuality is an ethically better standard for everyone, and so should not be taken as better only from "a woman's point of view," there are other key advantages to a gender-neutral standard. A gender-neutral standard allows us to avoid two objections that have been made against Pineau. Objectors have argued that because communicative sexuality does not really describe all of what women want, it does not express "a woman's point of view" at all. And, if its justification as a moral norm is based on the false notion that it expresses what all women actually want, it should be abandoned. The second objection is that men cannot be expected to understand sexuality from "a woman's point of view." Therefore, it is unfair to hold men responsible for taking such a perspective on sexuality.

Catharine Wells makes the first kind of objection (1996). She offers the fact that many women enjoy romance novels portraying the aggressive seduction model of good sex as evidence that at least some women want noncommunicative sex. Books such as Harlequin romances have long been a thorny issue for feminists. There are many reasons why a simple interpretation of some women's enjoyment of these books as a desire to be aggressively seduced, or raped, is problematic. Problems include that one does not necessarily like to do everything one enjoys reading about, that aggressive sex and rape lead to marriage and a happily ever-after scenario that diverges significantly from what can be expected in real life. Seducers and rapists "love" the women they rape in these books, while certainly rape, and often aggressive sex, is a product of hatred and disdain rather than love.

In my opinion, all of the responses above are plausible, and can be fully developed into arguments that reading a Harlequin romance and enjoying it does not mean that one wants to engage in the kind of sex portrayed in the book. However, I think this approach misses the key point. Even if there are women who want to be overpowered into submission, it is unreasonable for any particular man to assume that he is with such a woman. Pineau makes this point, but she misses its significance. The focus in rape cases should not be solely on what women can be said to want in the abstract, but on what a given individual has done to see what the other wants at a particular time and place. This makes men who engage in wordless overpowering sex guilty of rape. The crime of rape should focus on whether the alleged perpetrator actively tried to ascertain whether the other consented to the interaction. Guesswork based on stereotypes should be irrelevant. Hence, the focus should be not only on the beliefs of the alleged perpetrator, but on what he did to check that those beliefs were accurate in a particular situation, on what he did to make sure he was not committing rape. We do not need to ground this obligation to actively check for consent on false universalizations from a so-called "woman's point of view." Such appeals invite objections such as Wells's about what women actually desire that are irrelevant to the key issue. Sexual aggressors need to take more responsibility.

A gender-neutral standard of sexual decency allows us to avoid the other objection mentioned above as well, that it is unfair to expect men to understand sexuality from "a woman's point of view." David Adams (1996) has argued that it might be unfair to hold men responsible for understanding the "women's point of view" on sex. If men's and women's viewpoints on sex are very different, how can we expect men to be able to comprehend the situation from a woman's viewpoint? This objection works equally well whether the differences between "a man's point of view" and "a woman's point of view" on sex are considered to be the result of biology, socialization, or a mixture of the two. Adams claims that Pineau's account is problematic because she tries to have it both ways. She simultaneously holds a gendered account of sexual desire and expects men to understand what women want. Adams states:

> It is an assumption of Pineau's argument that a communicative sexual act could not be such that it would be unreasonable for a woman to have acquiesced to it — not possible that the sex be nonconsensual—and yet also be such that the defendant could have reasonably believed that it was consensual. This is to suppose that the dialectical starting points from which each person begins the inferences each will take, the epistemic paths each will pursue ultimately, do converge in a way that will show each to be in a like manner alive to the mutuality of desire. But if one takes seriously the fundamental feminist insight that the experiences one has and the way one conceptualizes them, that the beliefs one acquires, the inferential paths one takes through those beliefs, and the epistemic norms guiding one's selection can be influenced by one's gender identity—can track gendered features of the world—then it is possible to see how the understandings of communicative lovers could come apart, and come apart in ways that raise serious questions about the fairness of holding persons to a stringent epistemic duty. (p. 35)

The problem is that if we hold points of view on sexuality and "good sex" to be highly gendered, then it appears there is a problem holding people of the opposite gender responsible for understanding in heterosexual encounters. But, if gender-based approaches to sexuality are not acknowledged, arguments incorporating the idea of "a woman's point of view" would be unavailable. Appeals to a gender-neutral standard of sexual decency allow us to sidestep this kind of objection, which leads to pleas for excusing rapists, altogether.[3]

Fear

Even if the shift in standards under discussion is not taken as incorporating a woman's point of view, it may still generate fears that it is in fact unfair to men as a group, given patterns of socialization. The major fear is that since many men are not used to having to actively seek evidence of consent in sexual encounters, there is the possibility that they will commit sexual assault on the new standard without realizing it. I maintain that this problem is not nearly as large as it might at first appear. Angela Harris has argued that California's laws concerning sexual assault come quite close to legislating a standard of communicative sexuality, yet there has been no significant change, practically speaking (1996). Even if laws are clear that a defendant's belief in the consent of the complainant must be reasonable, as long as people consider being on a date as a component of reasonable belief of consent, as long as it is considered reasonable for someone to believe that in most cases when a woman says no this is only a token act, things will not change. Changes in what goes on in courts reflect attitudinal changes. There is always a gap between having a principle and deciding how it applies. Changes in the way rape is handled in courts is best seen as an indicator of already changing attitudes about rape. If those involved in the judicial system, including those who serve on juries, begin to hold defendants to a new standard, this is because attitudes have changed on a fairly widespread level. If this is so, defendants can be held responsible for knowing what prevailing attitudes are. Nevertheless, there remains the fear that someone (in this case a man) will be unaware of changes and commit rape without meaning to. How are we to deal with the fear that such a thing could happen?

In discussing this issue, I shall draw on the work of Keith Burgess-Jackson with regard to fair distribution of fear. Burgess-Jackson (1996) argues that fear of crime is a socially created burden. Since issues of distributive justice concern distribution of benefits and burdens made necessary by communal living, the distribution of fear is an issue of distributive justice and therefore is an issue for the state. He argues that although certain kinds of fear may be useful in protecting individuals from danger, fear itself is a burdensome mental state. Women in contemporary American society suffer a disproportionate share of the burden of fear due to fear of rape. This state of affairs is unjust and should be remedied.

Although fear can lead to self-protective action, Burgess-Jackson asserts that women's fear of rape is correlated with limitations on liberty in general and mobility in particular. Other costs include loss of self-confidence, self-respect, and self-esteem, nightmares and other sleep disorders, distrust of strangers and acquaintances, chronic anxiety, stress, depression, anxiety, inability to live alone, and increased dependence on men for protection. According to Burgess-Jackson, it is not merely the fact that fear is burdensome that makes women's fear of rape an issue of distributive justice. It is the fact that women, as a class, are significantly more burdened than men as a class. And, even in cases where women's fear does promote safety, it is unfair to deal with rape by making women afraid.

While I agree with Burgess-Jackson's analysis, I want to make a few additions and clarifications before applying it to men's fear. I believe that an additional source of the state's obligation is its own hand in promoting fear of rape in women that not only fails to help, but is extremely harmful. The following three examples come from my personal experiences as both a student and an instructor of women's self-defense. I have been present at safety workshops where police officers (agents of the state) suggested to women that if they fight back during attacks they will get hurt worse, something that statistics clearly indicate is false (Bart 1985). Another example includes encouraging women to be afraid of strangers and trusting of acquaintances, when women are most likely to be raped by someone they know (Robert and Jeanine Ferguson 1994). Finally, I have heard police officers encourage women to stay at home unless someone is with them, when statistically, women are more likely to be raped at home than anywhere else. These are all examples in which the state encourages women to be afraid in ways that do not make them safer.

A different kind of example is the racist fear of some white women that most black men would rape them, given the chance. Rape in America occurs within the context of white supremacy and within the historical context of American slavery. The myth of the white woman raped by the black man remains today, although almost all rape occurs between individuals of the same economic and racial background (Hall 1983). In sharp contrast with the myth of "the sexually pure white woman" is the myth of African American women as wanton and sexually promiscuous by nature, which justified the rape of African American women and made it unimportant or invisible. The purpose of these myths during slavery was to justify the rape of black women by white men and black male slave breeders and to justify the castration and lynching of black men accused of raping white women (Davis 1983; Hall 1983; hooks 1989, 1990).

Studies today indicate that white judges generally impose harsher sentences for rape when the victim is a white female rather than a black female, and the harshest sentences are reserved for black men found guilty of raping white women. The rape of black women by black men remains largely unaddressed (Hall 1983). It may be true that women's fear of rape should be reduced; the kinds of fear women have and the origins of such fear may well be very different.

I now turn to the issue of men's possible fear should standards of sexual responsibility shift. I have argued that much of women's fear regarding sexual assault is not valuable to them. However, men's potentially increased fear could prove quite valuable to them should standards change. Such fear would be valuable if it encouraged men to be extra careful that their sexual "partners" are consenting. It would help men avoid getting themselves into trouble, a direct benefit for them, and would help women avoid being sexually assaulted. This increased fear has the potential to be a win-win situation. However, just as in the case of women's fears, the issue turns out to be complex.

Burgess-Jackson acknowledges that other groups in society bear disproportionate burdens. He states that it is also unjust for the elderly, the poor, and urban residents to be disproportionately fearful. These considerations need to be dealt with in relation to men's fear of rape. Given America's racist history, it is highly problematic to claim that the burden of reducing women's fear of rape should fall on men. This may be true, but much more needs to be said. An adequate response to white women's racist fear of black men would not involve placing some additional burden on black men with regard to white women. Rather, it involves dealing with white women's racism. However, taking the rape of African American women seriously might well involve doing things that would increase fear in African American as well as white men. Redistribution of fear may be justified, but care in how and why fear is redistributed, and attention to patterns of dominance and oppression, is crucial.

A racially sensitive approach will require examination of patterns. Policy decisions will inevitably involve some strategic generalizations, given that it is almost impossible to say anything about a group that will be true of all of is members, and given the fact that issues of distributive justice require looking at groups in addition to individuals. This is why I have argued that it is not necessarily false universalization that is the problem with Pineau's use of "a woman's point of view," but that given what she wishes to accomplish, constructing such a position creates more problems than it solves. Effective arguments for increased responsibility in sexual interaction sensitive to issues of gender, race, class, and sexual preference, among other things, can be made using a gender-neutral standard of sexual decency, without appeals to "a woman's point of view."

Notes

1. For an interesting overview of this debate, see Goldstein, *Feminist Jurisprudence.*

2. This has caused some theorists, such as Andrea Dworkin (1991), to argue that under present circumstances, it is impossible for women to consent at all. However, for the purposes of this discussion, I will assume that if a woman believes that she is consenting, then she is.

3. For a stunning example of the creation of excuses, see Sommers, *Who Stole Feminism?* For a sensitive feminist analysis of these excuses, see Stoltenberg, *Refusing to Be a Man.*

References

Adams, David M. "Date Rape and Erotic Discourse." In *Date Rape: Feminism, Philosophy, and The Law*, edited by Leslie Francis. University Park: The Pennsylvania State University, 1996.

Bar On, Bat-Ami. "Marginality and Epistemic Privilege." In *Feminist Epistemologies*, edited by Linda Alcoff and Elizabeth Potter. New York: Routledge, 1993.

Bart, Pauline B. *Stopping Rape: Successful Survival Strategies.* New York: Pergamon, 1985.

Burgess-Jackson, Keith. *Rape: A Philosophical Investigation.* Aldershot, England: Dartmouth, 1996.

Cuomo, Christine. *Feminism and Ecological Communities: An Ethic of Flourishing.* New York: Routledge, 1998.

Davis, Angela Y. *Women, Race and Class.* New York: Random House, 1983.

De Lauretis, Teresa. "Upping the Anti- [*sic*] in Feminist Theory." In *Conflicts in Feminism*, edited by Marianne Hirsch and Evelyn Fox Keller. New York: Routledge, 1990.

Dworkin, Andrea. *Intercourse.* New York: Free Press, 1991.

Ferguson, Robert and Jeanine. *A Guide to Rape Awareness and Prevention.* Wethersfield, CT: Turtle Press, 1994.

Goldstein, Leslie Friedman, ed., *Feminist Jurisprudence.* Maryland: Rowman and Littlefield, 1992.

Griffin, Susan. "Rape: The All-American Crime." In *Women and Values*, 2d ed., edited by Marilyn Pearsall. Belmont, CA: Wadsworth, 1993.

Hall, Jacquelyn Dowd. "The Mind That Burns in Each Body: Women, Rape, and Racial Violence." In *Moral Controversies: Race, Class, and Gender in Applied Ethics*, edited by Steven Jay Gold. Belmont, CA: Wadsworth, 1993.

hooks, bell. *Talking Back: Thinking Feminist, Thinking Black.* Boston: South End Press, 1989.

___. *Yearning: Race, Gender, and Cultural Politics.* Boston: South End Press, 1990.

Husak, Douglas, and George Thomas III. "Date Rape, Social Convention, and Reasonable Mistakes." *Law and Philosophy* 11 (1992): 95–126.

Koss, Mary P., Thomas E. Dinero, Cynthia A. Seibel, and Susan Cox. "Stranger and Acquaintance Rape: Are There Differences in the Victim's Experience?" *Psychology of Women Quarterly* 12 (1988): 12.

Pineau, Lois. "Date Rape: A Feminist Analysis." In *Date Rape: Feminism, Philosophy, and the Law*, edited by Leslie Francis. University Park: The Pennsylvania State University Press, 1996.

___. "A Response to My Critics." In *Date Rape: Feminism, Philosophy, and the Law*, edited by Leslie Francis. University Park: The Pennsylvania State University Press, 1996.

Sommers, Christina Hoff. *Who Stole Feminism?* New York: Simon & Schuster, 1994.

Stoltenberg, John. *Refusing to Be a Man.* New York: Meridian, 1990.

Wells, Catharine Pierce. "Date Rape and Law: Another Feminist View." In *Date Rape: Feminism, Philosophy, and the Law,* edited by Leslie Francis. University Park: The Pennsylvania State University Press, 1996.

12

NANCY E. SNOW

Evaluating Rape Shield Laws

*Why the Law Continues to
Fail Rape Victims*

Introduction

During the 1970s, feminist reformers and law enforcement officials spearheaded an extensive array of substantive and evidentiary rape law reforms.[1] Among the evidentiary reforms was the passage of rape shield statutes, now in place in 49 states, the Federal government, and the military.[2] These laws are meant to exclude from consideration at trial evidence of the victim's past sexual conduct. The purposes of doing this are threefold: to protect the rape victim from humiliating and intimidating cross-examination about her sexual conduct; to prevent judges and juries from being prejudiced by sexual history evidence that might have little probative value; and to encourage the reporting of rape by making the victim's in-court experience less grueling and degrading.[3]

Recent studies of the impact of rape shield legislation conclude that its value has been largely "symbolic."[4] I take this to be a euphemism meaning that the three purposes of rape shield laws have not been achieved. A survey of the legal and social scientific literature on rape victims and the criminal justice system bears this out.[5] The question of this chapter is, "Why?" In the next section, I give additional background on rape shield statutes. The subsequent analysis identifies three kinds of reasons why shield laws continue to fail rape victims: loopholes in the laws themselves, the unequal power dynamics of cross-examination, and the persistence of myths that are prejudicial to rape victims. I then consider the respects in which the victim's trial experience is a "second rape." I suggest the possibility that victims have a constitutional right to a zone of privacy during cross-examination that might protect them on the witness stand. Finally, I raise the question, "What changes are needed for rape victims to receive justice without doing injustice to the accused?" I argue that establishing specialized criminal courts dealing with sex crimes would strengthen present reforms in rape law by working to exclude from trials prejudicial beliefs and attitudes about rape and rape-related offenses.[6]

Two words of warning. First, the suggestions made in *Changing the System* should not be viewed as a panacea for all of the ills that rape victims suffer at the hands of the justice system. Data indicate that multiple reforms are needed at numerous points in the criminal justice process, not just at trial, on which this chapter focuses.[7] Significant changes in the treatment of rape victims will likely result from a host of systemic reforms. Key to their success, I believe, is the eradication of false but pervasive beliefs and attitudes about rape, sex, and male and female sexuality. In this arena, education is the most powerful weapon in our arsenal.

Second, in this chapter, rape is defined as "sexual intercourse without the consent or against the will of at least one of the parties."[8] Consequently, the arguments presented here apply in any state in which "rape" is defined as nonconsensual intercourse. A distinction should be made between "aggravated" rape and "simple" rape.[9] An aggravated rape features extrinsic violence, such as a weapon or beating, involves multiple assailants, or occurs when there is no previous relationship between rapist and victim. A simple rape, often called "date" rape or "acquaintance" rape, occurs when none of the aggravating circumstances is present. Unfortunately, shield statutes have been needed to protect complainants in trials involving both kinds of crime.

More on Rape Shield Laws

The Historical Background[10]

The feminist critique that led to rape shield laws was a criticism of outmoded cultural myths that had been institutionalized in the law of evidence and routinely invoked in rape trials for centuries. As early as the eighteenth century, Sir Matthew Hale, Lord Chief Justice of the King's Bench, warned against the false rape complainant.[11] His admonition, that rape "is an accusation easily to be made and hard to be proved, and harder to be defended against by the party accused, tho never so innocent,"[12] found its way into judicial opinions and special jury instructions.[13]

This sentiment was echoed and expanded during the nineteenth century in John Wigmore's influential and still widely used treatise, *Evidence in Trials at Common Law*.[14] Wigmore went so far as to advise that no rape complaint should be brought to trial unless the complainant had been previously examined by a psychiatrist. His fear was that the sexual fantasies of mentally imbalanced or immature women would generate false accusations against innocent men. The frightening extent to which these views surfaced in judicial opinions and judges' instructions to juries, even into the 1970s and 1980s, is well documented.[15]

In addition to the myth of the false rape complainant, feminists objected to the myth of the unchaste woman. During the eighteenth, nineteenth, and well into the twentieth centuries, unchaste women, unlike unchaste men, were viewed by society as having bad moral character. Impugning a rape complainant's character for chastity was a common tactic among defense attorneys. To reveal a woman's unchastity in a court of law was tantamount to claiming that she was unworthy of the law's protection. The humiliation of having her sexual past exposed was sometimes considered a just punishment for past permissiveness. Moreover, consent to past sexual activity was often judged sufficient to warrant an inference to consent in the case at hand. ("If she did it before, she'll do it again.") Unchastity was also thought to undermine credibility, and in women, though not in men, was considered a form of dishonesty. In rape trials (though, interestingly, not in other kinds of trial), an unchaste woman who took the witness stand was thought likely to be a liar.[16]

Feminist reformers objected that times have changed. In the late twentieth century, a woman's sexual activity is no longer universally considered a character flaw, a reliable indicator of consent in all cases, or a reason for doubting her credibility. The law of evidence in rape trials, reformers argued, should reflect these cultural changes. Michigan passed the first rape shield law in 1974; by 1976, over half of the states had them in some form.[17]

Types of Rape Shield Laws

Harriet Galvin furnishes an excellent legal analysis of the bewildering array of shield laws.[18] She remarks, "Existing rape-shield statutes vary widely in scope and in procedural detail. Their single common feature is a rejection of the previous automatic admissibility of proof of unchastity."[19]

Galvin organizes shield statutes into four groups along a continuum from most-to-least restrictive.[20] Each of the groups raises complex legal issues. The Michigan law, and 25 statutes modeled on it, fall at the most restrictive extreme. They prohibit the introduction of any of the victim's sexual conduct as evidence, subject to enumerated restrictions. For example, Michigan allows evidence of the victim's past sexual conduct with the defendant and admits evidence of specific instances of sexual activity meant to show the origin of semen, pregnancy, or disease.[21] Like other legal scholars, Galvin believes that the Michigan approach is too restrictive. She argues that it is impossible to anticipate all contexts in which sexual conduct evidence could be relevant to a legitimate defense.[22] Other scholars question whether the stringency of the statutes violates the defendant's constitutional rights.[23]

The statutes of Texas and 11 other states lie at the opposite end of the spectrum.[24] They allow sexual conduct evidence subject to the discretion of the trial court judge under traditional standards of relevancy; that is, the probative value of the evidence must be deemed to outweigh its prejudicial effects. According to Galvin, the merit of this approach is that it encourages judges to consider the relevancy of sexual conduct evidence in *in camera* hearings before introduction at trial. However, its flaw is that it provides no substantive protection against the kinds of evidentiary bias that rape shield laws were meant to exclude.[25]

A third group of statutes, modeled on the Federal rape shield law and used in seven states, combines features of both the Michigan and Texas approaches in the effort to avoid the underinclusiveness and overinclusiveness of each.[26] In these statutes, sexual history evidence is generally prohibited, subject to enumerated exceptions, but a "catch-basin" provision is included to admit unexcepted sexual conduct evidence if "constitutionally required to be admitted," or "relevant and admissible in the interests of justice."[27] However, neither legislatures nor the Supreme Court have given guidance either as to when sexual conduct evidence is constitutionally required or when it is admissible in the interests of justice.[28]

Finally, a fourth group of statutes, which Galvin labels the "California approach," divides sexual conduct evidence into two categories.[29] Substantive evidence addresses the consent of the victim, whereas credibility evidence is offered to attack her believability. Some of the seven statutes following the California approach prohibit substantive evidence, subject to enumerated restrictions, whereas others prohibit credibility evidence, again, subject to enumerated restrictions. The problem with this approach, Galvin notes, is that evidence does not neatly separate into these two categories.[30]

Why Rape Shield Laws Continue to Fail Rape Victims

The following analysis identifies three kinds of reasons why shield laws continue to fail. One kind stems from loopholes in the statutes themselves. Another involves a central structural attribute of the adversarial trial, namely, the cross-examination of the complainant. The third kind of reason is prejudicial attitudes resulting from judges' and jurors' acceptance of a cluster of cultural myths. In practice, the three combine in complex ways to undermine the effectiveness of shield laws.

Loopholes in the Law

How well do shield laws exclude prior sexual conduct evidence from rape trials? Even a cursory glance at the various types of shield statutes suggests loopholes. One suspects, with Galvin, that the more discretion that is left to judges regarding the admissibility of sexual conduct evidence, the more potential there is for this kind of evidence to be admitted. Impact studies of rape shield laws in six jurisdictions tend to verify this.[31] Even in jurisdictions regulated by the most restrictive shield laws, such as Michigan (Detroit) and Illinois (Chicago), data indicate that the most probative types of evidence, for example, semen test results and evidence of a prior relationship between the victim and the defendant, stand a 50-50 chance of being admitted.[32] Further, data show that sexual history evidence of more questionable relevance stands a chance of being admitted in all six jurisdictions.[33] Studies also reveal a correlation between the restrictiveness of the shield statute and judgments of the likelihood of the admissibility of sexual conduct evidence.[34] This has led researchers to conclude that "A strong shield law may be a necessary condition if victims are to be afforded any protection"[35] and, "It apparently takes a strong shield law to counteract the assumption that a victim's prior sexual conduct is relevant to the issue of consent."[36]

Case law shows that defense attorneys try to introduce otherwise inadmissible sexual conduct evidence under other rubrics.[37] For example, one legal commentator chastises the 1994 decision of the Seventh Circuit Court of Appeals in *Stephens v. Miller*.[38] The higher court upheld an Indiana trial court's decision to exclude sexual conduct evidence from being introduced to show a "motive to fabricate." The defendant, Lonnie Stephens, wanted to introduce remarks about the complainant's prior sexual conduct that he had uttered during intercourse. His claim was that, angered by these remarks, the complainant had fabricated the charge of rape. Had it been admitted, as the commentator argues it should have, this evidence would have addressed the issue of the complainant's credibility. The defendant was convicted of attempted rape and sentenced to 20 years in prison.

Consider *State v. Lord.*[39] In Florida in 1989, Stephen L. Lord was acquitted of rape and kidnapping charges. His attorney, Timothy Day, repeatedly showed the jury the woman's clothing: a green tanktop and a white, lacy miniskirt with no underwear. The jury foreman said that the jury acquitted Lord because: "We felt she asked for it by the way she was dressed . . . [w]ith that skirt, you could see everything she had. She was advertising for sex."[40]

Perhaps in response to *Lord*, Florida's rape shield statute was amended in 1990 expressly to "exclude evidence presented to show that the rape victim's manner of dress incited the sexual battery."[41] But consider the sexual battery trial of William Kennedy Smith in 1991.[42] Roy Black, the defense attorney, sought to introduce into evidence the complainant's bra, which was decorated with lace and pearls. He maintained that it was "the single most importance piece of evidence" because it was undamaged, thereby undermining the complainant's claim that she had been tackled, pinned down, and raped.[43] Ignoring the rather obvious fact that a bra would not necessarily be damaged if a woman were attacked in that way, the judge admitted this and other evidence about her clothing but barred evidence that she had had an abortion and an illegitimate child. Smith was acquitted.

Another kind of loophole emerges in cases involving patterns of sexual conduct evidence. Several states admit evidence of the victim's sexual conduct with parties other than the defendant "if it establishes a pattern of prior conduct by the woman sufficiently similar to the defendant's version of the alleged rape."[44] In *State v. Shoffner* in 1983, the North Carolina Court of Appeals ordered a retrial on the grounds that a lower court had improperly excluded sexual conduct evidence of the victim with third parties that formed a pattern allegedly similar to her behavior with the two defendants, even though the court had heard testimony about her acts with the defendants prior to the rape and found evidence sufficient to convict.[45] The Court of Appeals claimed that three pieces of evidence had been improperly excluded: (1) evidence by a witness who claims to have seen the woman many times at a club attracting and touching men, (2) evidence of one episode of consensual sex with the brother of one of the defendants, and (3) evidence by a witness who testified to seeing the woman at an inn with two men standing in front of her, one of whom was zipping his pants.[46] The testimony, according to the court, suggested that the woman was the initiator or the "aggressor" in her sexual encounters. In the words of the court, her "*modus operandi* was to accost men at clubs, parties (public places) and make sexual advances by putting her hands 'all over their bodies.'"[47]

However, as Elizabeth Kessler observes, the woman's conduct with third parties displayed only two similarities to her behavior with the defendants: (1) She initiated the sexual advances and (2) they occurred outside the context of an ongoing relationship.[48] It appears that the North Carolina Court of Appeals sought to punish the victim for exercising her sexual autonomy, and in doing so, reinforced sexist myths about women's sexual passivity, dependency, and monogamy.

Similar sentiments surface in *State v. Colbath*, a 1988 New Hampshire case.[49] Even though New Hampshire's strict rape shield law prohibits introducing evidence of the victim's sexual conduct with third parties, the New Hampshire Supreme Court ruled that such evidence had been improperly excluded by the lower court. Then State Supreme Court Justice David Souter maintained that evidence of the woman's "provocative behavior" and "publicly inviting acts" toward a group of men shortly before the alleged assault by the defendant "could have been viewed as indicating the complainant's likely attitude at the time of the sexual activity in question."[50] Not only are the words "inviting" and "provocative" broad standards for judging the similarity of the woman's actions with the defendant and other men,[51] but Souter's opinion also ignores the fact that the woman and the defendant subsequently left the tavern where they had met to go to his trailer.[52] No matter how "provocative" and "inviting" her behavior had been in the tavern or later, she still had the right to change her mind about consensual sex with the defendant. The questions are: Did she change her mind and Is evidence of her prior sexual behavior toward a group of men relevant to determining that fact? Rape shield laws preclude evidence of prior sexual conduct on the ground that permitting it runs too great a risk of biasing jurors' deliberations. Unlike the trial court judge, Souter evidently thought the probative value of the complainant's prior sexual behavior outweighed its possible prejudicial effects. On retrial, however, the defendant, Richard Colbath, was convicted.[53]

Souter ordered the retrial based on his belief that the New Hampshire shield statute is too restrictive in its prohibitions of sexual conduct evidence and could result in violations of the accused's constitutional rights.[54] As noted earlier, some legal scholars worry whether restrictive shield statutes, such as New Hampshire's, violate the accused's Sixth Amendment right to a fair trial, in particular the compulsory process and confrontation clauses, which guarantee defendants the right to present evidence and to confront witnesses in their defense.[55]

Several observations should allay these fears to some extent. First, even the strictest shield statutes establish procedures allowing the defense to present potentially relevant sexual conduct evidence before the judge in a pre-trial *in camera* hearing. If the judge believes its probative value outweighs its possible prejudicial effects (the traditional standard of relevancy), the evidence is admissible. Second, as mentioned earlier, impact studies have revealed that, even in restrictive jurisdictions, relevant sexual history evidence has a good chance of being admitted.[56] Finally, if an innocent person is convicted due to the exclusion of relevant sexual conduct evidence, the defendant can appeal for a retrial in which the evidence is included, as in *Colbath*.

A final point before leaving this section. In *Lord*, *Shoffner*, and *Colbath*, the defense attorney and judges underscored the importance of the victim's attire and behavior with the defendant and with other men. This approach resembles a doctrine in tort law; namely, the doctrine of assumption of risk.[57] According to one version, if

> the plaintiff voluntarily enters into some relation with the defendant, with knowledge that the defendant will not protect him against one or more future risks that may arise from the relation . . . the legal result is that the defendant is simply relieved of the duty which would otherwise exist.[58]

That is, the plaintiff's knowing assumption of risk is a complete bar to legal action. Timothy Day in *Lord*, the North Carolina Court of Appeals judge in *Shoffner*, and Souter in *Colbath* suggest much the same thing. The victim assumed the risk of rape by her actions and dress. She thereby waived the right to complain.

Aside from questions of the kinds of knowledge and actions that are necessary or sufficient to waive a legal right, we can ask whether taking the "assumption of risk" approach in rape cases is desirable as a matter of public policy. Public policy concerns commonly extend beyond the realm of legal rights to include considerations of social efficiency, utility maximization, and quality of life, including the quality of our shared social environment. I have argued elsewhere that the practice of blaming rape victims for interacting socially with their rapists would have negative consequences for women as well as for the quality of social life.[59] If we are unwilling to embrace these consequences we ought not to blame victims in these cases. Similar remarks apply to using the assumption-of-risk approach in rape cases.

In addition to having the same negative consequences for women and our shared social life, I believe allowing the assumption-of-risk approach to prevail would have seriously negative implications for the legal system itself. Many people already feel disenfranchised from using the legal system. The poor, for example, often have access to legal resources only with great difficulty, and even then, the quality of those resources is frequently lacking.[60] The legal system has systematically and pervasively discriminated against blacks and other minorities.[61] As will be noted in the next section, women have suffered discrimination in both civil and criminal cases involving gender and, in their attempts to press charges of rape, have suffered discrimination at the hands of police and prosecutors.[62] Given the overwhelming evidence for these claims, it is not alarmist to believe that the integrity of our legal system is in jeopardy. Allowing the assumption-of-risk doctrine to prevail as a matter of public policy in rape cases, or even to insinuate itself into judicial reasoning, would only further discredit the law's integrity.

The Unequal Power Dynamics of Cross-Examination

Legal loopholes are not the only reasons why shield statutes fail. The unequal power dynamics of cross-examination present another host of problems. Horror stories abound. For example, Susan Griffin recounts the story of a woman who was raped in San Francisco in 1970.[63] She testified that her rapist, Jerry Plotkin, and three other men forced her into a car at gunpoint one night. She was taken to Plotkin's apartment where he and the others raped and sexually abused her. She was released but threatened with death if she reported the incident to the police. She did report the incident. Upon searching Plotkin's apartment, the police found a long list of women's names with hers on it. Her name had been crossed off. At trial, several other women testified that Plotkin had lured them into his apartment on false pretexts, then raped them.

One plank of Plotkin's defense was to portray the victim as sexually promiscuous and an unfit mother. The defense attorney noted that she was "familiar with liquor" and had worked as a "cocktail waitress." Twice he accused her of having sexual affairs with men at work. He tried to establish that she was living with a married man and contended that she had "spent the night" with another man who lived in her building. Before his questioning was cut off by the complainant's protest, he went as far as to claim that her children engaged in sex games. (The victim was divorced, and her children were in a foster home at the time of the trial.) At one point during cross-examination, she asked: "Am I on trial? . . . It is embarrassing and personal to admit these things to all these people. . . . I did not commit a crime. I am a human being."[64]

What happened to complainants on the witness stand before the advent of rape shield laws was planned moral abuse. Defense attorneys pried into the sexual past of victims with the intent of impugning their moral character. Questions were not cast in neutral terms but were loaded with insulting innuendo. Defense attorneys sought to connect complainants with the use of alcohol and drugs, "fast living," unfit motherhood, poor employment records, and other lapses generally deemed morally undesirable by society. "Character assassination" is not too strong a phrase. The point, however, was not just to smear the victim's character, thereby subverting her credibility and moral worth as a person, but to establish, if possible, the "contributory fault of the victim."[65] Engaging in certain activities, such as drinking or dancing with the defendant, hitchhiking, or wearing certain kinds of clothes, shows that the victim "had it coming," that she was "asking for it," and that she "got what she deserved."[66] Moreover, portraying the complainant as morally unsympathetic and essentially different from jurors was meant to block the possibility that members of the jury would compassionately identify with the victim's plight and thereby incline to render a verdict in her favor.

Such questioning was an integral part of the adversary system and was actively encouraged by prominent lawyers. In 1973, F. Lee Bailey and Henry B. Rothblatt published a guide for defense attorneys in rape trials, *Crimes of Violence: Rape and Other Sex Crimes.* They advise: "If you can totally destroy her character or reputation, as with proof of prior specific criminal or immoral acts, . . . launch your attack."[67] Thus, before the advent of shield laws, the adversary trial itself furnished the justificatory framework within which the abuse of the victim took place.

Fundamental features of the defense attorney's role and of the adversary trial have not changed. Canon 7 of the *Model Code of Professional Responsibility* states that "A lawyer should represent a client zealously within the bounds of the law."[68] In states with restrictive shield statutes, the law limits the introduction of sexual conduct evidence. However, consider Ethical Consideration (EC) 7-3 of the *Model Code of Professional Responsibility*: "while serving as an advocate, a lawyer should resolve in the favor of his client doubts as to the bounds of the law."[69] This almost seems to invite defense attorneys to seek ways to insinuate inadmissible sexual conduct evidence at trial. Even though a host of disciplinary rules sanctions intentional attempts to interject forbidden evidence,[70] Peter Hazelton remarks that, given the subjective nature of relevancy standards, the tradition of zealous advocacy, and the injunction to resolve doubts in the client's favor, "most lawyers can find some good faith argument for the weakest of claims."[71]

In a more radical vein, Gregory M. Matoesian argues that the cross-examination process itself is inherently patriarchal and thus, prejudicial to the victim.[72] Using elements of the sociological method of conversation analysis, Matoesian has analyzed tapes of actual cross-examinations of rape victims protected by shield statutes to reveal the unequal power dynamics of socially structured talk. The defense attorney and the victim are unequals not only because of their differing roles in the trial process. The structure of cross-examination itself allows the defense counsel to attempt to reconstruct the victim's self-presentation and the presentation of her testimony from a man's perspective. Defense counsel is free to try to disconnect elements that were originally united in her testimony, weave together initially disparate elements, recombine, overemphasize, underemphasize, and use innuendo, tone, demeanor, pauses, and gestures. The aim is to confuse and discredit the victim's self-presentation before the court as well as her perspective on the incident, thereby shifting the blame from defendant to victim.[73] The goal is to paint the victim a liar by making her account look more like the defendant's version of consensual sex.[74] Thus, an account of rape from a woman's viewpoint is made to look like consensual sex from a man's perspective. The subjective account of the woman is "corrected" and reinterpreted through the subjectivity of a man and then offered to judge and jury by the defense as "objective" truth—a value-neutral description of facts. According to Matoesian, "[P]atriarchal power . . . is being produced and reproduced in this exchange between the V [victim] and DA [defense attorney].[75] During cross-examination, not only is the victim's testimony reinterpreted from a patriarchal perspective, but her very self-presentation to the court—her right to control how she is perceived by others—is appropriated for the purposes of patriarchy.

One might object that one of the prosecutor's functions is to protect his client from irrelevant and misleading questioning. But even if, contrary to many trial records, prosecutors aggressively tried to shield complainants, this approach is limited for several reasons. First, if the judge shares commonly held prejudices, he might overrule the objection. Second, even if the objection were sustained, the defense has already made a prejudicial or insinuating remark for the court to hear. The psychological damage, especially in jury trials, is already done. Finally, defendants have more legal power in our system than victims.[76] The rights of defendants are constitutionally protected; the defense attorney is an advocate for his client's case. By contrast, the prosecutor is not an advocate for the victim, but instead is "an advocate for the state, and the interests of the state may often conflict with those of the victim."[77]

One might also object that defense attorneys are hard on victims of any crime during cross-examination. In other words, there is nothing specially abusive about the cross-examination that rape victims, as opposed to victims of other kinds of crime, receive. If so, I'm arguing, in effect, not specifically for rape shield statutes, but for "victim shield statutes"; that is, laws that would protect victims of any crime from abusive questioning.[78] I have not found empirical studies indicating that defense attorneys are, in fact, harder on rape victims than on other victims. Even without such studies, however, two points can be made.

First, there is plenty of anecdotal evidence, from trial records, press accounts, and the personal accounts of rape victims and others, that rape victims are subjected to more abusive questioning than are victims of other crimes.[79] In fact, one might suspect that the grueling character of rape victims' courtroom experience is a reason why rape is still underreported.[80] None of this should surprise us. Rape is a sensitive crime of a sexual nature. The very nature of the crime requires that the rape victim who takes the witness stand open herself to some degree to sensitive questioning. Although the personal lives of robbery and arson victims, for example, might be relevant to defense questioning, the sexuality of victims of these crimes is not liable to be opened to public scrutiny in the same kind of way as a rape victim's sexuality. Moreover, as I argue in the next section, common understandings of rape and of the experiences of rape victims are heavily influenced by outmoded cultural myths, sexual stereotypes, and false beliefs. Defense attorneys tap into these prejudices to portray the sexuality of rape victims in the most negative light possible. Since negatively depicted sexuality still carries a social stigma, the aim of defense attorneys is, in effect, to stigmatize rape victims. This is not to deny that victims of other crimes are also sometimes slurred. Defense attorneys sometimes seek to stigmatize robbery victims, for example, by blaming the victim. If someone leaves her wallet unattended on a lunch counter in a crowded restaurant and it is stolen, a defense attorney will probably allege that the victim "had it coming," or "got what she deserved." My point is that the social stigma attached to being depicted as careless about one's money or possessions is not as damaging to one's character as the stigma that still attaches to women who are portrayed as sexually promiscuous or "loose."

My second point is this. Suppose that one remains unconvinced that rape victims have it worse on the witness stand than other victims. If one believes that rape victims undergo grueling questioning, stigmatization, and character assassination, this must be true of victims of other crimes as well. Shouldn't we at least ask whether this kind of treatment is necessary and whether the prospect of such treatment might not discourage victims from pressing their claims? If cross-examination of victims on the witness stand discourages the reporting and prosecution of crimes, this is a reason for at least examining the situation. This is not an argument for "victim shield statutes." But if one believes that rape victims are subjected to abusive questioning that is no worse than that applied to other victims, the foregoing remarks suggest that the idea of protecting a zone of privacy for victims during cross-examination, through victim shield statutes if need be, is not terribly farfetched.

The Ongoing Power of Myths

Abusive defense tactics could not have worked without the presence of powerful cultural myths, primarily about women's and men's sexuality.[81] Not only was the law infused with biases against the credibility and mental stability of the rape complainant, courtesy of the likes of Hale and Wigmore, but society was and continues to be saturated with inconsistent myths that "good" women are sexually passive and essentially monogamous, that "bad" women are loose and licentious, and that somehow, all women, "good" and "bad," are at some level receptive to male sexual advances. (A notorious example is the "'no' means 'yes'" myth.)

Two other myths about sexuality deserve mention. One is that rape is committed by a small percentage of mentally aberrant men.[82] Studies have shown, however, that rapists and "normal" men are essentially similar. Attitudes and beliefs that lead to rape are extensions of normal sexual behavior and socialization, not products of sexual deviance.[83]

Another myth is that, at some point during the course of sexual arousal, men become unable to control their sexual urges. Thus, they cannot be held responsible for failing to stop sexual activity. In accordance with the contributory fault theory, women are to be blamed for unwanted sex because they apparently have more power than men to curb or encourage the intensity of male sexual arousal.[84]

The contributory fault theory also relies for its efficacy on the "just world" myth; that is, the need to believe that we live in an essentially just world.[85] To protect this belief, jurors tend to rationalize that, if bad things happen to people, the victims, including those of rape, must either be intrinsically evil or have brought the harm on themselves in some way.[86] Thus, we "blame the victim."[87]

Multiple studies have shown that judges and jurors "bought into" these myths, and that these false beliefs and attitudes, coupled with morally abusive defense tactics, affected the outcomes of many trials.[88] Rape law reform has not caused these myths to vanish. In a powerful article, Morrison Torrey argues that "jurors and judges who believe rape myths are not impartial."[89] Torrey presents the state with two "compelling reasons" to eliminate myth-based bias: (1) It denies the state and the rape victim a fair trial and (2) such sex discrimination undermines the integrity of the justice system.[90]

The "Second Rape" and the Victim's Privacy

In addition, the kind of cross-examination that victims were (and are) forced to undergo during trial is similar to rape. Thus, some commentators refer to the victim's trial experience as a "second victimization."[91] Both rape and cross-examination involve invasions of the victim's autonomy. Rape, of course, is a physical, as well as a mental and emotional, violation of the victim's autonomy. Rape denies the victim's autonomy and implies a negative judgment of her value. It is a morally objectionable objectification of the victim.[92] In Kantian terms, it is using the victim as a mere means to the rapist's ends. The rapist's total disregard of the victim's desires reduces her to the status of a tool or instrument. Similarly, the defense attorney's disregard of the victim's privacy, his indifference to truth, and his relative lack of concern with justice contribute to his treatment of the victim as a means to the end of securing his client's acquittal, thus reinforcing the hegemony of patriarchy. When cross-examination is intended to demean or denigrate the victim, the defense attorney's use of her as a tool is all the more blatant. This point can be put more strongly. In effect, the victim is a tool not just of the rapist, but also of the defense attorney. In order to get his "win," defense counsel is willing to "re-rape."

Invasions of privacy are central to the re-rape of the victim. Attempts to demean or humiliate a victim are most potent when attached to facts of the victim's life. Cross-examination to elicit irrelevant sexual history evidence violates the victim's moral right to privacy, construed as the right to control the dissemination of information about her private life. Moral privacy rights are rooted in the right to personal autonomy; that is, the right to have a personal sphere protected from the intrusion of others, including government.

In a groundbreaking article, Vivian Berger forcefully argues that the victim has the right to equal protection of the laws, and that morally abusive defense tactics place a special burden on victims of rape that is not borne by victims of other types of crime who seek justice.[93] This point is germane to the privacy issue. Victims of other kinds of crime need not open their private lives to public scrutiny in order to press their claims. Indeed, the point cuts across civil and criminal law.[94] Types of gender cases other than rape—for example, sexual abuse, sexual harassment, and sex discrimination cases—show the same unequal power dynamics of cross-examination. Complainants have not always been allowed to maintain a zone of privacy that is protected from unjustified, intrusive questioning.

To see the double standard, imagine a defense attorney probing a robbery victim's charitable past or making the victim feel guilty or unworthy of legal protection for having given away money in the past.[95] The promiscuous woman would be replaced by the profligate man. The man's charitable history might be relevant, but its relevance is outweighed by its prejudicial effect. Introducing it as evidence focuses the jury's attention on the victim's past instead of on the defendant's actions. But here, as in rape cases, the defendant, not the victim, is on trial.

Rape shield laws could be bolstered by showing that complainants have a constitutionally guaranteed right to a zone of privacy in cross-examination.[96] The intuitive idea is that, in making the charge of rape (or sexual harassment, and so on), the victim should not have to open her entire life to the court's scrutiny. One might point out that one effect of traditional standards of relevancy is to protect the victim's privacy. But traditional standards have clearly failed to protect victims' privacy in rape trials, as the need for shield statutes shows. Moreover, some judges manifest concern for the defendant's Sixth Amendment rights to confrontation and compulsory process (recall Souter's opinion in *State v. Colbath*). A complainant's ability to invoke a constitutionally guaranteed right to a zone of privacy in cross-examination could serve to equalize the competing claims of defendant and complainant. This would not make rape cases easier to decide. But it would ensure that victims' moral rights to privacy were respected during cross-examination.

Showing that complainants have a constitutionally guaranteed privacy right would not be easy. However, some fairly recent Supreme Court cases provide a promising line of precedent that might be used to give the beginnings of an argument sketch.[97] *Griswold v. Connecticut* traced a right to privacy out of the penumbra of several constitutional amendments to protect the right of married couples to use contraceptives without government intrusion.[98] The right was extended to unmarried couples in *Eisenstadt v. Baird*.[99] *Stanley v. Georgia* invoked, among other grounds, the right to privacy to ensure an individual's right to view pornography in his or her home.[100] Most famously, *Roe v. Wade* guaranteed women the right to have an abortion during the first and second trimesters of pregnancy, again drawing on the right to privacy.[101]

These cases delineate an ever-widening zone of privacy for the individual wherein government may not regulate certain kinds of sexual and reproductive choices. Governmental action with respect to these choices is limited; provided that no third parties are physically harmed, it is prohibited. But if governmental action in individual choices concerning the use of contraceptives, viewing pornography, and having an abortion is limited or even prohibited, how might one justify opening a woman's private life, including her sexual relationships, to public scrutiny in a court of law as an essential prerequisite for pressing a claim? If government does not have the right to regulate a person's sexual choices, on what grounds can it claim the right to scrutinize them in open court?

The most obvious answer is on grounds of the defendant's Sixth Amendment rights. But these rights are not unlimited.[102] They do not require irrelevant evidence to be admitted at trial. The law of evidence holds relevance as the presupposition of admissibility.[103] Conversely, evidence lacking probative value or whose probative value is outweighed by its prejudicial effects should be excluded. This is just what rape shield statutes require. Far from encroaching on a defendant's Sixth Amendment rights, shield statutes hold judges in rape trials to the same standards of relevancy applicable in other types of trial and, in doing so, protect the complainant's privacy. For one of the prejudicial effects of introducing past sexual history as evidence is that the victim's privacy is invaded.

Earlier it was suggested that showing the existence of a constitutionally guaranteed right to a zone of privacy in cross-examination might bolster rape shield statutes. The foregoing remarks, however, provide an alternative way of conceptualizing the relationship between the two. This is best explained by way of analogy. The Fourth Amendment protects citizens against unreasonable searches and seizures by government. It does not, however, say explicitly how this protection is to be afforded. For that, we must look to the exclusionary rule, a legal rule that excludes from presentation at trial evidence obtained in violation of certain legal procedures; for example, evidence obtained without a search warrant. There are disanalogies between the exclusionary rule and rape shield statutes, the most glaring being that the former developed at case law, whereas the latter are products of legislatures.[104] However, the important point is that, just as the exlusionary rule gives effect to a constitutionally guaranteed right against the government, so, too, shield statutes can be viewed as giving effect to an existing, but as yet unarticulated, constitutional right to privacy in certain trial circumstances.

In seeing what rape shield laws are intended to protect victims from, we can see what they are meant to furnish protection for: the victim's autonomy; her right to privacy; her right to be respected as an intrinsically valuable person and not be treated in a purely instrumental way, either by another person or by a process; her right to be perceived truthfully, that is, to not have her character defamed or her testimony distorted in the courtroom, or at least, to have a procedural right to be able to effectively counter attempts at defamation and distortion; and her right to use the legal system to receive justice without having to bear special burdens.

Changing the System: A Case for Specialized Sex Crimes Courts

How can the system be made fairer for rape victims without doing injustice to the accused? Some legal scholars contend that shield laws themselves should be revised.[105] Others argue that participants in the justice system need to be educated about the realities of rape.[106] Still others suggest substantive changes in rape law that reflect more egalitarian attitudes toward women's sexual autonomy.[107] Here I explore another possibility: establishing specialized criminal courts dealing only with sex crimes.

Specialized Courts and Why We Need Them

There are many specialized courts in the United States at both the state and Federal levels. They have existed for most of this century. Most are low-level and have at least one and usually two levels of review available.[108] These courts reflect the increasing specialization in society as a whole[109] and, in some instances, the sensitivity of the kinds of issues they address. Familiar examples include family courts, juvenile courts, and bankruptcy courts. Given the sensitivity and complexity of rape and other sex crimes as well as the burgeoning social scientific and legal literature on rape and related issues, arguably, the time has come to consider specialized sex crimes courts.

This view is reinforced by recognizing the state's interests in the reporting, detection, and deterrence of crime. Historically, rape has been an underreported crime.[110] Recent statistics from the U.S. Department of Justice show that "[i]n 1995 persons age twelve or older reported experiencing an estimated 260,000 attempted or completed rapes and nearly 95,000 threatened or completed sexual assaults other than rape."[111] However, in 1994 and 1995, only one third of victims said they reported the incident to a law enforcement agency.[112] To address this and other problems, sensitive crimes units dealing with sexual assault, domestic abuse, and child abuse already exist in District Attorney's offices in many urban areas.[113] A natural next step would be to introduce specialized sex crimes courts. Creating and maintaining viable sex crimes courts should encourage the reporting and ultimately, deterrence, of sex crimes by sending the public the message that these crimes will be treated more knowledgeably and fairly than in the past.

Elements of a Sex Crimes Court: Education,
Judges, Juries, and Counsel

The model of the specialized court is promising for several reasons. Foremost among them is its educational potential. Specialized courts require that the judge become an expert in a field. Even courts in which judges rotate on and off the bench, such as some family courts, stress the importance of ongoing education to the judge's ability to evaluate arguments.[114] Multidisciplinary education for judges about sex and sex crimes would thus be an important feature of a sex crimes court. It could take a number of forms, ranging from continuing education courses, to workshops and special seminars, to having mental health personnel and other professionals available to courts as nonpartisan consultants.[115] If, as Judge Richard Posner remarks, "judges know next to nothing about the subject beyond their own personal experience, which is limited,"[116] education of judges could help to debunk the myths about sexuality that currently hamper the system.

Mandatory juror education is also possible. Given that jurors routinely have to sit for several hours before being impaneled, why not require those who sit on specialized sex crimes courts to spend this time viewing an educational video? They could at least be alerted to the fact that their own sexual experiences do not necessarily provide reliable normative guides to the kinds of issues they will be asked to deliberate about.[117]

Further, by exploding myths, education has the potential for mitigating the effects on judges and jurors of defense tactics commonly used in rape trials. Instead of making legitimate arguments, defense attorneys continue to exploit the prejudices of judges and jurors to the disadvantage of rape victims. If these biases were eliminated or at least challenged, we can hope that such ploys would become less effective and eventually fall into disuse.

In part because of their emphasis on education, specialized courts provide the possibility of modified roles for judges and counsel. In an adversarial system, judges are the passive and allegedly impartial recipients of arguments presented by counsel. The adversarial model has ancient roots in the Anglo-American legal tradition.[118] The judge has knowledge of law, but relies on the parties to investigate and present the facts. The judge then applies the law to the facts, rendering a verdict or instructing the jury to do so.

This model is simplistic in several respects. The assumption seems to be that, aside from his knowledge of law, the judge functions as a sort of *tabula rasa*, bringing no antecedent beliefs or biases to the adjudication of a case. We have seen that this is false. Numerous judges bring sexist prejudices and inaccurate beliefs about rape and sex to bear on the disposition of rape cases or at least allow such prejudices to influence trials.

This shortcoming is related to another flaw in the model; namely, the assumption that relevant information neatly divides into two types: knowledge of law and knowledge of the facts of a particular case. Again, this is false. In many areas of law, specialized knowledge of information other than law or the facts of the case is needed for the court to render an informed, fair verdict. Examples include family law, commercial law, business law, tax law, patent law, real estate law, health law, and environmental law.[119]

Specialized courts allow judges to work toward an ideal of informed impartiality in adjudication. Informed impartiality opens the possibility of a more active role for judges in the investigation of facts and presentation of arguments normally left to counsel. I do not mean to suggest that judges should usurp the role traditionally played by counsel in the Anglo-American system. Counsel should still have primary responsibility for fact-finding and oral argument before the court. But, drawing on a repository of accurate information about rape, sex, and sexuality, judges should be freer to use this knowledge to intervene to redirect inquiry or to guide the course of questioning, especially when doing so supplies a corrective for creeping bias or protects the victim from degrading innuendo or interrogation.

One common objection to specialized courts is that allowing the judge a more active role risks unfairly truncating the truth-seeking process.[120] Bringing their own knowledge to bear, judges will incline toward hasty conclusions and prematurely curtail examination of possible lines of inquiry. But this can happen in any trial, and, as another scholar has argued elsewhere, any loss of impartiality caused by greater knowledge should be outweighed by gains in rationality.[121]

Besides, in sex crimes courts, two safeguards can address this concern. One is the possibility of permitting professional, nonpartisan consultants a prominent advisory role in court proceedings. If a judge closes a line of inquiry that the consultant thinks should be pursued, he or she should be able to register "on the record" disagreement. This provides a possible check on "judicial activism" at the time of trial, which could act in concert with a second safeguard: a system of review by higher courts. As mentioned, most specialized courts have one and usually two levels of review.[122] There is no reason to think that the decisions of low-level sex crimes courts should be the final word on a case in the system. For the plan to work, of course, appellate judges would also have to receive specialized education.

Conclusion: The Values We Seek

Complex concerns about values underlie debates about rape shield statutes. Deeply implicated are the values of fairness, autonomy, privacy, and respect. We would like to see rape complainants treated fairly by the justice system without depriving the accused of his constitutional right to a fair trial. We would like to see defense attorneys zealously represent their clients without deliberately disrespecting the victim, violating her personal privacy, or misportraying her character and choices. We would like to see a society in which women's sexual autonomy and privacy rights are respected and prized, both by individuals and by institutions. And we would like to see the criminal justice system effectively deter rape and other sex crimes, thereby making society a safer place, especially for women.[123]

As mentioned earlier, I believe that accomplishing these changes ultimately depends on our success at reeducating ourselves about men, women, sex, and rape—among many other topics. False beliefs and evaluations that continue to impede justice are deeply held and steeped in centuries of culture and tradition. For example, the beliefs that women are inferior to men, that women who accuse men of rape are likely to be liars or emotionally imbalanced, and that women should not be sexually autonomous, are parts of the larger interpretive frameworks supporting patriarchy that need to be challenged and revised. Similarly, the beliefs that torture would extract true testimony and that dunking would identify witches were once deeply held and jealously guarded.[124] They and the evaluations associated with them were parts of larger interpretive frameworks used to oppress some in order to maintain the power of others. As with those fictions and the oppressive power structures they supported, it is time for society and the criminal justice system to abandon other palliatives of times gone by and face reality.

ACKNOWLEDGMENTS   I am grateful to Lisa Peters, formerly of Marquette University Law Library, for research assistance in writing this chapter; to Eva M. Soeka, J.D., for very helpful comments on an earlier draft; and to Christine Wiseman, J.D., for informative conversation from a defense attorney's perspective. My special thanks go to Keith Burgess-Jackson for inviting me to contribute to this anthology and for searching criticisms of an earlier version of this chapter.

Notes

1. For good summaries of feminist law reforms, see Keith Burgess-Jackson, *Rape: A Philosophical Investigation* (Aldershot, England: Dartmouth, 1996), chap. 3; Nancy A. Crow-

ell and Ann W. Burgess, eds., *Understanding Violence Against Women* (Washington, DC: National Academy Press, 1996), pp. 124–9; Harriet R. Galvin, "Shielding Rape Victims in the State and Federal Courts: A Proposal for the Second Decade," *Minnesota Law Review*, 70 (1986), pp. 791-801; and Vivian Berger, "Man's Trial, Woman's Tribulation: Rape Cases in the Courtroom," *Columbia Law Review*, 77 (1) (January 1977). Throughout this essay, I use masculine pronouns for judges and rape defendants, most of whom are male, and feminine pronouns for rape victims, most of whom are female.

2. Galvin, "Shielding Rape Victims," pp. 906–7. At the time that Galvin's article was written, Utah and Arizona did not have rape shield statutes; as of 1996, only Utah did not have one. See Crowell and Burgess, *Understanding Violence*, p. 126.

3. John Lausch, "Note: *Stephens v. Miller*: The Need to Shield Rape Victims, Defend Accused Offenders, and Define a Workable Constitutional Standard," *Northwestern University Law Review*, 90 (1) (Fall 1995): 346–86; Galvin, "Shielding Rape Victims"; and Berger, "Man's Trial," 41–52.

4. Crowell and Burgess, *Understanding Violence*, pp. 126–7; Cassia Spohn and Julie Horney, *Rape Law Reform: A Grassroots Revolution and Its Impact* (New York: Plenum, 1992), p. 175; and Edward Felsenthal, "An Accuser's Past Is Fair Game Once Again in Many Sex Cases," *The Wall Street Journal*, 6 June 1997, pp. A1, A8.

5. See the last two sections of this chapter and accompanying notes.

6. For good analyses of rape-related offenses, see Burgess-Jackson, *Rape: A Philosophical Investigation*, chap. 6; and Crowell and Burgess, *Understanding Violence*, pp. 125–6.

7. See, for example, Lee Madigan and Nancy C. Gamble, *The Second Rape: Society's Continued Betrayal of the Victim* (New York: Lexington Books, 1991), pt. 3.

8. Nancy E. Snow, "Self-Blame and Blame of Rape Victims," *Public Affairs Quarterly* 8 (4) (October 1994): 377.

9. See Susan Estrich, *Real Rape: How the Legal System Victimizes Women Who Say No* (Cambridge: Harvard University Press, 1987), pp. 4–5.

10. For an excellent history of rape law that extends beyond the narrow history of evidentiary reform covered here, see Burgess-Jackson, chaps. 3 and 4.

11. Galvin, "Shielding Rape Victims," p. 792. See also J. Alexander Tanford and Anthony J. Bocchino, "Rape Victim Shield Laws and the Sixth Amendment," *University of Pennsylvania Law Review* 128 (1980): 546.

12. Sir Matthew Hale, *The History of the Pleas of the Crown*, vol. 1, ed. by W. A. Stokes and E. Ingersoll (Philadelphia: R. H. Small, 1847), p. 634.

13. Ibid., pp. 792–3 n. 139.

14. See John Henry Wigmore, *Evidence in Trials at Common Law*, vol. 3A, rev. James H. Chadbourn (Boston: Little, Brown, 1970), secs. 924 and 924A; ibid., vol. IA, rev. Peter Tillers (Boston: Little, Brown, 1983), sec. 62; see also Tanford and Bocchino, "Rape Victim Shield Laws," pp. 546–7; Galvin, "Shielding Rape Victims," pp. 777–81; Abraham P. Ordover, "Admissibility of Patterns of Similar Sexual Conduct: The Unlamented Death of Character For Chastity," *Cornell Law Review* 63 (1977): 94.

15. Wigmore, *Evidence in Trials*, notes to secs. 924A and 62.

16. Tanford and Bocchino, "Rape Victim Shield Laws," pp. 546–51.

17. Galvin, "Shielding Rape Victims," p. 765 n. 3.

18. Ibid., pp. 763–916.

19. Ibid., p. 773.

20. Ibid., pp. 773–6.

21. See Mich. Comp. Laws Ann. s. 750.520j (West 1991), quoted in Daniel Lowery, "The Sixth Amendment, the Preclusionary Sanction, and Rape Shield Laws: *Michigan v. Lucas,* 111 S. Ct. 1743 (1991)," *Cincinnati Law Review* 61 (1992): 297–8 n. 3.

22. Galvin, "Shielding Rape Victims," p. 774. Yet, having admitted this, it is puzzling that Galvin's own solution to the legal quandary of excessive restrictiveness is to propose a model statute enumerating more exceptions. The general strategy of adding exceptions seems to me unpromising, if only because eventually rape shield statutes will become too complex and unwieldy to be practicable.

23. This is probably the central constitutional issue raised by rape shield statutes. For a variety of perspectives, see Berger; Galvin, "Shielding Rape Victims"; Lausch, "Note: *Stephens v. Miller,*"; Lowery, "The Sixth Amendment,"; Ordover, "Admissibility of Patterns,"; Tanford and Bocchino, "Rape Victim Shield Laws,"; Clifford S. Fishman, "Consent, Credibility, and the Constitution: Evidence Relating to a Sex Offense Complainant's Past Sexual Behavior," *Catholic University Law Review* 44 (1994–1995): pp. 709–820; Elizabeth Kessler, "Pattern of Sexual Conduct Evidence and Present Consent: Limiting the Admissibility of Sexual History Evidence in Rape Prosecutions," *Women's Rights Law Reporter* 14 (1) (Winter 1992): pp. 79–96; and Frank Tuerkheimer, "A Reassessment and Redefinition of Rape Shield Laws," *Ohio State Law Journal* 50 (1989): pp. 1245–74.

24. Galvin, "Shielding Rape Victims," p. 774.

25. Ibid.

26. Ibid., pp. 774–5.

27. Ibid., p. 775.

28. Ibid.

29. Ibid., pp. 775–6.

30. Ibid.

31. Spohn and Horney, *Rape Law Reform*, p. 165. The six jurisdictions studied were: Detroit, MI; Cook County (Chicago), IL; Philadelphia County (Philadelphia), PA; Harris County (Houston), TX; Fulton County (Atlanta) GA; and Washington, DC. See ibid., p. 35.

32. See Ibid., p. 155.

33. See Ibid.

34. See Ibid., pp. 170–1.

35. Ibid., p. 170.

36. Ibid., p. 171.

37. Felsenthal, "An Accuser's Past," pp. A1, A8.

38. Lausch, "Note: *Stephen v. Miller,*" p. 347.

39. See Peter Hazelton, "Rape Shield Laws: Limits on Zealous Advocacy," *American Journal of Criminal Law* 19 (1991): p. 35. *State v. Lord* is the case. See ibid. n. 1 for an explanation of the lack of a citation for this case.

40. Quoted in ibid., p. 35.

41. Ibid., p. 36 n. 3.

42. Felsenthal, "An Accuser's Past," p. A8.

43. Ibid.

44. Kessler, "Pattern of Sexual Conduct Evidence," p. 82.

45. Ibid., p. 83.

46. Ibid.

47. Quoted in ibid.

48. Ibid.

49. Ibid., p. 84, and Felsenthal, "An Accuser's Past," pp. A1, A8.

50. Quoted in Kessler, "Pattern of Sexual Conduct Evidence," p. 84.

51. Ibid.

52. Ibid.

53. Felsenthal, "An Accuser's Past," p. A8.

54. Ibid.

55. See note 23, especially Tanford and Bocchino, "Rape Victim Shield Laws." At the time of this writing, the U.S. Supreme Court has not ruled directly on the constitutionality of rape shield statutes. However, in *Michigan v. Lucas* (1991), the Supreme Court held that precluding the introduction of sexual conduct evidence as a sanction for the defense's failure to comply with a ten-day notice and hearing requirement was not *per se* unconstitutional. See *Michigan v. Lucas*, 111 S. Ct. 1743 (1991); also Lowery, "The Sixth Amendment."

56. See text and accompanying notes 31–33.

57. See W. Page Keeton, ed., *Prosser and Keeton on the Law of Torts*, 5th ed. (St. Paul, MN: West, 1994), pp. 480–98. I am grateful to Eva M. Soeka for discussion of the ideas in this and the following paragraph.

58. Ibid., p. 481.

59. See Snow, "Self-Blame," pp. 388–9.

60. See, e.g., Russell W. Galloway, *Justice For All? The Rich and Poor in Supreme Court History 1790-1990* (Durham, NC: Carolina Academic Press, 1991); and Christopher E. Smith, *Courts and the Poor* (Chicago, IL: Nelson-Hall, 1991), esp. chap. 2, "The Poor and the Criminal Justice System."

61. See, e.g., Randall Kennedy, *Race, Crime and the Law* (New York: Pantheon Books, 1997).

62. On discrimination at the hands of police and prosecutors, see, e.g., Lynne Henderson, "Rape and Responsibility," *Law and Philosophy* 11 (1992):128–30, esp. nn. 6, 7, pp. 128–9; and Estrich, *Real Rape*, pp. 15ff.

63. See Susan Griffin, *Rape: The Power of Consciousness* (San Francisco, CA: Harper & Row, 1979), pp. 11–12.

64. Ibid., p. 12.

65. See Harry Kalven, Jr. and Hans Zeisel, *The American Jury* (Boston, MA: Little, Brown, 1966), pp. 249–54.

66. Ibid.; Hazelton, "Rape Shield Laws," p. 35; Estrich, *Real Rape*, p. 5; and Felsenthal, "An Accuser's Past," p. A8.

67. F. Lee Bailey and Henry B. Rothblatt, *Crimes of Violence: Rape and Other Sex Crimes*, vol. 2 (Rochester, New York: The Lawyers Co-Operative Publishing Co., 1973), p. 212.

68. Quoted in ibid., p. 49.

69. Quoted in ibid.

70. Ibid., pp. 50–1.

71. Ibid., p. 51.

72. See Gregory M. Matoesian, *Reproducing Rape: Domination through Talk in the Courtroom* (Chicago, IL: The University of Chicago Press, 1993). For a critique of the perils of using the adversary method in philosophy, see Janice Moulton, "A Paradigm of Philoso-

phy: The Adversary Method," in *Discovering Reality: Feminist Perspectives in Epistemology, Metaphysics, Methodology, and Philosophy of Science*, ed. Sandra Harding and Merrill B. Hintikka (Boston, MA: D. Reidel, 1983), pp. 149–64.

73. For more on defense attorneys' aims to discredit rape victims' testimony, see Susan Estrich, "Palm Beach Stories," *Law and Philosophy* 11 (1992): 5–33.

74. Morrison Torrey remarks that: "While undermining the credibility of the victim is a common tactic of defense lawyers in a variety of criminal cases, it is more prevalent in rape trials. In many rape prosecutions the victim, for all practical purposes, becomes a pseudo-defendant." Morrison Torrey, "When Will We Be Believed? Rape Myths and the Idea of a Fair Trial in Rape Prosecutions," *University of California Davis Law Review* 24 (1991):1059.

75. Matoesian, *Reproducing Rape*, p. 104.

76. See Spohn and Horney, *Rape Law Reform*, p. 174.

77. Ibid., p. 174.

78. I owe this point to Keith Burgess-Jackson.

79. Some of this anecdotal evidence is given in the text of this chapter. Far more is found in many of the references cited in the endnotes.

80. See text and accompanying notes 111 and 112.

81. For a summary of myths about rape victims, see Torrey, "When Will We Be Believed?," pp. 1025–27.

82. Ibid., pp. 1022–25.

83. Ibid.

84. Ibid., p. 1024, for research results consistent with this aspect of the contributory fault theory.

85. Ibid., pp. 1051-52; and Melvin Lerner, *The Belief in a Just World: A Fundamental Delusion* (New York, NY: Plenum, 1980).

86. See Torrey, "When Will We Be Believed?"

87. See Snow, "Self-Blame," pp. 380–92, where I argue that blaming rape victims can be justified only in a narrow range of cases.

88. See Torrey, "When Will We Be Believed?," pp. 1052ff.

89. Ibid., p. 1057.

90. Ibid.

91. On the criminal justice system as a second rape, see, e.g., Madigan and Gamble, *The Second Rape*, chap. 10; on general social attitudes toward rape, see Joyce E. Williams and Karen A. Holmes, *The Second Assault: Rape and Public Attitudes* (Westport, CT: Greenwood Press, 1981). See also Torrey, "When Will We Be Believed?," p. 1030: "the experience of a trial is grueling and frequently provokes responses similar to those caused by the actual rape."

92. See Martha Nussbaum, "Objectification," *Philosophy and Public Affairs* 24 (4) (Fall 1995):249–91.

93. See Berger, pp. 45–52. Torrey remarks that "the vicious treatment of rape victims during trial has prompted many lawyers to refuse to defend accused rapists." Torrey, "When Will We Be Believed?," p. 1059 n. 228. Quoting a 1990 article, Torrey points out that "The complainant stands trial along with the defendant in a way no other victim does." Ibid.

94. I am grateful to Eva Soeka for calling this to my attention.

95. I owe this analogy to Keith Burgess-Jackson.

96. I am grateful to Eva Soeka for suggesting that I develop this point.

97. See Sanford Levinson, "Privacy," in *The Oxford Companion to the Supreme Court of the United States*, ed. Kermit L. Hall (New York: Oxford University Press, 1992), pp. 671–8; and Michael W. McCann, "*Griswold v. Connecticut*," in ibid., pp. 351–3.

98. See *Griswold v. Connecticut* 381 U.S. 479 (1965).

99. See *Eisenstadt v. Baird* 405 U.S. 438 (1972).

100. *Stanley v. Georgia* 394 U.S. 557 (1969); see also Frederick Schauer, "*Stanley v. Georgia*," in Hall, *The Oxford Companion*, pp. 821–2.

101. *Roe v. Wade* 410 U.S. 113 (1973).

102. See Lowery, "The Sixth Amendment," pp. 299–300, and the discussion that follows, pp. 301–5.

103. See John W. Strong, *McCormick on Evidence*, 4th ed. (St. Paul, MN: West, 1992), pp. 338–41.

104. For the case history, see Thomas Y. Davies, "Exclusionary Rule," in Hall, *The Oxford Companion*, pp. 264–6.

105. See, for example, Galvin, "Shielding Rape Victims"; and Tanford and Bocchino, "Rape Victim Shield Laws."

106. See Torrey, "When Will We Be Believed?"; Toni M. Massaro, "Experts, Psychology, Credibility, and Rape: The Rape Trauma Syndrome Issue and Its Implications for Expert Psychological Testimony," *Minnesota Law Review* 69 (1985), pp. 395–470; and Pamela A. Wilk, "Expert Testimony on Rape Trauma Syndrome: Admissibility and Effective Use in Criminal Rape Prosecution," *American University Law Review* 33 (1983–1984), pp. 417–62.

107. For example, Stephen J. Schulhofer, "Taking Sexual Autonomy Seriously: Rape Law and Beyond," *Law and Philosophy* 11 (1992), pp. 35–94; and Lois Pineau, "Date Rape: A Feminist Analysis," *Law and Philosophy* 8 (1989), pp. 217–43.

108. See Ellen E. Sward, "Values, Ideology, and the Evolution of the Adversary System," *Indiana Law Journal* 64 (1989), pp. 338–9. An important exception to the claim that most specialized courts are low-level is specialized corporate business courts, which operate at a very high level. I am grateful to Eva M. Soeka, J.D., for calling this to my attention.

109. Ibid., p. 339.

110. See former President Carter, quoted in Hazelton, "Rape Shield Laws," p. 44; and former Representative Elizabeth Holtzman, quoted in Galvin, "Shielding Rape Victims," p. 764.

111. Lawrence A. Greenfeld, *Sex Offenses and Offenders: An Analysis of Data on Rape and Sexual Assault* (Washington, DC: U.S. Department of Justice Bureau of Justice Statistics, 1997), p. v.

112. Ibid.

113. I am grateful to Eva M. Soeka for pointing this out.

114. See Sward, "Values, Ideology," p. 339; and Margaret Beyer and Ricardo Urbina, *An Emerging Judicial Role in Family Court* (Washington, DC: American Bar Association, 1986).

115. For models, see Sward, "Values, Ideology," pp. 338–41; and Beyer and Urbina.

116. Richard A. Posner, *Sex and Reason* (Cambridge, MA: Harvard University Press, 1992), p. 1.

117. Thanks again to Eva Soeka for making this point.

118. See Sward, "Values, Ideology," pp. 319–26.

119. See *Marquette University Law School Bulletin 1997–1998*, pp. 10–11, for a list of

areas of concentration and required courses for each. For example, a concentration in family law requires a seminar on child abuse; one in business law requires a workshop on total quality management; health law requires a seminar on children with special health needs; and environmental law requires courses in air and water pollution, hazardous waste, and land use planning. Moreover, in addition to a J.D. degree, many tax lawyers also have a separate LL.M. degree, a Master of Law in Taxation, requiring courses in specialized areas. I owe this point to Vada Waters Lindsey, J.D., LL.M.

120. See Sward, "Values, Ideology," pp. 339–40.

121. Ibid., p. 339.

122. See text and accompanying note 108.

123. During 1993–1995, "an estimated 91% of the victims of rape and sexual assault were female." Greenfeld, "Sex Offenses and Offenders," p. 2.

124. On the use of torture to extract true testimony, see Cesare Beccaria, *On Crimes and Punishments,* trans. David Young (Indianapolis, IN: Hackett, 1986), chap. 16, "Torture," pp. 29–33, and accompanying notes, pp. 91–2; and Michel Foucault, *Discipline and Punish: The Birth of the Prison,* trans. Alan Sheridan (New York: Vintage Books, 1977), pp. 35–42. On the use of dunking to identify witches, see George Lyman Kittredge, *Witchcraft in Old and New England* (New York: Russell and Russell, 1929), chap. 15, "Cold Water," pp. 230–8.

A Chronology of Philosophical Publications on Rape

The criterion for inclusion on this list is disjunctive: Either the author is a philosopher or the essay was published in a philosophical journal or anthology. The dates are those of first publication rather than composition, since the latter (in most cases) is difficult to ascertain. Within each year, monographs are listed first, then contributions to anthologies, then journal articles.

1976

Curley, E. M. "Excusing Rape." *Philosophy and Public Affairs* 5 (summer): 325–60.

1977

Clark, Lorenne M. G., and Debra J. Lewis. *Rape: The Price of Coercive Sexuality*. Toronto: Women's Press.

Elliston, Frederick A. "Rape: Introduction." In *Feminism and Philosophy*, edited by Mary Vetterling-Braggin, Frederick A. Elliston, and Jane English, 309–12. Totowa, NJ: Littlefield, Adams.

Shafer, Carolyn M., and Marilyn Frye. "Rape and Respect." In *Feminism and Philosophy*, edited by Mary Vetterling-Braggin, Frederick A. Elliston, and Jane English, 333–46. Totowa, NJ: Littlefield, Adams.

Foa, Pamela. "What's Wrong with Rape." In *Feminism and Philosophy*, edited by Mary Vetterling-Braggin, Frederick A. Elliston, and Jane English, 347–59. Totowa, NJ: Littlefield, Adams.

Peterson, Susan Rae. "Coercion and Rape: The State as a Male Protection Racket." In *Feminism and Philosophy*, edited by Mary Vetterling-Braggin, Frederick A. Elliston, and Jane English, 360–71. Totowa, NJ: Littlefield, Adams.

1978

Bienen, Leigh. "Mistakes." *Philosophy and Public Affairs* 7 (spring): 224–45.

1979

None.

1980

Bleich, J. David, and Carol A. Tauer. "The Hospital's Duty and Rape Victims." *The Hastings Center Report* 10 (April): 25–7.

Hoagland, Sarah Lucia. "Violence, Victimization, Violation." *Sinister Wisdom* 15 (fall): 70–2.

1981

Duff, R. A. "Recklessness and Rape." *The Liverpool Law Review* 3: 49–64.

Meisel, Alan. "Confidentiality and Rape Counseling." *The Hastings Center Report* 11 (August): 5–7.

1982

Thornton, M. T. "Rape and Mens Rea." *Canadian Journal of Philosophy*, Suppl. Vol. 8: 119–46.

1983

None.

1984

Tong, Rosemarie. "Rape." In *Women, Sex, and the Law*, 90–123. Savage, MD: Rowman and Littlefield.

Davis, Michael. "Setting Penalties: What Does Rape Deserve?" *Law and Philosophy* 3 (April): 61–110.

1985

LeMoncheck, Linda. *Dehumanizing Women: Treating Persons as Sex Objects*. Totowa, NJ: Rowman and Allanheld.

Ruse, Michael. "Is Rape Wrong on Andromeda? An Introduction to Extraterrestrial Evolution, Science, and Morality." In *Extraterrestrials: Science and Alien Intelligence*, edited by Edward Regis, Jr., 43–78. Cambridge: Cambridge University Press.

O'Neill, Onora. "Between Consenting Adults." *Philosophy and Public Affairs* 14 (summer): 252–77.

1986

Harrison, Ross. "Rape—A Case Study in Political Philosophy." In *Rape: An Historical and Cultural Enquiry*, edited by Sylvana Tomaselli and Roy Porter, 41–56. Oxford: Basil Blackwell.

1987

Baber, H. E. "How Bad Is Rape?" *Hypatia* 2 (summer): 125–38.

1988

Baker, Brenda M. "Consent, Assault and Sexual Assault." In *Legal Theory Meets Legal Practice*, edited by Anne Bayefsky, 223–38. Edmonton, Alberta: Academic Printing and Publishing.

Schonsheck, Jonathan. "Human Nature, Innateness and Violence Against Women." In *Philosophical Essays on the Ideas of a Good Society*, edited by Yeager Hudson and Creighton Peden, 287–97. Lewiston, NY: Edwin Mellen Press.

Bar On, Bat-Ami. "Violence Against Women: Philosophical Literature Overview." *The American Philosophical Association Newsletter on Feminism and Philosophy* 88 (November): 8–11.

Bar On, Bat-Ami. "Violence Against Women: A Bibliography." *The American Philosophical Association Newsletter on Feminism and Philosophy* 88 (November): 11–3.

1989

Pineau, Lois. "Date Rape: A Feminist Analysis." *Law and Philosophy* 8 (August): 217–43.

1990

Schulhofer, Stephen J. "The Gender Question in Criminal Law." *Social Philosophy and Policy* 7 (spring): 105–37.

Beabout, Greg. "Abortion in Rape Cases." *Proceedings of the American Catholic Philosophical Association* 64: 132–8.

Cudd, Ann E. "Enforced Pregnancy, Rape, and the Image of Woman." *Philosophical Studies* 60 (September–October): 47–59.

Friedman, Marilyn. "'They Lived Happily Ever After': Sommers on Women and Marriage." *Journal of Social Philosophy* 21 (fall/winter): 57–65.

Sommers, Christina. "Do These Feminists Like Women?" *Journal of Social Philosophy* 21 (fall/winter): 66–74.

Friedman, Marilyn. "Does Sommers Like Women? More on Liberalism, Gender Hierarchy, and Scarlett O'Hara." *Journal of Social Philosophy* 21 (fall/winter): 75–90.

1991

Card, Claudia. "Rape as a Terrorist Institution." In *Violence, Terrorism, and Justice*, edited by R. G. Frey and Christopher W. Morris, 296–319. Cambridge: Cambridge University Press.

Sommers, Christina. "*Argumentum Ad Feminam.*" *Journal of Social Philosophy* 22 (spring): 5–19.

Bogart, J. H. "On the Nature of Rape." *Public Affairs Quarterly* 5 (April): 117–36.

1992

Scheman, Naomi. "Rape." In *Encyclopedia of Ethics*, edited by Lawrence C. Becker and Charlotte B. Becker, 2:1059–62. New York and London: Garland.

Wreen, Michael. "Abortion and Pregnancy Due to Rape." *Philosophia* 21 (April): 201–20.

McGregor, Joan. "Introduction [to Special Issue on Philosophical Issues in Rape Law]." *Law and Philosophy* 11: 1–3.

Estrich, Susan. "Palm Beach Stories." *Law and Philosophy* 11: 5–33.

Schulhofer, Stephen J. "Taking Sexual Autonomy Seriously: Rape Law and Beyond." *Law and Philosophy* 11: 35–94.

Husak, Douglas N., and George C. Thomas III. "Date Rape, Social Convention, and Reasonable Mistakes." *Law and Philosophy* 11: 95–126.

Henderson, Lynne. "Rape and Responsibility." *Law and Philosophy* 11: 127–78.

1993

French, Stanley G. "Interpersonal Violence: Power Relationships and Their Effects on Health." In *Interpersonal Violence, Health and Gender Politics*, edited by Stanley G. French, 3–26. Dubuque, IA, and Ottawa: Wm. C. Brown Communications.

Allen, Derek. "Relevance, Conduction and Canada's Rape-Shield Decision." *Informal Logic* 15 (spring): 105–22.

Brison, Susan J. "Surviving Sexual Violence: A Philosophical Perspective." *Journal of Social Philosophy* 24 (spring): 5–22.

Rendall, Steven. "Duction, or the Archaeology of Rape." *Philosophy and Literature* 17 (April): 119–28.

Hengehold, Laura. "Rape and Communicative Agency: Reflections in the Lake at L——." *Hypatia* 8 (fall): 56–71.

1994

Sommers, Christina Hoff. "Rape Research." In *Who Stole Feminism? How Women Have Betrayed Women*, 209–26, 297–300. New York: Simon and Schuster.

Murphy, Jeffrie G. "Some Ruminations on Women, Violence, and the Criminal Law." In *In Harm's Way: Essays in Honor of Joel Feinberg*, edited by Jules L. Coleman and Allen Buchanan, 209–30. Cambridge: Cambridge University Press.

McGregor, Joan. "Force, Consent, and the Reasonable Woman." In *In Harm's Way: Essays in Honor of Joel Feinberg*, edited by Jules L. Coleman and Allen Buchanan, 231–54. Cambridge: Cambridge University Press.

May, Larry, and Robert Strikwerda. "Men in Groups: Collective Responsibility for Rape." *Hypatia* 9 (spring): 134–51.

Hengehold, Laura. "An Immodest Proposal: Foucault, Hysterization, and the 'Second Rape'." *Hypatia* 9 (summer): 88–107.

Snow, Nancy E. "Self-Blame and Blame of Rape Victims." *Public Affairs Quarterly* 8 (October): 377–93.

Archard, David. "Exploited Consent." *Journal of Social Philosophy* 25 (winter): 92–101.

Burgess-Jackson, Keith. "Justice and the Distribution of Fear." *The Southern Journal of Philosophy* 32 (winter): 367–91.

1995

Burgess-Jackson, Keith. "Statutory Rape: A Philosophical Analysis." *The Canadian Journal of Law and Jurisprudence* 8 (January): 139–58.

Bogart, J. H. "Reconsidering Rape: Rethinking the Conceptual Foundations of Rape Law." *The Canadian Journal of Law and Jurisprudence* 8 (January): 159–82.

Davion, Victoria. "Rape, Group Responsibility and Trust." *Hypatia* 10 (spring): 153–6.

May, Larry, and Robert Strikwerda. "Reply to Victoria Davion's Comments on May and Strikwerda." *Hypatia* 10 (spring): 157–8.

McGregor, Joan. "What Can We Learn from Feminist Jurisprudence About Harm and Injury?" *The American Philosophical Association Newsletters on Feminism and Philosophy and Philosophy and Law* 94 (spring): 45–8.

West, Robin. "The Harms of Consensual Sex." *The American Philosophical Association Newsletters on Feminism and Philosophy and Philosophy and Law* 94 (spring): 52–5.

Soble, Alan. "In Defense of Bacon." *Philosophy of the Social Sciences* 25 (June): 192–215.

Burgess-Jackson, Keith. "Rape and Persuasive Definition." *Canadian Journal of Philosophy* 25 (September): 415–54.

Brison, Susan J. "On the Personal as Philosophical." *The American Philosophical Association Newsletter on Feminism and Philosophy* 95 (fall): 37–40.

Nussbaum, Martha C. "Objectification." *Philosophy and Public Affairs* 24 (fall): 249–91.

1996

Burgess-Jackson, Keith. *Rape: A Philosophical Investigation.* Aldershot, England: Dartmouth.

Francis, Leslie. Introduction to *Date Rape: Feminism, Philosophy, and the Law,* edited by Leslie Francis, vii–xix. University Park: The Pennsylvania State University Press.

Adams, David M. "Date Rape and Erotic Discourse." In *Date Rape: Feminism, Philosophy, and the Law,* edited by Leslie Francis, 27–39. University Park: The Pennsylvania State University Press.

Wells, Catharine Pierce. "Date Rape and the Law: Another Feminist View." In *Date Rape: Feminism, Philosophy, and the Law,* edited by Leslie Francis, 41–50. University Park: The Pennsylvania State University Press.

Pineau, Lois. "A Response to My Critics." In *Date Rape: Feminism, Philosophy, and the Law,* edited by Leslie Francis, 63–107. University Park: The Pennsylvania State University Press.

Harris, Angela P., and Lois Pineau. "A Dialogue on Evidence." In *Date Rape: Feminism, Philosophy, and the Law,* edited by Leslie Francis, 109–31. University Park: The Pennsylvania State University Press.

Silliman, Matthew R. "The Antioch Policy, a Community Experiment in Communicative Sexuality." In *Date Rape: Feminism, Philosophy, and the Law,* edited by Leslie Francis, 167–75. University Park: The Pennsylvania State University Press.

Tittle, Peg. "Sexual Activity, Consent, Mistaken Belief, and Mens Rea." Philosophy in the Contemporary World 3 (spring): 19–23.

Alexander, Larry. "Introduction to Issues 2 and 3: Symposium on Consent in Sexual Relations." Legal Theory 2 (June): 87–8.

Wertheimer, Alan. "Consent and Sexual Relations." Legal Theory 2 (June): 89–112.

Dripps, Donald. "For a Negative, Normative Model of Consent, with a Comment on Preference-Skepticism." Legal Theory 2 (June): 113–20.

Hurd, Heidi M. "The Moral Magic of Consent." Legal Theory 2 (June): 121–46.

Malm, H. M. "The Ontological Status of Consent and Its Implications for the Law on Rape." Legal Theory 2 (June): 147–64.

Alexander, Larry. "The Moral Magic of Consent (II)." Legal Theory 2 (September): 165–74.

McGregor, Joan. "Why When She Says No She Doesn't Mean Maybe and Doesn't Mean Yes: A Critical Reconstruction of Consent, Sex, and the Law." Legal Theory 2 (September): 175–208.

Sherwin, Emily. "Infelicitous Sex." Legal Theory 2 (September): 209–31.

West, Robin. "A Comment on Consent, Sex, and Rape." Legal Theory 2 (September): 233–51.

Bogart, John H. "Commodification and Phenomenology: Evading Consent in Theory Regarding Rape." Legal Theory 2 (September): 253–64.

Bar On, Bat-Ami. "Introduction [to Special Issue on Women and Violence]." Hypatia 11 (fall): 1–4.

Card, Claudia. "Rape as a Weapon of War." Hypatia 11 (fall): 5–18.

Schott, Robin May. "Gender and 'Postmodern War'." Hypatia 11 (fall): 19–29.

Cuomo, Chris J. "War Is Not Just an Event: Reflections on the Significance of Everyday Violence." Hypatia 11 (fall): 30–45.

Philipose, Liz. "The Laws of War and Women's Human Rights." Hypatia 11 (fall): 46–62.

Heberle, Renee. "Deconstructive Strategies and the Movement Against Sexual Violence." Hypatia 11 (fall): 63–76.

1997

LeMoncheck, Linda. "Appropriating Women's Bodies: The Form and Function of Men's Sexual Intimidation of Women." In Loose Women, Lecherous Men: A Feminist Philosophy of Sex, 155–215, 252–62. New York: Oxford University Press.

Archard, David. "Without Consent." Review of Rape: A Philosophical Investigation, by Keith Burgess-Jackson, and Carnal Knowledge: Rape on Trial, by Sue Lees. Radical Philosophy (January/February): 44–5.

Card, Claudia. "Addendum to 'Rape as a Weapon of War'." *Hypatia* 12 (spring): 216–8.

Soble, Alan. "Antioch's 'Sexual Offense Policy': A Philosophical Exploration." *Journal of Social Philosophy* 28 (spring): 22–36.

Calhoun, Laurie. "On Rape: A Crime Against Humanity." *Journal of Social Philosophy* 28 (spring): 101–9.

Davion, Victoria. "Rape Research and Gender Feminism: So Who's Anti-Male?" *Public Affairs Quarterly* 11 (July): 229–43.

Archard, David. "'A Nod's as Good as a Wink': Consent, Convention, and Reasonable Belief." *Legal Theory* 3 (September): 273–90.

Kittay, Eva Feder. "AH! My Foolish Heart: A Reply to Alan Soble's 'Antioch's "Sexual Offense Policy": A Philosophical Exploration'." *Journal of Social Philosophy* 28 (fall): 153–9.

May, Larry, and James Bohman. "Sexuality, Masculinity, and Confession." *Hypatia* 12 (winter): 138–54.

1998

Archard, David. *Sexual Consent*. Boulder, CO: Westview.

Francis, Leslie Pickering. "Rape." In *Encyclopedia of Applied Ethics*, edited by Ruth Chadwick, 3:791–8. San Diego: Academic.

Kazan, Patricia. "Sexual Assault and the Problem of Consent." In *Violence Against Women: Philosophical Perspectives*, edited by Stanley G. French, Wanda Teays, and Laura M. Purdy, 27–42, 207–10. Ithaca, NY, and London: Cornell University Press.

Lacey, Nicola. "Unspeakable Subjects, Impossible Rights: Sexuality, Integrity and Criminal Law." *The Canadian Journal of Law and Jurisprudence* 11 (January): 47–68.

Brett, Nathan. "Sexual Offenses and Consent." *The Canadian Journal of Law and Jurisprudence* 11 (January): 69–88.

Burgess-Jackson, Keith. "Wife Rape." *Public Affairs Quarterly* 12 (January): 1–22.

Burgess-Jackson, Keith. "A Chronology of Philosophical Publications on Rape." *The American Philosophical Association Newsletter on Philosophy and Law* 97 (spring): 105–7.

In press

Superson, Anita. "Rape." In *The Philosophy of Law: An Encyclopedia*, edited by Christopher B. Gray. New York: Garland.

Burgess-Jackson, Keith. "A Crime Against Women: Calhoun on the Wrongness of Rape." *Journal of Social Philosophy*.

Selected Bibliography

The works listed here are among the more prominent (and, in the judgment of the editor, most useful) in the philosophical, legal, historical, and scientific literature on rape, which is burgeoning. The bibliography is by no means exhaustive; it is meant to be illustrative and suggestive only. Readers interested in inquiring further into the topics addressed in this volume are advised to consult the notes and bibliographies of the works listed here as well as the endnotes accompanying the chapters. No attempt has been made to collect all endnote references in this space.

Bibliographies, Surveys, and Overviews

Barnes, Dorothy L., comp. *Rape: A Bibliography, 1965–1975.* Troy, NY: Whitston, 1977.

Bar On, Bat-Ami. "Violence Against Women: Philosophical Literature Overview." *The American Philosophical Association Newsletter on Feminism and Philosophy* 88 (November 1988): 8–11.

———. "Violence Against Women: A Bibliography." *The American Philosophical Association Newsletter on Feminism and Philosophy* 88 (November 1988): 11-13.

Burgess-Jackson, Keith. "A Chronology of Philosophical Publications on Rape." *The American Philosophical Association Newsletter on Philosophy and Law* 97 (spring 1998): 105–7.

Fogarty, Faith. "A Selective Bibliography." In *Forcible Rape: The Crime, the Victim, and the Offender,* edited by Duncan Chappell, Robley Geis, and Gilbert Geis, 356–82. New York: Columbia University Press, 1977.

Mathews, Joan. "Rape Bibliography." In *Rape: The First Sourcebook for Women,* by New York Radical Feminists, edited by Noreen Connell and Cassandra Wilson, 113–22. New York and Scarborough, Ont.: New American Library, 1974.

Vetterling-Braggin, Mary; Frederick A. Elliston; and Jane English. "Further References." In *Feminism and Philosophy,* edited by Mary Vetterling-Braggin, Frederick A. Elliston, and Jane English, 372–6. Totowa, NJ: Littlefield, Adams, 1977.

Ward, Sally K., Jennifer Dziuba-Leatherman, Jane Gerard Stapleton, and Carrie L. Yodanis, comps. *Acquaintance and Date Rape: An Annotated Bibliography.* Westport, CT: Greenwood, 1994.

Wilson, Carolyn F. *Violence Against Women: An Annotated Bibliography*. Boston: G. K. Hall, 1981.

Monographs and Treatises

Adler, Zsuzsanna. *Rape on Trial*. London and New York: Routledge and Kegan Paul, 1987.

Allen, Beverly. *Rape Warfare: The Hidden Genocide in Bosnia-Herzegovina and Croatia*. Minneapolis: University of Minnesota Press, 1996.

Allison, Julie A., and Lawrence S. Wrightsman. *Rape: The Misunderstood Crime*. Newbury Park, CA: Sage, 1993.

Amir, Menachem. *Patterns in Forcible Rape*. Chicago and London: The University of Chicago Press, 1971.

Archard, David. *Sexual Consent*. Boulder, CO: Westview, 1998.

Bailey, F. Lee, and Henry B. Rothblatt. *Crimes of Violence: Rape and Other Sex Crimes*. Deerfield, IL: Clark Boardman Callaghan, 1973.

Baron, Larry, and Murray A. Straus. *Four Theories of Rape in American Society: A State-Level Analysis*. New Haven: Yale University Press, 1989.

Bart, Pauline B., and Patricia H. O'Brien. *Stopping Rape: Successful Survival Strategies*. New York: Pergamon, 1985.

Beneke, Timothy. *Men on Rape*. New York: St. Martin's, 1982.

Bourque, Linda Brookover. *Defining Rape*. Durham, NC, and London: Duke University Press, 1989.

Brownmiller, Susan. *Against Our Will: Men, Women and Rape*. New York: Simon and Schuster, 1975.

Brundage, James A. *Law, Sex, and Christian Society in Medieval Europe*. Chicago and London: The University of Chicago Press, 1987.

Burgess-Jackson, Keith. *Rape: A Philosophical Investigation*. Aldershot, England: Dartmouth, 1996.

Cholakian, Patricia Francis. *Rape and Writing in the "Heptaméron" of Marguerite de Navarre*. Carbondale: Southern Illinois University Press, 1991.

Clark, Lorenne M. G., and Debra J. Lewis. *Rape: The Price of Coercive Sexuality*. Toronto: Women's Press, 1977.

Cuklanz, Lisa M. *Rape on Trial: How the Mass Media Construct Legal Reform and Social Change*. Philadelphia: University of Pennsylvania Press, 1996.

Dworkin, Andrea. *Intercourse*. New York: Free Press, 1987.

———. *Life and Death*. New York: Free Press, 1997.

Ellis, Lee. *Theories of Rape: Inquiries into the Causes of Sexual Aggression*. New York: Hemisphere, 1989.

Estrich, Susan. *Real Rape*. Cambridge, MA, and London: Harvard University Press, 1987.

Fairstein, Linda A. *Sexual Violence: Our War Against Rape*. New York: William Morrow, 1993.

Feild, H. S., and Leigh Bienen. *Jurors and Rape: A Study in Psychology and Law*. Lexington, MA: Lexington Books, 1980.

Finkelhor, David, and Kersti Yllo. *License to Rape: Sexual Abuse of Wives*. New York: Free Press, 1985.

French, Marilyn. *The War Against Women*. New York: Ballantine Books, 1992.

Funk, Rus Ervin. *Stopping Rape: A Challenge for Men*. Philadelphia: New Society, 1993.

Gordon, Margaret T., and Stephanie Riger. *The Female Fear: The Social Cost of Rape*. New York: Free Press, 1989.

Gravdal, Kathryn. *Ravishing Maidens: Writing Rape in Medieval French Literature and Law.* Philadelphia: University of Pennsylvania Press, 1991.

Griffin, Susan. *Rape: The Power of Consciousness.* San Francisco: Harper and Row, 1979.

Groth, A. Nicholas, with H. Jean Birnbaum. *Men Who Rape: The Psychology of the Offender.* New York and London: Plenum, 1979.

Hall, Rob. *Rape in America: A Reference Handbook.* Santa Barbara, CA: ABC-CLIO, 1995.

Koss, Mary P., and Mary R. Harvey. *The Rape Victim: Clinical and Community Interventions.* 2d ed. Newbury Park, CA: Sage, 1991.

LaFree, Gary. *Rape and Criminal Justice: The Social Construction of Sexual Assault.* Belmont, CA: Wadsworth, 1989.

Lees, Sue. *Carnal Knowledge: Rape on Trial.* London: Hamish Hamilton, 1996.

LeMoncheck, Linda. *Dehumanizing Women: Treating Persons as Sex Objects.* Totowa, NJ: Rowman and Allanheld, 1985.

Madigan, Lee, and Nancy C. Gamble. *The Second Rape: Society's Continued Betrayal of the Victim.* New York: Lexington Books, 1991.

Marsh, Jeanne C.; Alison Geist; and Nathan Caplan. *Rape and the Limits of Law Reform.* Boston: Auburn House, 1982.

Matoesian, Gregory M. *Reproducing Rape: Domination Through Talk in the Courtroom.* Chicago: The University of Chicago Press, 1993.

McCahill, T., L. Meyer, and A. Fischman. *The Aftermath of Rape.* Lexington, MA: Lexington Books, 1979.

Medea, Andra, and Kathleen Thompson. *Against Rape.* New York: Farrar, Straus and Giroux, 1974.

Millett, Kate. *Sexual Politics.* Garden City, NY: Doubleday and Company, 1970.

Pateman, Carole. *The Sexual Contract.* Stanford, CA: Stanford University Press, 1988.

Posner, Richard A. *Sex and Reason.* Cambridge: Harvard University Press, 1992.

Rape in America: A Report to the Nation. Arlington, VA: National Victim Center; and Charleston, SC: Crime Victims Research and Treatment Center, 1992.

Rise, Eric W. *The Martinsville Seven: Race, Rape, and Capital Punishment.* Charlottesville and London: University Press of Virginia, 1995.

Roberts, Cathy. *Women and Rape.* New York: New York University Press, 1989.

Roiphe, Katie. *The Morning After: Sex, Fear, and Feminism on Campus.* Boston: Little, Brown, 1993.

Rowland, Judith. *Rape: The Ultimate Violation.* London and Sydney: Pluto Press, 1986.

Russell, Diana E. H. *The Politics of Rape: The Victim's Perspective.* New York: Stein and Day, 1975.

———. *Sexual Exploitation: Rape, Child Sexual Abuse, and Workplace Harassment.* Beverly Hills, CA: Sage, 1984.

———. *Rape in Marriage.* Exp. and rev. ed. with a New Introduction. Bloomington and Indianapolis: Indiana University Press, 1990.

Sanday, Peggy Reeves. *Fraternity Gang Rape: Sex, Brotherhood, and Privilege on Campus.* New York and London: New York University Press, 1990.

Sanders, W. B. *Rape and Woman's Identity.* Beverly Hills, CA: Sage, 1980.

Schulhofer, Stephen J. *Unwanted Sex: The Culture of Intimidation and the Failure of Law.* Cambridge: Harvard University Press, 1998.

Schwendinger, Julia R., and Herman Schwendinger. *Rape and Inequality.* Beverly Hills, CA: Sage, 1983.

Scully, Diana. *Understanding Sexual Violence: A Study of Convicted Rapists.* Boston: Unwin Hyman, 1990.

Spohn, Cassia, and Julie Horney. *Rape Law Reform: A Grassroots Revolution and Its Impact.* New York and London: Plenum, 1992.

Temkin, Jennifer. *Rape and the Legal Process.* London: Sweet and Maxwell, 1987.

U.S. Department of Justice. Bureau of Justice Statistics. *Female Victims of Violent Crime.* Washington, DC: Government Printing Office, 1991.

——. Federal Bureau of Investigation. *Crime in the United States, 1991.* Washington, DC: Government Printing Office, 1991.

Warshaw, Robin. *I Never Called It Rape: The Ms. Report on Recognizing, Fighting, and Surviving Date and Acquaintance Rape.* Afterword by Mary P. Koss. New York: Harper-Perennial, 1994.

Williams, Joyce E., and Karen A. Holmes. *The Second Assault: Rape and Public Attitudes.* Westport, CT: Greenwood Press, 1981.

Anthologies and Symposia Proceedings

Alexander, Larry, ed. "Consent in Sexual Relations." *Legal Theory* 2 (June 1996): 87–164; *Legal Theory* 2 (September 1996): 165–264.

Bar On, Bat-Ami, ed. "Women and Violence." *Hypatia* 11 (fall 1996): 1–147.

Buchwald, Emilie, Pamela R. Fletcher, and Martha Roth, eds. *Transforming a Rape Culture.* Minneapolis: Milkweed Editions, 1993.

Burgess, Ann Wolbert, ed. *Rape and Sexual Assault: A Research Handbook.* New York and London: Garland, 1985.

——, ed. *Rape and Sexual Assault II.* New York and London: Garland, 1988.

——, ed. *Rape and Sexual Assault III: A Research Handbook.* New York and London: Garland, 1991.

Byers, E. Sandra, and Lucia F. O'Sullivan, eds. *Sexual Coercion in Dating Relationships.* New York: Haworth Press, 1996.

Chappell, Duncan, Robley Geis, and Gilbert Geis, eds. *Forcible Rape: The Crime, the Victim, and the Offender.* New York: Columbia University Press, 1977.

Francis, Leslie, ed. *Date Rape: Feminism, Philosophy, and the Law.* University Park: The Pennsylvania State University Press, 1996.

French, Stanley G., ed. *Interpersonal Violence, Health and Gender Politics.* Dubuque, IA and Ottawa: Wm. C. Brown Communications, 1993.

——, Wendy Teays, and Laura M. Purdy, eds. *Violence Against Women: Philosophical Perspectives.* Ithaca, NY, and London: Cornell University Press, 1998.

Grauerholz, Elizabeth, and Mary A. Koralewski, eds. *Sexual Coercion: A Sourcebook on Its Nature, Causes, and Prevention.* Lexington, MA: Lexington Books, 1991.

New York Radical Feminists. *Rape: The First Sourcebook for Women.* Edited by Noreen Connell and Cassandra Wilson. New York and Scarborough, Ont.: New American Library, 1974.

Parrot, Andrea, and Laurie Bechhofer, eds. *Acquaintance Rape: The Hidden Crime.* New York: Wiley, 1991.

Searles, Patricia, and Ronald J. Berger, eds. *Rape and Society: Readings on the Problem of Sexual Assault.* Boulder, CO: Westview, 1995.

Tomaselli, Sylvana, and Roy Porter, eds. *Rape: An Historical and Cultural Enquiry.* Oxford: Basil Blackwell, 1986.

Walker, Marcia J., and Stanley L. Brodsky, eds. *Sexual Assault: The Victim and the Rapist.* Lexington, MA: Lexington Books, 1976.

Williams, Mary E., and Tamara L. Roleff, eds. *Sexual Violence: Opposing Viewpoints*. San Diego: Greenhaven Press, 1997.

"Women, Law, and Violence." *Law and Social Inquiry* 19 (fall 1994): 829–1056.

Journal Articles

Abrams, Kathryn. "Sex Wars Redux: Agency and Coercion in Feminist Legal Theory." *Columbia Law Review* 95 (March 1995): 304–76.

Alexander, Larry. "Introduction to Issues 2 and 3: Symposium on Consent in Sexual Relations." *Legal Theory* 2 (June 1996): 87–8.

——. "The Moral Magic of Consent (II)." *Legal Theory* 2 (September 1996): 165–74.

Allen, Derek. "Relevance, Conduction and Canada's Rape-Shield Decision." *Informal Logic* 15 (spring 1993): 105–22.

Allen, Gina. "A Reply to Roy Schenk." *The Humanist* 39 (March/April 1979): 50–1.

Andre-Clark, Alice Susan. "Whither Statutory Rape Laws: Of *Michael M.*, the Fourteenth Amendment, and Protecting Women from Sexual Aggression." *Southern California Law Review* 65 (May 1992): 1933–92.

Archard, David. "Exploited Consent." *Journal of Social Philosophy* 25 (winter 1994): 92–101.

——. "'A Nod's as Good as a Wink': Consent, Convention, and Reasonable Belief." *Legal Theory* 3 (September 1997): 273–90.

Aswad, Evelyn Mary. "Torture by Means of Rape." *The Georgetown Law Journal* 84 (May 1996): 1913–43.

Baber, H. E. "How Bad Is Rape?" *Hypatia* 2 (summer 1987): 125–38.

Backer, Larry Catá. "Raping Sodomy and Sodomizing Rape: A Morality Tale About the Transformation of Modern Sodomy Jurisprudence." *American Journal of Criminal Law* 21 (fall 1993): 37–125.

Baker, Katharine K. "Once a Rapist? Motivational Evidence and Relevancy in Rape Law." *Harvard Law Review* 110 (January 1997): 563–624.

Balos, Beverly, and Mary Louise Fellows. "Guilty of the Crime of Trust: Nonstranger Rape." *Minnesota Law Review* 75 (February 1991): 599–618.

Bar On, Bat-Ami. "Introduction [to Special Issue on Women and Violence]." *Hypatia* 11 (fall 1996): 1–4.

Barry, Susan. "Spousal Rape: The Uncommon Law." *American Bar Association Journal* 66 (September 1980): 1088–91.

Barshis, Victoria R. Garnier. "The Question of Marital Rape." *Women's Studies International Forum* 6 (1983): 383–93.

Bart, Pauline B. "Rape as a Paradigm of Sexism in Society—Victimization and Its Discontents." *Women's Studies International Quarterly* 2 (1979): 347–57.

——. "Why Men Rape." *Western Sociological Review* 14 (1983): 46–57.

Beabout, Greg. "Abortion in Rape Cases." *Proceedings of the American Catholic Philosophical Association* 64 (1990): 132–8.

Becker, Judith V., Linda J. Skinner, Gene G. Abel, Roz Axelrod, and Joan Cichon. "Sexual Problems of Sexual Assault Survivors." *Women and Health* 9 (winter 1984): 5–20.

Berger, Vivian. "Man's Trial, Woman's Tribulation: Rape Cases in the Courtroom." *Columbia Law Review* 77 (1977): 1–103.

Berliner, Dana. "Rethinking the Reasonable Belief Defense to Rape." *The Yale Law Journal* 100 (June 1991): 2687–706.

Bernell, Laura. "Raped: Today and Yesterday." *Sojourner* 20 (March 1995): 12.

Bienen, Leigh. "Rape I." *Women's Rights Law Reporter* 3 (December 1976): 45–57.

——. "Rape II." *Women's Rights Law Reporter* 3 (spring/summer 1977): 90–137.

——. "Mistakes." *Philosophy and Public Affairs* 7 (spring 1978): 224–45.

——. "Rape III—National Developments in Rape Reform Legislation." *Women's Rights Law Reporter* 6 (spring 1980): 170–213.

——. "Rape IV." *Women's Rights Law Reporter,* Suppl. Vol. 6 (summer 1980): 1.

Bleich, J. David, and Carol A. Tauer, "The Hospital's Duty and Rape Victims." *The Hastings Center Report* 10 (April 1980): 25–7.

Bloch, Kate E. "A Rape Law Pedagogy." *Yale Journal of Law and Feminism* 7 (1995): 307–40.

Bogart, J. H. "On the Nature of Rape." *Public Affairs Quarterly* 5 (April 1991): 117–36.

——. "Reconsidering Rape: Rethinking the Conceptual Foundations of Rape Law." *The Canadian Journal of Law and Jurisprudence* 8 (January 1995): 159–82.

——. "Commodification and Phenomenology: Evading Consent in Theory Regarding Rape." *Legal Theory* 2 (September 1996): 253–64.

Bond, Susan B., and Donald L. Mosher. "Guided Imagery of Rape: Fantasy, Reality, and the Willing Victim Myth." *The Journal of Sex Research* 22 (May 1986): 162–83.

Bonilla, Margaret D. "Cultural Assault: What Feminists Are Doing to Rape Ought to Be a Crime." *Policy Review* (fall 1993): 22–9.

Boyle, Christine. "Sexual Assault in Abusive Relationships: Common Sense About Sexual History." *The Dalhousie Law Journal* 19 (fall 1996): 223–46.

Brereton, David. "How Different Are Rape Trials? A Comparison of the Cross-Examination of Complainants in Rape and Assault Trials." *The British Journal of Criminology* 37 (spring 1997): 242–61.

Brett, Nathan. "Sexual Offenses and Consent." *The Canadian Journal of Law and Jurisprudence* 11 (January 1998): 69–88.

Bridges, Judith S., and Christine A. McGrail. "Attributions of Responsibility for Date and Stranger Rape." *Sex Roles* 21 (August 1989): 273–86.

Brison, Susan J. "Surviving Sexual Violence: A Philosophical Perspective." *Journal of Social Philosophy* 24 (spring 1993): 5–22.

——. "On the Personal as Philosophical." *The American Philosophical Association Newsletter on Feminism and Philosophy* 95 (fall 1995): 37–40.

Bumiller, Kristin. "Rape as a Legal Symbol: An Essay on Sexual Violence and Racism." *University of Miami Law Review* 42 (September 1987): 75–91.

——. "Fallen Angels: The Representation of Violence Against Women in Legal Culture." *International Journal of the Sociology of Law* 18 (May 1990): 125–42.

Burgess-Jackson, Keith. "Justice and the Distribution of Fear." *The Southern Journal of Philosophy* 32 (winter 1994): 367–91.

——. "Statutory Rape: A Philosophical Analysis." *The Canadian Journal of Law and Jurisprudence* 8 (January 1995): 139–58.

——. "Rape and Persuasive Definition." *Canadian Journal of Philosophy* 25 (September 1995): 415–54.

——. "Wife Rape." *Public Affairs Quarterly* 12 (January 1998): 1–22.

——. "A Crime Against *Women*: Calhoun on the Wrongness of Rape." *Journal of Social Philosophy,* in press.

Burt, Martha R. "Cultural Myths and Supports for Rape." *Journal of Personality and Social Psychology* 38 (February 1980): 217–30.

——, and Rhoda Estep. "Apprehension and Fear: Learning a Sense of Sexual Vulnerability." *Sex Roles* 7 (May 1981): 511–22.

——, and Rochelle Semmel Albin. "Rape Myths, Rape Definitions, and Probability of Conviction." *Journal of Applied Social Psychology* 11 (May–June 1981): 212–30.

Busby, Karen. "Discriminatory Uses of Personal Records in Sexual Violence Cases." *Canadian Journal of Women and the Law* 9 (1997): 148–77.

Cairney, Kathleen F. "Addressing Acquaintance Rape: The New Direction of the Rape Law Reform Movement." *St. John's Law Review* 69 (winter/spring 1995): 291–326.

———. "Recognizing Acquaintance Rape in Potentially Consensual Situations: A Re-Examination of Thomas Hardy's *Tess of the D'Urbervilles.*" *American University Journal of Gender and the Law* 3 (spring 1995): 301–31.

Calhoun, Laurie. "On Rape: A Crime Against Humanity." *Journal of Social Philosophy* 28 (spring 1997): 101–9.

Calhoun, Lawrence G., James W. Selby, and Louise J. Warring. "Social Perception of the Victim's Causal Role in Rape: An Exploratory Examination of Four Factors." *Human Relations* 29 (June 1976): 517–26.

Card, Claudia. "Rape as a Weapon of War." *Hypatia* 11 (fall 1996): 5–18.

———. "Addendum to 'Rape as a Weapon of War'." *Hypatia* 12 (spring 1997): 216–8.

Carlin, David R., Jr. "Date Rape Fallacies." *Commonweal* 121 (25 February 1994): 11–2.

Carraway, G. Chezia. "Violence Against Women of Color." *Stanford Law Review* 43 (July 1991): 1301–9.

Carroll, Lisa A. "Women's Powerless Tool: How Congress Overreached the Constitution with the Civil Rights Remedy of the Violence Against Women Act." *The John Marshall Law Review* 30 (spring 1997): 803–36.

Casarino, Corinne. "Civil Remedies in Acquaintance Rape Cases." *Public Interest Law Journal* 6 (fall 1996): 185–201.

Chamallas, Martha. "Consent, Equality, and the Legal Control of Sexual Conduct." *Southern California Law Review* 61 (May 1988): 777–862.

Clutton-Brock, T. H., and G. A. Parker. "Sexual Coercion in Animal Societies." *Animal Behaviour* 49 (May 1995): 1345–65.

Cobb, Kenneth A., and Nancy R. Schauer. "Legislative Note: Michigan's Criminal Sexual Assault Law." *University of Michigan Journal of Law Reform* 8 (fall 1974): 217–36.

Comment. "Forcible and Statutory Rape: An Exploration of the Operation and Objectives of the Consent Standard." *The Yale Law Journal* 62 (December 1952): 55–83.

Comment. "Rape and Battery Between Husband and Wife." *Stanford Law Review* 6 (July 1954): 719–28.

Corns, Christopher Thomas. "Liability of Husbands for Rape-in-Marriage—The Victorian Position." *Criminal Law Journal* 7 (1983): 102–12.

Crenshaw, Kimberlè. "Mapping the Margins: Intersectionality, Identity Politics, and Violence Against Women of Color." *Stanford Law Review* 43 (July 1991): 1241–99.

Cudd, Ann E. "Enforced Pregnancy, Rape, and the Image of Woman." *Philosophical Studies* 60 (September–October 1990): 47–59.

Cuomo, Chris J. "War Is Not Just an Event: Reflections on the Significance of Everyday Violence." *Hypatia* 11 (fall 1996): 30–45.

Curley, E. M. "Excusing Rape." *Philosophy and Public Affairs* 5 (summer 1976): 325–60.

Davion, Victoria. "Rape, Group Responsibility and Trust." *Hypatia* 10 (spring 1995): 153–6.

———. "Rape Research and Gender Feminism: So Who's Anti-Male?" *Public Affairs Quarterly* 11 (July 1997): 229–43.

Davis, Martha S. "Rape in the Workplace." *South Dakota Law Review* 41 (1996): 411–64.

Davis, Michael. "Setting Penalties: What Does Rape Deserve?" *Law and Philosophy* 3 (April 1984): 61–110.

Denno, Deborah W. "Sexuality, Rape, and Mental Retardation." *University of Illinois Law Review* (1997): 315–434.

Dinovitzer, Ronit. "The Myth of Rapists and Other Normal Men: The Impact of Psychiatric

Considerations on the Sentencing of Sexual Assault Offenders." *Canadian Journal of Law and Society* 12 (spring 1997): 147–69.

Donat, Patricia L. N., and John D'Emilio. "A Feminist Redefinition of Rape and Sexual Assault: Historical Foundations and Change." *Journal of Social Issues* 48 (1992): 9–22.

Dripps, Donald A. "Beyond Rape: An Essay on the Difference Between the Presence of Force and the Absence of Consent." *Columbia Law Review* 92 (November 1992): 1780–809.

——. "More on Distinguishing Sex, Sexual Expropriation, and Sexual Assault: A Reply to Professor West." *Columbia Law Review* 93 (October 1993): 1460–72.

——, Linda Fairstein, Robin West, and Deborah W. Denno. "Men, Women and Rape." *Fordham Law Review* 63 (October 1994): 125–73.

——. "For a Negative, Normative Model of Consent, with a Comment on Preference-Skepticism." *Legal Theory* 2 (June 1996): 113–20.

Duff, R. A. "Recklessness and Rape." *The Liverpool Law Review* 3 (1981): 49–64.

Edmonds, Erin. "Mapping the Terrain of Our Resistance: A White Feminist Perspective on the Enforcement of Rape Law." *Harvard BlackLetter Journal* 9 (1992): 43–100.

Edwards, Daphne. "Acquaintance Rape and the 'Force' Element: When 'No' Is Not Enough." *Golden Gate University Law Review* 26 (spring 1996): 241–300.

Eidson, Rita. "The Constitutionality of Statutory Rape Laws." *UCLA Law Review* 27 (February 1980): 757–815.

Eskow, Lisa R. "The Ultimate Weapon? Demythologizing Spousal Rape and Reconceptualizing Its Prosecution." *Stanford Law Review* 48 (February 1996): 677–709.

Eskridge, William N., Jr. "The Many Faces of Sexual Consent." *William and Mary Law Review* 37 (fall 1995): 47–67.

Estrich, Susan. "Rape." *The Yale Law Journal* 95 (May 1986): 1087–184.

——. "Sex at Work." *Stanford Law Review* 43 (April 1991): 813–61.

——. "Palm Beach Stories." *Law and Philosophy* 11 (1992): 5–33.

——. "Teaching Rape Law." *The Yale Law Journal* 102 (November 1992): 509–20.

Feldberg, Georgina. "Defining the Facts of Rape: The Uses of Medical Evidence in Sexual Assault Trials." *Canadian Journal of Women and the Law* 9 (1997): 89–114.

Ferraro, Kenneth F. "Women's Fear of Victimization: Shadow of Sexual Assault?" *Social Forces* 75 (December 1996): 667–90.

Fishman, Clifford S. "Consent, Credibility, and the Constitution: Evidence Relating to a Sex Offense Complainant's Past Sexual Behavior." *Catholic University Law Review* 44 (spring 1995): 709–820.

Freeman, Michael D. A. "'But If You Can't Rape Your Wife, Who[m] Can You Rape?': The Marital Rape Exemption Re-examined." *Family Law Quarterly* 15 (spring 1981): 1–29.

Friedland, Steven I. "Date Rape and the Culture of Acceptance." *Florida Law Review* 43 (July 1991): 487–527.

Friedman, Marilyn A., and Larry May. "Harming Women as a Group." *Social Theory and Practice* 11 (summer 1985): 207–34.

Friedman, Marilyn. "'They Lived Happily Ever After': Sommers on Women and Marriage." *Journal of Social Philosophy* 21 (fall/winter 1990): 57–65.

——. "Does Sommers Like Women? More on Liberalism, Gender Hierarchy, and Scarlett O'Hara." *Journal of Social Philosophy* 21 (fall/winter 1990): 75–90.

Frieze, Irene Hanson. "Investigating the Causes and Consequences of Marital Rape." *Signs* 8 (spring 1983): 532–53.

Frohmann, Lisa, and Elizabeth Mertz. "Legal Reform and Social Construction: Violence, Gender, and the Law." *Law and Social Inquiry* 19 (fall 1994): 829–51.

Gans, Jeremy. "When Should the Jury Be Directed on the Mental Element of Rape?" *Criminal Law Journal* 20 (October 1996): 247–66.

Garcia, Luis T. "Exposure to Pornography and Attitudes About Women and Rape: A Correlational Study." *The Journal of Sex Research* 22 (August 1986): 378–85.

Geis, G. "Lord Hale, Witches, and Rape." *British Journal of Law and Society* 5 (1978): 26–44.

———. "Rape-in-Marriage: Law and Law Reform in England, the United States, and Sweden." *The Adelaide Law Review* 6 (1978): 284–303.

Gibson, Lorne, Rick Linden, and Stuart Johnson. "A Situational Theory of Rape." *Canadian Journal of Criminology* 22 (1980): 51–65.

Gilbert, Neil. "The Phantom Epidemic of Sexual Assault." *The Public Interest* (spring 1991): 54–65.

———. "Realities and Mythologies of Rape." *Society* 29 (May/June 1992): 4–10.

———. "Was It Rape? An Examination of Sexual Abuse Statistics." *The American Enterprise* 5 (September/October 1994): 68–77.

Gilligan, Francis A., Edward J. Imwinkelried, and Elizabeth F. Loftus. "The Theory of 'Unconscious Transference': The Latest Threat to the Shield Laws Protecting the Privacy of Victims of Sex Offenses." *Boston College Law Review* 38 (December 1996): 107–44.

Gold, Sally, and Martha Wyatt. "The Rape System: Old Roles and New Times." *Catholic University Law Review* 27 (1978): 695–727.

Gordon, Margaret T., Stephanie Riger, Robert K. LeBailly, and Linda Heath. "Crime, Women, and the Quality of Urban Life." *Signs* 5 (spring 1980): S144–60.

Gravdal, Kathryn. "Chrétien de Troyes, Gratian, and the Medieval Romance of Sexual Violence." *Signs* 17 (spring 1992): 558–85.

Griffin, Susan. "Rape: The All-American Crime." *Ramparts* 10 (September 1971): 26–35.

Harman, John D. "Consent, Harm, and Marital Rape." *Journal of Family Law* 22 (1983–84): 423–43.

Harris, Lucy Reed. "Towards a Consent Standard in the Law of Rape." *The University of Chicago Law Review* 43 (spring 1976): 613–45.

Hartsock, Nancy C. M. "Gender and Sexuality: Masculinity, Violence, and Domination." *Humanities in Society* 7 (winter-spring 1984): 19–45.

Hazelton, Peter M. "Rape Shield Laws: Limits on Zealous Advocacy." *American Journal of Criminal Law* 19 (fall 1991): 35–56.

Heberle, Renee. "Deconstructive Strategies and the Movement Against Sexual Violence." *Hypatia* 11 (fall 1996): 63–76.

Henderson, Lynne. "Rape and Responsibility." *Law and Philosophy* 11 (1992): 127–78.

Hengehold, Laura. "Rape and Communicative Agency: Reflections in the Lake at L———." *Hypatia* 8 (fall 1993): 56–71.

———. "An Immodest Proposal: Foucault, Hysterization, and the 'Second Rape'." *Hypatia* 9 (summer 1994): 88–107.

Hibey, Richard A. "The Trial of a Rape Case: An Advocate's Analysis of Corroboration, Consent, and Character." *The American Criminal Law Review* 11 (winter 1973): 309–34.

Hicks, Martin, and Gareth Branston. "Transsexual Rape—A Loophole Closed?" *The Criminal Law Review* (August 1997): 565–70.

Hirsch, Susan F. "Interpreting Media Representations of a 'Night of Madness': Law and Culture in the Construction of Rape Identities." *Law and Social Inquiry* 19 (fall 1994): 1023–56.

Hirshman, Linda R. "Moral Philosophy and the Glen Ridge Rape Case." *Harvard Journal of Law and Public Policy* 17 (winter 1994): 101–6.

Hoagland, Sarah Lucia. "Violence, Victimization, Violation." *Sinister Wisdom* 15 (fall 1980): 70–2.

———. "A Note on the Logic of Protection and Predation." *The American Philosophical Association Newsletter on Feminism and Philosophy* 88 (November 1988): 7–8.

"House of Delegates Redefines Death, Urges Redefinition of Rape, and Undoes the Houston Amendments." *American Bar Association Journal* 61 (April 1975): 465.

Hurd, Heidi M. "The Moral Magic of Consent." *Legal Theory* 2 (June 1996): 121–46.

Husak, Douglas N., and George C. Thomas III. "Date Rape, Social Convention, and Reasonable Mistakes." *Law and Philosophy* 11 (1992): 95–126.

Ingram, John Dwight. "Date Rape: It's Time for 'No' to Really Mean 'No'." *American Journal of Criminal Law* 21 (fall 1993): 3–36.

Isenberg, Beth Ann. "Genocide, Rape, and Crimes Against Humanity: An Affirmation of Individual Accountability in the Former Yugoslavia in the *Karadzic* Actions." *Albany Law Review* 60 (1997): 1051–79.

Jackson, Stevi. "The Social Context of Rape: Sexual Scripts and Motivation." *Women's Studies International Quarterly* 1 (1978): 27–38.

Johnson, Denise R. "Prior False Allegations of Rape: Falsus in Uno, Falsus in Omnibus?" *Yale Journal of Law and Feminism* 7 (1995): 243–76.

Karnezis, Kristine Cordier. "Modern Status of Admissibility, in Forcible Rape Prosecution, of Complainant's Prior Sexual Acts." *American Law Reports* 3d 94 (1979): 257–86.

Kasinsky, Renée Goldsmith. "Rape: A Normal Act?" *Canadian Forum* (September 1975): 18–22.

Kasubhai, Mustafa T. "Destabilizing Power in Rape: Why Consent Theory in Rape Law Is Turned on Its Head." *Wisconsin Women's Law Journal* 11 (summer 1996): 37–74.

Kelly, Katharine D. "'You Must Be Crazy If You Think You Were Raped': Reflections on the Use of Complainants' Personal and Therapy Records in Sexual Assault Trials." *Canadian Journal of Women and the Law* 9 (1997): 178–95.

Kennedy, Duncan. "Sexual Abuse, Sexy Dressing and the Eroticization of Domination." *New England Law Review* 26 (summer 1992): 1309–93.

Kersten, Joachim. "Culture, Masculinities and Violence Against Women." *The British Journal of Criminology* 36 (Special Issue 1996): 381–95.

Kesic, Vesna. "A Response to Catharine MacKinnon's Article 'Turning Rape into Pornography: Postmodern Genocide'." *Hastings Women's Law Journal* 5 (summer 1994): 267–80.

Kessler, Elizabeth. "Pattern of Sexual Conduct Evidence and Present Consent: Limiting the Admissibility of Sexual History Evidence in Rape Prosecutions." *Women's Rights Law Reporter* 14 (winter 1992): 79–96.

Kirkpatrick, Clifford, and Eugene Kanin. "Male Sex Aggression on a University Campus." *American Sociological Review* 22 (February 1957): 52–8.

Kittay, Eva Feder. "AH! My Foolish Heart: A Reply to Alan Soble's 'Antioch's "Sexual Offense Policy": A Philosophical Exploration'." *Journal of Social Philosophy* 28 (fall 1997): 153–9.

Kole, Susan M. "Statute Protecting Minors in a Specified Age Range from Rape or Other Sexual Activity as Applicable to Defendant Minor Within Protected Age Group." *American Law Reports* 5th 18 (1994): 856–91.

Konradi, Amanda. "Too Little, Too Late: Prosecutors' Pre-court Preparation of Rape Survivors." *Law and Social Inquiry* 22 (winter 1997): 1–54.

Korn, James H., Timothy J. Huelsman, Cynthia K. Shinabarger Reed, and Michelle Aiello. "Perceived Ethicality of Guided Imagery in Rape Research." *Ethics and Behavior* 2 (1992): 1–14.

Korn, James H., Timothy J. Huelsman, and Cynthia K. Shinabarger Reed. "Logic, Ethics, and Rhetoric of Research on Rape: A Reply to Mosher and Bond." *Ethics and Behavior* 2 (1992): 123–8.

Kutchinsky, Berl. "Pornography and Rape: Theory and Practice?" *International Journal of Law and Psychiatry* 14 (1991): 47–64.

Lanham, David. "Hale: Misogyny and Rape." *Criminal Law Journal* 7 (1983): 148–66.

Larson, Jane E. "'Even a Worm Will Turn at Last': Rape Reform in Late Nineteenth-Century America." *Yale Journal of Law and the Humanities* 9 (1997): 1–71.

Lebowitz, Leslie, and Susan Roth. "'I Felt Like a Slut': The Cultural Context and Women's Response to Being Raped." *Journal of Traumatic Stress* 7 (1994): 363–90.

LeGrand, Camille E. "Rape and Rape Laws: Sexism in Society and Law." *California Law Review* 61 (May 1973): 919–41.

Lewin, Miriam. "Unwanted Intercourse: The Difficulty of Saying No." *Psychology of Women Quarterly* 9 (June 1985): 184–92.

Lisak, David. "Sexual Aggression, Masculinity, and Fathers." *Signs* 16 (winter 1991): 238–62.

Livneh, Ernst. "On Rape and the Sanctity of Matrimony." *Israel Law Review* 2 (July 1967): 415–22.

Loh, Wallace D. "Q: What Has Reform of Rape Legislation Wrought? A: Truth in Criminal Labelling." *Journal of Social Issues* 37 (1981): 28–52.

Luginbuhl, James, and Courtney Mullin. "Rape and Responsibility: How and How Much Is the Victim Blamed?" *Sex Roles* 7 (May 1981): 547–59.

Lynch, Michael W. "Enforcing 'Statutory Rape'?" *The Public Interest* (summer 1998): 3–16.

MacKinnon, Catharine A. "Feminism, Marxism, Method, and the State: An Agenda for Theory." *Signs* 7 (spring 1982): 515–44.

———. "Feminism, Marxism, Method, and the State: Toward Feminist Jurisprudence." *Signs* 8 (summer 1983): 635–58.

———. "Reflections on Sex Equality Under Law." *The Yale Law Journal* 100 (March 1991): 1281–328.

———. "Turning Rape into Pornography: Postmodern Genocide." *Ms.* (July/August 1993): 24–30.

———. "Rape, Genocide, and Women's Human Rights." *Harvard Women's Law Journal* 17 (spring 1994): 5–16.

Malm, H. M. "The Ontological Status of Consent and Its Implications for the Law on Rape." *Legal Theory* 2 (June 1996): 147–64.

Marin, André. "When Is an 'Honest but Mistaken Belief in Consent' NOT an 'Honest but Mistaken Belief in Consent'." *Criminal Law Quarterly* 37 (July 1995): 451–60.

Marshall, W. L., and Laura Sona Hambley. "Intimacy and Loneliness, and Their Relationship to Rape Myth Acceptance and Hostility Toward Women Among Rapists." *Journal of Interpersonal Violence* 11 (December 1996): 586–92.

Martin, Patricia Yancey, and R. Marlene Powell. "Accounting for the 'Second Assault': Legal Organizations' Framing of Rape Victims." *Law and Social Inquiry* 19 (fall 1994): 853–90.

Massaro, Toni M. "Experts, Psychology, Credibility, and Rape: The Rape Trauma Syndrome Issue and Its Implications for Expert Psychological Testimony." *Minnesota Law Review* 69 (February 1985): 395–470.

Matoesian, Gregory M. "'You Were Interested in Him as a Person?': Rhythms of Domination in the Kennedy Smith Rape Trial." *Law and Social Inquiry* 22 (winter 1997): 55–93.

May, Larry, and Robert Strikwerda. "Men in Groups: Collective Responsibility for Rape." *Hypatia* 9 (spring 1994): 134–51.

———. "Reply to Victoria Davion's Comments on May and Strikwerda." *Hypatia* 10 (spring 1995): 157–8.

May, Larry, and James Bohman. "Sexuality, Masculinity, and Confession." *Hypatia* 12 (winter 1997): 138–54.

McCarthy, Sarah J. "Pornography, Rape, and the Cult of Macho." *The Humanist* 40 (September/October 1980): 11–20, 56.

McColgan, Aileen. "Common Law and the Relevance of Sexual History Evidence." *Oxford Journal of Legal Studies* 16 (summer 1996): 275–307.

McGregor, Joan. "Introduction [to Special Issue on Philosophical Issues in Rape Law]." *Law and Philosophy* 11 (1992): 1–3.

———. "What Can We Learn from Feminist Jurisprudence About Harm and Injury?" *The American Philosophical Association Newsletters on Feminism and Philosophy and Philosophy and Law* 94 (spring 1995): 45–8.

———. "Why When She Says No She Doesn't Mean Maybe and Doesn't Mean Yes: A Critical Reconstruction of Consent, Sex, and the Law." *Legal Theory* 2 (September 1996): 175–208.

McHugh, James T. "Traumatic Developments: Contractual Theory of Rape in America." *Feminist Legal Studies* 3 (August 1995): 237–47.

McNamara, Theresa A. "Act 10: Remedying Problems of Pennsylvania's Rape Laws or Revisiting Them?" *Dickinson Law Review* 101 (fall 1996): 203–31.

McSherry, Bernadette. "No! (Means No?)." *Alternative Law Journal* 18 (February 1993): 27–30.

Meisel, Alan. "Confidentiality and Rape Counseling." *The Hastings Center Report* 11 (August 1981): 5–7.

Miller, Beth C. "A Comparison of American and Jewish Legal Views on Rape." *Columbia Journal of Gender and Law* 5 (1996): 182–215.

Miller, Susannah. "The Overturning of *Michael M.*: Statutory Rape Law Becomes Gender-Neutral in California." *UCLA Women's Law Journal* 5 (fall 1994): 289–99.

Morris, A. Thomas. "The Empirical, Historical and Legal Case Against the Cautionary Instruction: A Call for Legislative Reform." *Duke Law Journal* (February 1988): 154–73.

Morris, Madeline. "By Force of Arms: Rape, War, and Military Culture." *Duke Law Journal* 45 (February 1996): 651–781.

Morris, Norval, and A. L. Turner. "Two Problems in the Law of Rape." *The University of Queensland Law Journal* 2 (1953): 247–63.

Mosher, Donald L., and Ronald D. Anderson. "Macho Personality, Sexual Aggression, and Reactions to Guided Imagery of Realistic Rape." *Journal of Research in Personality* 20 (March 1986): 77–94.

Mosher, Donald L., and Susan B. Bond. "'Little Rapes,' Specious Claims, and Moral Hubris: A Reply to Korn, Huelsman, Reed, and Aiello." *Ethics and Behavior* 2 (1992): 109–21.

———. "Ethics—Perceived or Reasoned from Principles? A Rejoinder to Korn, Huelsman, and Reed." *Ethics and Behavior* 2 (1992): 203–14.

Muehlenhard, Charlene L., and Lisa C. Hollabaugh. "Do Women Sometimes Say No When They Mean Yes? The Prevalence and Correlates of Women's Token Resistance to Sex." *Journal of Personality and Social Psychology* 54 (May 1988): 872–9.

Muehlenhard, Charlene L., Irene G. Powch, Joi L. Phelps, and Laura M. Giusti. "Definitions of Rape: Scientific and Political Implications." *Journal of Social Issues* 48 (1992): 23–44.

Murphey, Dwight D. "Feminism and Rape." *The Journal of Social, Political and Economic Studies* 17 (spring 1992): 13–27.

Naffine, Ngaire. "Possession: Erotic Love in the Law of Rape." *The Modern Law Review* 57 (January 1994): 10–37.

Nemeth, Charles P. "Character Evidence in Rape Trials in Nineteenth Century New York:

Chastity and the Admissibility of Specific Acts." *Women's Rights Law Reporter* 6 (spring 1980): 214–25.

Ni Aolain, Fionnuala. "Radical Rules: The Effects of Evidential and Procedural Rules on the Regulation of Sexual Violence in War." *Albany Law Review* 60 (1997): 883–905.

Note. "Recent Statutory Developments in the Definition of Forcible Rape." *Virginia Law Review* 61 (November 1975): 1500–43.

Note. "The Rape Corroboration Requirement: Repeal Not Reform." *The Yale Law Journal* 81 (June 1972): 1365–91.

Note. "To Have and to Hold: The Marital Rape Exemption and the Fourteenth Amendment." *Harvard Law Review* 99 (April 1986): 1255–73.

Nussbaum, Martha C. "Objectification." *Philosophy and Public Affairs* 24 (fall 1995): 249–91.

O'Donovan, Katherine. "Consent to Marital Rape: Common Law Oxymoron?" *Cardozo Women's Law Journal* 2 (1995): 91–107.

Olsen, Frances. "Statutory Rape: A Feminist Critique of Rights Analysis." *Texas Law Review* 63 (November 1984): 387–432.

O'Neill, Onora. "Between Consenting Adults." *Philosophy and Public Affairs* 14 (summer 1985): 252–77.

Palmer, Stephanie. "Rape in Marriage and the European Convention on Human Rights." *Feminist Legal Studies* 5 (February 1997): 91–7.

Pateman, Carole. "Women and Consent." *Political Theory* 8 (May 1980): 149–68.

Pelka, Fred. "Raped: A Male Survivor Breaks His Silence." *On the Issues* 22 (spring 1992): 8–11, 40.

Philipose, Liz. "The Laws of War and Women's Human Rights." *Hypatia* 11 (fall 1996): 46–62.

Pickard, Toni. "Culpable Mistakes and Rape: Relating Mens Rea to the Crime." *University of Toronto Law Journal* 30 (1980): 75–98.

Pineau, Lois. "Date Rape: A Feminist Analysis." *Law and Philosophy* 8 (August 1989): 217–43.

Podhoretz, Norman. "Rape in Feminist Eyes." *Commentary* 92 (October 1991): 29–35. Letters from readers and Podhoretz's replies, *Commentary* 93 (March 1992): 2–8.

Prevost, Earle G. "Statutory Rape: A Growing Liberalization." *South Carolina Law Review* 18 (1966): 254–66.

Price, Jason M. "Sex, Lies and Rape Shield Statutes: The Constitutionality of Interpreting Rape Shield Statutes to Exclude Evidence Relating to the Victim's Motive to Fabricate." *Western New England Law Review* 18 (1996): 541–76.

Puttkammer, Ernst Wilfred. "Consent in Rape." *Illinois Law Review* 19 (February 1925): 410–28.

Raitt, Fiona E., and M. Suzanne Zeedyk. "Rape Trauma Syndrome: Its Corroborative and Educational Roles." *Journal of Law and Society* 24 (December 1997): 552–68.

Razack, Sherene. "From Consent to Responsibility, from Pity to Respect: Subtexts in Cases of Sexual Violence Involving Girls and Women with Developmental Disabilities." *Law and Social Inquiry* 19 (fall 1994): 891–922.

Rector, Neil A., and R. Michael Bagby. "Criminal Sentence Recommendations in a Simulated Rape Trial: Examining Juror Prejudice in Canada." *Behavioral Sciences and the Law* 13 (winter 1995): 113–21.

Reed, Elizabeth J. "Criminal Law and the Capacity of Mentally Retarded Persons to Consent to Sexual Activity." *Virginia Law Review* 83 (May 1997): 799–827.

Remick, Lani Anne. "Read Her Lips: An Argument for a Verbal Consent Standard in Rape." *University of Pennsylvania Law Review* 141 (January 1993): 1103–51.

Rendall, Steven. "Duction, or the Archaeology of Rape." *Philosophy and Literature* 17 (April 1993): 119–28.

Reynolds, Janice M. "Rape as Social Control." *Catalyst* 8 (1974): 62–7.

Rich, Adrienne. "Compulsory Heterosexuality and Lesbian Existence." *Signs* 5 (summer 1980): 631–60.

Riger, Stephanie, Margaret T. Gordon, and Robert LeBailly. "Women's Fear of Crime: From Blaming to Restricting the Victim." *Victimology* 3 (1978): 274–84.

Rimonte, Nilda. "A Question of Culture: Cultural Approval of Violence Against Women in the Pacific-Asian Community and the Cultural Defense." *Stanford Law Review* 43 (July 1991): 1311–26.

Rise, Eric W. "Race, Rape, and Radicalism: The Case of the Martinsville Seven, 1949–1951." *The Journal of Southern History* 58 (August 1992): 461–90.

Roberts, Dorothy E. "Rape, Violence, and Women's Autonomy." *Chicago-Kent Law Review* 69 (1993): 359–88.

Rose, Vicki McNickle. "Rape as a Social Problem: A Byproduct of the Feminist Movement." *Social Problems* 25 (October 1977): 75–89.

Ross, Beverly J. "Does Diversity in Legal Scholarship Make a Difference? A Look at the Law of Rape." *Dickinson Law Review* 100 (summer 1996): 795–859.

Russell, Diana E. H. "Pornography and Rape: A Causal Model." *Political Psychology* 9 (1988): 41–73.

———, and Nancy Howell. "The Prevalence of Rape in the United States Revisited." *Signs* 8 (summer 1983): 688–95.

Ryan, Rebecca M. "The Sex Right: A Legal History of the Marital Rape Exemption." *Law and Social Inquiry* 20 (fall 1995): 941–1001.

Sanday, Peggy Reeves. "The Socio-Cultural Context of Rape: A Cross-Cultural Study." *Journal of Social Issues* 37 (1981): 5–27.

Schafran, Lynn Hecht. "Maiming the Soul: Judges, Sentencing and the Myth of the Nonviolent Rapist." *Fordham Urban Law Journal* 20 (spring 1993): 439–53.

———. "Writing and Reading About Rape: A Primer." *St. John's Law Review* 66 (fall 1993): 979–1045.

Schauer, Frederick. "Causation Theory and the Causes of Sexual Violence." *American Bar Foundation Research Journal* (fall 1987): 737–70.

Schenk, Roy U. "So Why Do Rapes Occur?" *The Humanist* 39 (March/April 1979): 47–50.

Scheppele, Kim Lane. "Just the Facts, Ma'am: Sexualized Violence, Evidentiary Habits, and the Revision of Truth." *New York Law School Law Review* 37 (1992): 123–72.

Schott, Robin May. "Gender and 'Postmodern War'." *Hypatia* 11 (fall 1996): 19–29.

Schulhofer, Stephen J. "The Gender Question in Criminal Law." *Social Philosophy and Policy* 7 (spring 1990): 105–37.

———. "Taking Sexual Autonomy Seriously: Rape Law and Beyond." *Law and Philosophy* 11 (1992): 35–94.

———. "The Feminist Challenge in Criminal Law." *University of Pennsylvania Law Review* 143 (June 1995): 2151–207.

Schultz, Terri. "Rape, Fear, and the Law." *The Chicago Guide* 21 (November 1972): 56–62.

Schwendinger, Julia R., and Herman Schwendinger. "Rape Myths: In Legal, Theoretical, and Everyday Practice." *Crime and Social Justice* 1 (spring-summer 1974): 18–26.

Scully, Diana, and Joseph Marolla. "'Riding the Bull at Gilley's': Convicted Rapists Describe the Rewards of Rape." *Social Problems* 32 (February 1985): 251–63.

Scutt, Jocelynne A. "Consent in Rape: The Problem of the Marriage Contract." *Monash University Law Review* 3 (June 1977): 255–88.

———. "Consent Versus Submission: Threats and the Element of Fear in Rape." *Western Australian Law Review* 13 (1977): 52–76.

Shah, Diane K. "Women Attack Rape Justice." *The National Observer* 10 (9 October 1971): 1, 21.

Sherwin, Emily. "Infelicitous Sex." *Legal Theory* 2 (September 1996): 209–31.

Shields, William M., and Lea M. Shields. "Forcible Rape: An Evolutionary Perspective." *Ethology and Sociobiology* 4 (1983): 115–36.

Shorter, Edward. "On Writing the History of Rape." *Signs* 3 (winter 1977): 471–82.

Shotland, R. Lance. "A Theory of the Causes of Courtship Rape: Part 2." *Journal of Social Issues* 48 (1992): 127–43.

Shulman, Alix Kates. "Sex and Power: Sexual Bases of Radical Feminism." *Signs* 5 (summer 1980): 590–604.

Simons, Andrew J. "Being Secure in One's Person: Does Sexual Assault Violate a Constitutionally Protected Right?" *Boston College Law Review* 38 (September 1997): 1011–49.

Sitton, Jaye. "Old Wine in New Bottles: The 'Marital' Rape Allowance." *North Carolina Law Review* 72 (November 1993): 261–89.

Slovenko, Ralph. "Statutory Rape." *Medical Aspects of Human Sexuality* 5 (March 1971): 155–67.

Smith, Joel E. "Constitutionality of 'Rape Shield' Statute Restricting Use of Evidence of Victim's Sexual Experiences." *American Law Reports 4th* 1 (1980): 283–305.

Smith, Rebekah. "Protecting the Victim: Rape and Sexual Harassment Shields Under Maine and Federal Law." *Maine Law Review* 49 (1997): 443–513.

Smuts, Barbara B., and Robert W. Smuts. "Male Aggression and Sexual Coercion of Females in Nonhuman Primates and Other Mammals: Evidence and Theoretical Implications." *Advances in the Study of Behavior* 22 (1993): 1–63.

Snow, Nancy E. "Self-Blame and Blame of Rape Victims." *Public Affairs Quarterly* 8 (October 1994): 377–93.

Soble, Alan. "In Defense of Bacon." *Philosophy of the Social Sciences* 25 (June 1995): 192–215.

———. "Antioch's 'Sexual Offense Policy': A Philosophical Exploration." *Journal of Social Philosophy* 28 (spring 1997): 22–36.

Sommers, Christina. "Do These Feminists Like Women?" *Journal of Social Philosophy* 21 (fall/winter 1990): 66–74.

———. "Argumentum Ad Feminam." *Journal of Social Philosophy* 22 (spring 1991): 5–19.

Soules, Michael R., Stephen K. Stewart, K. M. Brown, and Albert A. Pollard. "The Spectrum of Alleged Rape." *The Journal of Reproductive Medicine* 20 (January 1978): 33–9.

Stanchi, Kathryn M. "The Paradox of the Fresh Complaint Rule." *Boston College Law Review* 37 (May 1996): 441–77.

Stewart, Mary White, Shirley A. Dobbin, and Sophia I. Gatowski. "'Real Rapes' and 'Real Victims': The Shared Reliance on Common Cultural Definitions of Rape." *Feminist Legal Studies* 4 (August 1996): 159–77.

Svalastoga, Kaare. "Rape and Social Structure." *The Pacific Sociological Review* 5 (spring 1962): 48–53.

Syrota, G. "Rape: When Does Fraud Vitiate Consent?" *Western Australian Law Review* 25 (December 1995): 334–45.

Telling, David. "Rape—Consent and Belief." *Journal of Criminal Law* 47 (1983): 129–39.

Temkin, Jennifer. "The Limits of Reckless Rape." *The Criminal Law Review* (January 1983): 5–16.

Tetreault, Patricia A., and Mark A. Barnett. "Reactions to Stranger and Acquaintance Rape." *Psychology of Women Quarterly* 11 (September 1987): 353–58.

Thiessen, Del, and Robert K. Young. "Investigating Sexual Coercion." *Society* 31 (March/April 1994): 60–3.

Thomas, Keith. "The Double Standard." *Journal of the History of Ideas* 20 (April 1959): 195–216.

Thornhill, Randy, and Nancy Wilmsen Thornhill. "Human Rape: An Evolutionary Analysis." *Ethology and Sociobiology* 4 (1983): 137–73.

———. "The Evolutionary Psychology of Men's Coercive Sexuality." *Behavioral and Brain Sciences* 15 (June 1992): 363–421.

Thornton, M. T. "Rape and Mens Rea." *Canadian Journal of Philosophy*, Suppl. Vol. 8 (1982): 119–46.

Tittle, Peg. "Sexual Activity, Consent, Mistaken Belief, and Mens Rea." *Philosophy in the Contemporary World* 3 (spring 1996): 19–23.

Tomkovicz, James J. "On Teaching Rape: Reasons, Risks, and Rewards." *The Yale Law Journal* 102 (November 1992): 481–508.

Tompkins, Tamara L. "Prosecuting Rape as a War Crime: Speaking the Unspeakable." *Notre Dame Law Review* 70 (1995): 845–90.

Torrey, Morrison. "When Will We Be Believed? Rape Myths and the Idea of a Fair Trial in Rape Prosecutions." *U. C. Davis Law Review* 24 (summer 1991): 1013–71.

———. "Feminist Legal Scholarship on Rape: A Maturing Look at One Form of Violence Against Women." *William and Mary Journal of Women and the Law* 2 (fall 1995): 35–49.

Tur, Richard H. S. "Rape: Reasonableness and Time." *Oxford Journal of Legal Studies* 3 (winter 1981): 432–41.

Wald, Alexandra. "What's Rightfully Ours: Toward a Property Theory of Rape." *Columbia Journal of Law and Social Problems* 30 (spring 1997): 459–502.

Wallach, Shawn J. "Rape Shield Laws: Protecting the Victim at the Expense of the Defendant's Constitutional Rights." *New York Law School Journal of Human Rights* 13 (winter 1997): 485–521.

Walsh, Michael G. "Criminal Responsibility of Husband for Rape, or Assault to Commit Rape, on Wife." *American Law Reports 4th* 24 (1983): 105–31.

Warr, Mark. "Fear of Victimization: Why Are Women and the Elderly More Afraid?" *Social Science Quarterly* 65 (September 1984): 681–702.

———. "Fear of Rape Among Urban Women." *Social Problems* 32 (February 1985): 238–50.

Weihofen, Henry. "Victims of Criminal Violence." *Journal of Public Law* 8 (1959): 209–18.

Weis, Kurt, and Sandra S. Borges. "Victimology and Rape: The Case of the Legitimate Victim." *Issues in Criminology* 8 (fall 1973): 71–115.

Wells, Celia. "Swatting the Subjectivist Bug." *The Criminal Law Review* (April 1982): 209–20.

———. "Law Reform, Rape and Ideology." *Journal of Law and Society* 12 (spring 1985): 63–75.

Wertheimer, Alan. "Consent and Sexual Relations." *Legal Theory* 2 (June 1996): 89–112.

West, Robin. "Equality Theory, Marital Rape, and the Promise of the Fourteenth Amendment." *Florida Law Review* 42 (January 1990): 45–79.

———. "Legitimating the Illegitimate: A Comment on *Beyond Rape*." *Columbia Law Review* 93 (October 1993): 1442–59.

———. "The Harms of Consensual Sex." *The American Philosophical Association Newsletters on Feminism and Philosophy and Philosophy and Law* 94 (spring 1995): 52–5.

———. "A Comment on Consent, Sex, and Rape." *Legal Theory* 2 (September 1996): 233–51.

Whitney, Cheryl A. "Non-Stranger, Non-Consensual Sexual Assaults: Changing Legislation to Ensure That Acts Are Criminally Punished." *Rutgers Law Journal* 27 (winter 1996): 417–45.

Wicktom, Cynthia Ann. "Focusing on the Offender's Forceful Conduct: A Proposal for the Redefinition of Rape Laws." *George Washington Law Review* 56 (January 1988): 399–430.

Wiener, Robin D. "Shifting the Communication Burden: A Meaningful Consent Standard in Rape." *Harvard Women's Law Journal* 6 (spring 1983): 143–61.

Wise, Steven A. "State v. Heisinger: 'Statutory Rape's' Presumption of Incapacity to Consent—Rebuttable or Conclusive?" *South Dakota Law Review* 24 (spring 1979): 523–40.

Wood, Pamela Lakes. "The Victim in a Forcible Rape Case: A Feminist View." *The American Criminal Law Review* 11 (winter 1973): 335–54.

Wreen, Michael. "Abortion and Pregnancy Due to Rape." *Philosophia* 21 (April 1992): 201–20.

Wriggins, Jennifer. "Rape, Racism, and the Law." *Harvard Women's Law Journal* 6 (spring 1983): 103–41.

Young, Robert K., and Del Thiessen. "The Texas Rape Scale." *Ethology and Sociobiology* 13 (January 1992): 19–33.

Chapters of Monographs

Davis, Angela Y. "We Do Not Consent: Violence Against Women in a Racist Society." In *Women, Culture, and Politics*, 35–52. New York: Random House, 1989.

Dworkin, Andrea. "The Rape Atrocity and the Boy Next Door." In *Our Blood: Prophecies and Discourses on Sexual Politics*, 22–49. New York: Harper and Row, 1976.

LeMoncheck, Linda. "Appropriating Women's Bodies: The Form and Function of Men's Sexual Intimidation of Women." In *Loose Women, Lecherous Men: A Feminist Philosophy of Sex*, 155–215, 252–62. New York: Oxford University Press, 1997.

MacKinnon, Catharine A. "A Rally Against Rape." In *Feminism Unmodified: Discourses on Life and Law*, 81–4, 247–8. Cambridge, MA, and London: Harvard University Press, 1987.

———. "Sex and Violence: A Perspective." In *Feminism Unmodified: Discourses on Life and Law*, 85–92, 248. Cambridge, MA, and London: Harvard University Press, 1987.

———. "Sexuality." In *Toward a Feminist Theory of the State*, 126–54, 276–88. Cambridge, MA, and London: Harvard University Press, 1989.

———. "Rape: On Coercion and Consent." In *Toward a Feminist Theory of the State*, 171–83, 295–9. Cambridge, MA, and London: Harvard University Press, 1989.

Morgan, Robin. "Theory and Practice: Pornography and Rape." In *Going Too Far: The Personal Chronicle of a Feminist*, 163–9. New York: Vintage Books, 1978.

Paglia, Camille. "Rape and Modern Sex War." In *Sex, Art, and American Culture: Essays*, 49–54. New York: Vintage Books, 1992.

———. "The Rape Debate, Continued." In *Sex, Art, and American Culture: Essays*, 55–74. New York: Vintage Books, 1992.

Ploscowe, Morris. "Rape." In *Sex and the Law*, rev. and enl. ed., 155–81, 275–7. Introduction by Roscoe Pound. New York: Ace Books, 1962.

Sommers, Christina Hoff. "Rape Research." In *Who Stole Feminism? How Women Have Betrayed Women*, 209–26, 297–300. New York: Simon and Schuster, 1994.

Stoltenberg, John. "Rapist Ethics." In *Refusing to Be a Man: Essays on Sex and Justice*, 9–24, 211–2. Portland, OR: Breitenbush Books, 1989.

Tong, Rosemarie. "Rape." In *Women, Sex, and the Law*, 90–123. Savage, MD: Rowman and Littlefield, 1984.

Contributions to Anthologies

Adams, David M. "Date Rape and Erotic Discourse." In *Date Rape: Feminism, Philosophy, and the Law*, edited by Leslie Francis, 27–39. University Park: The Pennsylvania State University Press, 1996.

"Antioch College Sexual Offense Policy, The." In *Date Rape: Feminism, Philosophy, and the Law,* edited by Leslie Francis, 135–54. University Park: The Pennsylvania State University Press, 1996.

Baker, Brenda M. "Consent, Assault and Sexual Assault." In *Legal Theory Meets Legal Practice,* edited by Anne Bayefsky, 223–38. Edmonton, Alberta: Academic Printing and Publishing, 1988.

Bernatchez, Elise. "On Rape." In *Interpersonal Violence, Health and Gender Politics,* edited by Stanley G. French, 75–84. Dubuque, IA, and Ottawa, Ont.: Wm. C. Brown Communications, 1993.

Brundage, James A. "Rape and Seduction in the Medieval Canon Law." In *Sexual Practices and the Medieval Church,* edited by Vern L. Bullough and James Brundage, 141–8, 262–6. Buffalo: Prometheus Books, 1982.

Card, Claudia. "Rape as a Terrorist Institution." In *Violence, Terrorism, and Justice,* edited by R. G. Frey and Christopher W. Morris, 296–319. Cambridge: Cambridge University Press, 1991.

Dibbell, Julian. "A Rape in Cyberspace; Or, How an Evil Clown, a Haitian Trickster Spirit, Two Wizards, and a Cast of Dozens Turned a Database into a Society." In *Flame Wars: The Discourse of Cyberculture,* edited by Mark Dery, 237–61. Durham, NC, and London: Duke University Press, 1994.

Ellis, Kate, Sebern Fisher, Marian Meade, Vivian Neimann, Gloria Schuh, Mary Winslow, and Rosemary Gaffney. "Men and Violence." In *Radical Feminism,* edited by Anne Koedt, Ellen Levine, and Anita Rapone, 63–71. New York: Quadrangle Books, 1973.

Elliston, Frederick A. "Rape: Introduction." In *Feminism and Philosophy,* edited by Mary Vetterling-Braggin, Frederick A. Elliston, and Jane English, 309–12. Totowa, NJ: Littlefield, Adams, 1977.

Feldman-Summers, Shirley. "Conceptual and Empirical Issues Associated with Rape." In *Victims and Society,* edited by Emilio C. Viano, 91–104. Washington, DC: Visage Press, 1976.

Foa, Pamela. "What's Wrong with Rape." In *Feminism and Philosophy,* edited by Mary Vetterling-Braggin, Frederick A. Elliston, and Jane English, 347–59. Totowa, NJ: Littlefield, Adams, 1977.

Francis, Leslie. Introduction to *Date Rape: Feminism, Philosophy, and the Law,* edited by Leslie Francis, vii–xix. University Park: The Pennsylvania State University Press, 1996.

French, Stanley G. "Interpersonal Violence: Power Relationships and Their Effects on Health." In *Interpersonal Violence, Health and Gender Politics,* edited by Stanley G. French, 3–26. Dubuque, IA, and Ottawa, Ont.: Wm. C. Brown Communications, 1993.

Guskin, Alan E. "The Antioch Response: Sex, You Just Don't Talk About It." In *Date Rape: Feminism, Philosophy, and the Law,* edited by Leslie Francis, 155–65. University Park: The Pennsylvania State University Press, 1996.

Harris, Angela P. "Forcible Rape, Date Rape, and Communicative Sexuality: A Legal Perspective." In *Date Rape: Feminism, Philosophy, and the Law,* edited by Leslie Francis, 51–61. University Park: The Pennsylvania State University Press, 1996.

———, and Lois Pineau. "A Dialogue on Evidence." In *Date Rape: Feminism, Philosophy, and the Law,* edited by Leslie Francis, 109–31. University Park: The Pennsylvania State University Press, 1996.

Kamen, Paula. "Acquaintance Rape: Revolution and Reaction." In *"Bad Girls"/"Good Girls": Women, Sex, and Power in the Nineties,* edited by Nan Bauer Maglin and Donna Perry, 137–49. New Brunswick, NJ: Rutgers University Press, 1996.

MacKinnon, Catharine A. "Crimes of War, Crimes of Peace." In *Free Spirits: Feminist*

Philosophers on Culture, edited by Kate Mehuron and Gary Percesepe, 380–93, 513–8. Englewood Cliffs, NJ: Prentice Hall, 1995.

McGregor, Joan. "Force, Consent, and the Reasonable Woman." In *In Harm's Way: Essays in Honor of Joel Feinberg,* edited by Jules L. Coleman and Allen Buchanan, 231–54. Cambridge: Cambridge University Press, 1994.

Mehrhof, Barbara, and Pamela Kearon. "Rape: An Act of Terror." In *Radical Feminism,* edited by Anne Koedt, Ellen Levine, and Anita Rapone, 228–33. New York: Quadrangle Books, 1973.

Murphy, Jeffrie G. "Some Ruminations on Women, Violence, and the Criminal Law." In *In Harm's Way: Essays in Honor of Joel Feinberg,* edited by Jules L. Coleman and Allen Buchanan, 209–30. Cambridge: Cambridge University Press, 1994.

Peterson, Susan Rae. "Coercion and Rape: The State as a Male Protection Racket." In *Feminism and Philosophy,* edited by Mary Vetterling-Braggin, Frederick A. Elliston, and Jane English, 360–71. Totowa, NJ: Littlefield, Adams, 1977.

Pineau, Lois. "A Response to My Critics." In *Date Rape: Feminism, Philosophy, and the Law,* edited by Leslie Francis, 63–107. University Park: The Pennsylvania State University Press, 1996.

Ruse, Michael. "Is Rape Wrong on Andromeda? An Introduction to Extraterrestrial Evolution, Science, and Morality." In *Extraterrestrials: Science and Alien Intelligence,* edited by Edward Regis Jr., 43–78. Cambridge: Cambridge University Press, 1985.

Schonsheck, Jonathan. "Human Nature, Innateness and Violence Against Women." In *Philosophical Essays on the Ideas of a Good Society,* edited by Yeager Hudson and Creighton Peden, 287–97. Lewiston, NY: Edwin Mellen Press, 1988.

Shafer, Carolyn M., and Marilyn Frye. "Rape and Respect." In *Feminism and Philosophy,* edited by Mary Vetterling-Braggin, Frederick A. Elliston, and Jane English, 333–46. Totowa, NJ: Littlefield, Adams, 1977.

Silliman, Matthew R. "The Antioch Policy, a Community Experiment in Communicative Sexuality." In *Date Rape: Feminism, Philosophy, and the Law,* edited by Leslie Francis, 167–75. University Park: The Pennsylvania State University Press, 1996.

Taub, Nadine, and Elizabeth M. Schneider. "Women's Subordination and the Role of Law." In *The Politics of Law: A Progressive Critique,* rev. ed., edited by David Kairys, 151–76. New York: Pantheon Books, 1990.

Weis, Kurt, and Sandra S. Borges. "Rape as a Crime Without Victims and Offenders? A Methodological Critique." In *Victims and Society,* edited by Emilio C. Viano, 230–54. Washington, DC: Visage Press, 1976.

Wells, Catharine Pierce. "Date Rape and the Law: Another Feminist View." In *Date Rape: Feminism, Philosophy, and the Law,* edited by Leslie Francis, 41–50. University Park: The Pennsylvania State University Press, 1996.

Williams, Glanville. "Lords' Decision on the Law of Rape." In *The Philosophy of Law: Classic and Contemporary Readings with Commentary,* edited by Frederick Schauer and Walter Sinnott-Armstrong, 873–4. Fort Worth, TX: Harcourt Brace College, 1996.

Wolfgang, Marvin E., and Marc Riedel. "Racial Discrimination, Rape, and the Death Penalty." In *The Death Penalty in America,* 3d ed., edited by Hugo Adam Bedau, 194–205. New York: Oxford University Press, 1982.

Book Reviews

Archard, David. "Without Consent." Review of *Rape: A Philosophical Investigation,* by Keith Burgess-Jackson, and *Carnal Knowledge: Rape on Trial,* by Sue Lees. *Radical Philosophy* (January/February 1997): 44–5.

Bart, Pauline B. Review of *Intimate Violence: A Study of Injustice*, by Julie Blackman; *The Female Fear: The Social Cost of Rape*, by Margaret T. Gordon and Stephanie Riger; *Battered Women as Survivors*, by Lee Ann Hoff; *Women and Rape*, by Cathy Roberts; and *Fraternity Gang Rape: Sex, Brotherhood, and Privilege on Campus*, by Peggy Reeves Sanday. *Signs* 19 (winter 1994): 527–31.

Berger, Vivian. "Not So Simple Rape." Review of *Real Rape*, by Susan Estrich. *Criminal Justice Ethics* 7 (winter/spring 1988): 69–81.

Greer, Germaine. "What Is Rape?" Review of *Against Our Will: Men, Women and Rape*, by Susan Brownmiller. *The New Review* 2 (January 1976): 60–1.

Henderson, Lynne N. "What Makes Rape a Crime?" Review of *Real Rape*, by Susan Estrich. *Berkeley Women's Law Journal* 3 (1988): 193–229.

Manian, Maya. "Rethinking Rape." Review of *Date Rape: Feminism, Philosophy, and the Law*, edited by Leslie Francis. *Harvard Women's Law Journal* 20 (spring 1997): 333–40.

Scheppele, Kim Lane. "The Re-Vision of Rape Law." Review of *Real Rape*, by Susan Estrich. *The University of Chicago Law Review* 54 (summer 1987): 1095–116.

Steiker, Carol S. "Remembering Race, Rape, and Capital Punishment." Review of *The Martinsville Seven: Race, Rape, and Capital Punishment*, by Eric W. Rise. *Virginia Law Review* 83 (April 1997): 693–712.

Wells, Celia. Review of *Rape on Trial*, by Zsuzsanna Adler; *Real Rape*, by Susan Estrich; and *Rape and the Legal Process*, by Jennifer Temkin. *The Law Quarterly Review* 104 (July 1988): 479–82.

Encyclopedia Entries

Field, Martha A. "Rape: Legal Aspects." In *Encyclopedia of Crime and Justice*, edited by Sanford H. Kadish, 4:1356–64. New York: Free Press, 1983.

Francis, Leslie Pickering. "Rape." In *Encyclopedia of Applied Ethics*, edited by Ruth Chadwick, 3:791–8. San Diego: Academic, 1998.

Groth, A. Nicholas. "Rape: Behavioral Aspects." In *Encyclopedia of Crime and Justice*, edited by Sanford H. Kadish, 4:1351–6. New York: Free Press, 1983.

Scheman, Naomi. "Rape." In *Encyclopedia of Ethics*, edited by Lawrence C. Becker and Charlotte B. Becker, 2:1059–62. New York and London: Garland, 1992.

Superson, Anita. "Rape." In *The Philosophy of Law: An Encyclopedia*, edited by Christopher B. Gray. New York: Garland, in press.

Miscellaneous

MacKinnon, Catharine A. "The Palm Beach Hanging." *New York Times*, 15 December 1991, sec. 4, p. 15.

"Rape Is an Abuse of Power" (poem). Translated by Isabelle de Courtivron. In *New French Feminisms: An Anthology*, edited by Elaine Marks and Isabelle de Courtivron, 194–5. Amherst: The University of Massachusetts Press, 1980.

Smithyman, Samuel David. "The Undetected Rapist." Ph.D. diss., Claremont Graduate School, CA, 1978.

Statutes

Great Britain. Laws, Statutes, etc. *Statute of Westminster I*, 1275, 3 Edw. 1, ch. 13.
——. *Common Informers Act*, 1576, 18 Eliz., ch. 7.
——. *The Sexual Offences Act*, 1956, 4 & 5 Eliz. 2, ch. 69.
——. *The Sexual Offences Act*, 1967, ch. 60.
——. *The Sexual Offences (Amendment) Act*, 1976, ch. 82.
Violence Against Women Act of 1994. U.S. Code, title 42, ch. 136, secs. 13931–14040 (1995).

Cases

Adams v. Commonwealth, 219 Ky. 711, 294 S.W. 151 (1927).
Baxter v. State, 80 Neb. 840, 115 N.W. 534 (1908).
Bigliben v. State, 68 Tex. Crim. 530, 151 S.W. 1044 (1912).
Bixler v. Commonwealth, 712 S.W.2d 366 (Ky. Ct. App. 1986).
Black v. State, 119 Ga. 746, 47 S.E. 370 (1904).
Bloodworth v. State, 65 Tenn. (6 Baxt.) 614 (1872).
Boddie v. State, 52 Ala. 395 (1875).
Bradley v. State, 333 S.E.2d 578 (Ga. 1985).
Brooks v. Maryland, 24 Md. App. 334, 330 A.2d 670 (1975).
Brown v. State, 127 Wis. 193, 106 N.W. 536 (1906).
Brown v. State, 50 Ala. App. 471, 280 So. 2d 177, cert. denied, 291 Ala. 774, 280 So. 2d 182
    (1973).
Bryan v. State, 814 S.W.2d 482 (Tex. Crim. App. 1991).
Burke v. State, 624 P.2d 1240 (Alaska 1980).
Calhoun v. State, 85 Tex. Crim. 496, 214 S.W. 335 (1919).
Campbell v. United States, 176 F.2d 45 (D.C. Cir. 1949).
Cascio v. State, 147 Neb. 1075, 25 N.W.2d 897 (1947).
Coker v. Georgia, 433 U.S. 584 (1977).
Commonwealth v. Berkowitz, 609 A.2d 1338 (Pa. Super. Ct. 1992), 641 A.2d 1161 (Pa. 1994).
Commonwealth v. Burke, 105 Mass. 376 (1870).
Commonwealth v. Caracciola, 564 N.E.2d 774 (Mass. 1991).
Commonwealth v. Carpenter, 94 A.2d 74 (Pa. Super. Ct. 1953).
Commonwealth v. Cordeiro, 401 Mass. 843, 519 N.E.2d 1328 (1988).
Commonwealth v. Fogerty, 74 Mass. 487 (8 Gray) (1857).
Commonwealth v. Grant, 464 N.E.2d 33 (Mass. 1984).
Commonwealth v. McCay, 294 N.E.2d 213 (Mass. 1973).
Commonwealth v. Mlinarich, 345 Pa. Super. 269, 498 A.2d 395 (1985).
Commonwealth v. Rhodes, 510 A.2d 1217 (Pa. 1986).
Commonwealth v. Sheridan, 322 N.E.2d 787 (Mass. App. Ct. 1975).
Commonwealth v. Sherry, 386 Mass. 682, 437 N.E.2d 224 (1982).
Commonwealth v. Stephens, 143 Pa. Super. 394, 17 A.2d 919 (1941).
Commonwealth v. Vieira, 519 N.E.2d 1320 (Mass. 1988).
Commonwealth v. Williams, 439 A.2d 765 (Pa. Super. Ct. 1982).
Crump v. Commonwealth, 98 Va. 833, 23 S.E. 760 (1895).
Davis v. People, 112 Colo. 452, 150 P.2d 67 (1944).
Director of Public Prosecutions v. Morgan, 1976 App. Cas. 182, 2 W.L.R. 913, 2 All E.R. 347
    (H.L. 1975).

Doe v. Doe, 929 F. Supp. 608 (D. Conn. 1996).

Don Moran v. People, 25 Mich. 356 (1872).

Draughn v. State, 12 Okla. Crim. 479, 158 P. 890 (1916).

Eberhart v. State, 134 Ind. 651, 34 N.E. 637 (1893).

Finley v. State, 527 S.W.2d 533 (Tex. Crim. App. 1975).

Flores v. State, 69 Wis. 2d 509, 230 N.W.2d 637 (1975).

Frazier v. State, 86 S.W. 754 (Tex. Crim. App. 1905).

Getz v. State, 538 A.2d 726 (Del. 1988).

Gilliam v. State, 509 N.E.2d 815 (Ind. 1987).

Goldberg v. State, 41 Md. App. 58, 395 A.2d 1213 (Md. Ct. Spec. App. 1979).

Gordon v. State, 32 Ala. App. 398, 26 So. 2d 419 (1946).

Graham v. State, 67 S.W.2d 296 (Tex. Crim. App. 1933).

Green v. State, 611 P.2d 262 (Okla. Crim. App. 1980).

Grigsby v. Commonwealth, 299 Ky. 721, 187 S.W.2d 259 (1945).

Hacker v. State, 73 Okla. Crim. 119, 118 P.2d 408 (1941).

Hirdes v. Ottawa Circuit Judge, 180 Mich. 321, 146 N.W. 646 (1914).

In re Interest of J. D. G., 498 S.W.2d 786 (Mo. 1973).

In re W. E. P., 318 A.2d 286 (D.C. App. 1974).

Johnson v. Commonwealth, 5 Va. App. 529, 365 S.E.2d 237 (1988).

Johnson v. State, 625 S.W.2d 68 (Tex. Ct. App. 1981).

Johnston v. State, 673 P.2d 844 (Okla. Crim. App. 1983), cert. denied, 467 U.S. 1229 (1984).

King, The, v. Groombridge, 7 Car. & P. 582, 173 Eng. Rep. 256 (1836).

King v. State, 210 Tenn. 150, 357 S.W.2d 42 (1962).

Lancaster v. State, 168 Ga. 470, 148 S.E. 139 (1929).

Lannan v. State, 600 N.E.2d 1334 (Ind. 1992).

Lawson v. State, 17 Tex. App. 292 (1884).

Mares v. Territory, 65 P. 165 (N.M. 1901).

Marr v. State, 494 So. 2d 1139 (Fla. 1986).

Martin v. State, 504 So. 2d 335 (Ala. Crim. App. 1986).

Massey v. Commonwealth, 337 S.E.2d 754 (Va. 1985).

McGuinn v. United States, 191 F.2d 477 (D.C. Cir. 1951).

McIlwain v. State, 402 So. 2d 1194 (Fla. Dist. Ct. App. 1981).

McQuirk v. State, 84 Ala. 435, 4 So. 775 (1888).

Meloon v. Helgemoe, 564 F.2d 602 (1st Cir. 1977).

Michael M. v. Superior Court of Sonoma County, 450 U.S. 464 (1981).

Michigan v. Lucas, 500 U.S. 145 (1991).

Moss v. State, 208 Miss. 531, 45 So. 2d 125 (1950).

Olden v. Kentucky, 488 U.S. 227 (1988).

Owens v. State, 96 Nev. 880, 620 P.2d 1236 (1980).

Packineau v. United States, 202 F.2d 681 (8th Cir. 1953).

Pappajohn v. The Queen (1980), 111 D.L.R. 3rd 1.

Parsons v. Parker, 160 Va. 810, 170 S.E. 1 (1933).

Pendleton v. Commonwealth, 685 S.W.2d 549 (Ky. 1985).

People v. Abbot, 19 Wend. 192 (N.Y. 1838).

People v. Anderson, 144 Cal. App. 3d 55, 192 Cal. Rptr. 409 (1983).

People v. Barnes, 42 Cal. 3d 284, 721 P.2d 110, 228 Cal. Rptr. 228 (1986).

People v. Benson, 6 Cal. 221 (1856).

People v. Bowen, 609 N.E.2d 346 (Ill. App. Ct.), appeal denied, 616 N.E.2d 339 (Ill.), cert. denied, 114 S.Ct. 387 (1993).

People v. Bruce, 208 Cal. App. 3d 1099, 256 Cal. Rptr. 647 (1989).

People v. Burnham, 176 Cal. App. 3d 1134, 222 Cal. Rptr. 630 (1986).

People v. Castillo, 193 Cal. App. 3d 119, 238 Cal. Rptr. 207 (1987).

People v. Celmars, 332 Ill. 113, 163 N.E. 421 (1928).

People v. Collins, 25 Ill. 2d 605, 186 N.E.2d 30 (1962), cert. denied, 373 U.S. 942 (1963).

People v. Cox, 383 Ill. 617, 50 N.E.2d 758 (1943).

People v. Crispo, No. 3105-85 (N.Y. Sup. Ct. Oct. 16, 1988).

People v. Dailey, 405 N.Y.S.2d 986 (1978).

People v. Degnen, 70 Cal. App. 567, 234 P. 129 (1925).

People v. DeStefano, 467 N.Y.S.2d 506 (Suffolk County Ct. 1983).

People v. Dohring, 59 N.Y. 374 (1874).

People v. Dorsey, 104 Misc. 2d 963, 429 N.Y.S.2d 828 (Sup. Ct. 1980).

People v. Ellers, 18 Ill. App. 3d 213, 309 N.E.2d 627 (1974).

People v. Evans, 85 Misc. 2d 1088, 379 N.Y.S.2d 912 (Sup. Ct. 1975), aff'd, 55 A.D.2d 858, 390 N.Y.S.2d 768 (1976).

People v. Gould, 188 Colo. 113, 532 P.2d 953 (1975).

People v. Green, 183 Colo. 25, 514 P.2d 769 (1973).

People v. Greer, 374 N.Y.S.2d 224 (1975).

People v. Griffin, 117 Cal. 583, 49 P. 711 (1897).

People v. Guthreau, 162 Cal. Rptr. 376 (Ct. App. 1980).

People v. Hale, 142 Mich. App. 451, 370 N.W.2d 382 (1985).

People v. Hampton, 118 Cal. App. 3d 324, 173 Cal. Rptr. 268 (1981).

People v. Hayn, 341 N.E.2d 182 (Ill. App. Ct. 1976).

People v. Haywood, 118 Ill. 2d 263, 515 N.E.2d 45 (1987).

People v. Hearn, 300 N.W.2d 396 (Mich. Ct. App. 1980).

People v. Hill, 558 N.Y.S.2d 380 (N.Y. App. 1990).

People v. Hughes, 41 A.D.2d 333, 343 N.Y.S.2d 240 (1973).

People v. Ing, 65 Cal. 2d 603, 422 P.2d 590, 55 Cal. Rptr. 902 (1967).

People v. Iniguez, 872 P.2d 1183 (Cal. 1994).

People v. Jansson, 323 N.W.2d 508 (Mich. Ct. App. 1982).

People v. Jones, 28 Ill. App. 3d 896, 329 N.E.2d 855 (1975).

People v. Khan, 264 N.W.2d 360 (Mich. Ct. App. 1978).

People v. LaSalle, 103 Cal. App. 3d 139, 162 Cal. Rptr. 816 (1980).

People v. Liberta, 64 N.Y.2d 152, 474 N.E.2d 567 (1984), cert. denied, 471 U.S. 1020 (1985).

People v. Mackey, 46 Cal. App. 3d 755, 120 Cal. Rptr. 157, cert. denied, 423 U.S. 951 (1975).

People v. May, 213 Cal. App. 3d 118, 261 Cal. Rptr. 502 (1989).

People v. Mayberry, 15 Cal. 3d 143, 542 P.2d 1337, 125 Cal. Rptr. 745 (1975).

People v. M. D., 595 N.E.2d 702 (Ill. App. Ct.), appeal denied, 602 N.E.2d 467 (Ill. 1992).

People v. Medrano, 24 Ill. App. 3d 429, 321 N.E.2d 97 (1974).

People v. Nelson, 261 N.W.2d 299 (Mich. Ct. App. 1977), appeal denied, 281 N.W.2d 134 (Mich. 1979).

People v. Nye, 38 Cal. 2d 34, 237 P.2d 1 (1951).

People v. Payne, 282 N.W.2d 456 (Mich. Ct. App. 1979).

People v. Pelvino, 216 App. Div. 319, 214 N.Y.S. 577 (1926).

People v. Perez, 273 N.W.2d 496 (Mich. Ct. App. 1979).

People v. Perez, 194 Cal. App. 3d 525, 239 Cal. Rptr. 569 (1987).

People v. Quicke, 390 P.2d 393 (Cal. 1964).

People v. Rincon-Pineda, 14 Cal. 3d 864, 538 P.2d 247, 123 Cal. Rptr. 119 (1975).

People v. Romero, 171 Cal. App. 3d 1149, 215 Cal. Rptr. 634 (1985).

People v. Samuels, 250 Cal. App. 2d 501, 58 Cal. Rptr. 439 (1967).

People v. Serrielle, 354 Ill. 182, 188 N.E. 375 (1933).

People v. Stull, 338 N.W.2d 403 (Mich. Ct. App. 1983).

People v. Thompson, 117 Mich. App. 522, 324 N.W.2d 22 (1982).

People v. Varona, 192 Cal. Rptr. 44 (Ct. App. 1983).

People v. Walker, 150 Cal. App. 2d 594, 310 P.2d 110 (1957).

Peterson v. State, 90 Fla. 361, 106 So. 75 (1925).

Pleasant v. State, 15 Ark. 624 (1855).

Pomeroy v. State, 94 Ind. 96 (1883).

Preddy v. Commonwealth, 184 Va. 765, 36 S.E.2d 549 (1946).

Queen v. Ryan, 2 Cox C.C. 115 (1846).

Regina v. Flattery, 18 Cox C.C. 388 (1877).

Regina v. Fletcher, 8 Cox C.C. 131 (1859).

Regina v. Miller [1954], 2 W.L.R. 138 (1953).

Reidhead v. State, 31 Ariz. 70, 250 P. 366 (1926).

Rex v. Williams, [1923] 1 K.B. 340 (C.C.A.).

Reynolds v. State, 42 N.W. 903 (Neb. 1889).

Reynolds v. State, 664 P.2d 621 (Alaska Ct. App. 1983).

Roberson v. State, 501 So. 2d 398 (Miss. 1987).

Rubio v. State, 607 S.W.2d 498 (Tex. Ct. App. 1980).

Salerno v. State, 162 Neb. 99, 75 N.W.2d 362 (1956).

Satterwhite v. Commonwealth, 201 Va. 478, 111 S.E.2d 820 (1960).

Satterwhite v. State, 23 S.W.2d 356 (Tex. Crim. App. 1929).

Shapard v. State, 437 P.2d 565 (Okla. Crim. App.), cert. denied, 393 U.S. 826 (1968).

Shelby v. State, 541 So. 2d 1219 (Fla. Dist. Ct. App. 1989).

Stafford v. State, 104 Tex. Crim. 677, 285 S.W. 314 (1926).

Starr v. State, 205 Wis. 310, 237 N.W. 96 (1931).

State v. Alston, 310 N.C. 399, 312 S.E.2d 470 (1984).

State v. Atkins, 292 S.W. 422 (Mo. 1926).

State v. Bashaw, 296 Or. 50, 672 P.2d 48 (1983).

State v. Beishir, 646 S.W.2d 74 (Mo. 1983).

State v. Bell, 560 P.2d 925 (N.M. 1977).

State v. Bowen, 609 N.E.2d 346 (Ill. App. Ct. 1993).

State v. Boyd, 643 S.W.2d 825 (Mo. Ct. App. 1982).

State v. Budis, 125 N.J. 519, 593 A.2d 784 (1991).

State v. Camara, 113 Wash. 2d 631, 781 P.2d 483 (1989).

State v. Catron, 317 Mo. 894, 296 S.W. 141 (1927).

State v. Ciskie, 110 Wash. 2d 263, 751 P.2d 1165 (1988).

State v. Colbath, 540 A.2d 1212 (N.H. 1988).

State v. Cole, 20 N.C. App. 137, 201 S.E.2d 100 (1973).

State v. Davis, 190 S.W. 297 (Mo. 1916).

State v. Dill, 40 A.2d 443 (Del. Ch. 1944).

State v. Dombroski, 145 Minn. 278, 176 N.W. 985 (1920).

State v. Drake, 219 N.W.2d 492 (Iowa 1974).

State v. Dussenberry, 112 Mo. 277, 20 S.W. 461 (1892).

State v. Elmore, 24 Or. App. 651, 546 P.2d 1117 (1976).

State v. Ely, 114 Wash. 185, 194 P. 988 (1921).

State v. Etheridge, 352 S.E.2d 673 (N.C. 1987).

State v. Faehnrich, 359 N.W.2d 895 (S.D. 1984).

State v. Feddersen, 230 N.W.2d 510 (Iowa 1975).

State v. Fernald, 88 Iowa 553, 55 N.W. 534 (1893).

State v. Fontan, 624 So. 2d 916 (La. Ct. App. 1993).

State v. Gross, 351 N.W.2d 428 (N.D. 1984).

State v. Hancock, 874 P.2d 132 (Utah Ct. App.), cert. denied, 882 P.2d 1359 (Utah 1994).

State v. Hoffman, 228 Wis. 235, 280 N.W. 357 (1938).

State v. Jewett, 109 Vt. 73, 192 A. 7 (1937).

State v. Johnson, 316 Mo. 86, 289 S.W. 847 (1926).

State v. Jones, 39 La. Ann. 935, 3 So. 57 (1887).

State v. Koonce, 731 S.W.2d 431 (Mo. Ct. App. 1987).

State v. Kulmac, 644 A.2d 887 (Conn. 1994).

State v. Lamoureaux, 623 A.2d 9 (R.I. 1993).

State v. Lederer, 99 Wis. 2d 430, 299 N.W.2d 457 (1980).

State v. Lester, 70 N.C. App. 757, 321 S.E.2d 166 (1984), aff'd, 313 N.C. 595, 330 S.E.2d 205 (1985).

State v. Liddell, 685 P.2d 918 (Mont. 1984).

State v. Lint, 657 S.W.2d 722 (Mo. Ct. App. 1983).

State v. Longabardi, 5 Conn. App. 424, 499 A.2d 79 (1985).

State v. Lora, 213 Kan. 184, 515 P.2d 1086 (1973).

State v. Lung, 21 Nev. 209, 28 P. 235 (1891).

State v. McCune, 51 P. 818 (Utah 1898).

State v. McGuire, 124 Ariz. 64, 601 P.2d 1348 (Ariz. Ct. App. 1978).

State v. Mellis, 2 Wash. App. 859, 470 P.2d 558 (1970).

State v. Meloon, 116 N.H. 669, 366 A.2d 1176 (1976).

State v. Meyer, 37 Wash. 2d 759, 226 P.2d 204 (1951).

State v. Mezrioui, 602 A.2d 29 (Conn. App. Ct. 1992).

State v. Murphy, 6 Ala. 765, 41 Am. Dec. 79 (1844).

State v. Nagel, 75 N.D. 495, 28 N.W.2d 665 (1947).

State v. Ogden, 39 Or. 195, 65 P. 449 (1901).

State v. Oliver, 133 N.J. 141, 627 A.2d 144 (1993).

State v. Olsen, 138 Or. 666, 7 P.2d 792 (1932).

State v. Overman, 153 S.E.2d 44 (N.C. 1967).

State v. Patnaude, 438 A.2d 402 (Vt. 1981).

State v. Price, 215 Kan. 718, 529 P.2d 85 (1974).

State v. Probst, 623 So. 2d 79 (La. Ct. App. 1993).

State v. Reed, 479 A.2d 1291 (Me. 1984).

State v. Reinhold, 123 Ariz. 50, 597 P.2d 532 (1979).

State v. Richardson, 63 Mont. 322, 207 P. 124 (1922).

State v. Rider, 449 So. 2d 903 (Fla. 1984).

State v. Robinson, 539 A.2d 606 (Conn. App. Ct. 1988).

State v. Rusk, 289 Md. 230, 424 A.2d 720 (1981).

State v. Schlichter, 263 Mo. 561, 173 S.W. 1072 (1915).

State v. Selman, 300 So. 2d 467 (La. 1974), vacated in part, 428 U.S. 906 (1976).

State v. Settle, 111 Ariz. 394, 531 P.2d 151 (1975).

State v. Shoffner, 302 S.E.2d 830 (N.C. Ct. App. 1983).

State v. Sibley, 131 Mo. 519, 33 S.W. 167 (1895).

State v. Smith, 638 P.2d 1 (Colo. 1981).

State v. Smith, 85 N.J. 193, 426 A.2d 38 (1981).

State v. Smith, 210 Conn. 132, 554 A.2d 713 (1989).

State v. Smoot, 99 Idaho 855, 590 P.2d 1001 (1978).

State v. Stocker, 11 Or. App. 617, 503 P.2d 501 (1972).

State v. Taylor, 735 S.W.2d 412 (Mo. Ct. App. 1987).

State v. Thomas, No. B9198729 (Palo Alto Mun. Ct. Nov. 13, 1991).

State v. Thompson, 792 P.2d 1103 (Mont. 1990).

State v. Tuttle, 67 Ohio St. 440, 66 N.E. 524 (1903).

State v. Vicars, 186 Neb. 311, 183 N.W.2d 241 (1971).

State v. Whitener, 228 S.C. 244, 89 S.E.2d 701, cert. denied, 350 U.S. 861 (1955).

State v. Williams, 235 Kan. 485, 681 P.2d 660 (1984).

State v. Williams, 696 S.W.2d 809 (Mo. Ct. App. 1985).

State v. Wood, 59 Ariz. 48, 122 P.2d 416 (1942).

State v. Young, 55 N.D. 194, 212 N.W. 857 (1927).

State v. Zybach, 761 P.2d 1334 (Or. Ct. App. 1988).

State ex rel. J. F. S., 803 P.2d 1254 (Utah Ct. App. 1990), cert. denied, 815 P.2d 241 (Utah 1991).

State ex rel. M. T. S., 129 N.J. 422, 609 A.2d 1266 (1992).

State ex rel. Pope v. Superior Court, 113 Ariz. 22, 545 P.2d 946 (1976).

Stephenson v. State, 35 Ala. App. 379, 48 So. 2d 255 (1950).

Story v. State, 721 P.2d 1020 (Wyo. 1986).

Stringer v. State, 278 S.W. 208 (Tex. Crim. App. 1925).

Taylor v. State, 257 Ind. 664, 278 N.E.2d 273 (1972).

United States v. Kasto, 584 F.2d 268 (8th Cir. 1978).

United States v. Merrival, 600 F.2d 717 (8th Cir. 1979).

United States v. Saunders, 736 F. Supp. 698 (E.D. Va. 1990), aff'd, 943 F.2d 388 (4th Cir. 1991), cert. denied, 502 U.S. 1105 (1992).

United States v. Sheppard, 569 F.2d 114 (D.C. Cir. 1977).

United States v. Short, 4 C.M.A. 437, 16 C.M.R. 11 (1954).

United States v. Sneezer, 983 F.2d 920 (9th Cir. 1992).

United States v. Wiley, 492 F.2d 547 (D.C. Cir. 1973).

Valez v. State, 762 P.2d 1267 (Alaska Ct. App. 1988).

Vanderford v. State, 126 Ga. 753, 55 S.E. 1025 (1906).

Walter v. People, 50 Barb. (N.Y.) 144 (1867).

Warren v. State, 255 Ga. 151, 336 S.E.2d 221 (1985).

Waters v. State, 2 Md. App. 216, 234 A.2d 147 (1967).

Weishaupt v. Commonwealth, 315 S.E.2d 847 (Va. 1984).

Whitaker v. State, 199 Ga. 344, 34 S.E.2d 499 (1945).

Williams v. State, 51 Ala. App. 1, 282 So. 2d 349, cert. denied, 291 Ala. 803, 282 So. 2d 355 (1973).

Williams v. State, 254 Ark. 940, 497 S.W.2d 11 (1973).

Williams v. United States, 327 U.S. 711 (1946).

Wilson v. State, 49 Del. 37, 109 A.2d 381 (1954).

Wilson v. State, 264 So. 2d 828 (Miss. 1972).

Woods v. People, 55 N.Y. 515 (1874).

Index